AQA Law

AS

Second Edition

The College

Ramnoth Rc

Nick Price
Richard Wortley
Peter Smith
Jennifer Currer

Series editor
Richard Wortley

Nelson Thornes

Contents

Introduction

About this book

Nelson Thornes has developed this book to ensure that it offers you the best support for your AS course and helps you to prepare for your exams. You can be confident that this book has been reviewed by subject experts, and is closely matched to the requirements of your specification.

How to use this book

The book content is divided into chapters matched to the sections of the AQA Law specification for Units 1 and 2. Unit 1A (Law-making) and 1B (The legal system) cover Unit 1. Unit 2A (Criminal liability), 2B (Tort) and 2C (The law of contract) cover Unit 2.

The features in this book include:

In this topic you will learn how to:

Each chapter is made up of two or more topics. At the beginning of each of these topics, you will find a list of learning objectives that contain targets linked to the requirements of the specification.

Key terms

Terms that you will need to be able to define and understand.

Key cases

Cases that demonstrate a key legal concept.

Link

These refer you back to other points in the book that consider similar issues.

Activity

Things for you to do that will reinforce the information you have just learned.

Study tips

Hints to help you with your study and to prepare you for your exam.

Practice questions

Questions in the style that you can expect in your exam.

You should now be able to:

A bulleted list of learning outcomes at the end of each chapter summarising core points of knowledge.

Table of cases

Table of statutes

Introduction

Unit 1A together with Unit 1B constitutes Unit 1 of the AS specification. Unit 1A is about law-making and Unit 1B is about the legal system. Unit 1A and Unit 1B are examined together on one examination paper, which constitutes 50 per cent of the overall marks for the AS qualification and 25 per cent of the overall marks for the A2 qualification.

The Unit 1 examination is of 1.5 hours' duration. You must answer questions from three topics: one topic from Unit 1A; one topic from Unit 1B; and another topic, which may be from Unit 1A or 1B. There will be a choice of four topics in Unit 1A and four topics in Unit 1B.

Each topic is represented by one question, which has three parts. You must answer all parts of the question. Each part is normally worth 10 marks; the entire question is worth 30 marks, plus 2 marks for Assessment Objective 3.

All parts of each topic relate to the same topic area of the AQA Law AS specification – that is, the same chapter of this book. Parts (a) and (b) will normally be a test of your knowledge and understanding, and part (c) will normally be evaluative, requiring simple discussion of advantages and disadvantages of a topic.

Questions require essay-style answers. You should aim to include: correct identification of the issues raised by the question; sound explanation of each of the points; and relevant illustration. Illustration may be in many forms – for example, legislation, cases, research, statistics, and material from the media. Study tips are provided throughout each topic.

Unit 1A comprises four chapters:

1 **Parliamentary law-making:** concerned with how Parliament makes law, and how an idea can develop into a law.
2 **Delegated legislation:** explains how law is also made by bodies to which Parliament has delegated law-making powers.
3 **Statutory interpretation:** considers how judges approach the task of interpreting Acts of Parliament.
4 **Judicial precedent:** concerned with the explanation of law made by judges in cases that come before them in court.

1   Parliamentary law-making

In this topic you will learn how to:

- describe a range of influences on Parliament

- give appropriate examples of each influence

- evaluate the effectiveness of each influence.

Key terms

Parliament: made up of (1) the House of Commons, consisting of elected MPs; (2) the House of Lords, consisting of Lords who have either inherited their title or who have been appointed to the position; and (3) the Queen. All three parts have to agree on a law in order for it to be made and come into force.

Government: responsible for the day-to-day running of the country. It is drawn from MPs from the largest party in the House of Commons and a smaller number of Lords. The head of the Government is the Prime Minister, who is assisted by senior ministers in the Cabinet.

Law Commission: a full-time law reform body, independent of the Government. It was created by The Law Commission Act 1965. This Act gives the Commission its powers and duties.

Codification: bringing together all the law, both statutory and judge-made, into one new Act.

Consolidation: bringing all existing statutory laws into one new Act.

1 Influences on parliamentary law-making

Parliament is the supreme law-making body in the United Kingdom, and can make laws for England and – in some areas – for Wales, Scotland and Northern Ireland. Pressure on Parliament to make or reform the law comes from a variety of sources. Many laws are introduced by the **Government** to implement its political agenda. Other ideas come from the Law Commission, pressure groups and the media. There are many other pressures operating on Parliament, which candidates may wish to research even though they are outside the specification – for example, Royal Commissions and the European Union.

The Law Commission

The **Law Commission** is an independent, permanent and full-time law reform body set up by the Law Commission Act 1965. It has a full-time staff headed by five Law Commissioners, one of whom is the Chairman. The Chairman is responsible for promoting the work of the Law Commission, and is its public face and voice. The Chairman also oversees the repeal and consolidation aspects of the Commission's work. The Chairman is a High Court Judge and the other four Law Commissioners are well-qualified, experienced practising or academic lawyers. Each of the Law Commissioners is supported by a team, typically made up of barristers and solicitors, parliamentary draftsmen, researchers and administrative staff.

Under s3(1) of the 1965 Act, the role of the Law Commission is to 'keep under review all the law'. This includes in particular the codification and consolidation of the law, the repeal of obsolete law, and the simplification and modernisation of the law.

Codification

Codification is the bringing together of all the law on a particular topic into a single Act of Parliament. Unlike other countries, which typically have all the law on a particular topic in one document, the law in Britain has been developed piecemeal over hundreds of years by Parliament and judges. As a result the law is quite difficult to access and understand because to decide what the law is, it is necessary to research all possible sources of law. When it was first created, the Law Commission embarked on a major programme to codify contract law, landlord and tenant laws, family law and the law of evidence. In 1989 a draft Criminal Code was published, although it has yet to be implemented. The Law Commission has gradually accepted that its initial plans for codification were over-ambitious, and that codification of smaller areas is preferable. For example, the Criminal Law and Evidence team published its report on the Law of Murder and Homicide in November 2006, which was later incorporated into the Coroners and Justice Act 2009. This team is currently working towards the codification and simplification of the general principles of criminal law.

Consolidation

Consolidation brings all the statutory provisions relating to a particular area into one Act. As with codification, this makes the law more understandable and accessible to all those who use it. It does not necessarily require changes in the law. Examples of consolidation laws include the Education Act 1996 and the Powers of Criminal Courts (Sentencing) Act 2000.

While codifying and consolidation Acts make it easier to find out and understand what the law is, they require constant updating to truly fulfil their purpose. It is not usually very long before the Act is interpreted by the courts or is amended by further legislation, thus requiring cross-referencing to another source of law.

Repeal

Repeal of obsolete law is the removal of laws that have no further use. Many laws become out of date or irrelevant due to passage of time. It is important to remove these Acts, as they make research of the law more time-consuming and cause confusion. A Statute Law (Repeals) Bill was presented to both the Westminster and Scottish Parliaments in April 2012, recommending the removal of more than 800 old laws. With limited exceptions, once an Act of Parliament has been passed it can only be repealed or altered by another Act.

Through these processes of codification, consolidation and repeal, the law is simplified and modernised. However, it is also necessary to suggest changes to existing laws and to create new areas of law in response to social change and technical developments. For example, the Law Commission has suggested changes such as the Occupiers' Liability Act 1984, which made occupiers of land responsible for injury caused to trespassers while on their land, and the Computer Misuse Act 1990, which was passed to deal with the problem of computer hacking.

The Law Commission investigates matters referred to it by Government departments, and also decides for itself which areas to investigate. In addition, pressure may come from other sources – for example, the Criminal Attempts Act 1981 was a result of a Law Commission report prompted by academic pressure. Most areas of law considered by the Law Commission are politically non-contentious.

A Law Commission investigation will typically begin with research of the issue. A working paper is then produced, which sets out the current law, the problems within this, and the suggestions for reform. Consultation then follows of anyone interested in commenting on the issue. After the consultation, the Law Commission produces a report that includes a draft bill. The Government can then choose whether to introduce the draft bill into Parliament and implement the recommendations. Another example of a law passed to implement a Law Commission recommendation is the Law Reform (Year and a Day Rule) Act 1996, which abolished the previous requirement for a victim to die within a year and a day of the act which leads to the death in order for it to constitute murder.

Fig. 1.1 *A flow chart summarising a typical Law Commission investigation*

Advantages of the Law Commission

The Law Commission possesses considerable legal, non-political expertise. Its investigations are thorough, and as a result, its recommendations are well informed. The wording of the bill is accurate and deals effectively with the issue. This helps to avoid problems when the law is brought into force.

The Law Commission is an independent body. This ensures that all law is kept under review, and not just those areas the current Government wishes to focus on. The Law Commission may decide for itself to investigate a particular area, or a body other than the Government may ask it to do so.

Study tips

Note the use of examples – useful to include when explaining the influence of the Law Commission on Parliament.

The Law Commission drafts a bill to attach to its report to the Government. This means that the bill is based wholly on the Commission's findings, and that there will be less delay introducing the bill into Parliament.

Disadvantages of the Law Commission

A major disadvantage of the Law Commission is that many of its recommendations, about one third, are not implemented. The Government of the day is not obliged to introduce any of its proposals in Parliament. Often the nature of recommendations do not suit the political agenda of the Government.

The lack of power possessed by the Law Commission is further illustrated by the fact that the Government is not obliged to consult the Law Commission on any law it proposes to introduce into Parliament.

An investigation of the current law is often lengthy, and it can sometimes be years before a report is produced. An investigation may also be interrupted by investigations into other areas.

The Law Commission investigates more than one matter at a time. Often 20 or 30 areas are under review. Consequently, although investigations are thorough, they could perhaps be even more so.

The media and public opinion

The term 'the media' covers the channels by which information is transmitted. It includes newspapers, magazines, radio, television and internet sources. The media may both represent public opinion and influence public opinion. Members of the public can make their views known to Parliament by contacting the media, as well as by joining a pressure group and by writing to their Member of Parliament (MP.) In reverse, matters of concern can be highlighted to the public using the media. The media may be used by pressure groups to highlight their interest or cause, and bring about change. As MPs in the House of Commons are democratically elected by voters, it is inevitable that the media is able to exert considerable influence on reform of laws.

> **Key terms**
>
> **The media:** the channels through which information is communicated to the public.

There are sometimes direct campaigns in the media to reform a law. A famous example is the 'Name and Shame' campaign run by the *News of the World* newspaper in 2000, following the murder of a child by a paedophile. The paper gathered public support by regularly raising the issue. Perhaps the most influential tactic was naming convicted paedophiles, publishing their pictures and detailing where they lived. The government was forced to act because the population was becoming increasingly alarmed by the revelations. There was also the worry of individuals being harmed by the public. Indeed, on at least one occasion someone who was innocent was targeted. A law was passed requiring the police to maintain a register of convicted paedophiles. After being trialled in a few areas of the country, it was launched nationally.

Law reform is sometimes prompted by pressure from more than one of the influences operating on Parliament. An example is the Criminal Justice Act 2003. This reformed the 'double jeopardy' rule, by allowing a suspect to be re-tried for a crime for which he had been formally acquitted, if there was compelling new evidence. This law came into effect in April 2007. This change in the law was brought about by a media campaign after the suspects in the Stephen Lawrence were acquitted despite the overwhelming evidence against them. Eventually media pressure led to a government inquiry led by Sir William Macpherson, which in turn led to the Law Commission investigating and then recommending that the double jeopardy law be changed.

Advantages of the media

The media raises government awareness of certain matters, and helps to inform the Government of public concerns. Public opinion is often represented by pressure groups, and these pressure groups in turn are sometimes supported by the media.

Following the shooting of several young pupils at a school in Dunblane in 1996, an anti-handgun pressure group called the Snowdrop Campaign was set up. Many newspapers – for example, the *Daily Mail* – and television channels helped the Snowdrop Campaign to publicise its concerns to both the government and the public. This eventually led to legislation that banned handguns.

The media also raises public awareness, which is essential in order for the Government to feel pressured into making legislative reforms. The Government is ultimately answerable to the electorate, and fears losing favour with the public because this could lead to defeat in an election.

Disadvantages of the media

While radio and television channels are required to remain politically neutral, this is not the case with newspapers. Some newspapers, both tabloids and broadsheets, promote their own views. Sometimes the owners of newspapers hold particular political or moral views, and their papers, both broadsheets and tabloids, will promote those views. Some newspapers lend their support to a political party. *The Sun* traditionally supported the Conservative Party and reported favourably on the policies of the Thatcher Government.

Newspapers are in business to make a profit. They publish material that will sell copies and expand their readership, rather than merely keep the general public informed. They can easily whip up a public panic by reporting on matters that occur rarely yet worry people when they are reminded of them. This was clearly what happened with the *News of the World*'s 'Name and Shame' campaign.

Handguns to be banned in the UK

The British Government has announced plans to outlaw almost all handguns following the shocking massacre at Dunblane in Scotland.

On 13 March Thomas Hamilton walked into the gym at Dunblane Primary School and killed 16 young children and their teacher. He also injured 13 other children and three teachers. Hamilton, a former scout master, then shot himself.

Today's announcement follows publication of Lord Cullen's inquiry into the massacre which concluded Hamilton's horrific attack could not have been predicted.

But it made 23 recommendations to tighten rules on gun ownership and monitor those who work with children.

The proposal to ban all handguns – except .22 calibre target pistols – would leave Britain with some of the toughest laws on private possession of guns.

Home Secretary Michael Howard told a packed House of Commons he would make sure the measures were passed as quickly as possible through Parliament.

But the move has angered both those for and against private gun ownership.

The Snowdrop Campaign, set up by victims' families after Dunblane, wants to see a total ban on handguns and called the plan an 'unacceptable compromise'.

The opposition Labour Party welcomed the report and the Government's swift reaction to it but urged ministers to bring about a complete ban.

Shadow Home Secretary Jack Straw said politicians should have acted in a similar vein nine years ago after the Hungerford massacre.

Former Tory Cabinet Minister David Mellor also felt the proposals did not go far enough.

He asked, 'Isn't it time to conclude that, literally and metaphorically, the game is up for handguns now?'

But gun club owners warned thousands of jobs would be in jeopardy if the proposal became law.

Speaking to the *Daily Mirror* newspaper, Ross Armstrong, owner of Medway Shooting Club in Kent said, 'People are killed by drunk drivers but no one demands a ban on cars. Further restrictions suit no one.'

Pressure groups

Pressure groups are groups of people who share similar ideas and campaign for changes in the law. They can range from a small group of individuals to a large network of millions, in the case of popular charities such as the National Trust. Whatever their size, pressure groups try to influence Parliament to legislate on issues of interest to them.

These groups may use a variety of methods to obtain support for their campaign. These may include lobbying or talking to ministers or MPs, getting the public to sign a petition, running a publicity campaign with advertisements in the media, or more actively organising marches, demonstrations and strikes.

The main types of pressure groups are:

- sectional or interest groups, such as the British Medical Association (BMA) for doctors, the Law Society for solicitors, and the Bar Council for barristers
- cause groups, which promote a particular idea or belief (or cause), such as the environmental group Greenpeace and the human rights group Amnesty International
- insider groups (often sectional groups), which have direct contact with government ministers, MPs and other officials
- outsider groups, which do not have access to decision makers, and which may use direct action or barely legal methods to promote their cause.

The boundaries between the different types of group can change as time passes. For example, for several years Fathers 4 Justice (a group that campaigns for fathers' rights to see their children) was considered to be an outsider group, but more recently it has been consulted by the Government about proposed changes in family law.

The major sectional groups are often influential as they represent large or powerful groups of people, whose support the Government needs to gain or retain. These groups are often wealthy, and can afford to employ research staff and mount extensive publicity campaigns. Because of the wealth and influence of these groups, it is rare for the Government to introduce a law that directly affects the interests of the members of such a group without consulting it. The content of any law introduced may be influenced by this consultation process.

Cause groups are often considered outsider groups and are less likely to be consulted by, or have links with, overnment ministers. However, well-organised cause groups are often able to publicise their campaign and succeed in gaining some type of reform. The RSPCA is a long-established charity that has considerable support amongst the British public. The RSPCA has campaigned for animal welfare legislation for many years, using methods such as leafleting and multimedia advertising. The group was active in promoting the Animal Welfare Bill, which was passed as an Act in 2006. This Act requires animal owners to provide their pets with food, water, shelter, veterinary care and freedom to move about.

Sometimes, one person may campaign for a certain cause. Jamie Oliver has successfully used the media to publicise his crusade for healthier meals to be served in schools. A TV series was devoted to his cause and he gained the support of many sectional groups, including the National Union of Teachers and the British Medical Association. In 2006, the Department for Education and Skills issued The Education (Nutritional

Key terms

Pressure group: a group of people who campaign for reform of the law.

Standards for School Food) (England) Regulations, which came into force on 1 September 2007 and contained many provisions similar to those suggested by Jamie Oliver.

Table 1.1 *Characteristics of sectional and cause pressure groups*

Type of pressure group	Explanation	Illustration
Sectional	They exist to further the interests of a particular body of people.	BMA, Trade Union Congress, National Union of Teachers, Law Society
Cause	They exist to further a particular ideal.	Jamie Oliver – school dinners campaign – The Education (Nutritional Standards for School Food) (England) Regulations 2006. AllOut
Insider	They have access to decision makers.	BMA, Law Society
Outsider	They are unlikely to have access to decision makers.	Greenpeace, Amnesty International

Advantages of pressure groups

Through a broad range of tactics, pressure groups are able to raise public awareness of matters affecting their interest or cause. AllOut, a group working for international LGBT (lesbian, gay, bisexual, transgender) rights, primarily uses new media – rather than traditional advertising and leafleting – to publicise its campaign. AllOut produces online petitions, YouTube videos and social media content in order to spread knowledge of, and encourage protest against, institutionalised injustice and abuse suffered by LGBT people. The group also stages events, such as flash mobs, to support some of its campaigns.

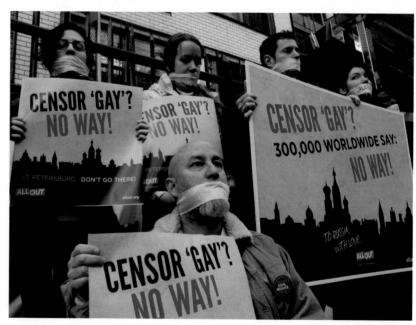

Fig. 1.2 *AllOut members stage protests all over the world to campaign against LGBT discrimination and abuse*

Pressure groups raise awareness, and remind Parliament of the importance of an issue. Parliament is sometimes consumed with debating issues on the Government's political agenda, so pressure groups perform a valuable role in keeping Parliament in touch with issues that members of the public believe to be important. Environmental pressure groups are a good example of this. In recent years, they have gained a greater influence on all political parties as the public has become increasingly concerned about global warming. For example, car tax rates have been changed in favour of smaller, more fuel-efficient vehicles.

Some pressure groups have huge memberships which exceed those of the main political parties. These large pressure groups – for example, the National Trust, which represents more than 2 million members – are able to raise awareness of issues of importance to large numbers of people.

Pressure groups must have sound knowledge of their interest or cause in order to put their point across convincingly. Therefore, law enacted as a result of influence from pressure groups should benefit from considerable expertise. Jamie Oliver is clearly an expert on nutrition, and able to advise on the key foods that should and should not be available to children at school.

Disadvantages of pressure groups

The main disadvantage of pressure groups is that they are inevitably biased in favour of their interest or cause. Campaigns by pressure groups may not present an objective, balanced argument. For example, Fathers 4 Justice rarely recognise that the courts and mothers are genuinely (even if sometimes mistakenly) attempting to achieve the best outcome for the children of the family.

Members of pressure groups often feel very passionately about their cause. This sometimes means they resort to undesirable tactics, involving criminal behaviour, to promote their cause. Examples include occasions when animal activists have damaged scientific laboratories that experiment on animals, and threatened workers and their families; and when members of the Countryside Alliance and Fathers 4 Justice demonstrated in the House of Commons.

Opinions held by a pressure group may only represent a small minority of the population. However, if the pressure group is well organised and influential, it can still be successful in changing the law.

Activity

Read the newspaper extract on page 6 and answer the following questions:

1. Why was the Snowdrop Campaign formed?
2. Is the Snowdrop Campaign a cause group or a sectional group?
3. Does the Snowdrop Campaign represent the views of everyone?
4. How did the legislation introduced by the then Conservative government fall short of that sought by the Snowdrop Campaign?
5. When and by what government were handguns eventually completely banned?

You should now be able to:

- understand a range of influences upon Parliament
- give examples of each influence
- evaluate each influence
- answer past paper questions on the topic of influences on Parliament.

Key terms

House of Commons: one of the two Houses of Parliament. This is the more powerful House, as its members are democratically elected.

Democracy: actions are carried out by the elected Government in the name of and on behalf of the electorate.

2 The legislative process

Parliamentary law-making

Laws made by Parliament are called Acts of Parliament. They are also referred to as 'statutes' and 'legislation'. In order to make an Act, a bill must be introduced to Parliament. The bill must then be debated and approved by both Houses of Parliament – the House of Commons and the House of Lords – and receive Royal Assent from the Queen.

Composition of the House of Commons

The **House of Commons** contains 650 members called MPs. Each MP represents a constituency. MPs are elected at general elections, which usually take place every five years. The Government is drawn from the party with the greatest number of elected MPs. The leader of the party with the greatest number of MPs is the Prime Minister. The Prime Minister and his chosen ministers make up the Cabinet, the central decision-making body of the Government. MPs from other political parties who are not part of the Government are called 'the opposition'.

Fig. 1.3 *The House of Commons*

The role of the House of Commons

The role of the Government is to make policy and to decide how to run the country. New policies require new laws. It is the role of the House of Commons to debate, scrutinise and vote on whether to approve the laws proposed by the Government. During debates, MPs are able to put forward the views of their constituents – the people they represent.

MPs also directly challenge Government ministers through rigorous questioning. In this way the Government is 'held to account'. The role played by the House of Commons ensures that the legislative process is democratic – that is, carried out in accordance with the ideals of **democracy**.

The House of Lords

There are approximately 700 members of the **House of Lords.** They are unelected and unpaid, and attendance is voluntary. Sitting in the House of Lords are:

- hereditary peers, who inherit their title
- life peers, who have been awarded a peerage because of their contribution to society or politics – for example, Lady (Margaret) Thatcher and Lord (Alan) Sugar; the life peerage ends on death and is not passed on to descendants
- 26 Bishops of the Church of England.

Key terms

House of Lords: one of the two Houses of Parliament. Membership is by appointment or hereditary.

The Crown: the King or Queen, who is also the Head of State. All laws passed by Parliament must be approved by the Crown before they come into force.

Fig. 1.4 *The House of Lords*

The role of the House of Lords

The role of the House of Lords is to complement the work of the Commons, and also to scrutinise and amend proposed legislation. Laws can be introduced in this House. In addition, the Lords pose questions to the Government, and debate policy issues and matters of current concern. Many peers also sit on specialist committees – for example, the European Union Committee, which has approximately 70 members and examines proposed European legislation.

The role of the Crown

The Crown is the title given to the monarch, who is the Head of State. Little real power remains with the monarchy. However, the Crown has three key functions in relation to parliamentary law-making:

- To open each parliamentary session – a traditional ceremonial event during which the monarch reads a speech, prepared by the Government, which outlines the legislative proposals to be considered in the coming session
- To give Royal Assent to all legislation
- To appoint and dismiss the Prime Minister, who is generally the leader of the party with the most MPs in the House of Commons.

Table 1.2 *A summary of the role of the Commons, the Lords and the Crown in the legislative process*

Role of the House of Commons	Role of the House of Lords	Role of the Crown
Where most new bills are introduced.	Where some bills are introduced.	To open each parliamentary session and announce the Government's legislative proposals.
To debate Government policy and hold the Government to account.	To scrutinise and amend proposed legislation including Government proposals.	To give Royal Assent to all legislation.
To scrutinise and amend proposed legislation.	To scrutinise proposed EU legislation.	
To debate matters of current concern.	To question the Government and debate legislative proposals.	
To represent the views of the electorate.	To debate policy issues and matters of current concern.	
	To delay legislation so as to allow further time to research and consult.	

Key terms

Bill: a draft law to be debated in Parliament.

Public bill: a bill affecting the general public.

Government bill: a bill introduced into Parliament by a government minister.

Types of bills

There are three main types of **bill**: public bills, private bills and hybrid bills.

Public bills

Public bills affect the general public. Some public bills apply to the whole of the UK, while others apply only to England and Wales. Since the establishment of the Scottish Parliament and the Welsh Assembly, power to make legislation on certain matters has been devolved to these bodies. Parliament has retained power to make law applicable to the whole of the UK in what are called 'reserved' matters, including defence and foreign affairs.

There are two types of public bills: government bills and private members' bills.

Government bills

The majority of bills introduced into Parliament each year are **government bills**. Most proceed to become Acts of Parliament as they are supported by the Government. Government bills are introduced into Parliament by the minister responsible for that area of policy.

Approximately a quarter of government bills are routine, and are introduced irrespective of which party is in power – for example, money bills that deal with collecting taxes. Government bills are introduced for a variety of reasons. They may be introduced:

- to honour manifesto promises – that is, promises made during election campaigns on issues such as health or education
- in response to a specific incident or matter of concern – for example, the Football Spectators Act 1989, as amended by the Football (Disorder) Act 2000, allows magistrates to ban potential trouble-making fans from travelling abroad for five days before an international match and until the match has been played
- in order to comply with international treaties – for example, the Treaty of Rome, which has prompted a vast amount of legislation on matters such as consumer and worker's rights
- following recommendation by a law reform body such as the Law Commission.

A bill may be introduced into Parliament without any previous consultation if the Government is clear about their plans. However, sometimes it is not clear, and it may wish to consult. It can do this by issuing Green or White papers.

A Green Paper is a consultation document issued by the Government before it introduces a bill. It contains outline policy proposals for debate and discussion before a decision is taken on the best option. A Green Paper will often contain several alternative policy options, and will invite comments from interested parties. As the title suggests, it is printed on pale green paper. An example is 'High Speed Rail', issued in March 2010, setting out the Government's proposals for a high-speed rail line from London to Birmingham and the North.

Fig. 1.5 *Vince Cable launches the Government's Green Paper on business finance at a press conference in 2010*

Following this consultation, the government may publish firmer recommendations in a White Paper. Sometimes the White Paper will be issued without a preceding Green Paper. A White Paper will set out the Government's firm policy plans, and it is likely that a bill will be introduced based on those proposals. An example of a White Paper is 'Putting victims first – more effective responses to anti-social behaviour', issued by the Home Office in May 2012. This set out the Government's plans to replace ASBOs and deal with anti-social behaviour. Only after this consultation will the Government decide whether to introduce a bill into Parliament.

Since 1997, the Government has promoted the introduction of draft bills into Parliament. These are examined by Select Committees in either House, or by a joint committee of both Houses. Draft bills enable consultation and pre-legislative scrutiny before the bills are formally introduced. An example is the draft bill to reform the House of Lords, which is being considered by a joint committee of both Houses. Another example is the draft Energy Bill, introduced in May 2012, which proposesto further the Government's objectives in meeting decarbonisation and renewable energy targets. It is being considered by the House of Commons Energy and Climate Change select committee.

Private members' bills

Private members' bills are introduced into Parliament by individual backbench MPs who are not part of the Government. Comparatively few private members' bills ever become law because of the shortage of parliamentary debate time allocated to them. The Government decides how this time is allocated, and so gives its own bills priority. Nevertheless, some notable examples of Acts introduced as private members' bills include the Murder (Abolition of Death Penalty) Act 1965 introduced by Sidney Silverman MP, and the Abortion Act 1967 introduced by David Steel MP.

Despite the fact that private members' bills rarely become law, they play an important role in raising public and government awareness of an issue, and often lead to future government legislation. An example of this is Ken Livingstone's Wild Animals (Hunting with Dogs) Bill. This failed in 2000, but was then introduced as a government bill, eventually becoming the Hunting Act 2004.

Private members' bills can also be introduced by peers in the Lords. An example of a bill introduced this way is Lord Joffe's Assisted Dying for the Terminally Ill Bill in 2006. Although this failed to progress beyond a second reading in the Lords, it did lead to much public debate on the issue.

Private bills

Private bills affect individuals, organisations or specific areas. These bills are introduced into Parliament through a petition by the individuals, organisations or local authorities concerned. They are rare compared with public bills. An example is the Edward Berry and Doris Eileen Ward (Marriage Enabling) Act 1980, the result of a personal bill, which was passed to allow a stepfather and stepdaughter to marry as long as they were adults when they first met.

Hybrid bills

Hybrid bills are so called because they are a cross between a public bill and a private bill. They are introduced by a government minister and, if enacted, will affect particular individuals, organisations or localities. An example of an Act that began life as a hybrid bill is the Channel Tunnel (Rail Link) Act 1996, which had a particular impact on landowners and residents in Kent. Another example is the Crossrail Act 2008 to build a new east to west rail link through central London.

The process through which a bill passes to become an Act of Parliament

To become an Act of Parliament, a bill must pass through both the House of Commons and House of Lords, and must receive Royal Assent. A bill can start in either House unless it is a money bill, which must start in the Commons.

Key terms

Private members' bill: a public bill introduced into Parliament by a backbench MP in the Commons or by a peer in the House of Lords.

Private bill: a bill affecting a particular individual or organisation, or a specific locality.

Study tips

Note that an explanation of the formal legislative process should include a description of each reading and stage.

Table 1.3 *A summary of the types of bill*

Type of bill	Explanation	Illustration
Public bills	Affect the general public. Two types: government bills and private members' bills. Government bills are introduced into Parliament by government ministers. Private members' bills are introduced by backbench MPs or peers.	Legislation that started as a government bill: the Football Spectators Act 1989 as amended by the Football (Disorder) Act 2000; the Children Act 2004; the Dangerous Dogs Act 1991. Legislation which started as a private members' bill: the Abortion Act 1967; the Murder (Abolition of the Death Penalty) Act 1965.
Private bills	Affect a particular person, organisation or locality.	The Edward Berry and Doris Eileen Ward (Marriage Enabling) Act 1980.
Hybrid bills	A cross between a public bill and a private bill. Introduced by a government minister but only affects a particular person, locality or organisation.	The Channel Tunnel (Rail Link) Act 1996.

First reading

The title and main aims of the bill are announced, and copies of it are distributed. There is no debate at this stage. Many private members' bills fail to progress beyond this stage. A date is set for the bill's second reading.

Second reading

The House debates the whole bill, focusing on its general principles. The minister or other promoter of the bill starts the debate. At the end of the debate, there is a vote for or against the bill progressing further. Should the bill progress beyond this stage, it is quite likely it will eventually become an Act of Parliament.

Committee stage

The bill is passed to a Standing Committee, which is made up of between 16 and 50 MPs selected to represent the proportions of the parties in the House. The MPs chosen will generally have a particular interest in the bill or specialist knowledge of its content. The Standing Committee scrutinises the bill line by line and clause by clause, and makes amendments as required to ensure it conforms to the general approval given by the House at the second reading. All amendments made to the bill are voted on. Some bills, for example money bills, are subjected to examination by the whole House at this stage. In the House of Lords, there are generally no specialist Standing Committees. The whole House scrutinises the bill.

Report stage

The Standing Committee reports any amendments made to the bill during the committee stage back to the whole House. Each amendment is debated, and a vote is taken to decide whether it should be accepted or rejected. The House may make additional amendments at this stage, provided these are approved by a vote. Should no amendments be made at the committee stage, there is no need for the report stage and the bill progresses directly to the third reading.

Third reading

This is a review of the whole bill, and a vote is taken to decide whether the bill should proceed to the other House. This stage is often a formality. As the bill has successfully completed its earlier stages, it is unlikely to fail. In the House of Lords, further amendments can be made at this stage.

After the third reading, the bill is passed to the other House where it goes through the same stages.

The limited power of the House of Lords

If the Lords propose amendments to a bill that has completed the process in the Commons, the bill is returned to the Commons for a stage called Lords Amendments Considered. At this stage, the Commons may approve or reject the Lords' amendments. Approximately 90 per cent of Lords' amendments are accepted by the Commons at this stage. In the event that the Lords do not approve a bill that has been passed by the Commons, then under the **Parliament Acts 1911 and 1949** the Lords can delay the passage of a money bill for one month and all other bills for one year. Once this time has elapsed, the Commons can send the bill for Royal Assent without the Lords' agreement. In order to exercise this power, the bill must be re-introduced into Parliament in the next session and pass successfully through all the stages again. Only four Acts have been passed using the Parliament Act: the War Crimes Act 1991; the European Parliamentary Elections Act 1999; the Sexual Offences (Amendment) Act 2000; and the Hunting Act 2004.

The supremacy of the House of Commons stems from the fact that it is a democratically elected body, answerable to the electorate. The Lords have retained the power to reject a bill that attempts to extend the duration of Parliament beyond five years.

Royal Assent

Once a bill has passed through both Houses, it requires Royal Assent to become law. It is not customary for the Monarch to assent in person; the last time this occurred was in 1854. Assent is now given by the Speaker in the House of Commons and the Lord Speaker of the House of Lords. The granting of Royal Assent is a formality. It has not been declined since Queen Anne refused to give assent to the Scottish Militia Bill in 1707. There is now a constitutional convention that assent will never be withheld, as this would jeopardise the future position of the monarchy.

On the day that Royal Assent is granted, the bill becomes an Act of Parliament. Most Acts come into force at midnight following Royal Assent. However, implementation of some Acts has to be delayed in order for necessary resources to be prepared and put into place: for example, the Police and Criminal Evidence Act 1984 was brought into effect in stages to give the police sufficient time to train personnel and acquire the equipment necessary for compliance with the Act. Acts of Parliament such as this are usually brought into force by delegated legislation, which is discussed in Chapter 2.

■ **Key terms**

Parliament Acts 1911 and 1949: these limit the power of the House of Lords to delay or defeat proposed legislation.

■ **Study tips**

An explanation of Royal Assent must be included in an explanation of the legislative process.

You should now be able to:

- describe the role of the House of Commons and House of Lords
- describe the different types of bill
- explain the legislative process
- answer past paper questions on the topic of the legislative process.

3 Advantages and disadvantages of parliamentary law-making

Advantages of parliamentary law-making

Scrutiny

The legislative process (passing through both Houses and receiving Royal Assent) is very thorough. There are three readings and two stages in each of the Houses of Parliament. This provides several opportunities for debate, scrutiny and amendment, ensuring that any mistakes or poor drafting can be corrected.

Democratic

Parliamentary law-making is democratic. MPs in the House of Commons are democratically elected to make laws. During the debates on the proposed law, each MP should have the opportunity to put forward the view of his or her constituents. Members of the House of Lords are not democratically elected, so they cannot veto a bill that has the approval of the Commons. Under the Parliament Acts 1911 and 1949, the delaying power of the Lords is limited to one month in respect of money bills and one year for other bills. The role of the Monarch, also unelected, has been reduced to a formality.

Government control

The Government has considerable control over parliamentary law-making. For example, it controls the parliamentary timetable for debates and is likely to win at each voting stage of the process unless a number of its own MPs vote against it. This is democratic because the Government is the preferred choice of a significant proportion of the population.

A government minister introducing a bill to Parliament has knowledge in his field of responsibility and the support of a civil service department with considerable expertise.

The House of Lords

The House of Lords acts as a checking mechanism. It can guard against laws being passed solely to fit the Government's political agenda. If the House of Lords exercises its power of delay there will be further opportunity for debate and amendment of the bill's provisions.

The House of Lords contains many peers with significant expertise in many different issues. Because of this, the quality of scrutiny and debate in the Lords is very high.

Members of the Lords are able to act independently when debating and voting. However, MPs often have to follow instructions from the party leadership.

Special rules exist in respect of money bills. For example, the whole House will sit at the committee stage in the House of Commons when a finance bill is being considered. This helps guard against unlawful taxation.

Flexibility

There are several types of bill which can be introduced in either House. This means that not only the Government but all MPs and Lords have the opportunity to propose new laws. This may be useful when the Government has not given thought to a particular matter, or does not want to be seen to introduce controversial legislation. Examples of potentially controversial legislation are the Abortion Act 1967, and the Marriage Act 1994, which allowed marriages to be made in places other than churches and registry offices.

In this topic you will learn how to:

- discuss the advantages of parliamentary law-making
- discuss the disadvantages of parliamentary law-making.

Disadvantages of parliamentary law-making

Undemocratic

Neither the House of Lords nor the Queen is elected. Arguably, the unelected House of Lords should not have the power to delay bills that have been approved by the democratically elected House of Commons. However, while the House of Commons is democratically elected, MPs are persuaded to vote with their party rather than in accordance with the wishes of their constituents. A Government with a large majority may be able to introduce any legislation it pleases, and is only answerable to the electorate every five years.

Government control

As the Government has a majority of MPs in the House of Commons, it can vote out any private members' bill that does not fit its political agenda. Very little parliamentary time is allocated to private members' bills. In comparison to government bills, very few private members' bills are enacted each year. In the 2009/10 parliamentary session, only five private members' bills made it into the statute book.

The Government is arguably too powerful, as it is able to bypass the House of Lords by invoking the Parliament Acts. The most recent example of this is the Hunting Act 2004. Any law desired by the Government may be passed despite the House of Lords' objections.

Slow

The process is slow. A bill has to go through many readings and stages in both Houses. This takes many months and is not appropriate when important laws need to be made quickly.

As Royal Assent is now no more than a formality, some argue that this stage is pointless and holds up the process unecessarily.

Dated processes, language and statistics

When drafting a bill, parliamentary draftsmen use words and phrases that are ambiguous, unclear, obscure and over-elaborate. This sometimes means it is up to the judiciary to decide what the Act is meant to say. Approximately 75 per cent of cases heard by the Supreme Court in its capacity as the final appeal court are about how words in an Act should be understood. Furthermore, the language used is often incomprehensible to the general public (and even to some lawyers!) Problems with the language and structure of Acts were originally identified in the Renton Committee's Report on Preparation of Legislation in 1975.

This report also suggested that the structure of many Acts was illogical, with sections of individual Acts having no obvious sequence and there being no clear connection between Acts dealing with the same topic. Similar problems were identified by the Hansard Society Commission led by Lord Rippon in 1992.

These language and structural problems make law inaccessible to ordinary people. It is also difficult to discover what the law on a particular issue is, and there is a problem with finding out which sections of an Act have come into force. Not all Acts become law at the point of Royal Assent. They may be brought into force by a government minister at a later date. In such situations, it becomes necessary to research regulations issued by the minister.

In addition, because of the principles of parliamentary sovereignty, once an Act has been passed it can only be replaced or amended by a later Act. For example, the Dangerous Dogs Act 1991 was found to be defective after it had been passed, and another amending Act had to be passed in 1996 to remedy the problems.

You should now be able to:

- explain the advantages and disadvantages of parliamentary law-making

■ **Activity**

Research the Christmas Day (Trading) Act 2004 on the internet. What disadvantages of the legislative process are apparent in this Act?

4 Parliamentary supremacy

Parliamentary sovereignty

The supremacy of Parliament was established in the 17th century. In 1689 the Bill of Rights was enacted, which deemed Parliament to be the supreme law-maker. Article IX states, 'the freedom of speech and debates or proceedings in Parliament ought not to be impeached or questioned in any court or place out of Parliament'. The Bill of Rights also declared that Parliament was to be freely elected every three years, that the levying of tax was subject to parliamentary consent and that it was illegal for the Monarchy to interfere with the law as enacted by Parliament – apart from to grant Royal Assent.

The meaning of **parliamentary sovereignty** was expressed clearly by A.V. Dicey, a 19th-century constitutional lawyer. In his work *Introduction to the Study of the Law of the Constitution*, first published in 1885, he wrote, 'The principle of parliamentary sovereignty means … that Parliament … has the right to make or unmake any law whatever; and, further, that no person or body is recognised by the law of England as having a right to override or set aside the legislation of Parliament.'

Parliamentary sovereignty means that:

- Parliament's power is unlimited and it can make law on any topic
- the validity of parliamentary law cannot be questioned by anybody, including the courts, the Church and the Monarchy
- no one Parliament can limit the law-making power of any future Parliament. It is impossible, therefore, for any Parliament to pass a permanent law, or in other words to entrench an Act of Parliament.

The effect of the European Union on parliamentary sovereignty

The United Kingdom (UK) joined the EEC (now the **European Union – EU**) on 1 January 1973. The **Treaty of Rome 1957** and subsequent amendment treaties, together with secondary legislation – that is, law made under the authority of the treaties – was given effect in the UK by the **European Communities Act (ECA) 1972**. The effect of s2(1) of the ECA is that all the provisions of EU law have the force of law in the UK. Section 2(4) has the effect of making UK Acts of Parliament subject to directly applicable EU law. Since the enactment of the ECA, Parliament is no longer the supreme law-maker in the UK. In the event of a conflict between an Act of Parliament and EU law, EU law prevails. As a result of this, membership of the EU challenges Dicey's theory.

In this topic you will learn how to:

- explain the doctrine of parliamentary supremacy
- consider limitations on the doctrine of parliamentary supremacy.

■ **Key terms**

Parliamentary sovereignty: Parliament is the supreme law-maker in the UK.

European Union (EU): a group of countries that have signed international treaties with the common purpose of creating an economic union.

Treaty of Rome 1957: the founding Treaty of the European Economic Community now known as the European Union.

European Communities Act (ECA) 1972: the Act of Parliament that incorporates EU law into UK domestic law. The effect of this Act is that Acts of Parliament are now subordinate to European Law.

Fig. 1.6 *The UK, as a member state of the European Union, must follow EU law*

The supremacy of European law over UK legislation was clarified by the European Court of Justice (ECJ) in *Costa* v *ENEL* (1964). The ECJ stated, 'The transfer by the states from their domestic legal system to the Community legal system of the rights and obligations arising under the Treaty carries with it a permanent limitation of their sovereign rights, against which a subsequent unilateral act incompatible with the concept of the Community cannot prevail.' This case clarified the requirement for both pre-existing domestic Acts and those made in the future to comply with EU law.

Arguably the greatest challenge to parliamentary sovereignty was that in **Ex parte Factortame No 2 (1991)**. The case was about the rights of Spanish fishermen to fish in British waters. The Spanish fishermen claimed that the Merchant Shipping Act 1988 was contrary to Community law, and sought interim relief from the provisions of the Act pending a trial of the issue. Both the Court of Appeal and House of Lords held that the 1988 Act should be enforced throughout the period in question, because no national court had the power to suspend an Act of Parliament. However, the ECJ decided that national courts were obliged to suspend the Act of Parliament in these circumstances. This decision thus gave the national courts the right to set aside an Act of Parliament, although in limited circumstances. This is clearly contrary to the principle of parliamentary sovereignty.

Following the ECJ decision in Factortame, when a piece of UK legislation is directly in conflict with EU law the UK court must follow the EU law. By virtue of the ECA, parliamentary sovereignty is now limited by all sources of European Union law. Unless the UK Parliament decides to withdraw the UK from the EU, an increasing amount of legislation will continue to be passed in order to comply with our membership obligations. This challenges UK parliamentary sovereignty, because Parliament is making law because the EU requires it to rather than of its own free will. In 1993, the Department of Trade estimated that one third of existing legislation had been enacted to implement EU law.

It is legally possible that the UK Parliament has surrendered sovereignty to the European institutions until it decides otherwise. By virtue of the doctrine of parliamentary sovereignty, the ECA can be repealed, as no Act of Parliament can be entrenched. In reality, this is unlikely to happen as the UK now has strong economic ties with the European Union.

Key cases

Ex parte Factortame No 2 (1991): the ECJ held that domestic courts must suspend domestic legislation while waiting for a ruling from the ECJ as to whether the domestic legislation contravenes European Community law.

The effect of the Human Rights Act 1998 on parliamentary sovereignty

The European Convention on Human Rights

Before the enactment of the **Human Rights Act (HRA) 1998**, the rights of citizens in the UK were safeguarded by the **European Convention on Human Rights (ECHR) 1950**, which is an international treaty created by the Council of Europe. The original purpose of the ECHR was to prevent a repeat of the atrocities committed against European citizens during the Second World War. The ECHR is concerned with the protection of human rights and fundamental freedoms. The UK signed the ECHR in 1950.

The Human Rights Act 1998

The Human Rights Act 1998 (HRA), which came into force in October 2000, incorporated the ECHR into UK domestic law. The main provision of the HRA, as far as parliamentary sovereignty is concerned, is that it requires all legislation passed by Parliament to be interpreted and given effect so far as is possible to comply with Convention rights. Section 19 of the Act requires a government minister to declare before a bill is given its second reading whether it is compatible with the HRA. In the event of incompatibility of existing legislation, the courts can quash or refuse to apply subordinate legislation (law made by bodies to whom Parliament has delegated law-making powers), and may make a declaration of incompatibility in respect of an Act of Parliament. This prompts a government minister to make a remedial order amending the legislation so that it is compatible with Convention rights.

Since the HRA came into force, there have been approximately 20 declarations of incompatibility made by the courts, and around six of these have been overturned on appeal by either the Court of Appeal or House of Lords. An example of a declaration of incompatibility that has led to a change in the law is *A and others* v *Secretary of State for the Home Department* (2004). In this case, the provisions of the Anti-Terrorism, Crime and Security Act 2001 were challenged. The Act provided that foreign nationals who were suspected international terrorists, and who could not be deported from the UK, could be held indefinitely without charge or trial. The House of Lords declared the 2001 Act to be incompatible with Arts 5 and 14 of the ECHR. The incompatibility was later remedied by the passing of the Prevention of Terrorism Act 2005.

It can be concluded that the effect of the HRA on parliamentary sovereignty is limited. The courts have the power to declare that domestic legislation is incompatible with the HRA, but do not have the power to declare the domestic legislation invalid. Any amendment or repeal of legislation must be done by Parliament. Similarly, while a government minister must declare whether domestic legislation being introduced is compatible with the HRA, there is no specific requirement that it must be.

Devolution

Following referendums in Scotland and Wales, and by the Scotland Act 1998 and the Government of Wales Act 1998, the Westminster Parliament has devolved certain powers to the Scottish Parliament and to the Welsh Assembly. This means that these Parliaments can make laws for their own countries, such as in education matters, without referring back to Westminster. As a result, the sovereignty of the Westminster Parliament has been removed in these areas. As with EU law, in theory the Westminster

Key terms

European Convention on Human Rights (ECHR) 1950: an international treaty signed by 47 European countries with the common purpose of protecting fundamental rights and freedoms of citizens.

Human Rights Act (HRA) 1998: an Act of Parliament that incorporates the European Convention on Human Rights into UK domestic law.

Devolution: the statutory granting of certain powers from the Westminster Parliament to the Parliaments of Scotland and Wales.

Parliament could repeal the Acts devolving power and regain its sovereignty. The Westminster Parliament has also retained powers to make laws in areas such as defence, which affect the whole of the UK.

Fig. 1.7 *The Scottish Parliament at Holyrood in Edinburgh*

The conditions of parliamentary sovereignty:

- Parliament can make law on any topic it wishes
- the validity of law passed by Parliament cannot be questioned by anyone, including judges
- Parliament cannot bind itself or future Parliaments
- existing and future UK legislation must comply with EU law. The effect of the European Communities Act is that UK legislation is subordinate to EU law
- parliamentary sovereignty is not ultimately affected by the Human Rights Act. Government ministers must declare whether new legislation derogates from the HRA but no justification for derogation is needed
- the Westminster Parliament has granted devolved powers to the Scottish Parliament and to the Welsh Assembly.

Activity

Copy and complete the table below.

Table 1.4

European body	Founding international treaty	Principal aims	Court in which treaty is upheld	UK legislation incorporating the treaty into UK law
European Union				
Council of Europe				

You should now be able to:

- describe the doctrine of parliamentary supremacy
- discuss the effect of EU law on the doctrine of parliamentary supremacy
- discuss the effect of the Human Rights Act 1998 on the doctrine of parliamentary supremacy
- discuss the effect of devolution on the doctrine of parliamentary supremacy
- answer exam questions on parliamentary sovereignty.

2 Delegated legislation

In this topic you will learn how to:
- describe how delegated legislation in general is made
- describe how each of the main types of delegated legislation are made.

Link

Primary legislation is law passed by Parliament. For more detail, see Chapter 1 (Parliamentary law-making), p3.

Key terms

Delegated legislation: a law made by a person or body to which Parliament has delegated (or given) law-making power.

Parent Act: this term can equally be used because the delegated legislation can be viewed as the offspring or product of the original Act.

Enabling Act: an original Act passed by Parliament that enables another person or body to make law.

1 Types of delegated legislation

The verb 'delegate' means to pass power, responsibility or authority to another person or body. **Delegated legislation** is law made by a person or body to which Parliament has delegated law-making power.

Most Acts passed by Parliament each year provide a framework for the law, but more detailed rules are often needed. Parliament does not have enough time or expertise to make all these more detailed laws. There is often only time in a parliamentary session to debate a limited number of new laws and policy issues, especially as Parliament also has to hold the Government to account. There are several reasons why details may need to be added:

- a new law may be required for a specific area of the country, for which case specialist local knowledge may be required.
- a new law on a technical matter, such as health or agriculture, will require specialist technical knowledge.
- sometimes, an emergency or a new situation may require a new law to be made very quickly. Parliament often does not possess the necessary specialist local or technical knowledge to make law quickly. Also, the formal legislative process (outlined in Chapter 1), requiring readings in both Houses of Parliament, is not suitable when there is an emergency.

For these reasons, it is necessary for Parliament to delegate law-making power to people and bodies who are better equipped to make the necessary, detailed legal reforms.

The parent (or enabling) Act

In order for Parliament to delegate its power to another, a **parent Act**, otherwise known as an **enabling Act**, must be passed. By this piece of primary legislation, Parliament gives authority to others to make law. The parent Act will enable further law to be made under this authority.

The parent or enabling Act contains the outline framework of the new law. Within the Act there will be authority for a specified person (such as a government minister) or body (such as a local authority) to make further, more detailed law. It is these provisions of the enabling Act that delegate the power to make law.

It is likely that the Act will specify the area within which law can be made, and any procedures that the delegated person or body must follow when making the delegated laws.

Law-making power is given to the person or body best equipped with the knowledge and resources to make the type of law required.

As with the law banning smoking in enclosed public spaces, power to make law on such a technical matter is given to a government minister, who has the support of a specialist civil service department.

If power is given to a local authority to make delegated legislation, they will have the required local knowledge. If it is given to another body, such as a train or bus company, it will be given to make laws in respect of their property (for example, to enforce the payment of fares).

Types of delegated legislation

Orders in Council

Historically, the Monarch ruled the country through the **Privy Council**. As the powers of the Monarchy were eventually reduced and Parliament emerged as the sovereign power, the powers of the Privy Council diminished. One of the remaining functions of the Privy Council is to make **Orders in Council**. Orders in Council are drafted by the Government and given formal approval by the Queen and the Privy Council.

There are currently over 420 members of the Privy Council; however, only three or four current government ministers attend meetings at which Orders in Council are made.

The Privy Council, in full, consists of current and former government ministers, senior politicians (for example, leading members of the opposition parties), members of the Royal Family, two Archbishops, senior judges, British Ambassadors, and leading individuals of the Commonwealth. Appointment is made by the Queen on the advice of the Government, and is for life.

Key terms

Privy Council: a body made up of senior current and former politicians, senior judges and members of the Royal Family.

Orders in Council: laws made by the Queen and Privy Council which are enforceable in courts.

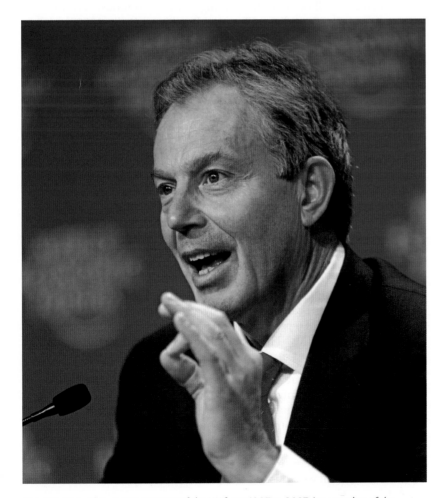

Fig. 2.1 *Tony Blair, Prime Minister of the UK from 1997 to 2007, is a member of the Privy Council*

Orders in Council are used in many situations, including:

■ transferring responsibilities between government departments, or from Westminster departments to the Scottish Parliament and the Welsh Assembly; this was done by the Scotland Act 1998 (Transfer of Functions to the Scottish Ministers etc.) Order 1999 and the National Assembly of Wales (Transfer of Functions) Order 1999

■ dissolving Parliament before an election

■ bringing an Act of Parliament into force

■ compliance with EU Directives – for example, the Consumer Protection Act 1987 (Product Liability) (Modification) Order 2000, which was passed to comply with a Product Liability Directive

■ dealing with foreign affairs – for example, the Afghanistan (United Nations Sanctions) Order 2001, which makes it an offence to make funds available to Osama Bin Laden or the Taliban or any person or body connected with Osama Bin Laden or the Taliban

■ in times of national emergency, when Parliament is not sitting. An example of an emergency situation in which an Order in Council was made, was after the terrorist attacks on 11 September 2001. The Terrorism (United Nations Measures) Order 2001, made on 10 October 2001 under the provisions of the United Nations Act 1946, made it an offence to provide funds to anyone involved in terrorism and allowed for the freezing of any such funds. A further example is The Extradition (Terrorist Bombings) Order 2002, which was made under the provisions of the Extradition Act 1989. It came into force on 27 August 2002 and allowed for persons suspected of terrorist activities to be extradited – that is, transferred from one country to another for questioning and trial. Another emergency situation that required an Order in Council was the fuel crisis in 2000. Truck drivers protesting about the price of fuel had blockaded some refineries, preventing fuel tankers from leaving, with the result that many petrol stations ran out of fuel. The Energy Act 1976 (Reserve Powers) Order 2000 was made under the provisions of the Energy Act 1976. It came into force on 11 September 2000 and enabled movement of fuel throughout the country. In the case of emergencies, powers are given by parent Acts which authorise the Queen and Privy Council to make law. Other examples of such parent Acts include the Emergency Powers Act 1920 and the Civil Contingencies Act 2004.

Statutory instruments

As seen by the example of implementing the smoking ban (see p31), **statutory instruments** are laws made by a government minister under the authority of a parent/enabling Act within the area of their ministerial responsibility. They are drafted by the legal department of the relevant government department.

Statutory instruments are often used to update a law; for example, a statutory instrument might be used to change the amount of a fine for a criminal offence. Another example is the regular increase in the amount of the national minimum wage under the National Minimum Wage Act 1998.

Sometimes wider powers are given to the government minister to fill in the necessary detail which is too complex to be incorporated into the Act.

Statutory instruments are often referred to as 'Regulations' or 'Orders'.

■ **Key terms**

Statutory instruments: laws made by Government ministers within the area of their responsibility. They are enforceable in the courts.

Statutory instruments are often made in the form of Commencement Orders. These are orders made by a government minister specifying when an Act or part of an Act must come into force. This is shown in the following example, which brings into force some of the Railways Act 2005.

2007 No. 62 (C. 2)
TRANSPORT
RAILWAYS
The Railways Act 2005 (Commencement No. 8) Order 2007
Made 16th January 2007
The Secretary of State makes the following Order in exercise of the powers conferred by section 60(2) of the Railways Act 2005:
Citation
1. This Order may be cited as the Railways Act 2005 (Commencement No. 8) Order 2007.
Commencement
2. (1) The provisions of the Railways Act 2005 specified in paragraph (2) shall come into force on 29th January 2007.
   (2) Those provisions are—
      (a) section 3 to the extent that it is not already in force;
      (b) section 4;
      (c) section 59(6) in so far as it relates to the provisions of Schedule 13 brought into force by this Order;
      (d) Schedule 4; and
      (e) in Part 1 of Schedule 13—
         (i) the entry relating to Schedule 4A of the Railways Act 1993 to the extent that it is not already in force; and
         (ii) the entry relating to paragraph 11 of Schedule 28 to the Transport Act 2000.
Signed by authority of the Secretary of State for Transport
Tom Harris
Parliamentary Under Secretary of State
16th January 2007

www.opsi.gov.uk

Sometimes several Commencement Orders may be made in respect of the same Act. For example, the Town and Country Planning Act 1971 was brought into force by 75 Commencement Orders! There is generally no time limit within which a Commencement Order must be made after an Act has been passed. This means that some Acts never actually come into force, an example being the Easter Act 1928, which specifies a fixed date for Easter.

Law that is made to comply with directives from the European Union is usually made in the form of a statutory instrument. For example:

- the Unfair Terms in Consumer Contracts Regulations 1999 were made in order to comply with the Unfair Terms in Consumer Contracts Directive 1993
- the Sale and Supply of Goods to Consumers Regulations 2002 were made in order to comply with the Sale of Consumer Goods Directive 1999.

Both of these regulations provide extra protection to consumers.

A large volume of law is made in the form of statutory instruments each year. In 2010, 2971 statutory instruments were made; in 2011, 3133 were made.

Statutory instruments can be enforced in the courts and are just as much part of the law of the country as Acts of Parliament. Some apply to the whole of the UK and others apply only to certain countries within the UK – for example, to England and Wales.

By-laws

By-laws are made by local authorities and public corporations or companies. They must be 'confirmed' (approved) by the relevant government minister, and are enforceable in the courts.

Local authorities can make laws that apply just within their geographical area. A County Council can pass laws affecting a whole county, while a City, Town or District Council may pass laws affecting that city, town or district. These laws may deal with many issues – for example, drinking alcohol in public places or the fouling of public areas by dogs.

Fig. 2.2 *These are common local authority by-laws*

A parent Act in respect of dog fouling is the Clean Neighbourhoods and Environment Act 2005, which replaced an earlier Act. Under the 2005 Act, a local authority can:

a   designate areas of land on which it is an offence for anyone to fail to remove dog faeces deposited by a dog for which he or she is responsible

b   to ban dogs from certain areas of land such as beaches, parks and children's playgrounds.

An example of a by-law made by Hastings Borough Council under the 2005 Act is shown below.

The Clean Neighbourhoods and Environment Act 2005:
The Fouling of Land by Dogs (Borough of Hastings) Order 2008

The Dog Control Orders (Prescribed Offences and Penalties, etc.) Regulations 2005 (S.I. 2006/1059)

The Fouling of Land by Dogs (Borough of Hastings) Order 2008

The Borough of Hastings hereby makes the following Order:

1. This Order comes into force on 25 March 2008.

Schedule 1

2. This Order applies to all land which is open to the air and to which the public are entitled or permitted to have access (with or without payment) within the Borough of Hastings (marked in red on a specific map)

Offence

3. (1) If a dog defecates at any time on land to which the Order applies and the person who is in charge of the dog, at that time, fails to remove the faeces from the land forthwith, that person shall be guilty of an offence unless:

   a. he has a reasonable excuse for failing to do so; or

   b. the owner, occupier or other person or authority having control of the land has consented (generally or specifically) to his failing to do so.

   (2) Nothing in this article applies to a person who:

   a. is registered as a blind person in a register compiled under section 29 of the National Assistance Act 1948; or

   b. has a disability which affects his mobility, manual dexterity, physical co-ordination or ability to lift, carry or otherwise move everyday objects, in respect of a dog trained by a prescribed charity and upon which he relies for assistance.

   (3) For the purposes of the article:

   a. a person who habitually has a dog in his possession shall be taken to be in charge of the dog at any time unless at that time some other person is in charge of the dog

   b. placing the faeces in a receptacle on the land which is provided for the purpose, or for the disposal of waste, shall be sufficient removal from the land

   c. being unaware of the defecation (whether by reason of not being in the vicinity or otherwise), or not having a device for or other suitable means of removing the faeces shall not be a reasonable excuse for failing to remove the faeces

   d. each of the following is a 'prescribed charity':
      i. Dogs for the Disabled (registered charity number 700454).
      ii. Support Dogs (registered charity number 1088281).
      iii. Canine Partners for Independence (registered charity number 803680).

Penalty

4. A person who is guilty of an offence under Article 3 shall be liable on summary conviction to a fine not exceeding level 3 on the standard scale.

Authority to make by-laws is given in several Acts of Parliament. Many by-laws are made under the authority of the Local Government Act 1972. For example, many local authorities make it an offence to drink alcohol or to skateboard or roller-skate in designated public places in their area, punishable with a fine. These designated areas have to have small signs supporting the prohibition; they are generally found on lampposts. See if you can find one in your area.

Public bodies and some companies are authorised to make laws regulating the behaviour of the public while on their property. For example, under the Railways Act 1993 railway companies can issue by-laws about the behaviour of the public on their stations and trains. By-laws made by public bodies and companies are enforceable in the courts. In *Boddington* v *British Transport Police* (1998) the defendant was caught smoking on the train in breach of a by-law made in 1965 by British Rail under the Transport Act 1962. The Magistrates' Court fined him £10 and the decision was upheld on appeal. Similar by-laws apply for the payment of fares and are enforceable by a penalty fare and/or fine.

Table 2.1 *A summary of the types of delegated legislation*

Type of delegated legislation Who makes it?	In what circumstances is it used?	Examples
Orders in Council. Made by the Queen and Privy Council.	To transfer responsibilitites between government departments. To dissolve Parliament.	National Assembly of Wales (Transfer of Functions) Order 1999.
	To bring Acts of Parliament into force. To comply with European Directives.	Consumer Protection Act 1987 (Product Liability) (Modification) Order 2000.
	To deal with foreign affairs.	Afghanistan (United Nations Sanctions) Order 2001.
	To deal with national emergencies.	Terrorism (United Nations Measures) Order 2001.
Statutory instruments. Made by government ministers.	To update and add detail to an Act of Parliament.	To increase the amount of a fine for a criminal offence, or change the annual amount of the national minimum wage.
	To bring an Act or part of an Act into force – a Commencement Order.	Railways Act 2005 Commencement Orders.
	To comply with directives from the European Union.	Sale and Supply of Goods to Consumers Regulations 2002.
By-laws. Made by local authorities and public corporations or companies.	To make laws for the good government of local areas.	By-laws made under the Clean Neighbourhoods and Environment Act 2005.
	To make laws regulating the behaviour of the public on property belonging to a public body or company.	By-laws restricting smoking on trains and stations, and imposing penalty fares for travelling on buses or trains without a valid ticket.

STATUTORY INSTRUMENTS

2006 No. 3368

PUBLIC HEALTH, ENGLAND

The Smoke-free (Premises and Enforcement) Regulations 2006

Made	13th December 2006
Laid before Parliament	18th December 2006
Coming into force	1st July 2007

The Secretary of State for Health, in exercise of the powers in sections 2(5), 10(1) and (2) and 79(3) of the Health Act 2006, makes the following Regulations:—

Citation, commencement, application and interpretation

1. (1) These Regulations may be cited as the Smoke-free (Premises and Enforcement) Regulations 2006 and shall come into force on 1 July 2007.

 (2) These Regulations apply in relation to England only.

 (3) In these Regulations 'the Act' means the Health Act 2006.

Enclosed and substantially enclosed premises

2. (1) For the purposes of section 2 of the Act, premises are enclosed if they—

 (a) have a ceiling or roof; and

 (b) except for doors, windows and passageways, are wholly enclosed either permanently or temporarily.

 (2) For the purposes of section 2 of the Act, premises are substantially enclosed if they have a ceiling or roof but there is—

 (a) an opening in the walls; or

 (b) an aggregate area of openings in the walls, which is less than half of the area of the walls, including other structures that serve the purpose of walls and constitute the perimeter of the premises.

 (3) In determining the area of an opening or an aggregate area of openings for the purposes of paragraph (2), no account is to be taken of openings in which there are doors, windows or other fittings that can be opened or shut.

 (4) In this regulation 'roof' includes any fixed or moveable structure or device which is capable of covering all or part of the premises as a roof, including, for example, a canvas awning.

Enforcement

3. (1) Each of the following authorities is designated as an enforcement authority for the purposes of Chapter 1 of Part 1 of the Act—

 (a) a unitary authority;

 (b) a district council in so far as it is not a unitary authority;

 (c) a London borough council;

 (d) a port health authority;

 (e) the Common Council of the City of London;

 (f) the Sub-Treasurer of the Inner Temple and the Under Treasurer of the Middle Temple; and

 (g) the Council of the Isles of Scilly.

Signed by authority of the Secretary of State for Health

Caroline Flint

Minister of State for Public Health Department of Health

13th December 2006

Activities

1 On page 31 is an extract of a recent piece of delegated legislation called a 'statutory instrument'. Answer the following questions about the extract:

   a Who was this piece of delegated legislation made by?

   b Under what piece of primary legislation (enabling Act) is it made?

   c To which part of the UK does the law apply?

   d Section 2 of the Health Act 2006 allows for the appropriate national authority to define, in delegated legislation, what 'enclosed premises' mean. How have they been defined?

   e How have 'substantially enclosed premises' been defined?

   f Who is responsible for enforcing the 'no smoking' ban?

   g Why was there a gap of six months between the making of the law and it coming into force?

2 Suggest which type of delegated legislation would be used in the following circumstances:

   a to transfer the responsibilities for university education from the Education Department to the newly created Department of Higher Education;

   b designating a new road;

   c a law introducing updated health and safety requirements;

   d increasing the amount of a fine for failing to travel with a valid train ticket;

   e declaring a 'state of emergency' to cope with widespread floods.

You should now be able to:

- identify the main types of delegated legislation
- describe how each of the main types of delegated legislation are made
- answer exam questions on the topic of creation of delegated legislation.

In this topic you will learn how to:

- describe parliamentary controls on delegated legislation
- describe judicial controls on delegated legislation
- evaluate the effectiveness of these controls.

2 Control of delegated legislation

We have seen that the power to make law is delegated to many different people/bodies. It is clear that some control must be exercised. Broadly speaking, there are two methods of control over delegated legislation: parliamentary control and judicial control.

Parliamentary control

The initial control Parliament exercises over delegated legislation is through the limits it sets in the parent/enabling Act. Only the people or bodies specified in the parent Act have power to make law, and the extent of that power is also specified. In addition, the parent Act will set out how the delegated legislation must be made and may establish certain procedures, such as consultation, that must be followed. Parliamentary supremacy is not compromised because Parliament ultimately remains in control of what law is made and how it is made. Although law-making is removed from the elected House of Commons through the parent Act, it specifies the limits of that power.

Parliament may repeal or amend the piece of delegated legislation. This control also upholds parliamentary supremacy, as Parliament can make or unmake any law. However, the effectiveness of this control is limited because, due to the volume of delegated legislation made each year, Parliament is not able to check it all.

All by-laws are confirmed or approved by the relevant government minister. For example, by-laws made by Hampshire County Council under the Children and Young Persons Act 1933, regulating the local employment of children, were approved by the Secretary for Health. This should ensure that all locally made law is overseen by those with knowledge of the technical issues involved. While local authorities are perhaps more aware than Parliament of local issues, the civil service department working for the minister possesses considerable technical expertise.

The Joint Select Committee on Statutory Instruments, more commonly known as the Scrutiny Committee, is made up of MPs and peers. Its role is to review statutory instruments and to refer provisions requiring further consideration to both Houses of Parliament. The main reasons for referring a statutory instrument back to the Houses of Parliament are:

- it appears to have gone beyond or outside the powers given under the parent/enabling Act
- it has not been made according to the method stipulated in the parent Act
- unexpected use has been made of the delegated power
- it is unclear or defective
- it imposes a tax or charge – only Parliament has the right to do this
- it is retrospective in its effect, and the parent/enabling Act did not allow for this.

This is arguably one of the more effective controls, as many statutory instruments are subject to some scrutiny. However, it is impossible for the Scrutiny Committee to review all statutory instruments because over 3000 are created each year. Furthermore, the powers of the Scrutiny Committee are limited in that it has no powers to amend the statutory instrument; it merely reports its findings back to either the House of Commons or the House of Lords. Research by the Hansard Society, reported in 1992, revealed that many of the Scrutiny Committe's findings were ignored.

The House of Lords Delegated Powers Scrutiny Committee checks all bills for any inappropriate enabling provisions. Any such provisions are brought to the attention of the House of Lords before the bill goes to the Committee stage (see p15). This is an effective control because, if the enabling provisions are made appropriately, it is more likely the law made under the authority of them will also be.

Most statutory instruments must be laid before Parliament. This requires the statutory instruments to be laid on the table of the House. The parent Act will state whether the statutory instrument must be laid before Parliament, and which method must be used. There are two methods of laying delegated legislation before Parliament.

First, there is **the positive (or affirmative) resolution procedure**. This means that the statutory instrument must be approved by one or both Houses of Parliament within a specified time, usually between 28 and 40 days, before it can become law. An example is the Human Rights Act 1998. Section 1(4) authorises the Secretary of State to make amendments to the Act as he thinks fit, to reflect the rights in protocols that have been ratified or have been signed with a view to ratification by the UK. By virtue of s20 any such amendments are subject to the affirmative resolution procedure.

The disadvantage of this form of control is that it is time-consuming, defeating one of the main objectives of delegated legislation, which is to save Parliament time. Furthermore, the statutory instrument cannot be amended by Parliament, only approved, annulled or withdrawn. The control is also limited in that, while it exists to control ministerial power, the Government, by virtue of its majority in the House of Commons, will usually win a vote. As a result of these disadvantages, the affirmative resolution is not used very often. However, statutory instruments subject to the affirmative resolution must always be debated by Parliament, and it is therefore more effective than some of the other controls. For this reason it is used for very important and potentially controversial issues.

Secondly, most statutory instruments are subject to the **negative resolution procedure**. The statutory instrument is laid before Parliament, usually for 40 days, during which time either House of Parliament can annul the instrument. All members of both Houses can put down a motion, known as a 'prayer', calling for annulment. There is then a debate and a vote. If either House votes to pass the annulment motion, the statutory instrument does not become law. More often, however, the statutory instrument is not annulled during the 40-day period, and so automatically becomes law.

It is arguable that this control is of limited effect, as there is no requirement for MPs to look at the statutory instrument. Most delegated legislation subject to this method is not challenged, and automatically becomes law after 40 days. However, this method of control does give an opportunity for any member of either House to raise objections. This in turn may provide for more debate and consideration to be given to the provisions of the statutory instrument.

Publication

The Statutory Instruments Act 1946 provides a defence to someone in breach of a statutory instrument if it has not been issued – published – by Her Majesty's Stationery Office. This means that all statutory instruments must be published in order to be fully effective.

Although publication does not mean that everyone will be aware of the statutory instrument, this requirement does at least mean that the public have access to it.

Questions

Another form of parliamentary control is that the responsible minister can be questioned by Parliament at Question Time or during debates. This method of control gives publicity to the delegated legislation due to the presence of the media in Parliament. It also makes the responsible minister explain and justify the legal provisions. However, questioning politicians is not always useful – politicians are notoriously skilled at not answering questions directly, and instead putting forward their own view.

Removing power

The final control is that Parliament may remove the power to legislate from the delegated person or body. This can be done by amending or repealing the parent or enabling Act.

This control upholds parliamentary supremacy. It should also mean that the delegated person or body takes care in the preparation of delegated legislation, knowing that their legislative power could be taken away. However, the volume of delegated legislation again limits the effectiveness of this control, as many provisions will inevitably remain unnoticed by Parliament.

Control by the judiciary

The validity of a piece of delegated legislation can be challenged in the High Court through the **judicial review** procedure. Judicial review was defined by Mr Justice Simon Brown – now Lord Brown – in *Ex parte Vijayatunga* (1988) as the 'exercise of the court's inherent power at common law to determine whether action is lawful or not'. Judicial review is not concerned with the merits of the delegated legislation or the reasons behind it, only whether it is lawful.

When the delegated legislation is made beyond the powers conferred by the parent/enabling Act, the delegated legislation can be declared *ultra vires* by the court and therefore void. **Ultra vires** means 'beyond the powers' or 'exceeding the authority of'. Any individual may challenge the validity of delegated legislation, provided he is affected by it.

There are two types of *ultra vires*: procedural *ultra vires* and substantive *ultra vires*.

Procedural ultra vires

Procedural ultra vires is concerned with how the delegated legislation is made. Some parent Acts specify procedures that must be followed. Any delegated legislation made without following these procedures can be declared *ultra vires* and therefore void. An example is *Agricultural, Horticultural and Forestry Training Board* v *Aylesbury Mushrooms Ltd* (1972), commonly known as the *Aylesbury Mushroom* case. An order against mushroom growers was declared void because a letter informing the Mushroom Growers' Association of the new law did not comply with the requirement in the parent Act to consult interested parties.

Substantive ultra vires

Substantive ultra vires is concerned with whether the content of the delegated legislation is within the limits set out in the parent Act. Any delegated legislation beyond these limits can be declared *ultra vires* and therefore void. In *A-G* v *Fulham Corporation* (1921), the parent Act gave the Corporation power to provide clothes-washing facilities for the public. In 1920, the Corporation set up a commercial laundry where council employees washed the residents' clothes. This was held to be *ultra vires* because the parent/enabling Act did not give authority to the Corporation to wash clothes for others. Another example is *Customs and Excise Commissioners* v *Cure and Deeley Ltd* (1962). The parent/enabling Act gave the Commissioners power to make laws concerning the collection of taxes. The Commissioners made a law deciding the amount of tax due when a tax return was submitted late. This was substantive *ultra vires*. The Commissioners had power to make laws concerning the collection of tax due, but not to rule on the amount of tax due.

Unreasonableness

The courts may also declare the delegated legislation to be *ultra vires* and therefore void on the basis that it is unreasonable. This judicial control was established in *Associated Provincial Picture Houses* v *Wednesbury Corporation* (1948), and is commonly known as 'Wednesbury unreasonableness'. It is often argued in judicial cases such as in *R (Rogers)* v *Swindon NHS Trust* (2006), when a woman with early-stage breast cancer was prescribed Herceptin by her doctor. The NHS Trust refused to provide this non-approved drug because (it said) her case was not exceptional. The Court of Appeal said this policy was irrational and unreasonable, and therefore unlawful. The Trust was unable to put forward any clear reasons for providing the drug for some patients and not for others.

Key terms

Judicial review: the procedure by which the High Court can ensure that the decision of a public body has been made lawfully.

Ultra vires: a court order which says that the delegated legislation is 'beyond the powers' set out in the parent Act.

Procedural *ultra vires*: the piece of delegated legislation has not been made using the procedures specified in the parent Act.

Substantive *ultra vires*: the content of the delegated legislation is beyond the limits set out in the parent Act.

Other circumstances where the delegated legislation may be declared void

Courts may also declare a piece of delegated legislation *ultra vires* and therefore void:

■ where it levies taxes

■ where it allows sub-delegation – no body to which law-making powers have been delegated has power to delegate to another body

■ where all interested parties have not been consulted as required by the parent/enabling Act

■ where the delegated legislation conflicts with European legislation.

Effectiveness of judicial control

Although there are quite a broad range of controls, the effectiveness of judicial control is limited. This is because the courts are dependent on cases being brought before them. It is quite rare that a person will question the validity of a law which it is claimed they have contravened. To do so requires considerable legal knowledge, financial resources and time. Even when a judge is presented with the opportunity to review a piece of delegated legislation, he or she cannot amend it, only declare it void. However, when delegated legislation is challenged in the courts, a judge is able to ensure that it has been made in accordance with the instructions set out by the democratically elected House of Commons within the parent Act. This upholds parliamentary supremacy because while a judge can declare a piece of delegated legislation to be void, he or she can only do so if it does not conform to the instructions given by Parliament.

Table 2.2 *A summary of the controls on delegated legislation*

Parliamentary controls	Judicial controls
The parent Act sets out the limits within which delegated law must be made or the procedures to be followed.	Procedural *ultra vires*. The delegated legislation is void because the procedures set out in the parent Act for creating it have not been followed, as in the *Aylesbury Mushroom Case* (1972).
Parliament can repeal or amend the delegated legislation.	
All delegated legislation, including by-laws, are made under the authority of government ministers.	Substantive *ultra vires*. The delegated legislation is void because the content exceeds the limits set out in the parent Act: for example, *Customs and Excise Commissioners* v *Cure and Deeley Ltd* (1962).
It is the role of the Scrutiny Committee to review statutory instruments and refer any requiring further consideration back to the Houses of Parliament.	Unreasonableness. The delegated legislation is void because it is so unreasonable: for example, *R (Rogers)* v *Swindon NHS Trust* (2006).
The House of Lords Delegated Powers Scrutiny Committee checks the enabling provisions of the parent Acts.	
The Statutory Instruments Act 1946 requires all statutory instruments (SIs) to be published.	
The affirmative resolution procedure. The SI is laid before Parliament and becomes law if approved by both Houses.	
The negative resolution procedure. The SI is laid before Parliament and automatically becomes law unless annulled.	
Ministers can be held to account at Question Time or during debates.	
Parliament can remove the power to make delegated legislation.	

Nuclear consultation was flawed

Queen's Bench Division
Published 20 February 2007
Regina (Greenpeace Ltd) v Secretary of State for Trade and Industry
Before Mr Justice Sullivan
Judgement February 16, 2007

Where it had been stated in a Government White Paper that there would be the fullest public consultation before making a decision on a matter of substantial public policy but information as to major relevant issues had emerged only after consultation had closed, then the decision-making process was fatally flawed.

Mr Justice Sullivan so held in the Queen's Bench Division in allowing the application of Greenpeace Ltd for judicial review by way of an order to quash the decision of the Secretary of State for Trade and Industry to announce Government support for the building of new civil nuclear power generation facilities.

Mr Nigel Pleming, QC and Ms Kassie Smith for Greenpeace; **Mr Richard Drabble, QC** and **Mr David Forsdick** for the secretary of state.

MR JUSTICE SULLIVAN said that a 2003 White Paper had said that a new nuclear build was not proposed and that there would be the fullest public consultation before a decision was made.

The consultation process was very seriously flawed. As an issues paper the Government's consultation paper was perfectly adequate. As the consultation paper on an issue of such importance and complexity it was manifestly inadequate.

It contained no proposals as such; even if it had, the information given to those consulted was wholly insufficient to enable them to make an intelligent response.

On both the economics and the waste issues all, or virtually all the information of any substance emerged only after the consultation period had concluded.

Elementary fairness required that those consulted should be given a proper opportunity to respond to the substantial amount of new evidence. There could be no proper consultation, let alone the fullest public consultation if the substance of these two issues was not consulted upon before the decision was made.

There was therefore procedural unfairness and a breach of legitimate expectation that there be the fullest public consultation before a decision was taken to support a new nuclear build. The application succeeded.

Solicitors: **Harrison Grant**, Kentish Town; **Treasury Solicitor**.

The Times, 20 February 2007

Activity

Read through the above report from *The Times* and answer the following questions:

1. Which organisation is challenging the Government?

2. In which court was the case heard?

3. Is this a case of procedural or substantive *ultra vires*?

4. What kind of order was requested?

5. What is the effect of the order granted by the judge?

6. Why might some people regard this order as an attack on the Government by the judge?

Activity

The Roads Act gives the Highways Minister power to make changes to the Highway Code by statutory instrument. A new Code is introduced which requires cyclists to wear helmets at all times while cycling and to cycle only in designated cycle lanes. The Order becomes law on the date stated on it, but will be annulled if either House passes a motion calling for its annulment within a certain time. This time period is 40 days including the day on which it was laid.

1 Is the Order subject to the affirmative or negative resolution procedure?

2 Members of the Keep Cycling Campaign consider that these changes are the biggest threat to cycling for decades. Advise them how these changes can be removed from the new Code.

You should now be able to:

- understand how delegated legislation is controlled by Parliament and the courts
- discuss the effectiveness of these controls
- attempt previous questions on controls of delegated legislation.

In this topic you will learn how to:

- discuss advantages of delegated legislation
- discuss disadvantages of delegated legislation.

3 Advantages and disadvantages of delegated legislation

Advantages of delegated legislation

Time-saving

Delegated legislation saves Parliament time. Parliament does not have enough time to pass all the new detailed and local laws required each year. There is often only enough time in the parliamentary session to pass all Government bills introduced. There is very little time left for other types of bills, and making over 3000 statutory instruments as well as local by-laws and emergency provisions each year would be impossible.

Delegated legislation can be passed quickly to deal with situations when they arise, and in emergencies. If it was necessary to follow the parliamentary procedure, it would take too long before the law was introduced. This would be wholly inappropriate and ineffective in emergency situations.

Produced with specialist knowledge

People with specialist knowledge are involved in the preparation of delegated legislation. Parliament does not necessarily possess this specialist knowledge. For example, local councils have greater knowledge of the local area. Bristol City Council has several by-laws relating to the Clifton and Durdham Downs. These by-laws regulate behaviour on the Downs and, amongst other things, prohibit vehicles and grazing. government ministers and their civil service departments have considerable technical knowledge within their particular area of responsibility. For example, the Cableway Installation Regulations 2004, made by the Transport Minister in order to comply with a European Directive, required detailed technical knowledge of cablecars, drag lifts and ski lifts, etc.

Parliamentary control

There is some control over delegated legislation. In Parliament, statutory instruments are subject to affirmative or negative resolutions or are scrutinised by the Scrutiny Committee. By-laws must be approved by the relevant minister, and a judge can declare void any delegated legislation that has gone beyond its powers. This range of control should ensure that all delegated legislation conforms to the requirements of the parent Act and therefore the will of Parliament.

Democratic

Delegated legislation is, to an extent, democratic. government ministers, who are responsible for issuing statutory instruments and who also approve by-laws, are elected. Local councillors, responsible for making by-laws, are also elected. Orders in Council are drafted by the Government, although they are approved by the Queen and Privy Council, neither of which is an elected body.

Disadvantages of delegated legislation

Partly undemocratic

The process of making delegated legislation is to some degree undemocratic. Delegated legislation is not debated by Parliament, except in the case of statutory instruments subject to the affirmative resolution procedure. Statutory instruments are drafted by unelected, permanently employed civil servants, and are often only rubber-stamped by the appropriate minister. As discussed above, the Queen and Privy Council are not elected, yet they approve Orders in Council.

Lack of publicity

Delegated legislation is insufficiently publicised. Because delegated legislation is not debated by Parliament, there is not the same opportunity for the press to raise public awareness of it as there is with an Act of Parliament. This, added to the fact that there is no general effective way to publicise delegated legislation, means that an enormous volume of law is passed without the public being aware of it. Much remains unpublicised after coming into force.

No effective control

There is a lack of proper control. Many of the parliamentary and judicial controls are limited in effect. For example, not all statutory instruments are subject to an affirmative or negative resolution, and those subject to the latter may be overlooked. Judicial controls are dependent on a person challenging the validity of the law, which rarely occurs due to limited knowledge, finance and time. Consequently, some delegated legislation that is *ultra vires* is never challenged, and so remains in force.

Contradicts the separation of powers

Some delegated legislation offends the doctrine of separation of powers. Under this doctrine there are three branches of power: the executive, the legislature and the judiciary. No one should be a member of more than one of the three branches of power, and the three branches should operate separately from each other. They should not perform each other's duties.

The executive is the Government and is responsible for formulating policy. In theory, Government ministers should not also be making law.

> **Study tips**
>
> A point can be argued both as an advantage and as a disadvantage. It is an advantage that delegated legislation is to an extent democratic, yet a disadvantage that it is to an extent undemocratic.

> **Study tips**
>
> This is another disadvantage with a contradictory advantage. It is an advantage that there is control, yet a disadvantage that there is a lack of control.

The legislature is the Houses of Parliament and is responsible for making law.

The judiciary should ensure the law passed by Parliament is applied. According to this theory, they should not be declaring whether the law is valid or not.

Risk of sub-delegation

There is a risk of sub-delegation where the person or body that has been given the power to make law may pass this power down to another. For example, statutory instruments are supposed to be made by Government ministers. In reality, they often merely rubber-stamp laws actually made by their civil servants.

Table 2.3 *A table identifying the advantages and disadvantages of delegated legislation*

Advantages of delegated legislation	Disadvantages of delegated legislation
It saves Parliament time.	There is a lack of publicity.
It is flexible.	Some delegated legislation offends the separation of powers.
It is made by people with local and technical expertise.	There is a risk of sub-delegation.
There is control over delegated legislation.	There is a lack of effective control.
It is, to an extent, democratic.	It is, to an extent, undemocratic.

You should now be able to:

- discuss advantages of delegated legislation
- discuss disadvantages of delegated legislation
- answer past paper questions on advantages and disadvantages of delegated legislation.

3 Statutory interpretation

Key terms

Statutory interpretation: the interpretation of Acts of Parliament by judges.

The literal rule: words or phrases in an Act are given their ordinary, natural or dictionary meaning. The literal rule does not allow a judge to create law. It requires application of the law as stated by Parliament.

Key cases

Whiteley v Chappell (1868); Fisher v Bell (1961): the literal rule of interpretation was used by the court in these cases, and produced an unexpected outcome.

1 Approaches to statutory interpretation

Acts of Parliament, sometimes referred to as 'legislation' or 'statutes', are usually drafted by parliamentary counsel (draftsmen). However, while it is the role of Parliament to create legislation, it is the role of the judges in court to apply it. Despite the best efforts of parliamentary draftsmen to make the Act as clear and as understandable as possible, some words may be ambiguous – that is, have more than one meaning – or may be unclear. Sometimes an Act may be deliberately drafted in broad terms to allow the Act to be flexible enough to cover unforeseen circumstances or matters which may arise in the future – for example, improved technology. These are some of the reasons that the judge may be required to interpret the Act/legislation/statute so as to provide for an appropriate outcome in the case before him/her – hence the term **statutory interpretation**.

While it is only the minority of Acts that pose such interpretation problems, 75 per cent of cases heard by the Supreme Court are concerned with statutory interpretation.

In addition to materials both inside and outside the Act, judges are assisted by certain 'rules' and presumptions. These 'rules' have been developed by the judges themselves and are not rules in the strict legal sense, but are alternative ways a judge can approach interpreting an Act. A judge will make certain presumptions when interpreting Acts of Parliament. The main presumptions are that Acts of Parliament are not retrospective (that is, they only apply to situations arising after the Act is passed), that the Crown is not bound, that there is no change in the common law unless the Act expressly states that there is, and that *mens rea* (a guilty mind) is required in criminal cases. Presumptions are beyond the scope of the AQA specification and will therefore not be considered further in this chapter.

The rules of interpretation

The literal rule

The literal rule requires the judge to give the word or phrase its natural, ordinary or dictionary meaning, even if this appears to be contrary to the intentions of Parliament. As Lord Reid said in *Pinner* v *Everett* (1969), 'In determining the meaning of any words or phrase in a statute, the first question to ask is always *what is the natural and ordinary meaning of that word or phrase* in its context in the statute.'

Application of the literal rule may lead to unexpected results that were not intended by Parliament. In **Whiteley v Chappell (1868)**, an Act made it an offence to impersonate 'any person entitled to vote at an election.' The defendant attempted to vote in the name of a deceased person, but the court held no offence had been committed because when 'any person entitled to vote' is interpreted literally, it does not include dead people.

Application of the literal rule also produced an unexpected result in **Fisher v Bell (1961)**. The defendant displayed flick knives in his shop window. He was charged under The Restriction of Offensive Weapons Act 1959. The Act made it an offence to 'sell or offer for sale' an offensive weapon. In contract law, the display of goods in a shop window is not an offer for sale but an invitation to treat; the display of goods thus invites the customer to make an offer to buy the goods. The court found the defendant not guilty despite the obvious aim of the Act being to prevent such behaviour.

The golden rule

This rule is an extension of the literal rule. It allows the court to look at the literal meaning of a word or phrase, but then avoid using a literal interpretation that would lead to an absurd result. There are two approaches taken to applying the golden rule: the narrow approach and the broad approach.

Where a word or phrase is capable of more than one literal meaning, the narrow application of the golden rule allows the judge(s) to select the meaning that avoids an absurdity. For example, in **Allen (1872)** the defendant remarried but this marriage would have been void because the woman was the niece of his first wife. However, he was charged under s57 Offences Against the Person Act 1861, which states whosoever being married shall marry again without the previous marriage being ended commits an offence. Allen argued that he could not be guilty because his second marriage was void in any case. The court decided that being married meant 'being validly married' but that 'shall marry' meant simply 'go through a marriage ceremony', which Allen had done. So, he was held to be guilty under the Act.

Where there is only one literal meaning of a word or phrase, but to apply it would cause an absurdity, then under the broad approach the court will modify this meaning to avoid the absurdity. In **Adler v George (1964)** the defendant was charged under the Official Secrets Act 1920 with obstructing a member of the armed forces 'in the vicinity of a prohibited place.' The defendant argued that he was actually in the prohibited place, not in the vicinity of it – that is, near to it. Had the court applied this literal interpretation of the phrase, the defendant would not have been guilty. The court therefore interpreted the phrase 'in the vicinity of' to include 'in' a prohibited place, to avoid the absurd result.

The golden rule provides an opportunity for judicial law-making. The narrow approach allows the judges to choose between two or more meanings of the words as stated by Parliament. The broad approach provides further scope for judicial law-making because it allows the judges to modify the meaning of the words as stated by Parliament.

The mischief rule

Under this rule, the court looks at the gap in the law that Parliament had felt it necessary to fill by passing the Act. It then interprets the Act to fill that gap and to remedy the 'mischief' Parliament had been aiming to remedy.

In *Heydon's Case (1584)* the judges said that the court should consider four things when attempting to interpret a statutory provision:

1 What was the common law before the Act was passed?
2 What was the defect or mischief for which the common law did not provide a remedy?
3 What remedy does the Act attempt to provide to cure the defect?
4 What is the true reason for the remedy?

Broadly speaking, therefore, the rule requires that where an Act has been passed to remedy a weakness or defect in the law, the interpretation that will correct that weakness or defect is the one that should be adopted.

The mischief rule was applied in **Smith v Hughes (1960)**. Under the Street Offences Act 1959 it is an offence to solicit 'in the street or public place'. Prostitutes solicited men from a balcony and through a window while in their home. The accused was found guilty of the offence even though she had not been in the street when the soliciting took place. Parker LCJ said that regard should be had to the mischief at which the Act was aimed. He said 'everybody knows this was an Act designed to clean up the streets'. The court held that, as the Act aimed to prevent people from being solicited whilst they were in the street or public place, it did not matter where the soliciting originated from.

The mischief rule provides scope for judicial law-making because it allows judges to decide what they think Parliament was trying to put right in the previous law. The judges do not focus on the words as stated by Parliament.

The purposive approach

The mischief rule involves the court looking back to the common law position before the Act was passed, to find the gap in the law that Parliament was trying to fill. The purposive approach focuses on what Parliament intended when passing the new law. The purposive approach is a modern version of the mischief approach. It is generally recognised by academics and the judiciary that the distinction between these two approaches is a minor technicality. In *Pepper (Inspector of Taxes)* v *Hart* (1993), Lord Browne-Wilkinson said 'the fine distinctions between looking for the mischief and looking for the intention in using words to provide the remedy are technical and inappropriate'.

In recent years, especially since the UK joined the European Union, the UK courts have increasingly used the purposive approach when interpreting legislation. Unlike UK legislation, European law is drafted in broad terms. In *Bulmer Ltd* v *J Bollinger SA* (1974), Lord Denning compared the two. 'The draftsmen of our statutes have striven to express themselves with the utmost exactness … In consequence the judges have followed suit. They interpret a statute as applying only to the circumstances covered by the very words. They give them a literal interpretation … How different is this treaty! It lays down general principles. It expresses its aims and purposes … All the way through the treaty there are gaps and lacunae [missing sections]. These have to be filled in by the judges, or by regulations or directives. It is the European way.'

In order to ensure the consistent application of European law throughout all the member states, judges in the UK recognise that when interpreting European legislation or domestic legislation enacted to comply with European law, the purposive approach to interpretation needs to be adopted. In *Bulmer Ltd* v *J Bollinger SA* (1974), Lord Denning said of the judge's role: 'No longer must they examine the words in meticulous detail. No longer must they argue about the precise grammatical sense. They must look to the purpose or intent. To quote the words of the European Court in the *Da Costa* case they must deduce from the wording and the spirit of the Treaty the meaning of the Community rules.' This preference for the purposive approach was extended to United Kingdom legislation by the House of Lords in *Pepper (Inspector of Taxes)* v *Hart* (1993). Lord Griffiths said, 'the days have long passed when the courts adopted a strict constructionist view of interpretation which required them to adopt the literal meaning of the language. The courts now adopt a purposive approach which seeks to give effect to the true purpose of legislation and are prepared to look at much extraneous material that bears on the background against which the legislation was enacted.'

> ### ▍Key cases
>
> **Smith v Hughes (1960):** the mischief rule was applied by the court.

Another influence operating on United Kingdom judges which encourages the use of the purposive approach is the Human Rights Act 1998. This Act provides that all United Kingdom legislation must be interpreted so as to be compatible with the European Convention on Human Rights (ECHR). The ECHR is drafted in broad terms, as is the law of the European Union. The European Court of Human Rights thus adopts a purposive approach when interpreting the ECHR, and this approach is now followed by United Kingdom judges when interpreting legislation in Human Rights Act cases.

Fig. 3.1 *A courtroom in the European Court of Human Rights, in Strasbourg, France*

While judges continue to use the literal, golden and mischief rules, there has clearly been a considerable shift from a preference for the literal rule to a preference for the purposive approach. This is in accordance with the recommendations of the Law Commission Report on the Interpretation of Statutes (1969), which has not to date been implemented. This report stated, 'The principles of interpretation would include: the preference of a construction which would promote the general legislative purpose over one which would not.'

Examples of cases in which judges have used the purposive approach include **Pepper (Inspector of Taxes) v Hart (1993)** and **Jones v Tower Boot Co. (1997)**.

In *Pepper (Inspector of Taxes)* v *Hart* (1993) the issue was how to interpret s63 of the Finance Act 1976. Teachers at an independent school for boys were having their children educated at the school for a fifth of the price charged to the public. This was a taxable benefit based on the 'cash equivalent' of the concession. Under s63 of the 1976 Act, the words 'cash equivalent' could be interpreted to mean either the additional cost of providing the concession to the teachers or the average cost of providing the tuition to the public and the teachers. The House of Lords referred to statements made by the Financial Secretary to the Treasury during the committee stage, which revealed that the intention of Parliament was to tax employees on the basis of the additional cost to the employer of providing the concession.

■ **Key cases**

Pepper (Inspector of Taxes) v Hart (1993); Jones v Tower Boot Co. (1997): the purposive approach was applied by the court.

In *Jones* v *Tower Boot Co.* (1997) the Court of Appeal had to decide whether the physical and verbal abuse of a young black worker by his workmates fell within 'the course of employment' under s32 of the Race Relations Act 1976. The employer had argued that these actions fell outside the course of the workmates' employment, because such behaviour was not part of their job. The Employment Appeal Tribunal agreed with the employer's argument and found that the employer could not therefore be held responsible to the young black worker for his workmates' behaviour. This decision was reversed by the Court of Appeal using the purposive approach to interpret s32. Parliament's intention when enacting the Race Relations Act was to eliminate discrimination in the workplace, and this would not be achieved by applying a narrow construction to the wording.

The purposive approach provides scope for judicial law-making because the judge is allowed to decide what he/she thinks Parliament intended the Act to say rather than what the Act actually says.

Activities

1 Answer the following questions concerning cases considered in this topic.

   a What rule of interpretation do you think influenced the Court of Appeal in *Jones* v *Tower Boot Co.*?

   b What would the outcome have been in *Smith* v *Hughes* had the court applied the literal rule?

   c What would the outcome have been in *Whiteley* v *Chappell* had the court applied the golden rule?

2 Explain, using examples, the rules judges may use when interpreting Acts of Parliament.

3 Taking into account the tips throughout this topic, make a bullet-point essay plan in respect of activity 2 above.

You should now be able to:

- explain the four approaches to statutory interpretation
- use cases to illustrate the rules of statutory interpretation
- attempt past paper questions on the topic of statutory interpretation.

---

2 Aids to interpretation

There are certain materials both inside and outside the Act that the judge can refer to, which help him/her interpret the words or provisions of the Act. These are known as 'aids to interpretation'. There are two types of aids: intrinsic aids and extrinsic aids.

Intrinsic aids

Intrinsic aids to interpretation are found within the Act itself. The judge may use other parts of the Act to understand the meaning of the word or phrase in question.

The long and/or short title of the Act may be referred to as guidance. The long title of the Abortion Act 1967 is 'An Act to amend and clarify the law relating to termination of pregnancy by registered medical practitioners'.

In this topic you will learn how to:

- state the different intrinsic aids to interpretation
- state the different extrinsic aids to interpretation
- give relevant examples of intrinsic and extrinsic aids to interpretation
- state the different rules of language
- give relevant examples for each rule of language.

Key terms

Intrinsic aids: aids found within the Act.

This was referred to by four of the five Law Lords who heard the appeal in *Royal College of Nursing of the United Kingdom* v *DHSS* (1981).

Older statutes may contain a preamble, which is a statement preceding the main body of the Act, setting out the purpose of the Act in detail. Newer Acts may contain an objectives or purposes section at the beginning of the Act. For example, the purposes section of the Climate Change and Sustainable Energy Act 2006 states:

1 Purposes

1 The principal purpose of this Act is to enhance the United Kingdom's contribution to combating climate change.

2 In performing functions under this Act, the relevant persons and bodies shall have regard to—
   a the principal purpose set out in subsection (1),
   b the desirability of alleviating fuel poverty, and
   c the desirability of securing a diverse and viable long-term energy supply.

3 In this section 'the relevant persons and bodies' means—
   a the Secretary of State;
   b any public authority.

www.opsi.gov.uk

Schedules appear as additions to the main body of the Act. These can be referred to in order to make some sense of the main text. In some cases it is necessary to refer to Schedules to understand the Act. For example, s2(1) of the Hunting Act 2004 provides 'Hunting is exempt if it is within a class specified in Schedule 1'. The exempt classes of hunting are then specified in Schedule 1.

Most modern Acts contain an interpretation definition section, which explains the meaning of key words used in the Act. For example, the Law Reform (Year and a Day Rule) Act 1996 provides that the defendant can be guilty of a fatal offence where the death follows more than a year and a day after the defendant's act or omission. Section 2(3) defines fatal offence as:

   a murder, manslaughter, infanticide or any other offence of which one of the elements is causing a person's death, or

   b the offence of aiding, abetting, counselling or procuring a person's suicide.

Punctuation is now recognised to have an effect on the meaning of words and can be taken into account in deciding the meaning of statutory provisions. In *Hanlon* v *The Law Society* (1981) Lord Lowry said:

   I consider that not to take account of punctuation disregards the reality that literate people, such as parliamentary draftsmen, punctuate what they write, if not identically, at least in accordance with grammatical principles. Why should not literate people, such as judges, look at the punctuation in order to interpret the meaning of the legislation as accepted by Parliament.

Extrinsic aids

Key terms

Extrinsic aids: aids to interpretation found outside the Act.

Extrinsic aids are materials found outside the Act that may be referred to by the judge.

Dictionaries can be used to find the literal meaning of words. In *Vaughan* v *Vaughan* (1973) the Court of Appeal had to interpret the word 'molest'.

The defendant had been the subject of injunctions in respect of previous violence towards his ex-wife, who was afraid of him. The defendant argued that pestering his ex-wife to resume their relationship by going to her home early in the morning and late at night, and also calling on her at work, did not amount to molesting her. The judges consulted the dictionary, which defined 'molest' as to 'cause trouble, vex, annoy, or put to inconvenience', and held that the defendant's behaviour did amount to molestation.

Previous Acts may be referred to. In *Wheatley* (1979) the Court of Appeal had to interpret the provisions of the Explosive Substances Act 1883. The long title of the Act was 'An Act to amend the law relating to explosive substances, amending the Explosives Act 1875'. The Court of Appeal therefore looked at the earlier Act to make sense of the 1883 Act.

Fig. 3.2 *Someone loitering outside a house at night*

The Interpretation Act 1978 provides a definition of certain words that are often used in Acts. For example, it provides that 'masculine shall include the feminine' and 'singular words include the plural unless a contrary intention appears within an Act'. Section 6 provides:

> In any Act, unless the contrary intention appears,
>
> **a** words importing the masculine gender include the feminine;
>
> **b** words importing the feminine gender include the masculine;
>
> **c** words in the singular include the plural and words in the plural include the singular.

The court may look at Reports of the Law Commission, Royal Commissions and other official law reform bodies. A Law Commission report can highlight what is wrong with the old law, and suggest options. Its report usually includes a draft bill, designed to update or improve the law.

International Treaties may be referred to in order to ascertain the overriding objective of the Treaty with which the Act is intended to comply. This will often arise when judges are interpreting EU law.

Since *Pepper (Inspector of Taxes)* v *Hart* (1993) the courts have been able to refer to the parliamentary debates recorded in Hansard. However, in this case, the House of Lords held that Hansard could only be referred to in certain circumstances:

- The wording in the Act must be ambiguous or obscure, or a literal interpretation would lead to an absurdity.
- Judges may look only at statements made by a minister or other promoter of the bill.
- The statements must be clear in order for them to be relied upon.

Since 1999, Acts have been issued with explanatory notes. These are not part of the Act, hence they are an extrinsic rather than an intrinsic aid. Explanatory notes are written by the Government department responsible for the Act, once the Act has been given Royal Assent.

Text books may be referred to for guidance on the meaning of a word or phrase. For example, in *Re Castioni* (1891) J. F. Stephen referred to his own text, *History of the Criminal Law of England*, when interpreting the words 'political crime'.

Table 3.1 *Examples of intrinsic and extrinsic aids*

Intrinsic aids: aids within the Act	Extrinsic aids: aids outside the Act
Long/short title	Dictionaries
Preamble/objectives/purposes section	Previous Acts
Schedules	Interpretation Act (1978)
Definition section	Reports of law reform bodies
Punctuation	Hansard
	International treaties
	Explanatory notes
	Textbooks

Study tips

As with the four rules of interpretation considered in Topic 1, you should use case illustration to explain these rules.

Key cases

Powell v Kempton Park Race Course (1899): the *ejusdem generis* rule was applied by the court.

Inhabitants of Sedgley (1837): the *expressio unius est exclusio alterius* rule was applied by the court.

Muir v Keay (1975): the *noscitur a sociis* rule was applied by the court.

The rules of language

In addition to the four main rules explained earlier, there are other rules of language, sometimes referred to as subsidiary rules.

The ejusdem generis *rule*

Under this rule, where general words follow particular words, the general words are interpreted to be of the same kind as the particular words. For example, in the phrase 'dogs, cats and other animals', the particular words are 'dogs' and 'cats'. The general words are 'other animals'. Under the *ejusdem generis* rule, the general words would be interpreted in line with the particular words. Therefore, since dogs and cats are domestic animals, then the general words of 'other animals' would be interpreted to mean other domestic animals.

In **Powell v Kempton Park Race Course (1899)**, the defendant company kept an open-air enclosure used by bookmakers, and racegoers who wished to place bets. Under a Regulation it was prohibited to keep a 'house, office, room or other place' for betting purposes. The court applied the *ejusdem generis* rule and held the defendant was not guilty because the enclosure was not a relevant place. The general words of 'or other place' following the specific words 'house', 'office' and 'room' referred to any defined spaces used for betting, which their enclosure was not.

Expressio unius est exclusio alterius

Translated, this means that the expression of one thing implies the exclusion of another. Where particular words are used and these are not followed by general words, the Act applies only to the instances specified (the particular words). For example, in **Inhabitants of Sedgley (1837)**, rates were charged on 'land, titles and coal mines'. Therefore rates could not be charged on any mine other than coal mines.

Noscitur a sociis

Under this 'rule', the meaning of a word is to be gathered from the context in which it is written. For example, the Refreshment Houses Act 1860 stated that all houses, rooms, shops or buildings kept open for 'entertainment' during certain hours of the night must be licensed. In **Muir v Keay (1975)** the defendant kept his café open to the public during the night without a licence. The court applied the *noscitur a sociis* rule and held that 'entertainment' in the context of the Act did not mean only musical or theatrical entertainment, but included other forms of enjoyment, such as drinking coffee late at night. Therefore the defendant had committed an offence under the Act.

Activities

1 The following are real cases. Decide the outcome of these cases by reference to the rules of language.

Wood v Commissioner of Police of the Metropolis (1986)
The court had to interpret the meaning of s4 of the Vagrancy Act 1824, which includes the phrase, 'any gun, pistol, hanger, cutlass, bludgeon, or other offensive weapon'. The defendant was in possession of a piece of glass that had fallen out of a door and was charged under this provision. Was he guilty?

Allen v Emmerson (1944)
Section 33 of the Barrow-in-Furness Corporation Act 1872 required 'theatres and other places of entertainment' to have a licence. The court had to decide whether a funfair required a licence. What do you think?

Pengelley v Bell Punch Co. Ltd (1964)
The court had to decide whether part of a factory floor used for storage fell within 'floors, steps, stairs, passages and gangways', as stated in s28 of the Factories Act 1961, and had to be kept free from obstruction. What do you think?

2 Look up the *Times* Law Report, 31 October 1990: *Cheeseman v Director of Public Prosecutions*. Answer the following questions.

a What extrinsic aid was referred to in order to decide the meaning of the word 'street'?

b According to that extrinsic aid, what did the court decide was the meaning of the word 'street'?

c Did the court decide that the public lavatory fell within the meaning of the word 'street'?

d What extrinsic aid was referred to in order to decide the meaning of the word 'passenger'?

e According to that extrinsic aid, what did the court decide was the meaning of the word 'passenger'?

f Did the court decide that the policemen were 'passengers'?

You should now be able to:

- explain the different aids to interpretation
- explain the different rules of language
- explain how cases illustrate the aids to interpretation and rules of language
- attempt past paper questions on the topic of aids to statutory interpretation.

3 Advantages and disadvantages of the rules of interpretation

Advantages of the literal rule

Under this rule, parliamentary sovereignty is respected – that is, the principle that Parliament is the supreme law-maker. Judges are given a restricted role. They must keep to the constitutional position of applying the law as set by Parliament.

In this topic you will learn how to:

- state the advantages and disadvantages of each rule or approach to statutory interpretation, using cases to illustrate them.

Law-making is left to those elected for the law-making role – that is, MPs in Parliament. Judges are not elected, and it is therefore not democratic for them to be involved in the creation or even modification of the law. If the law needs to be changed, then this is the responsibility of Parliament. Application of the literal rule can highlight to Parliament the problems with an Act, and then Parliament can amend the legislation. Literal interpretation in *Fisher* v *Bell* (1961) and *Partridge* v *Crittenden* (1968) prompted Parliament to amend the law so that invitations to treat are dealt with the same way as offers for sale. In *Partridge* v *Crittenden* (1968) the defendant had advertised some species of protected birds for sale. He was found not guilty because advertisements are invitations to treat and not offers for sale.

Disadvantages of the literal rule

As we have seen, the application of the literal rule can produce absurd results. Examples of absurd results include *Whiteley* v *Chappell* (1868) and *Fisher* v *Bell* (1961).

Application of the literal rule also produces unjust results. For example, in *London and North Eastern Railway* v *Berriman* (1946), an Act placed railway companies under a duty to provide a look-out man whenever a railwayman was 'repairing or relaying' the track. Mr Berriman's job was to top up the oil that lubricated the points on the line. His employer, a railway company, did not provide him with a look-out man or any other warning system, and Mr Berriman was killed by a train. Mr Berriman's widow claimed compensation, but was unsuccessful. The courts applied the literal rule and the words 'repairing and relaying' did not cover oiling points, since this was merely maintaining the line.

The literal rule cannot be said to always give effect to the intention of Parliament, as Parliament would not intend the Act to produce absurd or unjust results.

Where there is more than one possible dictionary definition of a word, the literal rule alone cannot provide the solution. Another interpretation rule or aid is required.

Application of the literal rule assumes that the parliamentary draftsmen will always do their job perfectly. This is virtually impossible, as not only will they sometimes be careless, as is human nature, but language has its limitations. In its Report on the Interpretation of Statutes (1969), the Law Commission said:

> To place undue emphasis on the literal meaning of the words of a provision is to assume an unattainable perfection in draftsmanship … ignores the limitations of language, which is not infrequently demonstrated even at the level of the House of Lords when Law Lords differ as to the so-called 'plain meaning' of words.

Advantages of the golden rule

Application of the golden rule prevents the absurd and unjust results that may be produced by application of the literal rule. Examples of cases where absurd or unjust results have been avoided by the use of the golden rule include *Re Sigsworth* (1935) and *Allen* (1872). In *Re Sigsworth* (1935) the judge had to apply the Administration of Estates Act 1925, which states that when a person dies without making a will the estate should be divided among the 'issue' – that is, that children of the deceased. The dead woman had only one son, but he had murdered her.

The court applied the broad application of the golden rule to avoid the absurd result whereby a murderer would inherit his victim's estate.

The application of the golden rule is more likely than the literal rule to produce a result that would have been intended by Parliament. Parliament would want to avoid absurd and unjust outcomes such as those in *Fisher* v *Bell* (1961) and *LNER* v *Berriman* (1946).

Disadvantages of the golden rule

There is no clear definition of what amounts to an absurd result. Use of the golden rule is therefore unpredictable, which in turn makes the outcomes of cases unpredictable. This makes it more difficult for lawyers to advise their clients on whether to pursue a case. For example, in *LNER* v *Berriman* (1946) and *Whiteley* v *Chappell* (1868), a different court might have chosen to avoid the absurd outcomes of these cases.

Too much power is given to judges, as they have to decide when and how to use this rule. They are not elected and so should not be empowered in this way. It is undemocratic.

The legal scholar Michael Zander has described this rule as a 'feeble parachute'. It allows the court to escape from problems caused by the literal rule, but the courts are still limited in what they can do.

Advantages of the mischief rule

Application of the mischief rule avoids absurd and unjust outcomes that might result from application of the literal rule. In *McMonagle* v *Westminster City Council* (1990) the court had to interpret the Local Government (Miscellaneous Provisions) Act 1982, which provided that it was an offence to use premises as a live sex encounter establishment without a licence from the local authority. The definition of 'sex encounter establishment' in the 1982 Act referred to performances, services and entertainments 'which are not unlawful'. The defendant claimed that his use of the premises for peep shows was unlawful and that therefore he could not be convicted. The House of Lords said that, in order to avoid the absurd result whereby a person could be convicted if the use of the premises was lawful but not if the use was unlawful, the words 'which are not unlawful' should be ignored. The guilty verdict was upheld.

The mischief rule promotes flexibility, enabling the law to be applied as intended by Parliament as opposed to merely applying the law as stated in the Act. It was the flexibility promoted by this rule, through the focus on what Parliament meant rather than what is stated in the Act, that allowed the judges to make the decision in *Smith* v *Hughes* (1960) (considered on p43). In his judgment, Parker LCJ specifically referred to what the Act was intended to do.

In 1969 the Law Commission described this rule as a 'rather more satisfactory approach' than the literal and golden rules, and suggested it should be the only rule used.

Disadvantages of the mischief rule

The main criticism of the mischief rule is that it gives far too much power to the unelected judiciary to decide what it thinks Parliament meant to say, rather than what the law actually says.

In some cases, it can be argued that the judiciary has updated the legislation. It is the role of Parliament to update legislation through an amending Act. In *Royal College of Nursing of the United Kingdom* v *DHSS* (1981) the House of Lords had to interpret the Abortion Act 1967. Section 1(1) states that no criminal offence is committed 'when a pregnancy is terminated by a registered medical practitioner'. In 1967 abortions had been surgical and carried out by doctors. In 1972 medically induced abortions were introduced, which involve a doctor inserting a catheter into the womb and then nurses administering fluid into the womb via a pump or drip to induce labour. The nurses acted upon instructions from the doctor, but the doctor was not always present. As it was the fluid that induced the labour, the abortions were effectively carried out by nurses.

The question for the Lords was whether this method of abortion was within the provisions of the 1967 Act – that is, is the pregnancy terminated by a 'registered medical practitioner'? The Court of Appeal held that such abortions were unlawful, but the House of Lords reversed the decision, reinstating the decision of the first instance judge. Out of the nine judges overall who heard the case, five thought the induced abortions were unlawful. The majority of the House of Lords justified the decision on the basis that the mischief at which the Act was aimed was the unsatisfactory and unclear state of the old law, under which many abortions were carried out in unhygienic conditions. Therefore, the Act could apply to the situation whereby a registered medical practitioner retained overall responsibility. The dissenting Law Lords felt that the majority were rewriting the Act. Lord Edmund-Davies referred to the decision as 'redrafting with a vengeance'.

It is not always easy to discover the mischief that the Act was intended to remedy. Discovering the mischief requires research of the old law and the reports concerning how the law should be reformed. The old law may be contained partly in legislation and partly in cases. Reports may contain many different viewpoints on how the new law should remedy the mischief. For these reasons it may be difficult to identify the precise intention of Parliament.

The mischief rule is considered to be out of date for the following reasons:

- It was laid down in the 16th century, when common law was the main source of law.
- In the 16th century, parliamentary supremacy was not as established as it is now.
- In the 16th century, Acts contained lengthy preambles which spelt out the mischief the Act was intended to remedy.
- Judges in the 16th century usually drafted Acts on behalf of the King, so were well qualified to decide the mischief the Act was meant to remedy.
- In the 16th century, drafting was not the exact science that it is today.

Advantages of the purposive approach

Advantages of the purposive approach are much the same as those of the mischief rule. However, there is another important advantage of this rule. The purposive approach is the approach to interpretation used in courts in other EU countries. Since the UK joined the EU in 1972, UK courts have increasingly used the purposive approach. This is bringing the UK more into line with its European counterparts. The judiciary now recognises that when interpreting Acts which have been passed to comply with European Union law, the correct approach to use is the purposive approach.

In some situations, the purposive approach is more likely to give effect to the intention of Parliament than the more restrictive literal approach. In *Coltman* v *Bibby Tankers* (1987) the court had to interpret the meaning of the word 'equipment' in the Employers' Liability (Defective Equipment) Act 1969. An employee had been killed when a ship provided by the employer sank. The question was whether a ship was 'equipment'. The Act defined 'equipment' as 'any plant and machinery, vehicle, aircraft and clothing'. The House of Lords applied a purposive approach and held the employer liable on the basis that a ship was equipment. Had a more restrictive literal approach been taken, the employer would not have been liable.

In general, Lord Denning preferred the purposive approach to the literal approach. In *Magor and St Mellons* v *Newport Corporation* (1950) he said:

> We do not sit here to pull the language of Parliament and of ministers to pieces and make nonsense of it. That is an easy thing to do and it is a thing to which lawyers are too often prone. We sit here to find the intention of Parliament and of ministers and carry it out, and we do this better by filling in the gaps and making sense of the enactment than by opening it up to destructive analysis.

Table 3.2 *Advantages and disadvantages of the rules of interpretation*

Rule	Advantages	Disadvantages
Literal rule	Respects parliamentary sovereignty. Leaves law-making to democratically elected Parliament.	Produces absurd/unjust outcomes. Does not always give effect to Parliament's intentions. Sometimes there is more than one dictionary definition. Assumes perfection from draftsmen.
Golden rule	Prevents absurd/unjust outcomes. More likely to give effect to Parliament's intentions.	Uncertainty as to what is an absurd outcome. Too much power to the judiciary. Michael Zander – 'feeble parachute'.
Mischief rule	Avoids absurd/unjust results. Promotes flexibility. Preferred approach of the Law Commission.	Too much power to unelected judiciary. Used by judges to update legislation. Not always easy to identify the mischief. Out of date.
Purposive approach	Consistent with European approach. Gives effect to Parliament's intentions. Denning: preferable to destructive analysis.	Too much power to unelected judiciary. Judicial decisions based on policy.

Disadvantages of the purposive approach

As with the mischief rule, the purposive approach gives too much power to the unelected judiciary. It leaves it up to a judge to decide the intention of the democratically elected Parliament, rather than merely applying the law as stated by Parliament.

In some situations, judges can further overstep their role by making decisions based on public policy – a matter that should be left to Parliament. In *Fitzpatrick* v *Sterling Housing Association Ltd* (1999) the House of Lords used the purposive approach to interpret the word 'family' in the Rent Act 1977 to include a homosexual relationship. This was a majority decision. The dissenting judges stated that recognition of homosexual relationships was a matter of public policy and therefore for Parliament to decide.

You should now be able to:

■ understand the advantages and disadvantages of each of the rules of interpretation and use cases to illustrate

4 Judicial precedent

Key terms

Stare decisis: 'to stand by what has been decided'.

1 The doctrine of judicial precedent

The doctrine of judicial precedent is based upon the principle of **stare decisis**, meaning 'to stand by what has been decided'.

Under this doctrine, legal principles made by judges in the higher courts set a precedent to be followed by that court, and all courts below it, in future cases of similar fact.

For the system to operate successfully, three things are required:

1 a settled court structure
2 a *ratio decidendi*
3 accurate records of the decisions made by the superior courts.

The court structure

It is necessary for there to be a settled court structure, as the judges need to know which decisions they are bound to follow. The UK court structure/hierarchy as it stands today was largely established by the Judicature Acts 1873–75. The House of Lords was made the final appeal court in 1876 under the Appellate Jurisdiction Act. The Supreme Court was created in 2009 to replace the House of Lords as the final appeal court.

In addition to the court structure established by these Acts, it is important to consider the European Court of Justice and the Judicial Committee of the Privy Council.

The European Court of Justice

The European Court of Justice (ECJ) is not part of the UK court structure. It does not hear national cases. However, under Art 234 of the Treaty of Rome 1957, a UK court may refer a point of European law to the ECJ for interpretation. The interpretation made by the ECJ is binding on all courts throughout the European Union. Once the ECJ has decided how a piece of European law must be interpreted, all English courts and other courts throughout the European Union must interpret that piece of law in that same way.

Fig. 4.1 *The main courtroom of the European Court of Justice, Luxembourg*

The ECJ is not, however, bound by the doctrine of precedent. It does not have to follow its own previous decisions but does, nevertheless, try to be consistent.

The Judicial Committee of the Privy Council

The Judicial Committee of the Privy Council (JCPC), like the ECJ, is not part of the UK court structure. The decisions of the JCPC are not binding on UK courts, but are persuasive. This means that judges in the UK courts do not have to follow the decisions of the JCPC, but may do so if they choose.

The importance of the JCPC in the doctrine of precedent lies in the fact that it is the final appeal court for many Commonwealth countries. Another reason why decisions of this court are so highly regarded is that it is staffed by the same judges that decide cases in the Supreme Court.

The Supreme Court

The Supreme Court stands at the top of the English court structure, and its decisions are binding on all lower courts. It is the final appeal court in the United Kingdom for both criminal and civil cases. The creation of the Supreme Court was provided for by the Constitutional Reform Act 2005.

Fig. 4.2 *The Supreme Court is housed in the Middlesex Guildhall building, London*

Until 1966, the then House of Lords regarded itself as bound by its own previous decisions, unless the previous decision was made **per incuriam** – that is, through lack of care – a mistake for example, where the previous decision was made without reference to a relevant Act of Parliament or precedent. This was the approach as stated by the House of Lords in *London Street Tramways* v *London County Council* (1898).

In the **1966 Practice Statement** issued by the Lord Chancellor, Lord Gardiner stated that the House of Lords would in future be free to depart from its own previous decision 'where it appears right to do so'. However, the Practice Statement emphasised that this freedom should be used 'sparingly' in order to maintain certainty and consistency in decisions.

An example of the House of Lords departing from its previous decision is **British Railways Board v Herrington (1972)**, when it departed from its own previous decision made in *Addie* v *Dumbreck* (1929). In *Addie*, the House of Lords held that an occupier of premises did not have a duty to prevent injury/death to children who trespassed on his/her land. Although this decision was repeatedly criticised, it was not until after the Practice Statement of 1966 that the House of Lords could depart from it. Even then, it was another six years after the Practice Statement before a case of similar fact reached the House of Lords. In *BRB* v *Herrington* (1972) the House of Lords held that an occupier of land owes child trespassers a duty to protect them from injury. Another example of the use of the Practice Statement is **Hall v Simons (2000)**. The House of Lords held that advocates – lawyers representing a client in court – should no longer be immune from being sued for negligent performance in court. This decision overruled the earlier decision of the House of Lords in *Rondel* v *Worsley* (1967). The Supreme Court uses the Practice Statement in the same way as its predecessor, the House of Lords.

The Court of Appeal

The Court of Appeal (CA) is directly below the Supreme Court in the English court structure. It is bound by the decisions of the Supreme Court. It is divided into two divisions: the Civil Division and the Criminal Division. Decisions made by the Civil Division are binding on all the courts below it in civil cases, and decisions made by the Criminal Division are binding on all the courts below it in criminal cases. Each division is usually bound by its own decisions, with some exceptions (set out below), but the two divisions do not bind each other.

As a general rule, the Court of Appeal is bound by its own previous decisions. However, in *Young* v *Bristol Aeroplane Co.* (1944), the CA listed the circumstances in which it could refuse to follow one of its own previous decisions:

- If its previous decision conflicts with a later Supreme Court decision, then the CA must follow the decision of the Supreme Court.
- If there are two conflicting previous CA decisions (which in theory should not happen but in reality sometimes does) then the CA must choose between them. The rejected decision then loses its binding force.
- If its previous decision was made *per incuriam*, that is, through lack of care, in ignorance of relevant legislation or case law. In this situation, the *per incuriam* decision will again lose its binding force.

Key cases

British Railways Board v Herrington (1972): the House of Lords used the Practice Statement to overrule its decision in *Addie v Dumbreck* (1929).

Hall v Simons (2000): the House of Lords used the Practice Statement to overrule its decision in *Rondel v Worsley* (1967).

Fig. 4.3 *The Royal Courts of Justice building houses the Court of Appeal and the High Court*

A case in which the CA had to decide which of two conflicting previous decisions to follow is **Parmenter (1991)**. The defendant had caused serious injuries to his baby son while handling him very roughly. It could not be proved that the defendant had foreseen the risk of injury, so his conviction for inflicting grievous bodily harm under s20 of the Offences Against the Person Act 1861 was quashed. The CA then had to decide whether the defendant could be convicted of assault occasioning actual bodily harm under s47.

In *Spratt* (1990) the CA had decided that foresight of harm was required for a conviction under s47. However, on the same day as *Parmenter* (1991), in *Savage* (1991) another court of the CA had decided that foresight of harm was not required. In *Parmenter* (1991) the CA chose to follow the decision in *Spratt* (1990).

The defendant could not be found guilty under s47 because foresight of harm was required. However, the case was then appealed to the House of Lords, which reversed the decision and held that the decision in *Savage* (1991) was correct. The defendant could be found guilty under s47 because foresight of harm was not required.

The CA Criminal Division has one more exception, this being where it considers the previous decision was wrong and will do injustice to the defendant. In such circumstances the CA Criminal Division may not follow it. Criminal appeals need more flexibility than civil appeals, because the liberty of the individual is at stake. It is important to remember in this respect that criminal convictions result not only in a sanction but also a criminal record.

The High Court

The High Court has two roles. It is a court of first instance, meaning it is a trial court as well as an appeal court. The High Court is divided into three divisions: the Family Division, the Chancery Division and the Queen's Bench Division. Each of these three divisions has its own Divisional Court.

Lower courts and the High Court itself are bound by decisions made in *appeal* cases in the Divisional Courts of the High Court. However, the exceptions set out in *Young v Bristol Aeroplane Co*. (1944) also apply to the Divisional Courts of the High Court.

In criminal appeals heard in the Divisional Court of the Queen's Bench Division, the additional exception concerned with avoiding injustice and the liberty of the individual also applies.

First instance decisions of the High Court must be followed by the lower courts, but need not be followed by other High Court Judges. However, these decisions are highly persuasive and are usually followed.

The lower courts

The Crown Court, County Courts and Magistrates' Courts do not set binding precedents, although the decisions of the Crown Court are persuasive. Because of this, the decisions of these courts are not usually recorded in law reports.

Table 4.1 *The civil and criminal court structure*

The civil courts	The criminal courts
European Court of Justice Binds lower courts on matters of European law.	**Supreme Court** Binds all lower courts. Generally follows its own decisions except when using the Practice Statement.
Supreme Court Bound by the European Court of Justice. Binds all lower courts. Generally follows its own decisions except when using the Practice Statement.	**Court of Appeal (Criminal Division)** Bound by the Supreme Court. Generally follows its own decisions, but takes a more flexible approach than the Civil Division in order to protect the liberty of the individual.
Court of Appeal (Civil Division) Bound by the European Court of Justice and the Supreme Court. Binds all lower courts. Bound by its own decisions except in the circumstances outlined in *Young v Bristol Aeroplane Co*. (1944).	**Queen's Bench Divisional Court** Bound by the Supreme Court and Court of Appeal. Generally bound by its own decisions, but takes a flexible approach in order to protect the liberty of the individual.
Divisional Courts of the High Court Bound by the European Court of Justice, the Supreme Court and the Court of Appeal. Binds all lower courts. Bound by its own decisions except in the circumstances outlined in *Young v Bristol Aeroplane Co*. (1944).	
High Court Bound by the European Court of Justice, the Supreme Court, the Court of Appeal and the Divisional Courts. Binds all lower courts.	**Crown Court** Bound by the Supreme Court Court of Appeal and the Queen's Bench Divisional Court. Not bound by its own decisions and does not bind another court.
County Court Bound by the European Court of Justice, the Supreme Court, the Court of Appeal, the Divisional Courts and the High Court. Not bound by its own decisions and does not bind any lower court.	
Magistrates' Court Bound by the European Court of Justice, the Supreme Court, the Court of Appeal, the Divisional Courts and the High Court. Not bound by its own decisions and does not bind any other court.	**Magistrates' Court** Bound by the Supreme Court, Court of Appeal and the Queen's Bench Divisional Court. Not bound by its own decisions and does not bind another court.

Ratio decidendi

The legal principle upon which the decision of the court is based is known as the **ratio decidendi**, meaning 'the reason for deciding'. In each case, the judge will listen to the legal arguments put forward by the parties and come to his/her decision. In his/her judgment (the speech made by the judge at the end of the case) the judge will explain the legal reason for the decision. It is this legal reason that forms the *ratio decidendi*. The *ratio decidendi* must be followed in future cases of similar fact by the same court and all courts below it.

An example of a *ratio decidendi* is provided by the case of **Howe (1987)**. The House of Lords held the defendant was guilty of murder because the defence of duress, which he had pleaded, was not available to a defendant charged with murder. A further example is provided by **Brown (1993)**. The defendants were found guilty of offences under ss47 and s20 of the Offences Against the Person Act 1861 because the defence of consent, which they had pleaded in respect of their sado-masochistic practices at a private party, was not available to defendants charged with such offences.

Another example of a *ratio decidendi* is provided by **Donoghue v Stevenson (1932)**, often referred to as 'the snail in the ginger beer' case. The facts were that the claimant went to a café with her friend. Her friend bought her a drink of ginger beer. The drink was delivered to the table in

Key terms

Ratio decidendi: the legal reason for the decision.

Key cases

Howe (1987): the *ratio decidendi* of this case is that duress is not a defence to a charge of murder.

Brown (1993): the *ratio decidendi* of this case is that consent is not a defence to charges under ss47 and s20 of the Offences Against the Person Act 1861.

Donoghue v Stevenson (1932): the *ratio decidendi* of this case is that manufacturers owe a duty of care to the consumers of their products.

an opaque (dark glass) bottle. Some of the drink from the bottle was poured into a glass and the claimant drank it. She then poured the remaining contents into the glass and a decomposed snail emerged from the bottle. The claimant suffered shock and gastroenteritis (a stomach bug). She could not bring a legal action against the café in contract law because she had no contract with it, as her friend had bought the drink. Instead, she sued the manufacturer for negligence. The House of Lords decided that her claim should succeed. The *ratio decidendi* was that manufacturers owe a duty of care to the ultimate consumers of their products. This was an **original precedent**, which judges can create when a new situation arises and/or where there is no existing precedent or legislation.

Unfortunately, judges rarely make it clear what the *ratio decidendi* of their decision is. Judgments are not set out with clear headings. Therefore, it is up to the lawyers and judges reading the judgment to discover the *ratio decidendi*. Furthermore, in the appeal courts, decisions are often given by more than one judge. Even if all the judges reach the same decision in the case, they may each give a different reason for their decision. In such cases, it is difficult to decide which reason forms the *ratio*.

Obiter dicta

Obiter dicta (a plural noun; singular *obiter dictum*) are things said 'by the way', or 'other things said'. These statements are not crucial to the outcome of the case. In the judgment, the judge may discuss not only the *ratio decidendi* but also other matters. He/she may speculate on what the outcome of the case would have been if the facts were slightly different. For example, in **Howe (1987)** the *ratio decidendi* of the case was that duress is no defence to murder. The House of Lords expressed the opinion that duress is also no defence to attempted murder. This opinion was clearly made *obiter*, because it did not relate directly to the facts of the case, as Mr Howe was charged with murder not attempted murder. Similarly, in **Brown (1993)** the *ratio decidendi* of the case was that consent is no defence to sado-masochistic practices. The House of Lords also expressed the opinion (the *obiter dicta*) that consent was a defence in other circumstances such as ritual circumcision, tattooing, ear and body piercing and violent sports.

Obiter dicta are important because they can be persuasive (see under 'Binding and persuasive precedent' below). Should a judge choose to follow the *obiter dicta* of an earlier case, that *obiter dictum* becomes the *ratio decidendi* of the later case. For example, in *Gotts* (1992) the defendant was charged with attempted murder and pleaded the defence of duress. Following the *obiter dicta* of *Howe* (1987), the House of Lords held that the defendant was guilty on the basis that duress is no defence to attempted murder. Similarly, in *Wilson* (1996) the defendant was charged under s47 and pleaded the defence of consent. He had branded his initials on his wife's body with a hot knife with her approval. Following the *obiter dicta* of *Brown* (1993), the Court of Appeal held the defendant was not guilty, on the basis that this was a form of body decoration similar to tattooing, and that consent was therefore a defence.

Binding and persuasive precedent

A **binding precedent** is a precedent that *must* be followed. The *ratio decidendi* of a case is a binding precedent. It is binding on courts of the same level and on all courts below.

Key terms

Original precedent: a precedent is created to deal with a new situation or when there is no existing law.

Obiter dicta: things said 'by the way' or 'other things said'.

Binding precedent: a precedent that must be followed.

Key cases

Howe (1987): *obiter dicta* in this case state that duress is not a defence to a charge of attempted murder.

Brown (1993): *obiter dicta* in this case state that consent can be a defence to a charge of a non-fatal offence under the Offences Against the Person Act 1861 in certain circumstances.

A **persuasive precedent** is a precedent that *may* be followed by judges in future cases of similar fact, should they so choose. As we have seen, one form of persuasive precedent is *obiter dicta*. There are other types of persuasive precedent.

Decisions of lower courts may be persuasive. For example, decisions of the Court of Appeal may be followed by the Supreme Court in later cases of similar fact.

Decisions of Scottish courts, courts of other countries such as the US, and especially decisions of courts in Commonwealth countries such as Australia, New Zealand and Canada, are persuasive. This is because these countries have legal systems based on the UK legal system, due to previous or continuing dependence. In **R v R (1991)**, the Court of Appeal, and then the House of Lords, followed a previous decision made by the Scottish courts holding that a man can be guilty of raping his wife. Another example is *Lister* v *Hesley Hall* (2001). The House of Lords held that a residential school was vicariously liable (that is, legally answerable) for the sexual abuse of several former pupils by the warden of the school. The barrister representing the former pupils drew the House of Lords' attention to two recent decisions of the Canadian Supreme Court in support of his clients' case. The House of Lords then chose to follow the approach of the Canadian Supreme Court in these two cases, and in so doing overruled the previous decision of the Court of Appeal in *Trotman* v *North Yorkshire County Council* (1999).

Decisions of the Judicial Committee of the Privy Council, which is the final appeal court for Commonwealth countries, are highly persuasive. The court is equivalent in rank to the Supreme Court, and it is staffed by the same judges who sit in the Supreme Court. A case that illustrates the considerable influence of the Judicial Committee of the Privy Council is *Holley* (2005). The case was about the defence of provocation, which, at the time, could reduce a murder charge to voluntary manslaughter (the defence has since been abolished and replaced by a new statutory defence of 'loss of control'). This decision was in conflict with the decision of the House of Lords in Smith (Morgan) (2000). The decision in *Holley* (2005) raised the question of whether the courts should still be following the decision in *Smith (Morgan)* (2000). However, the Privy Council in this case comprised nine Law Lords, six of whom were in the majority, and the Court of Appeal followed the Privy Council decision rather than the House of Lords decision in three cases, these being *Mohammed* (2005), *James* (2006) and *Karimi* (2006).

Dissenting judgments are also persuasive. In the appeal courts – that is, the Court of Appeal and the Supreme Court – the case is heard by more than one judge. Sometimes the decision is reached by only a majority of the judges. In this situation, the judges in the minority will give their reasons for reaching a different decision. This is called a dissenting judgment. An example of a dissenting judgment that was followed in a later case is that of Lord Denning in **Candler v Crane Christmas (1951)**, in which he expressed the opinion that a person who suffers financial loss as a result of a negligent mis-statement ought to be able to recover compensation. This judgment was followed in *Hedley Byrne* v *Heller and Partners* (1966), and now forms the basis of the law regarding negligent mis-statement.

Table 4.2 *Types of persuasive precedent*

Type of persuasive precedent	Illustrative material
Obiter dicta – things said by the way	*Howe* (1987) – duress is not a defence to a charge of attempted murder
	Brown (1993) – consent can be a defence to a charge of actual or grievous bodily harm in certain circumstances
Decisions of lower courts	*Miliangos* v *George Frank (Textiles) Ltd* (1976) – the House of Lords was influenced by the decision of the Court of Appeal in *Schorsch Meier GmbH* v *Hennin* (1975)
Decisions of leading foreign courts	*Lister* v *Helsey Hall* (2001) – the House of Lords followed the decision of the Canadian Supreme Court
	R v *R* (1991) – the House of Lords followed the approach of the Scottish courts
Decisions of the Judicial Committee of the Privy Council	*Holley* (2005) – this JCPC decision has now been followed by the Court of Appeal despite conflicting House of Lords authority in 2000.
Dissenting judgments – the decisions of the minority judges	*Hedley Byrne* v *Heller and Partners* (1966) – that decision followed Lord Denning's dissenting judgement in *Candler* v *Crane Christmas* (1951)

Law reports

It is crucial to the operation of the doctrine of precedent that accurate records be kept of the decisions of the higher level courts, because it must be possible for the binding and persuasive precedents to be found. Records of the decisions of the higher level courts are kept in law reports.

Until the mid-19th century, law reports were published privately. Standards varied and some reports consisted of little more than incomplete jottings of lawyers or students. However, law reporting became more comprehensive and systematic when the Incorporated Council of Law Reporting was established in 1865. This organisation is responsible for a series of reports known as the Appeal Cases (AC), which reports cases heard in the Supreme Court, Court of Appeal and all three divisional courts of the High Court. The ICLR also publishes the Weekly Law Reports which, as the name suggests, are published weekly and thus help legal practitioners keep up-to-date with legal developments.

There are also private series of law reports, such as the All England Law Reports, published by Butterworths since 1936. This series is published weekly and covers cases heard in the superior courts.

Some series of law reports are more specialised, focusing on a particular area of law. Examples of such series include the Family Law Reports, the Industrial Relations Law Reports and the European Human Rights Reports.

Law reports are also published by the media. Some newspapers have their own law reports. The most notable are *The Times* Law Reports; however, law reports are occasionally published in the *Guardian* and the *Independent*. Law reports may also be found in journals such as the *New Law Journal* and the *Law Society Gazette*.

Records of decisions are also kept online. Some reports are available on subscription websites, such as LEXIS and JUSTIS. However, many reports are freely available on the internet. The Supreme Court, the European Court of Justice, the European Court of Human Rights and some leading foreign courts publish their decisions within hours of being made.

Purity ring is not intimately linked to religious belief

Queen's Bench Division
Published July 23, 2007
Regina (Playfoot) (a Child) v Millais School Governing Body
Before Mr Michael Supperstone, QC
Judgment July 16, 2007

A school's refusal to allow one of its pupils to wear a purity ring, demonstrating her commitment to sexual abstinence prior to marriage, did not infringe her right to freedom of thought, conscience and religion protected by the European Convention on Human Rights.

Mr Michael Supperstone, QC, sitting as a deputy Queen's Bench Division, so held when dismissing the claim of Lydia Playfoot, suing by her father as next friend, for judicial review of the refusal of Millais School, Horsham, West Sussex, to let her wear a purity ring. Mr Paul Diamond instructed directly, for the claimant; Mr Jonathan Auburn for the school.

HIS LORDSHIP said that the claimant sought judicial review of the decision of the school which she attended not to permit her to wear a purity ring as a symbol of her commitment to celibacy before marriage.

She contended that that decision unlawfully interfered with her right to manifest her religion or beliefs contrary to Article 9.1 of the Human Rights Convention.

The issues between the parties were: whether the wearing of the ring was a manifestation of the claimant's religious belief, whether refusing to permit her to wear the ring interfered with her freedom to manifest her belief, and, if so, whether such interference was justified by Article 9.2.

Guidance as to what amounted to manifestation was to be found in decisions of the House of Lords in *R (Shabina Begum)* v *Governors of Denbigh High School* (The Times March 23, 2006; [2007] 1 AC 100) and *R (Williamson)* v *Secretary of State for Education and Employment* (The Times February 25, 2005; [2005] 2 AC 246).

In *Williamson*, it was held that in deciding whether a person's conduct constituted manifesting a belief and practice for the purposes of Article 9 it was necessary to identify the scope of the practice.

If the belief took the form of a perceived obligation to act in a specific way, then, in principle, doing that act pursuant to that belief was itself manifestation of that belief in practice. In such cases the act was intimately linked to the belief.

The claimant was under no obligation by reason of her belief to wear the ring and, in his Lordship's judgement, the act of wearing it was not intimately linked to the belief in chastity before marriage.

In any event, the claimant's Article 9 rights had not been interfered with because she voluntarily accepted the school's uniform policy and there were other means open to her to practise her belief without undue hardship or inconvenience.

Moreover, the rules on uniform and the school's decision to enforce them were proportionate.

Solicitors: Miss Diane Henshaw, Chichester.

The Times, *23 July 2007*

Most law reports, such as the one above, follow a similar structure. A law report will usually include the name of the case, the court in which the case was heard, the names(s) of the judge(s) and the date of the hearing. There then follows a summary of the facts and legal issues and the decision of the court in which the case was first heard (court of first instance). There is a list of cases and statutes referred to, and the names of the counsel appearing in the case. Finally, there is the judgment, in which the judge will consider the arguments and legal issues cited by the counsel for each side and give his/her conclusion.

The formal rule is that a law report must be vouched for by a barrister or solicitor with rights of audience, who was present in court when the judgment was delivered. This is often demonstrated by the appearance of the person's name at the end of the report. This confirms accuracy and authenticity.

Activities

1. Using the law report on p63, make a note of:
   - the name of the case
   - the court that heard the case
   - the name of the judge who heard the case
   - the facts, the legislation and the previous decision referred to
   - the *ratio decidendi* of the case.

2. Find a law report either on the internet or in a recent copy of *The Times*. Make a note of:
   - the name of the case
   - the court that heard the case
   - the names of the judge(s) who heard the case
   - the facts of the case, legislation and previous decisions referred to
   - the *ratio decidendi* of the case.

You should now be able to:

- explain the elements of the doctrine of precedent
- attempt past paper questions requiring a description of the doctrine of precedent.

In this topic you will learn how to:

- define the terms 'overruling', 'distinguishing' and 'disapproving'
- identify and explain cases illustrating those terms.

Key terms

Distinguishing: the judge does not follow the decision in an earlier case because the facts are materially different.

2 Methods of avoiding judicial precedent

We have seen that the Supreme Court, and the Court of Appeal and High Court, may in certain circumstances avoid following precedent. The Supreme Court may use the Practice Statement, and the Court of Appeal and the High Court can use the exceptions set out in *Young* v *Bristol Aeroplane Co.* (1944). In addition, there are some mechanisms that the judges in these courts and other courts may use to depart from a precedent.

Distinguishing

Distinguishing is the main device used by judges in all courts to avoid a binding precedent. No two cases will have exactly the same facts. When this is the case, the judge is not bound to follow a precedent; it can be distinguished and may form a precedent itself. The first case will remain a binding precedent for a case with similar facts. This device of distinguishing can be illustrated by two examples.

In **Balfour v Balfour (1919)** the Court of Appeal decided that an agreement between husband and wife – that the husband should pay the wife £30 per month – was not a legally binding agreement that could be enforced by the courts. This was because there is a presumption against an intention to create legal relations in domestic situations, when the married couple are living together – or in legal language, 'living in amity'. As a result of this *ratio*, the wife failed to enforce the agreement against her husband.

This decision was distinguished in **Merritt v Merritt (1971)**, where an agreement was made between a husband and wife after they had separated. He agreed to sign their house over to her if she continued to pay the mortgage. She did pay the mortgage but the husband refused to sign over the house, relying on the principle from *Balfour* that their agreement was not legally binding. The Court of Appeal disagreed with the husband's argument by distinguishing *Balfour*. Their separation meant that the presumption against an intention to apply legal relations did not apply, and their agreement was legally enforceable. This is now a precedent that applies alongside the precedent of *Balfour*.

Other examples are the cases of *R v Brown (1993)* and **R v Wilson (1996)**, referred to previously in relation to *ratio* and *obiter*. In *Brown* the House of Lords decided (by a majority) that consent to suffer serious injuries in the course of sado-masochistic activities is no defence to charges of s20 Offences Against the Person Act or to charges of actual bodily harm. In *Wilson* the Court of Appeal was able to distinguish the *ratio* in *Brown* as Mr and Mrs Wilson were a married couple. Mr Wilson's defence of consent to a charge of ABH was accepted as the court decided that the branding of his wife with a hot knife (at her request) was a form of body decoration, similar to tattooing.

Fig. 4.4 Balfour *v* Balfour *and* Merritt *v* Merritt

Overruling

Overruling is the procedure whereby a court higher up in the hierarchy sets aside a legal ruling established in a previous case.

One example is *Hedley Bryne* v *Heller and Partners* (1964), where the House of Lords overruled the decision of the Court of Appeal in *Candler v Crane Christmas* (1951) and decided that there can be liability for making a negligent mis-statement. This illustrates that a higher court can overrule an earlier decision of a lower court. Another example is *Herrington*, where the House of Lords used the 1966 Practice Statement to overrule its previous decision in *Addie v Dumbreck (1929)*, and allowed a claim by a trespasser for injury suffered on an occupier's land.

Study tips

It is important that you understand that the 1966 Practice Statement only applies to the House of Lords, and the exceptions in *Young* v *Bristol Aeroplane Co.* (1944) only apply to the Court of Appeal and High Court.

Key cases

Balfour v Balfour (1919): the Court of Appeal decided that an agreement between husband and wife in a domestic circumstance was not legally binding.

Merritt v Merritt (1971): the CA distinguished the earlier case of *Balfour* v *Balfour* (1919).

R v Wilson (1996): the Court of Appeal distinguished the case of *R v Brown* (1993).

This shows that an appeal court can overrule a previous decision of its own, which it later considers wrong. In this case, the decision in *Addie* v *Dumbreck* was considered to be wrong as social conditions had changed in the 40 years since the ruling was made.

Disapproving

Disapproving is not a method of avoiding precedent, but rather a mechanism that allows a departure from precedent in a future case. When a judge disapproves of a precedent, he/she makes clear that he/she believes the precedent is wrong. These disapproving comments are persuasive, and may be followed by judges in future cases who wish to avoid the precedent. For example, the *ratio decidendi* of the House of Lords in *Anns* v *Merton London Borough Council* (1978) was that purchasers of defective buildings could recover compensation from local authorities when the defects were caused by the negligent failure of the local authority to inspect the foundations during construction. This decision was heavily disapproved before the House of Lords overruled it 12 years later in *Murphy* v *Brentwood District Council* (1990).

Table 4.3 *Methods of departure from precedent*

Method	Explanation	Illustration
The Practice Statement 1966	The Supreme Court can depart from its own decisions 'when it appears right to do so'.	*British Railways Board* v *Herrington* (1972) departed from *Addie* v *Dumbreck* (1929) *Hall* v *Simons* (2000) departed from *Rondel* v *Worsley* (1967)
The exceptions in *Young* v *Bristol Aeroplane Co.* (1944)	The Court of Appeal can depart from its own decisions in three circumstances: i when the decision conflicts with a House of Lords decision ii when the decision was made *per incuriam* iii when there are two conflicting decisions.	*Parmenter* (1991)
Distinguishing	The binding decision is not followed because the facts of the cases are materially different.	*Merritt* v *Merritt* (1971) distinguished *Balfour* v *Balfour* (1919) *Evans* v *Triplex Safety Glass* (1936) distinguished *Donoghue* v *Stevenson* (1932)
Overruling	The precedent in an earlier case is found to be incorrect and is replaced by a new rule which becomes a binding precedent for the future.	*Hedley Byrne* v *Heller and Partners* (1964): the House of Lords overruled the decision of the Court of Appeal in *Candler* v *Crane Christmas* (1951)
Disapproval	Comments of a persuasive nature are made indicating the judge's belief that the precedent is wrong.	*Anns* v *Merton London Borough Council* (1978)

Activity

1 Consider whether *Donoghue* v *Stevenson* should be distinguished in the following circumstances:
   a A person suffers sickness having found a baby mouse in the empty bottle of cola he had just drunk.
   b A person suffers food poisoning having eaten half a bar of chocolate containing raisins, some of which turn out to be dead flies.
   c A girl has half of her hair burnt off by a faulty hairdryer.
   d A woman suffers a broken ankle when the heel of her new shoe falls off.
   e A man suffers multiple injuries when his car engine blows up.

You should now be able to:

- understand the ways of avoiding precedent
- use cases to illustrate the ways of avoiding precedent
- attempt past paper questions requiring a description of the doctrine of precedent.

3 Advantages and disadvantages of the doctrine of judicial precedent and the methods of avoiding precedent

Advantages of the doctrine of precedent

Consistency

The doctrine of precedent brings consistency to the UK legal system, in that cases with similar facts will be treated in the same manner. It prevents judges making random decisions, and promotes justice and equal treatment. The law remains the same, which helps people plan their affairs.

Predictability

Lawyers are able to advise their clients with some degree of certainty. They can tell their client, for example, that a proposed course of action is likely to be upheld by the court, or that they will probably lose their case and should therefore settle out of court or cease their legal action. Predictability is also important in deciding who should qualify for help in funding legal action. The Government does not fund cases that have little chance of success, as this would be a waste of taxpayers' money. Also, a lawyer will advise whether a case should or should not proceed if payment is on a no-win no-fee arrangement.

Flexibility

Judges can sometimes develop the law – for example, by overruling an outdated precedent. The House of Lords can also use the Practice Statement. This means that the law can be developed in areas not considered important or not considered at all by Parliament. For example, the decision in *Herrington* updated the rule in occupiers' liability to trespassers. Updating decisions may prompt Parliament to review the legislation and bring it into line with precedent. Parliamant eventually introduced the Occupiers' Liability Act 1984, putting the law on occupiers' liability onto a statutory footing.

Detailed practical rules

There is a wealth of detail contained in cases reported in law reports. The principles set out in the cases are a response to real-life situations, and can be a guide to future litigants.

Original precedents

The doctrine of precedent allows for new or 'original' precedents to be created. This occurs when there is no previous decision on the matter before the court, and there is sometimes no legislative provision. An original precedent therefore makes legal provision on a matter for which there was previously no law. In **Gillick v West Norfolk and Wisbech Area Health Authority (1985)**, the House of Lords had to decide whether or not girls under the age of 16 could be prescribed contraceptives

In this topic you will learn how to:

- state the advantages and disadvantages of the doctrine of precedent
- use examples relevant to those advantages and disadvantages
- state the advantages and disadvantages of the methods of avoiding precedent
- use examples relevant to those advantages and disadvantages.

Key cases

Gillick v West Norfolk and Wisbech Area Health Authority (1985): the House of Lords made an original precedent holding that girls aged under 16 could be prescribed contraceptives without parental consent.

without parental consent. The matter had not previously arisen before the courts, and Parliament had provided no guidance. The Lords decided that girls could be prescribed contraceptives in such circumstances, provided they were able to understand the issues involved.

Disadvantages of the doctrine of precedent

Complexity

The judgments are often complex and it is sometimes difficult to decide what the *ratio decidendi* of a case is. Furthermore, in the Supreme Court and Court of Appeal there is often more than one judgment to consider and a common *ratio* has to be decided by the judges in future cases. In addition, each judge may give a different reason for the decision. An example is **R v Brown (1993)** when all five judges in the House of Lords gave different reasons for their decisions. The court eventually found Brown and others not guilty by a 3–2 majority.

Volume

It is difficult for anyone to research the law. Hundreds of judgments are made every year, so to discover the precise law on a matter, a person may have to search through many volumes of law reports. The complete official law reports are estimated to run to almost half a million pages. Also, some law reports are very long and detailed. For example, in *R v Brown* (1993), the report extends to more than 50 pages of close type.

Key cases

R v Brown (1993): all five judges in the House of Lords gave different reasons for their decisions. The court eventually found Brown and others guilty by a 3–2 majority.

Fig. 4.5 *The law is difficult to research*

Uncertainty

By not always following a binding precedent, the courts can create uncertainty amongst lawyers as to how a case will be resolved. This uncertainty will not be resolved until the final decision is reached.

For example, in *Herrington*, his lawyers could not be certain that he would win his case and be able to claim compensation from British Rail for his injurie until the House of Lords gave its judgment. Some lawyers may not be prepared to test the appeal courts' willingness to depart from precedent, and so will not advise their clients to take a case to appeal.

Rigidity

An unjust precedent can lead to further injustices. Once an appeal court sets an unjust precedent, it cannot be changed unless and until a case of similar facts goes to appeal. For example, in 1736 Sir Matthew Hale had written in his work *History of the Pleas of the Crown*, that a husband cannot be guilty of raping his wife as, by their marriage, the wife gave up all her property to her husband and irrevocably consented to sexual intercourse with him. This ruling was obviously unfair but it was only

Study tips

Any of the illustrative material from Topic 2 can be used here when explaining why uncertainty is a disadvantage.

when the case of **R v R (1991)** came to the House of Lords that the ruling was altered and a husband could be guilty of raping his wife. The rigid statement of Sir Matthew Hale had stood for over 250 years before it was changed.

Unconstitutional/ Undemocratic

It is often argued that judges are overstepping their constitutional role by actually making the law rather than simply applying it. It is the role of Parliament to create the law and the role of the judiciary to enforce/apply the law as set by Parliament. Only persons who are elected – that is, the Government and MPs – should be able to create law. The judges are not elected and should therefore not engage in law-making.

Retrospective effect

Unlike legislation made by Parliament, the law created by judges is backward-looking. It applies to events that occurred before the case came to court. This is unfair, because the parties involved would rightly have considered themselves to be acting within the law (legally) at the time. For example, in *R v R* (1991) the husband had not been acting illegally when he subjected his estranged wife to sexual intercourse without her consent. His conduct only became illegal some time after the event, when the House of Lords reached its decision. The retrospective effect of case law can be compared to the prospective effect of legislation (law made by Parliament). Legislation usually only applies to events occurring after it has come into effect.

Lack of research

Unlike legislation, which is made with the benefit of research by interested and knowledgeable bodies, there is no opportunity for a judge to commission research or consult experts on the likely outcomes of their decisions. Judges are confined to making their decisions on the basis of the arguments presented in the course of the case.

> **Key cases**
>
> **R v R (1991):** the House of Lords overruled previous decisions and held that marital rape is a crime.

Table 4.4 *Advantages and disadvantages of precedent*

Advantages of precedent	Disadvantages of precedent
Consistency	Complexity: *R v Brown* (1993)
Predictability	Volume: *R v Brown* (1993)
Flexibility: *R v R* (1991)	Uncertainty – due to methods of departure. Use illustrative material from Topic 2
Detailed practical rules	Rigidity: *R v R* (1991)
Original precedent – to deal with new situations or where there is no existing law: *Gillick* v *West Norfolk and Wisbech AHA*	Unconstitutional
	Undemocratic
	Retrospective: *R v R* (1991)
	Lack of research

You should now be able to:

- explain the advantages and disadvantages of the doctrine of precedent
- use examples to support your explanation of the advantages and disadvantages of the doctrine of precedent.

Practice questions

Unit 1A questions in the AQA exam

Unit 1A together with Unit 1B constitutes Unit 1 of the AS specification. Unit 1A is about law-making and Unit 1B is about the legal system. Unit 1A and Unit 1B are examined together on one examination paper, which constitutes 50 per cent of the overall marks for the AS qualification and 25 per cent of the overall marks for the A2 qualification.

The Unit 1 examination is of 1.5 hours' duration. You must answer questions from three topics: one topic from Unit 1A; one topic from Unit 1B; and another topic, which may be from Unit 1A or 1B. There will be a choice of four topics in Unit 1A and four topics in Unit 1B.

Each topic is represented by one question, which has three parts. You must answer all parts of the question. Each part is normally worth 10 marks; the entire question is worth 30 marks, plus 2 marks for Assessment Objective 3.

All parts of each topic relate to the same topic area of the AQA Law AS specification – that is, the same chapter of this book. Parts (a) and (b) will normally be a test of your knowledge and understanding, and part (c) will normally be evaluative, requiring simple discussion of advantages and disadvantages of a topic.

Questions require essay-style answers. You should aim to include:

- correct identification of the issues raised by the question
- sound explanation of each of the points
- relevant illustration.

Illustration may be in many forms – for example, legislation, cases, research, statistics, and material from the media.

Chapter 1: Parliamentary law-making

These example questions are taken from past exam papers. You must answer all three parts of the question.

Example question 1 (AQA, May 2011)

a) Describe any **one** influence operating on Parliament in the law-making process. *(10 marks)*

b) Describe the law-making procedure in Parliament. *(10 marks)*

c) Briefly discuss advantages **and** disadvantages of the parliamentary law-making procedure.
(10 marks + 2 marks for AO3)

Example question 2 (AQA, January 2012)

a) Outline the process in the House of Commons **and** the House of Lords in the making of an Act of Parliament. *(10 marks)*

b) Describe the Law Commission **or** the media **or** pressure groups as an influence operating on Parliament in the law-making process. *(10 marks)*

c) Discuss advantages of the process of parliamentary law-making.
(10 marks + 2 marks for AO3)

Example question 3 (AQA, May 2012)

a) Briefly explain what is meant by the doctrine of parliamentary sovereignty. Outline **one** limitation on this doctrine.
(10 marks)

b) Outline the following:
   - The nature and purpose of Green and White papers
   - The law-making process in the House of Commons.
(10 marks)

c) Discuss disadvantages of the law-making process in Parliament. *(10 marks + 2 marks for AO3)*

Chapter 2: Delegated legislation

These example questions are taken from past exam papers. You must answer all three parts of the question.

Example question 1 (AQA, May 2012)

a) Statutory instruments, Orders in Council and by-laws are all forms of delegated legislation. Briefly describe any **two** of these forms. *(10 marks)*

b) Describe parliamentary controls on delegated legislation. *(10 marks)*

c) Discuss why Parliament delegates law-making power. *(10 marks + 2 marks for AO3)*

Example question 2 (AQA, January 2012)

a) There are different forms of delegated legislation, including statutory instruments, Orders in Council and by-laws. Describe any **one** form of delegated legislation. *(10 marks)*

b) Explain why Parliament needs to delegate law-making power. *(10 marks)*

c) Discuss disadvantages of delegated legislation. *(10 marks + 2 marks for AO3)*

Example question 3 (AQA, January 2011)

a) Outline what is meant by statutory instruments **and** by-laws. *(10 marks)*

b) Describe judicial controls on delegated legislation. *(10 marks)*

c) Discuss the reasons for the use of delegated legislation in the English legal system. *(10 marks + 2 marks for AO3)*

Chapter 3: Statutory interpretation

These example questions are taken from past exam papers. You must answer all three parts of the question.

Example question 1 (AQA, May 2012)

a) Outline external (extrinsic) aids to interpretation **and** **one** of the rules of language. *(10 marks)*

b) Describe the golden rule of statutory interpretation. *(10 marks)*

c) Briefly discuss advantages **and** disadvantages of the golden rule. *(10 marks + 2 marks for AO3)*

Example question 2 (AQA, January 2012)

a) Outline the purposive approach to statutory interpretation **and** outline **one** of the rules of language. *(10 marks)*

b) Outline the literal rule of statutory interpretation. *(10 marks)*

c) Briefly discuss advantages **and** disadvantages of the literal rule. *(10 marks + 2 marks for AO3)*

Example question 3 (AQA, May 2011)

a) In the context of statutory interpretation, briefly describe what is meant by **two** of the following:
   - rules of language
   - external (extrinsic) aids
   - internal (intrinsic) aids. *(10 marks)*

b) Describe **either** the literal rule **or** the mischief rule. *(10 marks)*

c) Briefly discuss advantages **and** disadvantages of the literal rule **or** of the mischief rule. *(10 marks + 2 marks for AO3)*

▨ Chapter 4: Judicial precedent

These example questions are taken from past exam papers. You must answer all three parts of the question.

Example question 1 (AQA, May 2011)

a) With reference to judicial precedent, briefly explain the meaning of *ratio decidendi* **and** *obiter dicta*. *(10 marks)*

b) Explain how judges **either** in the Supreme Court **or** in the Court of Appeal can avoid following precedent. *(10 marks)*

c) Discuss advantages of the use of judicial precedent. *(10 marks + 2 marks for AO3)*

Example question 2 (AQA, January 2012)

a) In the system of judicial precedent, briefly explain the role of law reports **and** what is meant by *ratio decidendi*. *(10 marks)*

b) Outline **two** ways in which judges can avoid a binding precedent. *(10 marks)*

c) Discuss disadvantages of judicial precedent. *(10 marks + 2 marks for AO3)*

Example question 3 (AQA, May 2012)

a) Outline the main features of judicial precedent. *(10 marks)*

b) Outline the process of overruling **and** briefly explain how judges in the Supreme Court can avoid following a binding precedent. *(10 marks)*

c) Discuss **either** advantages **or** disadvantages of judicial precedent. *(10 marks + 2 marks for AO3)*

The legal system

Introduction

Unit 1B together with Unit 1A constitutes Unit 1 of the AS specification. Unit 1A is about law-making and Unit 1B is about the legal system. Unit 1A and Unit 1B are examined together on one examination paper, which constitutes 50 per cent of the overall marks for the AS qualification and 25 per cent of the overall marks for the A2 qualification.

The Unit 1 examination is of 1.5 hours' duration. You must answer questions from three topics: one topic from Unit 1A; one topic from Unit 1B; and another topic, which may be from Unit 1A or 1B. There will be a choice of four topics in Unit 1A and four topics in Unit 1B.

Each topic is represented by one question, which has three parts. You must answer all parts of the question. Each part is normally worth 10 marks; the entire question is worth 30 marks, plus 2 marks for Assessment Objective 3.

All parts of each topic relate to the same topic area of the AQA Law AS specification – that is, the same chapter of this book. Parts (a) and (b) will normally be a test of your knowledge and understanding, and part (c) will normally be evaluative, requiring simple discussion of advantages and disadvantages of a topic.

Unit 1B comprises four chapters:

5 The civil courts and other forms of dispute resolution: this gives an outline of civil courts and a description and evaluation of ways in which civil disputes are resolved without going to court.

6 The criminal courts and lay people: this gives an outline of the criminal court structure and a description and evaluation of the role and work of lay magistrates and of jurors.

7 The legal profession and other forms of advice and funding: this looks at how lawyers qualify, and the work they do. It also looks at how civil and criminal cases are paid for, and where legal advice can be obtained.

8 The judiciary: this looks at the different types of judges and how they qualify, and considers the concept of their independence.

The civil courts and other forms of dispute resolution

1 Outline of civil courts and appeal system

Fig. 5.1 *The civil court structure*

Courts of first instance

Civil disputes are generally between individuals, partnerships, companies and/or local or national Government departments. Any or all of the above may disagree about, for example, a contract, a negligence claim, or a landlord and tenant relationship.

The dispute will be between the **claimant** and the **defendant**. The claimant will issue proceedings in a civil court by giving to the court a description of the claim on a set form, together with the court fee. This claim is then sent to the defendant for a response, usually in the form of a defence to the claim.

There are two main civil courts in which civil claims may be issued: the County Court and the High Court. The Magistrates' Court is primarily a criminal court, but does have some civil **jurisdiction**.

These courts are known as courts of first instance, as claims may be commenced and decided there. If the decision of the court is disputed, then a party may be able to ask a higher court to reconsider the case – known as an appeal (see 'Appeal hearings', on p77).

There are currently 216 County Courts in England and Wales, which hear lower level civil disputes. Trials in the High Court (which has jurisdiction to hear all types of civil disputes) may be in London or may be heard in one of the 26 High Court District Registries in England and Wales. The High Court generally hears the higher level civil cases.

Magistrates' Court

The Magistrates' Court has jurisdiction over most family matters (except divorce). It can deal with the recovery of unpaid council tax and charges for water, gas and electricity. It can also hear appeals from the local authority about granting licences for gambling or the sale of alcohol.

County Court

The County Court deals with many types of civil disputes, including cases on contract, tort (for example, negligence), bankruptcy, property and divorce.

Civil cases are divided into three types: cases involving less than £5000 are transferred to the small claims track and are dealt with and heard by District Judges; cases involving between £5000 and £25,000 are transferred to the fast track and are generally heard by a Circuit Judge; cases over £25,000 are usually transferred to the multi-track and may be heard by a Circuit Judge or may be transferred to the High Court – if, for example, the case concerns professional negligence and/or there is a complicated point of law in issue.

There are proposals to increase the amounts of claims heard by the Small Claims Court and County Court, but at the time of writing no increase has come into force.

High Court

The High Court has three divisions: the Queen's Bench Division, the Family Division and the Chancery Division. These divisions are then sub-divided into the court where civil claims may be issued and the court where appeals from lower civil courts will be heard (see 'Appeal hearings' below). There are approximately 120 High Court Judges.

- Queen's Bench Division: this is the main court, and deals primarily with contract and tort cases. There are currently 74 High Court Judges sitting in this court. The cases are often heard in the **Royal Courts of Justice** in The Strand, London, but may be heard in one of the High Court's District Registries around the country. Cases allocated to the multi-track may be heard in this court, rather than the county court, due to the legal complexity of the case, the large amount of money involved, or if the case is of a certain type – for example, professional negligence or claims against the police.
- Family Division: this court deals with all aspects of family matters, including divorce, related children and financial claims, adoption and care proceedings.
- Chancery Division: historically, this court dealt with cases in which the rules of **equity** could be used. The modern version of this court deals with cases such as partnership disputes, company law, disputes about wills or trusts, bankruptcy, the sale of land and the creation of mortgages. There are currently 17 judges who sit in the Chancery Division. Cases will be heard at the Royal Courts of Justice, or in one of the eight specified Chancery centres around the country.

Appeal hearings

An appeal is when a party to a civil case is dissatisfied with the court's decision and requests a higher court to review the earlier decision. Following the **Access to Justice Act 1999**, the majority of appeals will only be allowed to proceed if either the original court or the appeal court has given such authorisation. Permission is only granted if it involves a matter of importance or if the appeal has a good chance of success.

The High Court as appeal court

As mentioned above, the High Court is both a court of first instance and an appellate court (a court of appeal).

Study tips

Ensure you can distinguish between the three divisions of the High Court, and the different types of cases dealt with in those divisions. The High Court is both a court of first instance and a court of appeal.

Key terms

Royal Courts of Justice: based in The Strand in London, this is where High Court Judges mainly sit.

Equity: a branch of law that developed from the end of the 13th century. It is based on the court's application of 'fairness' to a decision in a case, in response to the occasional unfairness of the inflexible rules of common law.

Access to Justice Act 1999: amended the law on appeals in order to restrict the number and type of appeals allowed to proceed.

■ **Key terms**

Case stated: a means by which a case may be reviewed by a higher court at the request of an inferior court in order for a point of law to be confirmed or clarified.

Leave to appeal: when a party wishes to appeal and authority for the appeal must be obtained, either from the original court or from the appeal court.

Justices of the Supreme Court: judges who sit in the Supreme Court.

■ Queen's Bench Divisional Court: in cases of judicial review, this court may review the decisions made by local authorities and national Government departments and by tribunals. Judicial review is a consideration by this court whether the rules of fairness have been broken in the decision-making process. This court may also hear appeals on a point of law by way of **case stated** from a Magistrates' Court, Crown Court. These will be criminal cases. Finally, a party who claims to be unlawfully detained may apply for a 'writ of *habeas corpus*' for the decision to detain to be overturned.

■ Family Divisional Court: this court hears appeals from the decisions of Magistrates' and County Courts in respect of family-related matters.

■ Chancery Divisional Court: this court hears appeals on decisions made in bankruptcy and insolvency cases originally decided in the County Court.

The Court of Appeal

There are currently 37 judges (known as Lords Justices of Appeal) who sit in the Court of Appeal. The most senior civil appeal judge is the Master of the Rolls. The Court of Appeal has a Civil Division, which specialises in civil cases.

In general terms, the Court of Appeal hears appeals from:

■ the County Court (District Judge or Circuit Judge)

■ the High Court in its capacity as a first instance court (all three Divisions)

■ the High Court in its capacity as an appellate court (all three Divisions)

■ the Employment Appeal Tribunal.

These appeals are generally heard by three to five judges, although appeals may be heard by two judges if, for example, the parties agree. In the majority of cases, **leave to appeal** to the Court of Appeal is required.

The appeal is not a re-hearing of the original trial with the calling of witnesses, etc., but a review of the case. Barristers in Court of Appeal hearings must provide, in advance, written and concise statements of their arguments to the court and the opposing barrister. This saves time and cost to all parties. These statements are called 'skeleton arguments'.

The court will look at the judges' reasons for their decision to see whether the judge has correctly interpreted and applied relevant rules of law.

The Supreme Court

The Constitutional Reform Act 2005 created the Supreme Court to replace the House of Lords, and this change took place in October 2009. The Supreme Court has no connection with Parliament. It has its own building, staff and budget, and the appointment process of Justices has been reformed. It is the final court of appeal in civil law for England, Scotland, Wales and Northern Ireland.

There are 12 judges of this court, called **Justices of the Supreme Court**. The Supreme Court hears about 200 cases each year, the majority of which are civil. These cases are on matters of general public importance. Most appeals are heard by three or five Justices of the Supreme Court. Leave to appeal must be obtained from the original court or from the Supreme Court itself.

The majority of the appeals are from the Civil Division of the Court of Appeal. However, there is a 'leap-frog' procedure provided by the Administration of Justice Act 1969. If a High Court Judge certifies the case as suitable for the Supreme Court and the Supreme Court agrees to grant leave to appeal, the case will go straight from the High Court to the Supreme Court. The case must be on a point of law, and one:

- of public importance in relation to the statutory interpretation of an Act of Parliament or a piece of **delegated legislation**
- when the trial judge is bound by a **precedent** of the Court of Appeal or Supreme Court.

The Court of Appeal has a civil and criminal division, and hears many more cases per year than the Supreme Court: the Court of Appeal hears about 2000 cases a year. Decisions of the Court of Appeal are more likely, therefore, to have an impact on the general public.

Generally, the Supreme Court is restricted in the cases it decides to those that involve important legal issues.

Key terms

Delegated legislation: a law made by a person or body other than Parliament but with the authority of Parliament.

Precedent: the principle that an inferior court must follow the earlier decision of a higher court.

Parties: the people who are in dispute with each other.

Activities

1. Alan wishes to sue Ben for £12,500 for a negligence claim following an accident. Advise Alan of the court to be used to commence the claim and the track to which the claim will be allocated. How would your advice be different if the claim were for £72,500?

2. Carol wishes to divorce David and claim residence (formerly known as 'custody') in respect of the child of the family. David is a wealthy businessman and Carol has just inherited a large amount of money from a long-lost relative. Advise Carol of the two courts in which she may start the proceedings.

3. Alan was unsuccessful in his claim against Ben for £72,500. Advise Alan on the different civil courts in which his appeal may be heard.

You should now be able to:

- outline the civil court structure
- describe the jurisdiction of each court
- attempt past paper questions on the civil court structure.

2 Other forms of civil dispute resolution

Reasons for alternatives to the court system

When **parties** are involved in a dispute that cannot be resolved, the parties will often apply to the civil courts for a decision. Topic 1 of this chapter outlined the types of civil courts available, and the jurisdiction of each court.

However, for many reasons, these courts are not always the most suitable or appropriate method to resolve such disputes. The civil courts are, for example, expensive and slow and have to follow specific procedures. Alternative methods for resolving such disputes have developed, or been created, which are often less costly and speedier than the courts, as well as being less procedural.

In this topic you will learn how to:

- state reasons why there is a need for other forms of dispute resolution
- describe the people involved in each of the other forms of dispute resolution
- outline the procedures in each of the other forms of dispute resolution
- allocate types of dispute to each form.

Tribunals

Since the late 1940s there has been a growth in parliamentary legislation affecting individuals in their private lives. Examples are laws affecting employment rights, social security benefits, housing, education, immigration and mental health.

These laws inevitably result in disputes – for example, whether an individual is entitled to a particular State benefit. A system had to be constructed to allow these disputes to be resolved. The court system could not cope with the number of disputes so **tribunals** were created to allow the public access to fast and inexpensive ways of resolving disputes that may otherwise have clogged up the civil courts.

In 1957, the Franks Committee on Tribunals reviewed how tribunals were working and recommended that tribunals should be based on, for example:

- independence (from Government)
- openness (all hearings should, if possible, be in public)
- accessibility (so that all parties could understand the procedure involved, and legal representation was not essential).

As a result of this Committee's report, the Tribunal and Enquiries Act 1958 created the Council of Tribunals to review the running and workings of tribunals. The Council has 15 members, who observe cases and deal with complaints. The Council cannot insist on reforms, but may make recommendations. After a recommendation, the Government set up the Leggatt Committee in 2001, which advised that all tribunals should be dealt with under the Tribunals Service from April 2006.

Types of dispute dealt with by tribunals

There are many tribunals, but they may be classed as two main types: **administrative** and **domestic**.

Administrative tribunals deal with disputes between the individual and the State. The tribunal will apply the relevant law to the dispute between the parties. Examples include:

- the Social Security Appeal Tribunal, which deals with disputes arising out of claims for State benefits such as Jobseeker's Allowance, Income Support and Incapacity Benefit
- the Immigration and Asylum Tribunal, which deals with disputes over rights to enter and remain in the UK
- the Mental Health Review Tribunal, which deals with applications by patients for release from secure hospitals.

However, some administrative tribunals deal with disputes between individuals. Examples include:

- Rent Tribunals, which deal with disputes between landlords and tenants over levels of rent
- Employment Tribunals, which deal with disputes between employers and employees on unfair dismissal, discrimination and redundancy.

Domestic tribunals are 'in-house' tribunals often set up by professional bodies. The tribunal will apply the rules of the particular organisation to the dispute between the parties. Examples include:

- the Solicitors Disciplinary Tribunal, which decides whether solicitors have broken professional rules

Key terms

Tribunal: less formal than a court, it is an alternative way to resolve a dispute where legislative rules indicate a specific route of resolution

Administrative tribunals: deal with disputes between an individual and the State, or with another individual.

Domestic tribunals: deal with disputes between an organisation and one of its members.

- the Bar Council, which covers the same areas, but in relation to barristers
- the General Medical Council, which covers the medical profession
- the Football Association, which deals with disputes between members of the Association.

People involved

Most tribunals consist of three members, namely a legally trained chairperson (for example, a qualified lawyer) and two lay members, who are selected from a panel of persons who have expertise in the matter under dispute. For example, an Employment Tribunal hearing will consist of a legally qualified chairperson, now called an Employment Judge, plus two lay members who have experience of industry and commerce, and who represent the views of the employee and of the employer.

Some tribunals will have a chairperson who has expertise in the area of the parties' dispute, rather than a legal qualification.

Generally, parties are encouraged to represent themselves rather than using lawyers. The parties will attend, as will their witnesses.

Procedure

The parties and their witnesses give evidence. All will be available for questioning by the other party and by the chairperson and lay members.

The panel's judgement is based on the law, evidence and arguments put to them, though they are not bound by strict rules of judicial precedents as the courts would be.

A party does not need to employ a lawyer for representation at the tribunal. The party may choose to represent himself or herself, be represented by a friend or by someone with an understanding of his or her complaint, such as a trade union member.

Tribunals are free: no fees are charged, in order to keep the system available to all. There is a proposal to charge a fee to launch a claim in an Employment Tribunal from April 2013.

If a party chooses to be represented by a lawyer, it is most unlikely that public funding will be available. A few exceptions include the Mental Health Review Tribunal and the Employment Appeal Tribunal. Unlike in the civil courts, each party must meet their own legal costs, regardless of who wins the case. This helps to discourage people from using lawyers and maintains the lower cost compared to a civil court. However, costs can be ordered if a party or their representative has behaved 'unreasonably' during the case.

Most tribunals are obliged to give reasons for their decisions, which has allowed for more tribunal decisions to be challenged on appeal. The appeal may be to another tribunal – for example, appeals against decisions of an Employment Tribunal pass to the Employment Appeal Tribunal and finally to the Court of Appeal. Appeals can only be made on a point of law.

Tribunals must follow the rules of natural justice. This means, for example, that both parties must be given time to prepare the case and be given a fair hearing. The Queen's Bench Division of the High Court can look at a tribunal's decision if there are claims that the rules of natural justice have not been followed.

Alternative Dispute Resolution

Lord Woolf conducted a two-year investigation into means of reforming the civil justice system. His reports in 1997 proposed streamlining the civil court procedure and recommended the greater use of **Alternative Dispute Resolution (ADR)**. The Civil Procedure Rules 1998, passed as a result of Lord Woolf's proposals, place a duty on the courts to encourage the use of ADR. The Court of Appeal has held that the courts do not have the power to force parties to try ADR, as this would be a breach of a person's right to a fair trial under Art 6 of the European Convention on Human Rights. This can be seen in *Halsey* v *Milton Keynes General NHS Trust* (2004). However, if a party unreasonably refuses to try ADR and then wins the case at court, that successful party may not be awarded their costs to be paid by the losing party – see *Dunnett* v *Railtrack plc* (2002).

Arbitration

Arbitration is where the parties refer the dispute to a third party, who will act like a judge and give a decision on the dispute, which is called an award.

The arbitrator will usually be a person with both legal and specialist knowledge of the subject matter of the dispute – for example, a surveyor may arbitrate in a building dispute between a builder and developer. Arbitration is governed by the Arbitration Acts 1979 and 1996, which set out rules for arbitration and the various grounds for appeal from an arbitrator's award.

Types of dispute dealt with by arbitration

Arbitration may arise in a number of ways:

■ Most large commercial contracts will contain an arbitration clause allowing for arbitration to occur if a dispute arises under the contract.

■ A number of trade and professional organisations offer an arbitration facility. For example, the Association of British Travel Agents (ABTA) can arbitrate between a holidaymaker and a travel company on a disagreement about a package holiday. Most disputes may use the arbitration process and the **Chartered Institute of Arbitrators (CIA)** can suggest and supply an independent arbitrator, if requested.

■ If a claim is started at the Employment Tribunal, a copy of the employee's claim and employer's response is sent automatically to the **Advisory, Conciliation and Arbitration Service (ACAS)**. The ACAS representative is an expert in employment law and can, if the parties agree, act as an arbitrator.

People involved

The arbitrator is independent of the parties and is usually an expert in the area of the dispute. The parties may name a specific arbitrator in their contract, or name a professional body that can appoint the arbitrator should a dispute arise. An example would be the CIA or, if the dispute involved building, the professional body for surveyors – the Royal Institute of Chartered Surveyors.

The parties will present their case to the arbitrator (see 'Procedure' below), a process that may involve witnesses.

Procedure

Arbitration is covered by the Arbitration Act 1996. The arbitration agreement must usually be in writing, but how the arbitration proceeds is open to the parties to agree. The parties may include an arbitration clause in their original contract, committing them to arbitration in the event of a dispute. This is known as a *Scott* v *Avery* clause. The clause will specify who will act as arbitrator (where the parties choose one themselves) or the process for appointing one (for example, nomination by the CIA).

Where this type of clause has been included within a contract, the court will refuse to deal with any dispute unless and until it has gone to arbitration.

The Act sets out the powers of the parties to shape the process according to their needs, together with the powers of the arbitrator. Both the parties and the arbitrator agree the arbitration hearing procedure together. The hearing can be set at a time and place of mutual convenience to the parties and the arbitrator. The hearing is carried out in private. The process usually involves each party putting forward its own arguments and evidence, either in writing or orally. Witnesses may be called to give evidence and be cross-examined.

The arbitrator makes the final decision (the award), which is binding on the parties. An arbitrator has the power, for example, to order one party to pay money to the other. This order can be enforced through the courts.

The process of arbitration is free, but the arbitrator will charge a fee, which may be shared or paid by just one of the parties. The parties are allowed to be represented by a lawyer if they wish, but this is discouraged.

There is no automatic right of appeal. However, under s68 of the Arbitration Act 1996, a party may appeal to the High Court if there is a 'serious irregularity' – for example, the arbitrator did not carry out the arbitration in the manner as agreed by the parties. Under s69 of the 1996 Act, a party may appeal on a point of law that arises in the arbitration decision.

Mediation

Mediation is a process by which a third party acts as a messenger between the parties to assist in resolving the dispute. The parties do not have to meet and the **mediator** will pass on the offers, counter-offers and general comments between the parties.

The mediator helps the parties define the issues under dispute, and the emphasis is on the parties themselves creating a solution to the dispute. The mediator does not act as adviser to either party, who must make their own judgements on the offers made.

Mediators may be selected from mediation bodies such as the Centre for Dispute Resolution (which has approximately 300 trained mediators).

Types of dispute dealt with by mediation

The Family Law Act 1996 has encouraged separating couples to use mediation instead of court action. If a party wishes to obtain public funding for legal advice and representation, it must have attempted mediation first. The mediation may cover disputes over children, property and finance.

There are now a growing number of mediation services aimed at resolving small disputes. For example, the West Kent Independent Mediation Service offers a free service from trained voluntary mediators to try to resolve neighbour disputes over noise and boundaries.

> ### Study tips
> Remember that the parties agree to arbitration in the original contract and it is not forced on them. The parties may choose the arbitrator or the manner in which the arbitrator is chosen.

> ### Key terms
> **Mediator:** an independent third party who will assist the parties in their attempt to resolve the dispute.

People involved

The mediator will organise the mediation at a time and place convenient to all parties. The parties attend with legal advisers (if any). The mediator will pass on information from one party to another. The parties may be in separate rooms from each other if they prefer.

Procedure

Mediation takes place in private and in a neutral setting. Procedures vary, but typically each party puts forward its position, followed by private meetings between the mediator and each party in turn. The mediator acts as a go-between, whereby the two parties in dispute communicate and negotiate through the mediator. The mediator remains neutral and does not suggest any solutions to the problem, and cannot force settlement on the parties. The mediator encourages both parties to reach an agreement.

Each party may be legally represented, but this is discouraged. Each party must meet their own legal costs but public funding is available for family mediation. Witnesses are rarely involved in mediation.

If the parties reach an agreement then this may be written down and, if the parties agree, the agreement becomes legally binding. The agreement is enforceable by the civil courts should either party fail to follow the terms of the agreement. If no agreement is reached, the matter may be taken to court or a tribunal.

Conciliation

This is a similar process to mediation. However, the **conciliator** is able to intervene in the process, actively suggest terms of settlement and comment on terms put by one party to another. It is important for the parties to realise that the conciliator is neutral and is not acting as their representative (such as a lawyer).

Types of dispute dealt with by conciliation

ACAS (see p82) operates a conciliation scheme in industrial disputes, for example in Employment Tribunal cases. In a tribunal case, ACAS will be sent a copy of the employee's claim and employer's response. The ACAS representative is an expert in employment law and, with the parties' agreement, can act as a conciliator in the dispute.

People involved

The conciliator will organise the conciliation at a time and place convenient to all parties. The parties attend with legal advisers (if any). The conciliation will proceed as mediation except for the conciliator's added powers of intervention.

Procedure

The procedure is very similar to mediation. The conciliator and the parties will meet and the conciliator will listen to the grievances and will make suggestions on how the problem can be resolved. If the parties agree then the agreement may be made legally enforceable. If no agreement is reached, the matter may be taken to court or a tribunal.

Mediation and conciliation are very similar. Remember the subtle differences between the two, and that ACAS is a good choice as an example of both arbitration and conciliation.

■ **Key terms**

Conciliator: an independent third party who will actively assist the parties in their attempt to resolve the dispute. The conciliator will suggest terms of settlement to the parties, and advise on offers put forward by the parties during negotiations.

Negotiation

Negotiation is usually the first method in trying to resolve a dispute. The parties can communicate directly with each other to try and agree matters without going to court. This communication may be face to face, by letter, telephone, email, text, etc.

If either or both of the parties are legally represented, the lawyer(s) may continue to negotiate throughout their involvement, either with the other lawyer or directly with the other party. Many cases are settled on the morning of a court hearing. Negotiation may also be carried out by non-legally qualified representatives on behalf of the parties. For example, in an employment dispute the employee can be represented by a trade union official.

Types of dispute dealt with by negotiation

Any dispute may be resolved by negotiation. Mediation and conciliation are forms of negotiation, but using third parties to assist in the process.

Low-key disputes are best resolved by negotiation without expensive court action. A neighbour disagreement or a dispute between an electrician and a homeowner are examples of when a negotiated settlement would be appropriate.

People involved

The only people involved are the parties themselves or their representatives, if they have them.

Procedure

There is no fixed procedure, but often a meeting will commence with each party stating their position. For a successful negotiation, the parties must focus on the issues rather than personalities. A successful negotiation is likely to require each party to compromise their position to a certain extent.

There are no costs involved with negotiation unless representatives are involved, in which case it is likely that the parties will pay the costs of their representatives.

Lawyers will often encourage their clients to reach an agreement without resorting to the court, and/or try to negotiate on behalf of the clients. Obviously, it is cheaper and quicker to reach an agreement without involving lawyers.

▪ **Key terms**

Negotiation: an informal method of dispute resolution. It may take place between the parties or between their representatives.

▪ **Study tips**

Remember that tribunals and the four types of ADR are outside the civil court justice system. They are alternative ways of resolving civil disputes. Each type of ADR is separate from the other, and the parties will not move from one type to another automatically. Negotiation may lead to mediation or conciliation or arbitration if negotiation is unsuccessful.

▪ **Activity**

Make a table with a column for each form of ADR. List the types of dispute dealt with, the people involved, the procedure, any costs involved, what result can be achieved, and whether an appeal is possible.

You should now be able to:

- understand the other forms of civil dispute resolution

- explain the operation of each form

- attempt past paper questions on other forms of dispute resolution.

Key terms

Public funding: the State paying for, or contributing to, the costs and expenses incurred by a party to a case (formerly known as Legal Aid).

Remedies: what the successful claimant is awarded by the court at the trial.

Civil Procedure Rules (CPR): introduced into all civil courts in April 1999, they were the result of a review of the civil justice system by Lord Woolf. Their purpose is the 'overriding objective' – namely to simplify the system, reduce costs and delay.

3 Advantages and disadvantages of forms of civil dispute resolution

The civil courts: advantages

Legal expertise/experience

Judges sitting in the county or High Court have acquired experience of the law and the legal system over many years, both as lawyers acting for parties and as judges. They will be able to guide the parties through the court process. Their decision will be supported by research of the facts with a detailed description of the law used to reach the decision.

Availability of public funding

The Community Legal Service oversees the granting of public funding for civil cases. **Public funding** is available for some civil cases – for example, a financial claim related to divorce.

Remedies

The civil court has the power to award the successful party a variety of **remedies**. Compensation (known as 'damages') may be ordered to be paid from the defendant to the claimant. The court also has the power to order a party to cease an act or activity (an 'injunction') or to complete a contract ('specific performance'). These remedies are enforceable by the court.

New procedure under the **Civil Procedure Rules (CPR)**:

■ Pre-action protocols: since 1999, parties must now complete certain procedures before issuing a court case. These procedures cover a full exchange of relevant information – for example, the disclosure of an accident book in a place of work. This enables the parties to consider the merits of their respective claims before issuing a claim.

■ Emphasis on encouraging settlement: the civil courts must now actively encourage the parties to try and achieve a settlement without continuing with the case – for example, by the use of ADR (see Topic 2, p79).

■ Case management by judges: judges order the parties, and their lawyers, to complete certain formalities by set dates – for example, the exchange of witness statements. This means the case will proceed at a reasonable speed.

■ Part 24 strike-out provisions: the CPR allow the court to strike out (dismiss) a claim at any time after the claim is issued. This stops the defendant from incurring unnecessary legal costs in a claim that has no merit.

■ Part 36 offers to settle: the CPR allow the parties to make offers to settle the claim to the court and to the other party in a simple and effective manner. Cases may be compromised (settled) without the need for a trial.

The civil courts: disadvantages

Lack of technical knowledge

Judges may have limited knowledge of the subject-matter of the dispute, as it may be of a technical or specialist nature. The judge will have to rely on the view of an expert appointed by the court rather than on his/her own expertise – for example, a surveyor in a building dispute.

Slow process

Despite the CPR, the civil justice system is still slow and delays do occur. For example, in cases allocated to the 'fast track' (see Chapter 13, Unit 2) the final hearing must be within 30 weeks, but this track only covers cases where the claim is less than £25,000. Larger claims will take longer to come to trial.

Case management by judges is not wholly effective, as judges are very reluctant not to allow a party to continue with their case even if they have not met deadlines.

Lack of flexibility in court process

The parties have little control over the court process and procedure. Evidence at a trial is restricted by technical rules, and hearings are set by the court, which may be inconvenient to either or both parties. The court is limited in the remedies it may award – for example, a letter of apology may be part of a suitable remedy but the court is unable to order this.

Need for lawyers

Due to the complexity of the law and the procedure in the civil courts, lawyers are generally required by parties. A party may represent themselves but will inevitably be at a disadvantage.

General cost

Parties must pay fees, which can run into hundreds of pounds, to the court when commencing a claim. Lawyers' costs are high, as are expert witnesses, who may be required to give evidence. There is a general rule in civil cases that the loser will pay the winner's costs as well as their own.

Under pre-action protocols, parties will now incur costs at an early stage in the case, which may finally prove unnecessary. For example, a claimant in a personal injury case has to incur the cost of a full medical report before beginning a case, and may then discover that the defendant is not liable.

Adversarial process

The English civil court system is still based on winning a case, whether on a legal, factual or procedural point. The CPR attempted to banish tactical manoeuvring by lawyers, but such tactics still exist.

Publicity

Most cases heard in the civil courts are open to the public and the press. This may make the experience of resolving a dispute in the courts an even more stressful and embarrassing experience.

Tribunals: advantages

Expertise

A tribunal **chairperson** and members usually have expertise in the matter under dispute. For example, in an Employment Tribunal the chairperson will be a judge or an experienced lawyer in employment disputes, and the lay members have practical experience of business due to their respective connections with employers and employees.

Reasons for decisions

Tribunals must give reasons for their decisions. This allows the parties and the public to understand why a particular decision has been reached, and that the decision should be based on legal grounds.

Activity

At this stage, make a mind-map or spidergram of the advantages and disadvantages of the civil court justice system.

Key terms

Chairperson: usually a legally qualified individual who leads a tribunal, with the assistance of two legally unqualified persons (lay members).

Cost

Legal representation is not essential. Tribunals do not charge a fee for entering a claim. Each party usually pays their own legal costs, rather than the losing party paying all the costs of both parties. Public funding is available in a few tribunals – for example, before a Mental Health Review Tribunal.

Informality

Two of the tribunal members are lay persons, and neither they nor the chairperson wears an official outfit. This lack of formality allows for a more relaxed environment and the parties can present their case with confidence, without the necessity for legal representation.

Flexibility

Because tribunals do not operate strict rules of **judicial precedent**, they are more flexible in their decision-making. This allows the tribunal to judge each case on its own merits. Strict **rules of evidence** do not apply in tribunal hearings, though decisions are based on legal rules.

Speed

Tribunal cases are usually heard quickly. The hearing date is fixed within a short period of the start of the claim, giving details of place, date and time. The final hearing is usually completed within one day.

Privacy

Proceedings taken before a tribunal are often not as highly publicised as court hearings. It is unlikely that members of the public wll be present in a hearing.

Congestion

Tribunals relieve congestion in the civil court system. If the volume of cases heard by tribunals were heard in the civil courts, the court system would be overloaded, which would cause further delays.

Tribunals: disadvantages

Influence of chairperson on lay members

The chairperson is usually a legally qualified person. The chairperson may influence the lay members of the tribunal panel because of this expertise and professional experience.

Lack of availability of public funding

Generally, public funding is not available for legal representation before a tribunal. This affects the more disadvantaged members of society, as the other party may be able to afford legal representation. For example, in an Employment Tribunal an employer will probably be able to afford a lawyer while the (former) employee may not. The tribunal system was created to assist the weaker members of society and this defect devalues the system.

Appeals procedure

There are different rights and routes of appeal from different tribunals, which may make the process complicated and require legal representation. For example, an appeal from an Employment Tribunal is to the Employment Appeal Tribunal (but only on a point of law). However, all tribunal decisions may be reviewed by the High Court under

---

the principle of judicial review if, for example, there has been a breach of natural justice.

Inconsistencies in decisions

Tribunals are not bound by the rules of judicial precedent, nor by strict rules of evidence. As a result, tribunal decisions will sometimes be inconsistent, which creates uncertainty for parties in a case.

Publicity

Because of the lack of publicity for tribunals, cases of public importance are not given the attention and consideration they deserve.

Formality

Following the recommendations of the Franks Committee, the chairperson must be legally qualified and judges are now used in the Employment Tribunal. This has led to greater formality of proceedings, which are sometimes conducted in the same way as a court hearing. The attendance of lawyers, representing their clients, also makes the procedure and atmosphere more formal.

Arbitration: advantages

Expertise

Arbitrators will have specialist knowledge of the relevant area under dispute, which allows fair and speedy decisions. For example, the arbitrator in a building dispute is likely to be a surveyor.

Privacy

The proceedings are conducted in private and the evidence and decision are not publicised in the media. The parties may not want their domestic or business affairs to be made public.

Convenience

The parties agree the time, date and venue to meet with the arbitrator.

Enforceability of the award

Arbitration will result in a conclusion to the dispute between the parties. The award made by the arbitrator is binding on the parties. This means the parties must comply with the terms of the award and, if they do not, the court will enforce it.

Informality

The process is likely to be less formal than the courts. There are no complicated rules of evidence and the use of lawyers is discouraged. For example, in a dispute about a package holiday dealt with through ABTA, the parties may represent themselves and need not have a detailed knowledge of the relevant law in order to achieve a successful conclusion.

Speed

Arbitration is quicker than using the civil courts. The pre-hearing procedure will be shorter, and the hearing will usually take only one day or part of a day.

Cost

There are no court fees, and the use of lawyers is discouraged, which saves on legal costs.

Cost-saving to the State

The use of arbitration frees the court from dealing with many disputes. Many small disputes (for example, package holiday cases or employment disputes) may be dealt with by arbitration, as may many large disputes of a technical nature (for example, the building dispute that arose over the new Wembley Stadium).

Arbitration: disadvantages

Lack of legal expertise

The arbitrator will often lack the legal expertise possessed by a judge. Where a dispute hinges on a difficult point of law, the arbitrator may not be able to judge the matter, due to this lack of legal knowledge.

Inconsistencies in decisions

The arbitrator is not bound by rules of judicial precedent. Each case is judged on its own merits, providing no real guidelines for future disputes. This can lead to inconsistent decisions and conclusions. It may be difficult for a party to predict the result of an arbitration.

Cost

The costs may be high. This is due to the length of time that some disputes may take to be resolved, and to the possibility that arbitrators may charge high fees for their professional services. For example, a surveyor will charge an hourly or daily rate to act as an arbitrator in a building dispute.

Appeals

Under ss68 and 69 of the 1996 Act, appeals may be made on limited grounds to the High Court (see Topic 2). This prolongs the arbitration process and increases costs, which are factors arbitration is supposed to resolve.

Lack of awareness/popularity

There is a low take-up rate for arbitration. Some cases are not appropriate for arbitration, and some parties may not want to try it because they do not understand it or have faith in it. Cases dealt with by arbitration have not increased since the CPR reforms introduced by Lord Woolf in April 1999, which aimed to promote more use of all forms of alternative dispute resolution.

Mediation: advantages

Speed and convenience

The process is quicker than the ordinary courts. The meeting will be arranged at the earliest date that is agreeable to the parties. The parties can arrange the date, time and venue for the meeting, rather than wait for the court to fix a hearing date. The process allows the parties to continue their business or personal relationship after the mediation is completed.

Lack of formality

The process is less formal than the courts. There are no complicated rules of evidence, and the use of lawyers is discouraged. For example, in a family dispute, the parties can use the mediator but may always negotiate directly if both agree to do so.

Empowerment

The system empowers the parties because it does not force a decision upon them, but encourages them to reach a mutual agreement. The process generally leads to both parties being satisfied with the outcome. Mediation has been encouraged by the courts, and even if a case involves a decision or a point of law it does not make it unsuitable for mediation.

Cost

The process is not expensive. There are no court fees, and the use of lawyers is discouraged. For those who qualify, public funding is available for mediation in family cases.

Expertise

Mediators are usually specialists in the area of dispute. They are also normally trained in the art of mediation (for example, by the Centre for Dispute Resolution). Lord Woolf said, 'Skilled mediators are now able to achieve results satisfactory to both parties in many cases which are quite beyond the powers of the lawyers and the courts to achieve.'

Privacy

The proceedings are conducted in private, and the decision is not publicised in the media. This enables the parties to keep their business and domestic disputes between themselves.

Mediation: disadvantages

Imbalance of power

One party is usually weaker than the other, whether financially or emotionally. That party is susceptible to intimidation by the stronger party, whereas this would not be allowed in a courtroom setting. An example of this would be one party in a personal relationship still having the power to inhibit the other in a mediation situation.

Lack of legal expertise

Mediators may not be legal experts. When the resolution of a dispute involves a difficult or complicated point of law, the mediator may not have the ability to deal with the mediation in an appropriate manner.

Lack of certainty

There is no certainty as to the outcome of the mediation. This is because the mediation does not have to conform to the rules of precedent, and because one or both parties may choose not to accept offers made to compromise the dispute. The Paul McCartney and Heather Mills divorce is an example of an unsuccessful mediation resulting in increased costs, publicity and a court hearing.

Enforceability

It is difficult to facilitate the resolution of a dispute between parties who may have strong emotions – for example, in a family case. Unless the parties agree otherwise, the mediation settlement is not binding and the parties cannot enforce the agreement in the courts. Therefore, mediation may not lead to a satisfactory conclusion. This means time and costs will have been wasted, and the dispute will have to proceed to court in any event. It was said in *Halsey* v *Milton Keynes General NHS Trust* (2004) that the courts cannot require the parties to a dispute to enter into mediation, as this would breach the right to a fair trial.

Conciliation: advantages

Pro-active element of conciliator

The conciliator is independent of the parties and has the power and ability to suggest and advise on offers made by parties during conciliation. This allows the parties the security of knowing the advice came from a neutral source. This may mean the dispute is settled on agreed terms.

Expertise

The conciliator has expert knowledge and experience of the types of disputes under conciliation. For example, ACAS conciliators are experts in the area of employment law. They can confidently comment on, and suggest compromises for, settlement of employment disputes. As with mediation, advantages of conciliation also include speed and convenience, lack of formality, lower cost and increased privacy.

Conciliation: disadvantages

Imbalance of power

One, or both, of the parties may feel the conciliator is not neutral in his or her comments and/or suggestions. This may lead to a non-resolution to the dispute.

The other disadvantages are similar to mediation.

Negotiation: advantages

Speed

The process is often quicker than using civil courts. The parties meet at a mutually convenient time, which is probably shortly after the dispute arises. Time has not passed, so both parties will be familiar with the reasons for the dispute arising.

Formality

The process is less formal than the courts. Simple negotiation is a process by which the parties discuss the issues between themselves, probably face to face. The terms of settlement may be in any form acceptable to the parties, and may be in a form not allowed or sanctioned by the court process. For example, an employer might agree to supply a letter of apology to a (former) employee, a neighbour might agree to allow a third party to prune an overhanging tree, or a business might allow a customer a choice of products from its stock.

Cost

The process is the least expensive of all forms of ADR. There are no court or legal fees, unless solicitors are instructed at a later date. The only expense may be the parties' time, postage or the cost of a telephone call.

Privacy

The proceedings are conducted in private. The agreement is not publicised in the media. The parties are secure in the knowledge that the settlement is confidential, and that no one outside the agreement need know about the dispute or its compromise.

Negotiation: disadvantages

Imbalance of power

There can be an imbalance of power. As with the other forms of alternative dispute resolution, one party is often weaker than the other and is acting less voluntarily. Not all parties wish to resolve their disputes by negotiation. Some disputes are not appropriate for this method of alternative dispute resolution, and some parties may not want to use it – for example, due to serious personality clashes or reluctance to admit fault.

Lack of legal expertise

There may be a lack of legal expertise if lawyers are not used. However, lawyers could be consulted on a point of law, or might be instructed if no agreement is reached. The parties may agree a settlement of the dispute which is not practical or enforceable. The dispute may then resurface and the parties may have little choice but to instruct solicitors for advice.

Lack of certainty

There is lack of certainty, as the negotiation process does not follow rules of precedent. The parties have no security that there will be a successful negotiation, and the process may itself re-ignite the dispute between the parties.

Enforceability

The agreement negotiated between the parties may become enforceable by the civil courts. However, the parties involved may have no appreciation of this point. One party may believe the agreement is a binding agreement, but the other may feel it is not enforceable by the civil court unless agreed otherwise. This can cause confusion and upset.

Activities

1. Pick a type of ADR and a dispute to be resolved. List the advantages and disadvantages of the process to be undertaken compared to a civil action in the courts.

2. Divide into two groups. Group 1 should argue that the civil court justice system is the preferable forum to resolve a civil dispute. Group 2 should argue that ADR generally, and/or a particular type of ADR, is a better option.

3. Divide into four groups. Group 1 is the neighbour to Group 2, and there is a falling-out concerning late, loud parties held by Group 1, which annoy Group 2. Group 3 is the mediator or conciliator, and must assist the parties to reach a compromise. Group 4 is neutral, and takes notes on the reasons for the success or failure of the mediation/conciliation process.

You should now be able to:

- understand the ways of resolving civil disputes
- answer examination questions on civil dispute resolution.

The criminal courts and lay people

In this topic you will learn how to:

■ draw a diagram of the criminal court structure showing appeal routes

■ state the jurisdiction of each court

■ describe the appeal process.

Link

For more information on the Criminal Appeal Structure, see Chapter 11 (The criminal courts: procedure and sentencing), p192.

1 Outline of criminal courts and appeal system

The outline in this section will provide the background to the work that is done by lay people in the criminal court system. The court structure has been explained in Chapter 5, and should now be reviewed.

This topic concentrates on the jurisdiction (the powers and types of case dealt with) of the Magistrates' Court and the Crown Court in criminal matters.

The overall criminal court structure can be seen in the diagrams set out below.

Fig. 6.1 *Criminal appeal structure: Magistrates' Court trial*

Fig. 6.2 *Criminal appeal structure: Crown Court trial*

This chapter looks at the lay people who perform a central role in the criminal courts, either as magistrates or as jurors.

The Magistrates' Court jurisdiction

Whilst the Magistrates' Court has some limited civil jurisdiction, most of its work is dealing with criminal offences involving adult defendants. This includes: issuing arrest and search warrants; deciding on **bail**; conducting sending for trial hearings where **indictable offence** cases, such as murder, are transferred to the Crown Court; trying **summary offences** such as assault; and trying **either-way offences** that are to be tried summarily, such as theft.

The magistrates also deal with young offenders in the Youth Court. This is a specialised form of Magistrates' Court. Unlike the Magistrates' Court, the Youth Court is not open to the general public, and only those directly involved in the case will normally be in court. It deals with almost all cases involving young people under the age of 18. A hearing in the Youth Court is similar to one in the Magistrates' Court, although the procedure is adapted to take account of age of the defendant. The magistrates who sit in the Youth Court receive specialist training on dealing with young people.

The Crown Court jurisdiction

The Crown Court deals exclusively with serious criminal cases. The work includes: trying indictable offences such as murder; trying either-way offences that are to be tried on indictment, such as theft; sentencing where the case has been sent by the Magistrates' Court to the Crown Court for sentence (usually because the magistrates' sentencing powers are limited); and appeals from the Magistrates' Court against conviction or sentence.

Appeals from the Crown Court go to the Court of Appeal (Criminal Division). Possible grounds for appeal include misdirection of law or facts, failure to refer to a defence, inappropriate comments by the judge, or jury irregularity. The Court of Appeal will allow an appeal (and possibly order a new trial) if it considers the conviction unsafe. Where the Court of Appeal quashes a conviction on a point of law, and the verdict of the jury shows that it was satisfied that some other offence had been committed, the Court of Appeal may substitute a conviction for that other offence.

You should now be able to:

- outline the criminal court structure
- describe the jurisdiction of each court
- attempt past paper questions on the criminal court structure.

Key terms

Bail: release of a defendant from custody, until his or her next appearance in Court.

Indictable offence: a criminal offence that can only be tried by the Crown Court.

Summary offence: a criminal offence that can only be tried by a Magistrates' Court.

Either-way offence: an offence, such as theft, for which the accused will be tried by the Magistrates' Court or in the Crown Court, where the defendant will be tried by jury.

Study tips

Make sure you answer any question on the jurisdiction of criminal courts accurately. In particular, the different appeal structures from the Magistrates' Court and Crown Court can be confusing.

Activity

Draw a chart comparing the appeal structure for a summary offence, an either-way offence and an indictable offence.

2 Magistrates

Magistrates are also known as Justices of the Peace. They can be traced back to 1195, when Richard I required some of his knights to preserve the peace in unruly areas. They were responsible to the King for ensuring that the law was upheld; they preserved the 'King's Peace' and were known as Keepers of the Peace. In 1327, an Act of Parliament set out the appointment of men in every county to 'guard the peace'. The term 'Justice of the Peace' was first used in 1361, and the role has developed since then.

There are just under 29,000 lay magistrates in England and Wales. They are unpaid, except for expenses, although the annual training budget is

In this topic you will learn how to:

- describe the qualification, selection and appointment of a magistrate
- describe the training, role and powers of magistrates.

approximately £500 per head. The magistracy is comprised of roughly equal numbers of men and women. It is supposed to reflect society as a whole, so it is expected to have a race and gender balance that reflects the make-up of the country and, more importantly, of the local area in which magistrates sit. They are all part-time, but give a commitment to be able to sit as a magistrate at least 26 half-days a year. About 1600 new magistrates are appointed each year. This level of appointment does not just include growth in the number of magistrates, but also turnover, as magistrates retire or are otherwise unable to continue in the role.

The statistics can be seen in Table 6.1 below.

Table 6.1 *Numbers of Justices of the Peace in England and Wales*

Year	Total	Men	Women
1990	28,667	16,090	12,577
1991	29,062	16,098	12,964
1992	29,441	16,105	1,336
1993	29,686	16,087	13,599
1994	30,054	16,151	13,903
1995	30,088	16,045	14,043
1996	30,326	15,951	14,375
1997	30,374	15,858	14,516
1998	30,361	15,713	14,648
1999	30,260	15,561	14,699
2000	30,308	15,544	14,764
2001	28,735	14,639	14,096
2002	24,526	12,439	12,087
2003	28,344	14,392	13,952
2004	28,705	14,555	14,150
2005	28,253	14,256	13,997
2006	28,865	14,519	14,346
2007	29,816	15,007	14,809
2008	29,419	14,672	14,747
2009	29,270	14,472	14,798

www.official-documents.gov.uk

Link

For more information on District Judges (Magistrates' Courts), see Chapter 8 (The judiciary), p139.

Lay magistrates sit as a bench of three magistrates and have a role in all criminal cases in some way, dealing with the entire criminal process for 95 per cent of all cases. In 2009, 1.6 million cases were heard in Magistrates' Courts, with 1.3 million convictions. Many of these cases involved more than one hearing, so the workload is enormous. There are some full-time, paid, legally qualified magistrates, called District Judges (Magistrates' Courts). This chapter will focus on the lay magistrates.

How magistrates are qualified, selected and appointed

Qualifications and eligibility to be a magistrate

Lay magistrates require no special qualifications. The first requirement is to have the correct personal qualities and to be able to commit the time and effort to being a magistrate. There are six general personal qualities that applicants to become a magistrate should possess. These are:

1   To be of good character, including having personal integrity, keeping confidences and the respect and trust of others.

2   To have understanding and communication. This is needed, as a magistrate will have to understand documents, identify facts, follow evidence and concentrate for long periods of time. A magistrate also needs to be able to communicate effectively, both in court and out of court.

3   To have social awareness, including an appreciation and acceptance of the rule of law, respect for people from different ethnic, cultural or social backgrounds, and an understanding of their local community.

4   To be mature and of sound temperament. This will include an awareness and understanding of people, and a sense of fairness, as well as humanity and courteousness.

5   Being of sound judgement. This requires the ability to think logically, to weigh arguments and come to a sound decision, as well as having an open mind, being objective, and recognising and controlling prejudices.

6   Having commitment and reliability. This includes being committed to serving the community, and making the necessary time commitment. The applicant must be willing to undergo training, and be in sufficiently good health to undertake magistrate duties on a regular basis. Support of family and employer is essential.

The second requirement is the willingness to take the Oath of Allegiance. British nationality is not a requirement, although those who are in the process of seeking asylum cannot be appointed as a magistrate. Even then, certain professions or occupations are ineligible, because they may be incompatible with the magistrates' duty to be impartial. These professions and occupations include the police and the armed forces; and it is also relevant if the magistrate has been selected as a prospective candidate for election to the House of Lords, or any other parliament or assembly. There is discretion in this area, but the key is whether there is likely to be a conflict of interest, so the list of excluded occupations could be extended in individual cases. These guidelines also apply to the occupation of the potential magistrate's spouse, partner and even close relatives. The guidance notes for applicants give more details, as it would be unacceptable if previous occupations or professions prevented a person from becoming a magistrate. Applicants also have to disclose whether they are a freemason.

The third requirement relates to criminal convictions and civil claims. In a way, this is an extension of the quality of good character and integrity. Applicants must disclose any convictions, however minor, including motoring offences for which a fixed penalty was payable and even police cautions. Disclosure is also required of other criminal or civil orders, including details of divorce and maintenance orders. The Rehabilitation of Offenders Act 1974 does not apply to the application, so even minor motoring offences that are 20 years old have to be disclosed. The effect of this is that anyone who, or whose spouse or partner has been convicted of a serious offence or even a number of minor offences will not be appointed if the Advisory Committee (which advises on the appointment of magistrates) believes that the public would not have confidence in them as a magistrate. For these purposes, a serious offence is regarded as anything other than a minor motoring conviction for which one received points on one's licence and/or a fine, although very old convictions of this nature are not regarded as serious.

There is no formal age requirement, except that applicants must be a minimum of 18 years old. Magistrates retire from the bench at the age of 70, and five years' service is normally expected before retirement. This means that anyone aged over 65 is unlikely to be appointed.

Selection of a new magistrate

The selection process has a number of stages. When new magistrates are needed, there is usually an advertisement placed in the area where the need has arisen. This is often part of a local campaign to recruit more magistrates. There are public awareness days in some courts, so that potential magistrates can learn more about what is involved. A person can apply to be a magistrate in either their home or work locality.

There is a standard application form available from the Ministry of Justice, which can also be downloaded or printed from its website. A DVD is included in the application pack. A person who has decided to apply to be a magistrate must complete an application form. This is straightforward, and reflects the eligibility criteria. It can be completed online, or as a hard copy.

Once the form is submitted, it is checked to make sure that, in general, the applicant is eligible to apply. If the applicant is eligible, an invitation to a first interview is sent by the Advisory Committee. The local Advisory Committees consist of local people, including some magistrates.

If successful at the first interview, there is a second interview at which practical examples of the sort of cases magistrates deal with are discussed. At this stage, background checks are made for conflicts of interest. In making their recommendations, Advisory Committees consider the suitability of candidates and the number of vacancies. The view of the Advisory Committee is then sent to the Lord Chancellor, who will make the appointments.

Appointment of a new magistrate

Magistrates are appointed by the Secretary of State and Lord Chancellor on behalf of, and in the name of, the Queen. New magistrates will then meet their colleagues and begin their training.

Training of magistrates

Training is supervised by the Judicial Studies Board, which decides the key areas in which magistrates need instruction. The training itself is carried out locally, often by the clerk of the court. All magistrates are trained before sitting, and continue to receive training throughout their service.

Magistrates' training is based on competences. These are what a magistrate needs to know and needs to be able to do so that he/she can fulfil the role. The competences are:

▓ Managing yourself: this focuses on some of the basic aspects of self-management in relation to preparing for court, conduct in court and ongoing learning

▓ Working as a member of a team: this focuses on the team aspect of decision-making in the Magistrates' Court

▓ Making judicial decisions: this focuses on impartial and structured decision-making

▓ Managing judicial decision-making: this is only for the chair of the bench, and focuses on working with the clerk, managing the court and ensuring effective, impartial decision-making.

1 **Initial Training** Before sitting in court, a new magistrate will undergo introductory training on the basics of the role. After this, s/he will sit in court with two experienced magistrates.

2 **Mentoring** Each new magistrate has a specially trained magistrate mentor to guide them through their first months. There are formal mentored sittings in the first 12–18 months of service, where the new magistrate will review his/her learning progress and talk over any training needs.

3 **Core Training** Over this first year, further training, visits to penal institutions and/or observations take place, to equip magistrates with the key knowledge they need.

4 **Consolidation Training** At the end of the first year, consolidation training builds on the learning from sittings and core training. This is designed to help magistrates plan for their ongoing development and prepare for their first appraisal.

5 **First Appraisal** About 12–18 months after appointment, the new magistrate is appraised. This will see whether the new magistrate is demonstrating that s/he fits the competences. When successful, the magistrate is deemed fully competent.

Magistrates continue training throughout their magisterial career, in order to maintain their competency and to receive update training on new legislation and procedures.

The role and powers of magistrates

The Lord Chancellor's Directions for Advisory Committees on Justices of the Peace state that 'Each bench should broadly reflect the community it serves in terms of gender, ethnic origin, geographical spread, occupation and political affiliation.' This enables the magistrates to act in an appropriate manner to ensure that the community in which they serve can deal with local issues.

A magistrate is required to sit for at least 26 half-days each year. Magistrates normally work as part of a bench of three magistrates. There is a chairman and two wingmen, who are often less experienced than the chairman. As magistrates are not legally trained, they always have access to the advice of a qualified legal adviser. This is a justices' clerk or assistant clerk, who is also responsible for effective case management and the avoidance of delay in court.

The legal adviser explains the relevant points of law and legal procedures to the magistrates, and gives advice on possible sentencing options. The actual decisions are made by the magistrates alone, as they decide on guilt or innocence based on the findings of fact that they make. Similarly, the magistrates decide on a sentence, but must act within their powers. The adviser will make sure that the magistrates are aware of the latest guidelines and policies on sentencing, but the magistrates make the decision and the chairman of the bench announces it to the court.

Assault – actual bodily harm	Offences Against the Person Act 1861 s.47 Triable either way – see Mode of Trial Guidelines Penalty: Level 5 and/or 6 months

CONSIDER THE SERIOUSNESS OF THE OFFENCE
(INCLUDING THE IMPACT ON THE VICTIM)

IS DISCHARGE OR FINE APPROPRIATE?

IS IT SERIOUS ENOUGH FOR A COMMUNITY PENALTY?

GUIDELINE: → IS IT SO SERIOUS THAT ONLY CUSTODY IS APPROPRIATE?

ARE YOUR SENTENCING POWERS SUFFICIENT?

THIS IS A GUIDELINE FOR A FIRST-TIME OFFENDER PLEADING NOT GUILTY

 ## CONSIDER AGGRAVATING AND MITIGATING FACTORS, CULPABILITY AND HARM

for example	for example
Abuse of trust (domestic setting) Deliberate kicking or biting Extensive injuries (may be psychological) Headbutting Group action Offender in position of authority On hospital/medical or school premises Premeditated Victim particularly vulnerable Victim serving the public Weapon *This list is not exhaustive*	Minor injury Provocation Single blow *This list is not exhaustive*

If offender is on bail, this offence is more serious

If offender has previous convictions, their relevance and any failure to respond to previous sentences should be considered – they may increase the seriousness. The court should make it clear, when passing sentence, that this was the approach adopted.

TAKE A PRELIMINARY VIEW OF SERIOUSNESS, THEN CONSIDER OFFENDER MITIGATION

for example
 Age, health (physical or mental)
 Co-operation with police
 Evidence of genuine remorse
 Voluntary compensation

CONSIDER YOUR SENTENCE

Compare it with the suggested guideline level of sentence and reconsider your reasons carefully if you have chosen a sentence at a different level. Consider a reduction for a timely guilty plea.

DECIDE YOUR SENTENCE
NB. COMPENSATION – Give reasons if not awarding compensation

© The Magistrates' Association **14** Published October 2003 and revised December 2006

Fig. 6.3 *Extract from sentencing guidelines in adult bench book*

The adviser carries out many administrative roles, such as: preparing for court sessions and making sure that all relevant papers and exhibits are ready; reading charges to the court; dealing with the paperwork for legal aid and completing bail forms; managing court schedules; and training magistrates. This means that the magistrates can concentrate on the evidence in the case and the appropriate sentence, rather than being burdened with tasks that require specialist knowledge and expertise.

Out of the courtroom, magistrates may have to sign police warrants authorising arrest of suspects, search of premises and extensions of custody up to a maximum of 96 hours.

Magistrates hear less serious criminal cases and commit serious cases to the Crown Court, where the case will be heard by a judge and/or jury. Magistrates cannot impose sentences of imprisonment of more than six months (or 12 months for consecutive sentences) or fines exceeding £5000. Magistrates can also sit in the Crown Court with a judge to hear appeals from Magistrates' Courts against conviction and/or sentence.

You should now be able to:

- understand the workings of lay magistrates
- attempt past paper questions on lay magistrates.

Activities

1. Explain how lay magistrates are chosen and appointed.

2. Describe, in outline, the work of lay magistrates.

3. Identify and discuss the advantages and disadvantages of using lay magistrates in the criminal justice process.

4. In small groups, discuss whether you would like to be appointed a magistrate. List the positive and negative points to your view of becoming a magistrate.

In this topic you will learn how to:

- describe the qualification and selection of jurors
- describe the role of jurors.

3 Jurors

Trial by jury has been a feature of English law for hundreds of years. The way in which the jury operates has developed over the years, and is now seen as central to the administration of justice for serious criminal offences. Whilst there are other, more limited, roles for the jury, this section deals exclusively with the jury in criminal trials.

Nearly 500,000 people are summoned for jury service each year. This is normally for a period of two weeks, but there is no guarantee that there will be a trial to hear on any particular date. Some trials are lengthy, and service continues until the trial ends. On occasions when the trial has a high media profile, there is a danger that once the jury has retired to consider its verdict, the jurors may be exposed to reports that might influence the verdict. In such cases, the jury stays together until the verdict is reached; if this is overnight, the jury is accommodated in a hotel and kept away from media reports.

If a person does not reply to the summons, fails to attend without good reason, or is not available or unfit through drink or drugs when called, that person may be prosecuted. Similarly, those who absent themselves without good reason when on jury service may be prosecuted.

Jury service is one of the most important civic duties. All members of the public are expected to perform this duty if called upon to do so. However, some people are not eligible, or are disqualified from jury service, while others may be asked to have their service deferred because their personal circumstances make it difficult to carry out their duty at the time. Whilst a person might be summoned for jury service more than once, a few people are excused further jury service after completing a trial. Since electronic records were created in 1999–2000, the Jury Central Summoning Bureau's database shows that by 2006, the most that any one person has served on a jury is four times, and that was only one person.

The juror's role in the criminal justice system is to decide, based on the evidence presented, whether a defendant is guilty or not guilty of the crime with which he or she has been charged. A jury trial takes place only in the Crown Court. A jury is made up of 12 jurors, who should come to a unanimous decision, although this can be reduced to 11:1 or 10:2 in some situations. As with magistrates, jurors are unpaid, except for expenses and some compensation for loss of earnings, and are not expected to have any legal knowledge.

Qualification and selection of jurors

Eligibility

Jurors are chosen at random from the electoral roll to serve on a jury at a Crown Court reasonably close to where the juror lives. According to the Juries Act 1974, any person is eligible for jury service provided they fulfil certain conditions. This means that a person may be summoned if all the conditions set out below are satisfied:

- He or she is aged at least 18 and under 70 on the day on which the jury service is due to start.
- He or she is registered on the electoral roll.
- He or she has lived in the UK, Channel Islands or Isle of Man for at least five years after the age of 13.

The jury summons is prepared on a random basis by a computer. This is dealt with by the Jury Central Summoning Bureau.

Disqualification

A person is not qualified for jury service whilst on bail, or following certain convictions for criminal offences, or suffering from a mental disorder or other mental health problem. The following situations disqualify a person from jury service, and are set out in the Criminal Justice Act 2003:

- Bail: if a person summoned is on bail for a criminal offence.
- Conviction: if a person summoned has ever been sentenced to:
    - **a** imprisonment, detention or custody for life; or
    - **b** imprisonment for public protection or detention for public protection; or
    - **c** five or more years' imprisonment or youth custody; or
    - **d** certain extended sentences in Scotland.
- Conviction: if a person summoned has in the past ten years:
    - **e** served any part of a sentence of imprisonment, or a sentence of detention; or
    - **f** had a suspended sentence passed on them; or
    - **g** had various community orders imposed, such as a community rehabilitation order, a community punishment order, a community punishment and rehabilitation order, a drug treatment and testing order.
- Mental disorders or mental health problems: if the person summoned:
    - **h** suffers from, or has suffered from, a mental disorder or mental health problem, and as a result is a resident in a hospital or other similar institution; or
    - **i** regularly visits the doctor for treatment for the mental disorder or mental health problem; or

j has a guardian under the Mental Health Act 1983; or

k as a result of mental health problems, the court has decided that they are not capable of managing their own affairs or property.

It should also be noted that a juror can be discharged from his duties if the judge considers that, because of physical disability (such as deafness) or insufficient understanding of English, the juror would not be able to perform his or her duties properly.

Deferral

Anyone can apply for deferral of their jury service. If the application is successful, the effect is that the jury service is carried out later within the following 12 months. The new dates may be given as soon as an application for deferral is accepted. The application for deferral needs to be a good reason, such as examinations, a date for an operation in a hospital, or a holiday that has already been booked. Most applications for deferral are granted, but anyone refused deferral can appeal to the head of the Bureau. Jury service can only be deferred once up to a maximum of 12 months from the original date. Home Office research into deferral of jury service found that almost three-quarters of all deferrals were for either work commitments or holidays. Guidelines are being produced to ensure consistency in deferral and excusal of jury service.

Excusal

As an alternative to deferring, a person can be excused from serving as a juror at any time during the following 12 months. Excusal effectively takes a person off the list for jury service for 12 months, and therefore requires a further random selection before the person is summoned again. It is only available in exceptional circumstances.

A person may be excused if he or she has been on jury service in the criminal courts (not a coroner's jury) in the previous two years. This also applies where the court has excused someone for further jury service for a period that has not yet ended. This can occur after a particularly long or distressing trial. This ensures that no individual should feel overburdened by the duty.

A full-time member of the armed forces may also be excused, if the commanding officer certifies to the Jury Summoning Officer that absence would prejudice the efficiency of the service. The list of those who have a right to be excused jury service or to apply for discretionary refusal is:

- those who are over 65 years of age
- those who have served within the last two years
- those whose religious beliefs are incompatible with jury service
- full-time members of the armed forces
- certain members of the medical profession
- representatives of the Assembly of the European Communities (Euro MPs)
- Members of Parliament.

Lawyers and the police are not excused from jury duty. This may create difficulties within the jury panel as they may be seen by other jurors as knowing the process or some of the procedures involved in the case. Other jurors may rely on them for explanations of the law or procedures in the case.

Jury service is a serious commitment, and those who do not fulfil their commitment are dealt with seriously.

> **Study tips**
>
> Do not confuse disqualification, deferral and excusal – it's easy to do this!

Female juror, 51, sent to jail for 56 days after abandoning robbery trial to take a week's holiday

A woman juror who abandoned a four-week robbery trial to jet off on holiday to Malta was jailed last night for 56 days for contempt of court. Janet Chapman, 51, said she thought it would be fine to travel abroad for a week because her doctor had signed her off work due to a bad back. The next day she phoned the court and left a telephone message saying: 'Hello, this is Janet Chapman... I won't be attending court for a period of up to two weeks. I have got to return to the doctor's next Tuesday. I have got sciatica. Thank you. Bye.' She then flew off to enjoy some winter sun on a £669 week-long holiday in Malta with her long-time partner Raymond Pritchard.

But she had a nasty surprise when she touched down at Liverpool Airport as a welcoming party of police officers was waiting to arrest her. Judge Anthony Russell QC said: 'It is clear you deliberately deceived the court for your own ends and pleasure. Your assertion that you were unaware that you could not go away on holiday whilst absent from jury duty due to what you maintain was illness is ludicrous. I am satisfied that if you really suffered back pain of such severity that that you could not continue your jury service you would not have been able to endure the travel to Malta. I am driven to the conclusion that you pretended to your doctor that you had a back problem in order that you could take a holiday in Malta.'

Preston Crown Court heard potential jurors were told to indicate if they had a holiday or hospital admission which would leave them unable to sit on a serious robbery trial. At the start of the trial of robbery suspect Raymond Mallen, Chapman did not notify the court why she should not be part of the jury. He was accused of being part of an organised gang which carried out a series of high value cash-in-transit robberies across the North West of England. Evidence had been heard and Judge Stuart Baker was about to begin summing up when Chapman phoned the courts and left her message. Yesterday she told the court the holiday last month had been a birthday surprise from her partner and she had only learned about the trip the night before they flew out. Chapman, a deputy manager at a children's residential home, said that having suffered a back injury and been signed off sick from work she didn't think she would have to attend the trial. She said: 'On the Monday morning I couldn't get out of bed. I went to the doctor that night. I was signed off for a week. I didn't think I was doing anything wrong.'

Her partner, Raymond Pritchard, told the court he booked the £669 holiday in January, but had not told her about it until the night before. Judge Russell said it had been a serious contempt of court. He said: 'You have manifestly failed to perform your public duty. Further, it is clear that you deliberately deceived the court for your own ends and pleasure, namely taking a holiday in Malta.' The case

carried on and Mallen was convicted of conspiracy to rob and jailed for 12 years. Various gang members have now been jailed for a total of more than 80 years in all. Last night Mr Pritchard choked back tears at his semi-detached property on the outskirts of Blackpool and said the mistake would cost them dear.

He said: 'Obviously we did not know what the consequences would be. I have never stepped into a court of any kind until today. This could well lose my wife her job. She works with children and it is a job she loves. Janet has never done anyone any harm. Then to come home from holiday and get arrested at the airport, it was terrible. I have not heard from her since she was jailed I don't know when she will be able to phone me. 'I think what has happened is like using a jack hammer to crack a nut. I don't know how she will cope behind bars ... I just told her to survive it.' Last year juror Matthew Banks, 19, was jailed for 14 days after phoning a court and saying he was ill so he could go and watch a West End musical with his mother. He was released four days later on appeal. Detective Chief Inspector Lee Halstead, said: 'His Honour Judge Russell QC, the Recorder of Preston, has sent a clear message that as a member of the public, fulfilling your responsibility on jury service is a fundamental cornerstone of the British criminal justice system, and is to be taken seriously.'

Daily Mail, 5 April 2012

Jury vetting and challenges

Article 6(1) of the European Convention on Human Rights requires trial by an independent and impartial tribunal. Jury vetting, where the members of the jury are checked before service, would appear to be contrary to that principle.

There are strict rules about jury selection:

- members of a jury should be selected at random from the panel of jurors in waiting, subject to any right of challenge
- the Juries Act 1974 and the Juries (Disqualification) Act 1984 identify those groups of people who are disqualified from or ineligible for service on a jury

the prosecution can only challenge a jury member by a request to stand by or a challenge for cause – in other words, showing a reason why that person should not serve.

There are two types of jury vetting allowed, where checks of a juror may be made:

- a **Criminal Records Bureau (CRB) check**, which is now automatically conducted on each juror to assess qualification against jury service criteria
- a more detailed check known as an **'authorised jury check'**, which may involve a CRB check, Special Branch records check, and sometimes a Security Services check. An authorised jury check can only be authorised by the Attorney General, and should only be used in cases involving national security.

Challenges for cause can be made by the prosecution and defence, and are used when an individual juror is challenged. This may be if the juror is recognised by one of the parties in the case, is considered to be disqualified, or exceptionally is considered to be biased – for example, with possible racist views.

Challenges to the array are when the whole jury panel is objected to, perhaps because it is considered unrepresentative.

Any challenge has to be made before the jury is sworn in.

The role and process of the jury

The jury system offers to the defendant the opportunity of being tried by his or her equals. The role of the jury can be seen as simply to return verdicts of guilty or not guilty. This is done by deciding the facts. The jury must apply the law, as explained by the judge in his summing up, to those facts, and give their verdict. The verdict should be initially unanimous – that is, all 12 jurors should reach the same verdict. However, a majority verdict can be accepted by the judge when all the jurors cannot agree. In this situation, the judge decides that the jury's decision is acceptable if at least ten of the jurors agree. A majority decision can only occur when the judge has allowed the jury to deliberate for at least two hours.

The jury is independent and should be free from bias. The random nature of the selection of jurors by the computer starts the process. When the juror reaches court, there is another random element in the selection of the individual trial for which that juror may be involved. When jurors arrive at court, they go to the assembly area. This is a room in the courthouse where jurors have to check in at the start of their service and have their identity confirmed. The assembled potential jurors are shown a DVD explaining their role as a juror and what happens in a courtroom.

When a court is ready to select a jury, a court official chooses a group of people at random from those in the jury assembly area. More people are called into the courtroom than the 12 required to make up the jury – usually 15 people are called forward. This is to allow for the random selection process to continue, to make sure that no one is a juror on a case with which they have a connection. If a case is expected to go on for more than two weeks, this allows for some people who will be unable to serve on the jury for an extended period.

An average trial lasts about a day and a half. Jurors may be called to sit on more than one trial, which may mean more than one per day. However, this depends on the number of trials going ahead, the size of the the juror pool at the court, and the random selection of jurors from that pool. At all times other than in the courtroom, the jury will be kept apart from lawyers, witnesses and all other people involved in the trial.

During the trial, jurors will listen to the evidence and look at the exhibits, such as items involved in the crime, photographs, diagrams and CCTV images. A juror can take notes, but these can only be used in the courtroom and the jury room. They cannot be taken home. At the end of the trial, the notes will be destroyed, because the whole process of the jury's deliberation is secret.

When the evidence has been completed and the lawyers have finished their speeches, the judge sums up the case to the jury and explains the law. The jury then retires to the jury room to consider the verdict. Each juror can only take into the jury room any notes made during the trial, a copy of the indictment (the list of the offences with which the defendant is charged), and any exhibits submitted during the trial that are allowed to be taken (typically photographs and diagrams). Jurors may not have access to mobile phones or computers, to ensure secrecy and discussions based purely on evidence.

You should now be able to:

- understand the operation of the jury
- attempt past paper questions on juries.

Activities

Discuss the two points below:

1. Whether barristers, solicitors and judges should be eligible to serve on a jury.

2. Whether serving police officers should be eligible to serve on a jury.

In this topic you will learn how to:

- state the advantages and disadvantages of the use of lay magistrates

- give examples relevant to those advantages and disadvantages

- state the advantages and disadvantages of the jury

- give examples relevant to those advantages and disadvantages.

4 Advantages and disadvantages of using lay people in the criminal courts

There are many advantages and disadvantages of using lay people in the criminal justice system. The key advantages and disadvantages are set out below, but there are many other arguments that can be made. For most of the advantages or disadvantages stated, it is possible to argue the opposite view: for example, the cost of replacing magistrates with judges is shown as an advantage of having magistrates; it could be argued that the cost is relatively small if the result of the spending were a better criminal justice system. It is a useful exercise to think what the counter-arguments are for each advantage or disadvantage as you read this topic.

The advantages of the use of magistrates

Cost

Magistrates are unpaid, apart from their expenses. This means that the large majority of criminal cases are tried without the need for a judge, Recorder or District Judge (Magistrates' Court), whose salary would be over £100,000 each. It is estimated that the annual saving is in the region of £100m. This figure takes into account the cost of the legal adviser in the court, which would not be necessary for full-time salaried judges; an administrator for each court would still be needed.

Local knowledge

Magistrates' local knowledge is invaluable when it comes to understanding exactly where an offence took place. In Crown Court, much time can be taken explaining exactly where the location of a crime was and where, in relation to the event, a witness was standing. Most importantly, the decisions made in court can take into account local problems that can be helped by sensitive sentencing.

An example of this arises from that fact that, under the Drugs Act 2005, police can drugs test people arrested for a variety of 'trigger' offences such as theft, robbery or taking a motor vehicle. This was put into effect as a pilot scheme in three police areas where high levels of drug-related crime existed. Those who tested positive for drugs were obliged to attend a compulsory drug assessment and were helped into treatment and other support. The scheme could be backed up by appropriate sentencing for those charged and convicted.

The approach of using local knowledge was seen in the case of *Paul* v *DPP* (1989), where the court had to decide whether a kerb-crawler was 'likely to cause nuisance to other persons in the neighbourhood'. The magistrates knew that the neighbourhood was a residential area in which kerb-crawling had become a problem. The defendant was convicted, and on appeal, Lord Justice Woolf said this was the sort of case that was particularly appropriate for trial by magistrates with local knowledge.

On the other hand, many local Magistrates' Courts have closed in recent years, and more closures are planned. Knowledge of the local area and witnesses will be less of a problem in the future.

Availability of judges

If all magistrates were replaced by judges, approximately 1000 judges would have to be appointed. This would require an entirely new approach to the appointment of judges, as the pool of candidates would be nowhere near large enough.

Can deal with the issues that arise

Over 90 per cent of defendants plead guilty, and most trials deal with issues of conflicting evidence rather than questions of law. Magistrates are perfectly able to decide who is telling the truth and can also decide whether behaviour is reasonable in all the circumstances, such as when self-defence is pleaded. In many ways they are better able to do this as they reflect a cross-section of society better than the judiciary. This can be seen by comparing the respective statistics on race and gender.

Public confidence

The public has great confidence in the magistrate system, even though there is perhaps less confidence in magistrates than in the judiciary. Studies in 2000 and 2001 suggest that the public would neither understand nor support any moves to lessen the role of lay magistrates, who are seen as an example of active citizenship within the criminal justice system.

The disadvantages of the use of magistrates

Unrepresentative of society

Surveys reveal that the magistracy fundamentally remains socially unrepresentative, as it is disproportionately white, middle class, professional and wealthy. This situation varies from town to town, and in general the local magistracy reflects at least to some extent the local racial mix. Also, the magistracy is now nearly gender equal. Efforts continue to attract appropriate magistrates, so the old adage that magistrates are 'middle class, middle aged and middle minded' is no longer entirely true.

The magistracy remains disproportionately middle-aged in comparison to the population. Despite the reduction in the minimum age for a magistrate, only about four per cent are under 40 years old, and over 50% are aged 60 or over. Approximately two thirds of magistrates have managerial or professional backgrounds, compared to one third of the population. The vast majority of defendants in the Magistrates' Court are under 25 years old.

Controversy flares over magistrate aged 19

Kate O'Hara

A 19-YEAR-OLD law student has become one of Britain's youngest magistrates, the *Yorkshire Post* can reveal.

But the appointment of Lucy Tate to the Pontefract bench has caused resentment among some of her fellow justices, who believe a 19-year-old cannot possibly have enough life experience to carry out the role properly.

Miss Tate is studying for a law degree in Leeds, and has had only one sitting as a magistrate so far.

She was recruited after a £4m Government advertising campaign two years ago to recruit more young people and ethnic minority candidates to the bench.

Magistrates without legal qualifications deal mainly with minor criminal offences and some family cases. The minimum age was reduced from 27 to 18 in 2004.

Miss Tate is even younger than the 20-year-old man from north Sussex who became the country's youngest magistrate last year.

One magistrate told the *Yorkshire Post*: 'It is an absolute folly to have somebody so young making such important decisions.

'Some of the magistrates in Pontefract feel very disillusioned about what has happened and they just can't see where the Government is coming from by wanting to take people on so very young.

'It was all hushed up when she was sworn in because it was felt there might be bad publicity. There probably will be – what life experience does she have at 19?'

The chairman of the local advisory committee responsible for recruiting magistrates, Sue Vogan, said: 'Lucy was an exceptional candidate, and came through a rigorous recruitment process. The committee were very impressed with her personal maturity and judgment.

'Of course, the magistracy should reflect the community it serves and we can only emphasise that Lucy's appointment was based solely on merit having met all the selection criteria. The Lord Chancellor requires that advisory committees recruit people from a wide range of experiences and backgrounds.'

Miss Tate did not want to speak to the *Yorkshire Post* but issued a statement which said: 'I was very pleased to be appointed, and look forward to serving as a magistrate. I have had my first sitting, which was fascinating, and am grateful for the training and support which I have received, as all new magistrates do.

'I don't see myself as a role model, but rather as someone who wants to serve the local community in a useful and positive way.'

www.yorkshirepost.co.uk

However, there are an increasing number of young magistrates, but some people take the view that they lack experience. An example can be seen in the article set out above.

Inconsistent

Two of the major criticisms of magistrates have been inconsistency between neighbouring benches in the sentences they impose, and bail refusal rates. Research in the 1980s and 1990s pointed out such inconsistencies. Since then, there have been increased efforts to be more consistent without losing the ability to vary sentences to suit the needs of the individual offender and crime. The sentencing guidelines and revised principles on bail are major reasons for improvement. However, inconsistencies remain between sentencing in neighbouring benches. In 2005, research was undertaken in the Bath and Bristol area:

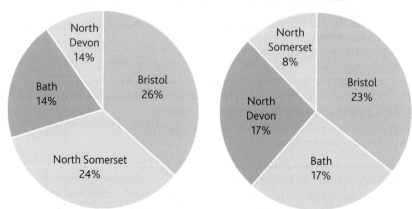

Fig. 6.4 *Percentage of those convicted given custodial sentences by magistrates for actual bodily harm by region*

Fig. 6.5 *Percentage of those convicted given custodial sentences by magistrates for domestic burglary by region*

Varying circumstances may justify these differences, of course, but justice should be consistent across the country and not vary unduly according to the views of local magistrates.

Case-hardened and biased

Magistrates often hear very similar cases, with similar evidence and with the same witnesses. For example, a magistrate may have 30 or more TV licence evaders to deal with in a session. This can lead to a suspicion that the evidence is not really considered and that the convictions are rubber-stamped, particularly if the defendant is not present. It is inevitable that the same police officer witnesses will appear to give evidence, given the local nature of the courts. The magistrates could be suspected of knowing and always believing the police witnesses, particularly when a defendant is not properly represented. This leads to suspicions that magistrates may be too ready to believe the police, and may be unlikely to accept the defendant's evidence. One quite old example of this is the case of **Bingham Justices ex p Jowitt (1974)**, where a motorist was charged with exceeding the speed limit. The only evidence was given by the motorist and a police officer. The evidence was contradictory. The magistrates found the motorist guilty. The chairman of the magistrates said, 'My principle in such cases has always been to believe the evidence of the police officer.' The conviction was quashed on appeal, as any reasonable person would suspect that the chairman of the magistrates was biased and that there had not been a fair trial.

It should be noted that fewer than 1 in 100 Magistrates' Court cases is appealed successfully on any ground whatsoever. This figure should be seen in the context of a very low acquittal rate, which results from the Crown Prosecution Service not bringing cases to court that are unlikely to secure a conviction. For many categories of offence, the Crown Prosecution Service has achieved a conviction rate of over 90 per cent in parts of the country. In July 2007 there were just over 30,000 prosecutions across 42 Crown Prosecution Service areas for motoring offences. The conviction rate was 90.2 per cent. For burglary, there were over 2300 prosecutions, with a conviction rate of 85.7 per cent (including 100 per cent in Cumbria). For drugs offences, there were nearly 4300 prosecutions, with a conviction rate of 93.6 per cent (several CPS areas had 100 per cent conviction rates). With such statistics, it is not surprising that there is a cynical view of bias.

Reliance on legal adviser

There is a suggestion that magistrates rely too much on their legal adviser. Whilst the adviser is not allowed to help the magistrates decide on a sentence, a defendant who sees the adviser constantly conferring with the magistrates and going in and out of the magistrates' retiring room may form the view that the magistrates are not in fact making the decisions. If you visit a Magistrates' Court, you can form your own opinion on this.

The advantages of the use of the jury

A balance against State interference in criminal trials

Lord Devlin, writing on jury trials, made the point that juries provide a balance against the power of the Government: 'The first object of any tyrant in Whitehall would be to make Parliament utterly subservient to his will; and the next to overthrow or diminish trial by jury, for no tyrant could afford to leave a subject's freedom in the hands of twelve of his countrymen.' A jury can find defendants not guilty even if they are

> ### Key cases
>
> **Bingham Justices ex p Jowitt (1974):** magistrates showed bias in favour of police evidence. This is an isolated example of magistrates being case-hardened and ignoring their neutral stance.

obviously guilty and the judge tells them to convict the defendant. This right was first seen in 1670, when the Quakers Penn and Meade were charged with riot, which allowed them to have a jury trial. The jury, led by a man called Bushel, refused to convict. The judge was so incensed that he committed the entire jury to Newgate prison until released under a writ of *habeas corpus*. The trial, which took place at the Old Bailey, established the independence of a jury to return a true verdict without fear of the consequences.

A modern example of this is the trial of Clive Ponting. He was an assistant secretary at the Ministry of Defence, and the civil servant responsible for 'the policy and political aspects of the operational activities of the Royal Navy' during the time of the Falkland Islands conflict. Ponting had to draft replies and answers on the sinking of an Argentinian warship, *The General Belgrano*, by the Royal Navy on 2 May 1982. Because he believed that the Government was deliberately misleading the Commons, a select committee and the public, and thought this was unethical, he acted out of professional conscience in sending two documents to an MP who would be horrified by the Government's action. Ponting was then prosecuted under the Official Secrets Act 1911. The prosecution lost the case, not because they were not correct in law, but because the jury refused to convict.

This result can be seens as a perverse verdict. A perverse verdict is one that could not reasonably be expected on the evidence given. On the one hand it is an advantage, as the jury was putting the interests of the defendant above the interests of the State. However, it is a disadvantage when juries make decisions that go against all the evidence in a case, as the public could then lose confidence in the jury system.

A jury sometimes gives a perverse verdict

As we have seen in the Clive Ponting case, a jury sometimes comes to a perverse verdict, often as a view of public opinion and the justice of bringing a prosecution. Another example is the case of Kronlid. On the night of 29 January 1996, three women – Andrea Needham, Joanna Wilson and Lotta Kronlid – broke through the perimeter fence that surrounds the British Aerospace factory at Warton in Lancashire, where planes were being prepared for sale to the Indonesian government. At that time, Indonesia was in dispute over East Timor and many people were killed in the conflict. The women slipped past security guards to a hangar containing a Hawk jet, and forced opened its door. Then, using household hammers, they smashed the £12m plane's sophisticated electronics.

The women draped the aircraft with banners bearing the slogans 'Swords into Ploughshares' and 'Peace and Justice in East Timor'. They also left a video in the cockpit explaining the reasons for their actions. They then used a telephone in the hangar to call Angie Zelter (a conspirator with them), a press agency and security. They made no attempt to escape.

They were charged with causing nearly £2m of criminal damage to the plane. The defence stated that the attack 'was not a publicity stunt, but an act of last resort by women of principle who had so far unsuccessfully campaigned against the sale of the Hawks'. The prosecution told the court that the women's 'genuine and sincere' beliefs were irrelevant to the issues in the case. However, the jury of seven men and five women cleared them of the charges. This is clearly another example of a perverse verdict.

Juries are racially balanced

Research published in 2007 by the Ministry of Justice shows that there are no differences between white, black and minority ethnic people in responding positively to being summoned for jury service, and that black and minority ethnic groups are not significantly under-represented among those summoned for jury service or among those serving as jurors. The research also found that racially mixed juries' verdicts do not discriminate against defendants based on their ethnicity.

Public participation in the criminal justice system

The fact that juries are drawn from the general public reinforces the view that the criminal justice system serves society as a whole, and is not totally removed from society as a Government agency might be. A report for the Home Office in 2004 found that over half of those included in the survey who received a jury summons claimed to be 'enthusiastic' or 'very enthusiastic', while just under one third of respondents claimed to be 'reluctant' or 'very reluctant'. Reluctance was usually because of the inconvenience of serving on a jury, rather than the principle of it. Many jurors found the experience reinforced their confidence in the criminal justice system.

The disadvantages of the use of the jury

Juries do not have to give reasoned verdicts

Whilst it can be argued that not having to give reasons for the verdict speeds up the process and reinforces the secrecy of the jury room, it does mean that individual jurors can give their verdict on a whim. This could be a result of 'going with the flow' to finish the trial quickly or it could be to produce a genuinely perverse result. Juries deliberate in private and no one can inquire into what happened in the jury room. The only time that the public finds out what happens in the jury room is when a juror complains and this leads to a retrial, as in the 1994 case of insurance broker Stephen Young. He was granted a retrial after it emerged that some members of the jury at Hove Crown Court had consulted an ouija board in a hotel during an overnight stay in a break from their deliberations. This irregularity led to a retrial.

The jury is not truly representative of the public

The jury represents the public, but people are disqualified or ineligible. Reluctant jurors will try to get their jury service excused or deferred. Once those excused have been added in, it is likely that the jury will have a higher proportion of older people (most people with criminal convictions that result in their exclusion are under 25; mothers of young children are often excused jury service). Jury vetting may also affect the representative make-up of the jury.

Lack of ability to do the job

It is often suggested that jurors do not really understand the nature of the proceedings in a criminal trial. Lawyers make a point of ensuring the evidence is given in such a way that all jurors will understand the case being made. For many jurors this is seen as trying too hard, and some become suspicious that they are not really being told the truth. The real problem is claimed to be with long and complex fraud trials, where there is now provision for a judge to sit without a jury in order to avoid any problems of juror ability. All these arguments are based on conjecture, as the actual workings of real jurors cannot be studied because of jury secrecy. This is seen in the 1986 Report of the Fraud

Trials Committee, which stated that the Committee was disadvantaged in determining whether or not jurors could understand the technical evidence and complex issues in fraud trials because they were prohibited from discussing this issue with jurors in such trials.

The effect of jury service on jurors

Most jurors find the experience interesting, and are reassured about the high standard of the criminal justice system. However, for some jurors the experience can be very distressing, particularly where the case has similarities to a personal experience. There is some follow-up counselling, but a system was only set up in 2007. Members of Crown Court juries struggling to cope with horrific cases are now put in direct touch with the Samaritans through court staff. Contact numbers and leaflets are now available in jury rooms, after the launch of the partnership between the Samaritans and the Courts Service. Feelings of distress may not surface until some time after the trial. Although Samaritan volunteers are not allowed to talk to jurors about their deliberations, they can discuss their feelings and emotions without disclosing jury room secrets.

Activities

1 Identify and discuss the advantages and disadvantages of using lay people to decide cases in the Magistrates' Court.

2 Identify and discuss the advantages and disadvantages of using lay people to decide cases in the Crown Court.

You should now be able to:

- understand the advantages and disadvantages of using lay people in the criminal justice system
- answer examination questions on magistrates and jurors.

The legal profession and other sources of advice and funding

Key terms

Bar Council: the professional body for barristers in England and Wales.

Barrister: one branch of professional lawyers whose main work is to give specialist legal advice and represent people in court.

Queen's Counsel (QC): a barrister appointed to senior rank.

1 The legal profession

The legal profession consists of two main branches: barristers and solicitors. They are collectively known as 'lawyers'. They have rights of audience (that is, the right to appear and speak on behalf of their clients) in court. There are also legal executives, who are usually specialist employees of solicitors. Legal executives might work in areas such as conveyancing, debt recovery or wills. A legal executive does not have the same rights of audience in court as a solicitor or barrister.

Barristers

Barristers have existed since the 13th century. For many years they were the only profession that had the right to represent people in the higher courts, but this monopoly has ceased. Barristers cannot form partnerships, but use common facilities and support services in chambers (originally rooms, now effectively offices). England and Wales is divided into regions or 'circuits' for the purposes of the administration of justice, and barristers attach themselves to a circuit.

The **Bar Council** is the professional body for barristers in England and Wales. It provides representation and services for the Bar, and guidance on issues of professional practice. The Bar Standards Board was established in January 2006, and separated the Bar Council's regulatory and representative functions. It is responsible for regulating barristers – for example, by setting entry qualifications and discipline.

Barristers of at least ten years' standing may apply to become **Queen's Counsel (QC)**. They undertake work of an important nature, and are referred to as 'silks', a term derived from the gown that QCs wear in court. Solicitors can now also apply to be a QC: the appointment as QC is often seen as a stepping stone to applying to be a judge. These senior lawyers are made Queen's Counsel in recognition of their outstanding ability. There are also a number of honorary QCs appointed each year from nominations made. These are appointments of people who do not intend to practise in the courts as a QC, but whose work in the law is deemed to deserve recognition.

Qualification

There are three stages to becoming a barrister: the academic stage, the vocational stage and pupillage.

- The academic stage sets the minimum educational requirement for becoming a barrister. This is a qualifying degree in law at the minimum of a 2:ii. A qualifying law degree's requirements are set out by the Bar Council and the Law Society jointly, as required by the Courts and Legal Services Act 1990. This sets out a minimum law content for the degree course followed at a university. If a person's degree is in a subject other than law, or does not comply with the requirements for a law degree, a one-year conversion course must be completed. This conversion course is either the Common Professional Examination (CPE) or an approved Graduate Diploma in Law (GDL) course. This is so that all persons starting the next stage of training have a common basic foundation in legal principles. It is for this reason that some law degrees do not qualify for exemption from taking a conversion course.

▨ Before starting the vocational stage, a person must join one of the four Inns of Court: Lincoln's Inn, Inner Temple, Middle Temple and Gray's Inn. The Inns are societies that provide various activities and support for barristers and student barristers. They also provide the use of a library, dining facilities, common rooms and gardens. Most importantly, the Inns alone have the power to call a student to the Bar, and admission to an Inn is required before registration on the Bar Professional Training Course, the main part of the vocational stage of qualifying as a barrister. The purpose of the Bar Professional Training Course is to ensure that students intending to become barristers acquire the skills and knowledge of procedure and evidence that will be required for the more specialised training in pupillage. The course runs for one academic year full-time or for two years part-time.

Fig 7.1 *Inner Temple is one of the four Inns of Court*

▨ The final stage is **pupillage**. At this stage, the pupil barrister undertakes practical training under the supervision of an experienced barrister. Pupillage is divided into two parts: the first is non-practising. In this six-month period pupils shadow, and work with, their supervisor barrister. During the second, practising, six-month period, pupils – with their supervisor's permission – can carry out legal services and have rights of audience in court. There is great competition for pupillage, and so a mini-pupillage is a useful starting point. This is a short period of work experience (usually one or two weeks) in a set of chambers. Some chambers require applicants to undertake an assessed mini-pupillage as part of the recruitment process, and others use it as one of their selection criteria. All applicants to the Bar are advised to undertake at least one mini-pupillage by the Bar Standards Board.

Training

Once a person has successfully completed the Bar Professional Training Course, he or she can be called to the bar. This usually takes place towards the end of the first six months of pupillage. As with most professions, there is a requirement for continuing training and updating. Barristers need to update and develop specialist areas of knowledge and improve their skills, particularly as there is increasing competition in the market for legal services.

The **Bar Standards Board** has set up an Education and Training Committee, which is responsible for setting the standards of education and training that people must pass before being able to practise as barristers, together with the further training requirements that barristers must comply with throughout their careers. At present, in the first three years of practice, a barrister must complete 45 hours of continuing professional development, including at least nine hours of advocacy training and three hours of ethics on the New Practitioners' Programme. After the first three years of practice, barristers are required to undertake 12 hours of continuing professional development each year under the Established Practitioners' Programme. There is a wide range of courses available to cover most specialisms, such as sentencing, aspects of tax law, and patents and design law.

Pay

The Bar Council sets a minimum rate to be paid to pupils. In 2012, this is £12,000 per annum plus reasonable travel expenses. Once qualified, a barrister will have typical earnings as a self-employed barrister in a range from £25,000 to £150,000 gross within five years. There are huge disparities in annual earnings at the Bar, with some junior barristers working in criminal law earning as little as £50 per day, before deduction of tax and chambers' charges. It should also be noted that barristers rely on the solicitors appointing them to pay the fee. This is because the arrangement for representation is between solicitor and barrister, and not between the barrister and the person he or she represents. The fee is agreed by their clerk and is often paid at the end of a trial. This means much work is done several months before payment. Some solicitors used to be very unreliable at paying the barrister's fee; more recently, the Law Society has made it clear that solicitors should pay promptly. Despite this, many young barristers actually receive little or no income in the first year of practice.

Barristers' clerks were originally paid purely on commission. Today, the majority of chambers offer a pay package. This is a mixture of salary and bonus based on the income of the barristers. This has to be paid for on a proportional basis by all the barristers in the chambers. This could cost each barrister up to 15 per cent of all earnings, although each set of chambers has its own method of spreading the cost of running the chambers. Clerks organise work for the barristers in their chambers and provide administrative support.

Work

Barristers are usually self-employed, although there is an increasing number who are employed directly by large organisations and some who work in law centres. Barristers can now work for firms of solicitors. The Bar is a referral profession and barristers are usually instructed by a professional on the behalf of a client. However, the Bar Council has relaxed its rules relating to direct access and there are now four routes to accessing a barrister.

1 Professional client access

Solicitors, European lawyers and certain legal advice centres can instruct a barrister on behalf of a client or themselves.

2 Public access barristers

Public access barristers can be instructed directly by a member of the public or a business to give legal advice or representation in court. They are normal barristers who have completed a special course. Once qualified, they can provide legal advice and representation directly to members of the public, without the need for a solicitor.

Key terms

Bar Standards Board: the independent regulatory board of the Bar Council. It is responsible for regulating barristers.

Barristers' clerk: the person (who may be one of a team) responsible for running the business activities and administration of a barristers' chambers.

What can public access barristers do?

Public access barristers are able to:

- represent a person in court or before a tribunal
- give legal advice
- negotiate a settlement
- investigate and collect evidence
- draft formal court documents, such as a statement of case or witness statements
- draft routine legal documents – for example, leases, wills, deeds or contracts.

What can't public access barristers do?

Public access barristers are not allowed to:

- actually issue proceedings or applications in court – the barrister can draft these documents, but the client will have to arrange the issue and service of the documents
- instruct an expert witness to give evidence in support of the case
- send letters on behalf of the client
- take responsibility for handling their client's affairs generally, or the day to day management of a case
- handle client's money
- act for those entitled to public funding from the Legal Services Commission (legal aid).

3 Arbitration and Mediation representative

A barrister can work as a representative in Arbitration and Mediation if he or she has completed specialist training.

4 Organisations with licensed access

Organisations can apply to the Bar Council to be licensed to instruct barristers directly, because they have expertise in particular areas of the law. Financial services companies and firms of clinical negligence insurers are typical examples of those with licensed access.

Barristers are specialists, yet have a varied workload that includes drafting documents and giving legal opinions. Barristers specialising in criminal law are likely to spend a great deal of time in court, whereas civil practitioners will probably attend court less often. Now that civil procedure encourages the use of alternative methods of dispute resolution, barristers may find that some time is spent in preparing and advising on this. Similarly, an increasing amount of time is spent in tribunals, but the vast majority of time is spent drafting documents and giving opinions as to the best way to progress a legal problem. For many barristers, much of their work is preparing for and then appearing in court. The key benefit of the barrister is that he or she is independent and objective, and trained to advise clients on the strengths and weaknesses of their case.

Day in the life of a criminal barrister

As a very junior criminal barrister, life is a mixture of waiting around and exciting performance. It's a bit like being a trapeze artist: incredibly hard work and great fun. There are hours of preparation outside court time, so weekends and evenings are never free from work, but there is nothing like standing up in court and doing your best to ensure that both parties get a fair trial.

Bar Council

Background of barristers

Barristers are the smaller branch of the legal profession. The breakdown of the profession shows that it is male-dominated and largely white.

Table 7.1 *Bar statistics 2010*

Called to the Bar			
Total 1852	Men 876	Women 977	Ethnic Minority 819

Pupillage (to July 2006)			
Total 444	Men 241	Women 181	Ethnic Minority 58

Self-Employed Bar			
Total 12,420	Men 8443	Women 3977	Ethnic Minority 1203

www.barcouncil.org.uk

Activity

What do the figures in Table 7.1 tell you:

1. about those training to be barristers?
2. about qualified barristers?

Solicitors

Usually, the first port of call for someone needing legal advice is a **solicitor**. Solicitors are the general practitioners of the legal world, dealing with all kinds of legal problems. Solicitors are readily available within geographical reach of most people. Most solicitors are in private practice, working in firms ranging in size from those with hundreds of staff, to a small office in the high street as sole practitioners (one person working on their own in their own business), and in firms of every size in between. Solicitors, unlike barristers, can form partnerships. The sole practitioner has chosen not to work in a partnership, but still may employ other solicitors or legal executives. Other solicitors have jobs in local government, law centres, the civil service, commerce and industry.

Qualification

There are three parts to becoming a solicitor: the academic training, which gives the fundamentals of legal knowledge; the vocational training, which provides the practitioner fundamentals; and the training contract. There are three starting points to academic training.

 The first route is the law graduate route, which requires a person to successfully complete a qualifying law degree. The content of a qualifying law degree is set out in the Joint Statement on Qualifying Law Degrees prepared jointly by the **Law Society** and the Bar Council under the Courts and Legal Services Act 1990. However, to qualify as a solicitor, a person must achieve the required pass mark for each of the foundations of legal knowledge subjects. This is 40 per cent, regardless of the pass mark set by the educational institution itself. It should also be noted that the degree remains valid for seven years, after which it becomes stale. This is to ensure that solicitors have up-to-date basic legal knowledge.

Key terms

Solicitor: a legal professional who advises clients about the law, and acts on behalf of clients in legal matters.

Law Society: the representative body for solicitors in England and Wales.

The second route is the non-law graduate route, in which a student graduates from a non-law degree course and then completes a Common Professional Examination (CPE) course or a Graduate Diploma in Law (GDL) course.

The final route has different regulations for those who are non-graduates and those who are members of the **Chartered Institute of Legal Executives (CILEX)**. This route is not available for a person who wishes to become a barrister. A person who is a non-graduate may be able to undertake a CPE course or a GDL course if that person is a mature student or holds certain other academic or vocational qualifications. A mature student must be over 25 years of age and have considerable experience in a suitable area of work as well as a good general education. Acceptance is at the discretion of the Law Society. This also applies to people who hold a degree from outside the United Kingdom.

In this route, the person must pass equivalent examinations in the foundations of legal knowledge and a further legal subject. Provided that the person is an CILEX Member or Fellow, these examinations can be taken within the CILEX framework. This route may also exempt a CILEX member who wants to become a solicitor from needing to undertake a **training contract**.

Vocational training is common to all those seeking to qualify as a solicitor, whichever route they started from. This is the Legal Practice Course, which provides the professional training for a solicitor. The main purpose of the course is to learn how to apply the law to the needs of clients. At the end of the Legal Practice Course, a trainee solicitor will be able to enter a training contract with the necessary knowledge and skills to undertake appropriate tasks under proper supervision during the contract. The course includes legal knowledge, skills and ethics.

The Legal Practice Course has some compulsory areas of study: Business Law and Practice; Property Law and Practice; and Civil and Criminal Litigation. There are also topics known as pervasives, which appear throughout the course at appropriate times. These focus on Probate and Administration, Professional Conduct and Client Care and Financial Services, Revenue Law and Solicitors' and Business Accounts, EU Law and Human Rights. There are also some optional, or elective, topics, which vary depending on the potential solicitor's interests and the specialisms of the institution offering the course. The skills needed to be a solicitor are also part of the course, and include practical legal research, writing and drafting documents, advocacy and interviewing. The course can be taken on a full- or part-time basis with a number of providers across England and Wales.

A training contract is a period of practice-based training. The idea is that the trainee will gain practical training under supervision, and learn to apply a range of skills through working in a solicitor's office or the legal department of another organisation. As with a barrister's pupillage, trainees are paid with minimum amounts set. In 2011, this was a minimum of £18,590 in central London and £16,940 elsewhere. This is normally two years of full-time work, but can be part-time over a longer period.

On a training contract, the trainee solicitor will work in at least three areas of law, such as personal injury law, conveyancing, company law, environmental law or criminal litigation. The areas will depend on the nature of the firm or organisation and the interests of the trainee. Skills are developed through working on clients' cases, although with close supervision. The trainees' work will be regularly reviewed, and as time goes on the trainee will deal with clients and learn to handle cases without supervision.

On completion of these three parts of the training, the trainee will be admitted as a solicitor and will receive his/her practising certificate. This licence to work as a solicitor must be renewed annually.

Training

Solicitors, as with most professions, have a requirement for continuing professional development to be undertaken. This is designed to make sure that the solicitor is up to date with law and other matters essential for his/her work. The **Solicitors Regulation Authority** requires that all solicitors complete at least 16 hours of continuing professional development activities per year. These activities might be a tax law update, a study of the latest anti-money-laundering regulations, or a reading of the solicitors' new code of conduct. In addition, new solicitors must complete the Law Society's Management Course Stage 1 by the end of their third year in practice. This is a one-day course that deals with basic aspects of management that are essential to managing a firm. Solicitors must keep a record of all continuing professional development undertaken.

Work

Solicitors work in a range of roles and areas. The vast majority of solicitors (more than 88,000) work in private practice – that is, as a firm of solicitors. These range from sole practitioners to multinational firms with hundreds of partners and offices across the world. Most solicitors in private practice work with individual clients – either private individuals or businesses.

A solicitor in a large firm will usually carry out work that is quite specialised. By contrast, a solicitor in a small firm may be involved in a great range of activities. Solicitors deal with a wide variety of legal problems, such as: helping to buy and sell property; personal injury claims; advising on matrimonial problems such as divorce, or financial disputes between partners; and immigration problems. They also represent people in court or instruct a barrister to represent them.

Solicitors do more work in court than is often imagined. In civil matters, they represent their clients at most interlocutory hearings – that is, hearings before trial. They also often appear in County Court cases on a variety of matters. In criminal cases, they often represent their client in the Magistrates' Court: indeed, this is a typical function of the duty solicitor, who will be the representative that usually makes a defendant's first bail application. Many solicitors now act as advocates for their firm, requiring less need to instruct barristers.

Businesses need help and advice in areas such as employment law, contracts and property leases. Bigger clients may be involved in company mergers and acquisitions. Some firms of solicitors have offices overseas, which may involve advising local clients on English, EU or foreign law, or representing a UK person or business abroad.

This vast range of work is affected by the public perception of what amounts to a legal matter that a solicitor should be dealing with. For example, if a person has a problem with the Inland Revenue, a decision has to be made whether to go to a solicitor, an accountant or other adviser.

Traditionally, solicitors have only been able to operate as sole practitioners or partnerships where the firm has been owned only by solicitors. However, the rules have changed and now other non-legal firms are able to buy into and run legal firms, as the article on page 120 explains.

Key terms

Solicitors Regulation Authority: the independent regulatory body for solicitors.

Study tips

Make sure you can distinguish training from a training contract.

Study tips

Use extracts from articles and contacts with solicitors and barristers to give real examples of the work each does.

Wait for ABSs is over: Tesco law is here

Alternative business structures will bring subtle, but significant changes in the way law is practised

Thank goodness the wait is finally over. On Wednesday, the Solicitors Regulation Authority (SRA) finally unveiled the first three businesses to receive an alternative business structure (ABS) licence. This was meant to have happened last October, and recently the SRA made itself a hostage to fortune by saying it would be by the end of February, but at last we've got there.

The regulator needed a big name to get the ball rolling, and the Co-operative obliged. Its reward was a visit on Wednesday from Justice Minister Jonathan Djanogly to mark the big day. The Co-op's ambitions to expand its legal offering have been far from a secret – in the past six years it has built a £25m-plus, 500-person legal business without needing to be an ABS, but the licence opens up more opportunities.

They include launching a fixed-fee family law service later this year, handling legal aid work, and offering face-to-face legal advice through the Co-op's bank network (it is currently done on the phone and online). If the Co-op succeeds in its bid for 632 Lloyds branches, for which it is the preferred bidder, then that would give it around 1000 possible locations from which to provide legal advice. That's a scary thought for high street solicitors, whose big selling point is the ability to give a personal, local service.

Then again, the other two new licensees are a high street firm in Oxfordshire, John Welch and Stammers, and a sole practitioner in Kent, Lawbridge Solicitors. Both are bringing in non-lawyer partners as their practice managers (in the case of Lawbridge, the solicitor's wife).

These two licences show that ABSs are not just about enabling new competition and external investment, nor do they exclude the smallest legal practices. While the prospect of law firms accepting private equity cash or floating on the stock market consumes the media, the new regime also allows for more subtle but no less significant changes in the way law is practised.

A perfect example of this is Artesian Law, a recently opened SRA-regulated firm specialising in criminal law. Nothing unusual there, except that six of its seven partners are barristers and it is being run like a regular chambers (where traditionally the barristers are self-employed). Artesian is going to become an ABS so that the non-lawyer practice manager can become managing partner, while it has the flexibility to do the solicitor work involved in litigation and bid for legal aid contracts, should the partners wish to in future.

Partner Dan Jones says the change in status has not affected them: "We are a close knit bunch, and are enjoying pulling together – promoting Artesian is actually promoting each other with benefit for us all."

They will not be the last. The heavy pressures that legal aid reform is putting on the way criminal defence lawyers operate, particularly at the bar, are driving innovation. We can expect to see considerable changes to their business structures in the next year or two. More broadly, the government is putting its faith in ABSs as one way to ameliorate the effect of the legal aid cuts.

In a recent parliamentary debate, Djanogly argued that while the legal aid, sentencing and punishment of offenders bill will probably mean a reduction in the number of firms and lawyers doing legal aid, the government is "creating the conditions that will allow legal aid providers to flourish". He said the significance of the ABS model, "and the commercial opportunity that it represents, cannot be overstated".

In the meantime, innovation continues from businesses that do not need to become ABSs to open up the legal market. QualitySolicitors (QS) – arguably the biggest talking point in the legal profession of the last two years – launched a £15m advertising campaign with a 90-second John Lewis-style spot just before the results of the *Dancing on Ice* final were announced last Sunday. It has booked no fewer than 8000 adverts in May.

A fast-growing network of traditional law firms under the QS banner, the aim is to build the first national legal brand with straightforward service standards and Saturday opening. It took private equity investment last autumn – QS itself is not a law firm and so does not need to be an ABS – and aims to be in 1000 locations by the end of the year.

The battle for the consumer legal market is well and truly on. Choice will not be a problem for the public and for lawyers it may stimulate more demand. It will be for the SRA and other regulators to ensure that, in the fight for market share, standards do not fall.

www.guardian.co.uk/law/2012/apr/02/abs-tesco-law-here

Background of solicitors

There are roughly ten times as many solicitors as there are barristers, although approximately 25 per cent of solicitors do not currently hold a practising certificate. Those who do not hold a practising certificate are still qualified solicitors, but are not authorised to act as a solicitor. This could be as a result of a career change or a career break. There has been a rapid growth in the number of solicitors over recent years, with an even greater rise in the proportion of female solicitors and those from ethnic minorities. This is much the same as the changes in barristers.

In 2010, there were 117,862 solicitors holding practising certificates. Women account for nearly half of all working solicitors. 48% of male solicitors in private practice are partners in law firms whereas only 21% of women have achieved that level. Around 11% of practising solicitors are from black and ethnic minority backgrounds.
(Source: *The Guardian*, 4 April 2011)

Legal executives

Legal executives are members of the Chartered Institute of Legal Executives (CILEX). This organisation was formerly known as ILEX before it received a Royal Charter in January 2012. The aim was to provide a professional body recognising the work done by non-solicitors working in a solicitors' office. Legal executives are qualified lawyers specialising in a particular area of law, and have at least five years' experience of working under the supervision of a solicitor. There are currently around 24,000 legal executives who are members of CILEX. Their status as professionals is recognised throughout the legal profession and the courts. Whilst their right to appear in court is limited, Fellows of CILEX with more than four years' post-qualification experience are equated with similarly experienced solicitors in terms of assessment of costs in court cases.

The role of egal executive lawyers is expanding. They will be able to become partners or managers in firms with external ownership and investment (known as Alternative Business Structures) and set up their own firms. They will be also be able to apply for some judicial posts and become Chairs of Tribunals.

> **Key terms**
>
> **Legal executive:** a qualified lawyer who specialises in a particular area of law but is not a solicitor or barrister.

Qualification

Most trainee legal executives combine study for the CILEX qualification with practical experience of working in a law firm or legal department of a company or local authority, usually being given day release from work to study. There are many starting points for qualifying as a legal executive, the routes varying depending on existing qualification. The usual minimum is four GCSEs at grade C or above, including English language. At the highest level, a person can begin qualification with a degree.

At the lower level, there is a Level 3 Professional Diploma in Law and Practice (equivalent to A Level) and for a full qualification there is the Level 6 Professional Higher Diploma in Law and Practice assessed at honours degree level.

Training

Continuing Professional Development is compulsory following qualification. A minimum of 16 hours is required for Fellows, 12 hours for graduate members and 8 hours for Associate members. CPD can be undertaken in both specialist and non-specialist areas of work, and it has to be recorded each year.

Work

Legal executives specialise in a particular area of law, such as conveyancing, wills, matrimonial matters or general litigation. Their day-to-day work is similar to that of a solicitor earning fees for the firm of solicitors for which they work. Quite often all the work on a particular matter will be handled by a legal executive rather than a solicitor. Legal executives are usually expert in one field of work and concentrate exclusively on that type of work with their own clients. They may have some rights of audience in court, including certain unopposed applications in the County Court, in County Court arbitrations and in front of tribunals.

Activities

1 Make a table comparing how solicitors, barristers and legal executives are trained and how they qualify.

2 Make a table comparing the work of solicitors, barristers and legal executives in and out of court.

3 Read the article from *The Times* below. Discuss the points raised in the article about the life of a solicitor.

All take and no give? I'm afraid I'm off

Edward Fennell

The Law Society is worried about the high turnover of recently qualified staff, so why are so many people voting with their feet?

When people cease liking their jobs – and there is the prospect of another, better job elsewhere – they leave. And that is what has been happening at scores of large law firms. Young lawyers have been leaving in droves.

Getting hold of exact details is not easy. Understandably, individual firms are reluctant to talk about their figures. Nonetheless, just how serious the problem is was revealed by the most recent PricewaterhouseCoopers (PWC) annual law firm survey. This announced that 'staff turnover levels are high, averaging 20 per cent for some top 25 firms. The turnover is highest in London and in the three to five years' postqualification experience [PQE] category. There are undoubtedly work-life balance issues here.'

Analyse the details of the survey and the findings are revealing – maybe even shocking. For example, at the three to five years' PQE stage almost half the top 25 firms had a turnover of between 16 and 20 per cent. More spectacularly, at almost one in five firms the turnover rate was more than 30 per cent. Even among the one to three-year PQE lawyers the turnover was between 26 and 30 per cent at a quarter of firms.

The indications are that turnover tends to be highest where younger lawyers have fewer flexible benefits and where maternity and childcare rights are stripped down to the minimum. As to sabbaticals? Forget it.

'The lack of flexibility in terms of both benefits and work arrangements has, perhaps, contributed towards firms suffering from high staff turnover,' PWC commented, adding archly that 'they may need to give further consideration to the value that employees put on flexibility in the workplace.'

It was anxieties about the scale of departures from firms that prompted in part the Law Society to undertake its Quality of Life investigation (lawsociety.org.uk/newsandevents/news/majorcampaigns/view). As it said when the programme was announced: 'The Law Society has launched a project on staff retention and job satisfaction aiming to drive forward the thinking on this subject through research and a sharing of experience. We'll cover issues such as the working practices that affect employees' decisions to stay or move on, the extent to which firms should adapt to fit with employees' life choices and the impact on the firms and employees that decide to adopt different working practices.' In defence of the employers, the society went on to claim that firms are starting to 'address urgently' issues of staff retention – not least because it is vital to their growth, innovation and competitiveness. 'Retaining staff and recruiting at mid-career level are becoming increasingly difficult. The pool of high-quality talent is not growing. In the services sector, businesses rely on the quality of their people. Turnover costs are around £150,000 for every £50,000 of salary.'

While some staff turnover is inevitable, there is clearly an emerging consensus that it has reached a worryingly high level. Firms are losing not merely the also-rans but, potentially, very able people in whom they have invested heavily.

Robert Sully, who works for Cripps Harries Hall in Tunbridge Wells, is typical of those who got away. He comes across as very bright, articulate, able and ambitious. Yet after six years of hard toil he left a well-known City name almost entirely because of work-life balance reasons. 'There was a macho atmosphere that came from the partners,' he says. 'I was doing well in the firm and that, maybe, was my downfall. I was staying very late night after night and the partners' attitude was, "So, what's the problem?" Personally I can't see how it's a good thing to have tired young lawyers working on a deal, but that was the general atmosphere. It's not so much the policies within the firms that matter but their culture.'

With a child on the way Sully decided that the time had come to leave the City but build on his experience in a positive way. He now works reasonable hours, lives five minutes from the office and does jobs that are comparable to his previous City life. 'The difference is,' he says, 'that if you are still working here at 9 o'clock at night people ask what's the matter with you.'

Source: The Law Society

The Times, 8 May 2007

You should now be able to:

- discuss the qualification, training and work of different branches of the legal profession

- take an overview of the make-up of the different branches of the legal profession

- attempt past paper questions on the legal profession.

2 Funding and other sources of legal advice

The law is open to everyone, but legal services can cost a great deal of money. Most people will need to use legal services at some time in their life, yet not everyone will be able to afford the services they need. The purpose of this topic is to investigate the sources that are available, and then, in the next topic, evaluate the provision of legal services.

Litigation – the threat of and the process of taking legal action against another person or organisation in a dispute – can be extremely expensive. A person is primarily responsible for paying his/her lawyer's costs resulting from the litigation. It is often the case that the losing party will pay for the winning party's costs and expenses of pursuing the claim. However, that may not amount to all the legal fees and expenses, so the winner will still have a bill to pay.

It is difficult to estimate the costs in advance, as there are many variables. For example, expert evidence might be required, the defendant may fight to have his day in court when the matter could have been settled early, or unexpected legal issues might arise.

These are questions that cannot be answered when a solicitor is first instructed. However, a good solicitor will know the probable or possible outcomes of the case, and will explain the potential liability for paying the legal costs and discuss the funding options.

What might appear to be a simple case can go on for a long time at great expense when lawyers become involved. For example, *Cockbone v Atkinson, Dacre and Slack* was a standard divorce case, in which problems occurred and one of the parties argued that a solicitor had been negligent. The extract below sets out the events.

Cockbone v *Atkinson, Dacre and Slack*

The marriage between Mr Clive Cockbone ('the Husband') and his wife, Mrs Patricia Cockbone ('the Wife') was dissolved by a decree absolute pronounced on 25 September 1989, leaving outstanding the Wife's claim for ancillary relief. (He and the Wife were married in August 1958. They had five children. The Wife left the farm in

In this topic you will learn how to:

- describe different methods an individual can use to fund legal services

- describe the financial limits on each method of State funding

- describe the sources of legal advice apart from a solicitor or barrister.

February 1988.) In connection with that claim, on 20th June 1991, the Husband retained Atkinson, Dacre and Slack ('the Solicitors') to act for him.

The claim was settled at the Harrogate county court on 22nd August 1991 on terms that the Husband should pay £250,000 to the Wife by instalments, the unpaid part being secured on his farm in the meantime. An order to that effect was made, pursuant to s33A Matrimonial Causes Act 1973, by District Judge Grills on the same day. On 10th April 1992 the Husband, appearing in person, was refused leave to appeal from that order. In May and June 1995 the Husband started proceedings in the Leeds county court against, amongst others, the Solicitors claiming damages for negligent handling of his case, and for the use of undue pressure and blackmail inducing him to enter into the settlement and to consent to the order. On 30th October 1997 His Honour Judge McGonigal, sitting as a deputy judge of the Queen's Bench Division, struck out the Husband's claim against the Solicitors on the grounds that they were immune from suit in respect of their actions and advice leading to the settlement on 22nd August 1991. This is an appeal of the Husband from that order.

www.bailii.org

Note the length of time that a straightforward case took to be resolved. Even after the divorce was finalised, there was a further civil case that went to the House of Lords along with *Hall* v *Simmons* (2000) to consider the question of a lawyer's liability for negligent work.

Private funding

There are three main ways of paying for your own legal services. The first is paying the bill out of your own resources, using your own money. The second way is when an insurance company will pay the bill. It is quite common to have legal expenses insurance with your house and contents insurance or car insurance. The final way is a conditional fee agreement. Most personal injury claims are made using this agreement with your solicitor.

Own resources

This is what is done when you use a solicitor to make a will or undertake the conveyancing when buying or selling a house. Most individuals will not be able to afford to do this for more complex or lengthy legal work. Businesses have more need to pay directly for legal work, as most successful businesses have worked out that it makes better financial sense to seek advice first rather than have lawyers sort a problem out later.

The solicitor's work is charged to the client at an hourly rate, plus expenses such as court fees. The hourly rate will vary with the location of the solicitors – central London is usually most expensive – and the level of seniority and expertise of the solicitor. Solicitors' costs in the Guide to Summary Assessment of Costs used by the courts reflect this. For 2010, the recorded costs varied from up to £409 per hour for solicitors with over eight years' post-qualification experience, including at least eight years' litigation experience, working in central London; to £111 per hour for trainee solicitors, paralegals and fee earners of equivalent experience working in areas where overheads are lower, such as Teesside or Devon.

Some work, such as conveyancing or making a will, may be done for a fixed cost.

These sums soon make a solicitor's bill quite large. As has been seen in the extract above relating to *Cockbone* v *Atkinson, Dacre and Slack*, litigation can drag on at potentially great cost. In *Hall* v *Simons* (2000), the solicitors' bill that was unpaid had been sent in 1988 for about £10,500, and related to a building dispute where the sums involved totalled a little over £20,000.

Insurance

Insurance is the first part of risk-sharing using a legal expense insurer. A **'before the event' policy** is an insurance policy that can be taken out, usually with an annual premium, to provide cover for a possible future legal problem. This is often part of a home contents or car insurance policy. However, some of these policies are limited in what they cover and may include restrictions on choice of solicitor, the hourly rates that will be paid, and other related expenses.

Conditional fees

This is effectively risk-sharing with lawyers, and is part of the change to the funding arrangements set up by the Courts and Legal Services Act 1990, to combat the huge cost of public legal funding. Before these changes, solicitors were not allowed to offer clients any risk-sharing arrangement. However, there are now a number of types available. Around 2.5 million people in the UK suffer accidental injuries every year. Public funding through legal aid for these costs was withdrawn in 2000, leaving these people with the option of paying for legal action themselves or risk-sharing in some way.

The first type of risk-sharing with lawyers is a **conditional fee agreement**. This is often known, inaccurately, as a 'no win, no fee' arrangement. This is where the solicitor makes no charge if the case is lost. However, the disbursements (the costs incurred by the solicitor on behalf of the client, such as court fees or fees for medical reports) and the opponents' legal charges will still have to be paid. If the case succeeds, the solicitor charges a 'success fee' on top of the normal hourly rate. The loser may be ordered to pay at least part of these charges, including the success fee. Insurance is normally taken out at the client's expense to cover this risk with an 'after the event' policy.

An **'after the event' insurance policy** is designed to help to cover the cost of litigation once the dispute has arisen. If the premium is affordable, then it can provide some peace of mind against the possibility of the total litigation costs if you lose the case. There are also potential limitations to the amount payable under this type of policy. With some insurance policies, the client must pay the solicitor's bill and then reclaim the money from the insurance company, which can be difficult for some people.

The second is a contingency fee arrangement. Again, a person is not charged if he or she loses, but the fee, if he or she is successful, is a percentage of what is recovered. However, this arrangement cannot be used for cases which require court proceedings.

There are also other possible arrangements, such as a discount conditional fee, where an hourly rate is agreed as being payable if the case is won but the rate is reduced if the outcome is unsuccessful. Such an agreement could also provide for a success fee.

Key terms

'Before the event' policy: an insurance policy that provides cover for a possible future legal problem.

Conditional fee agreement: an agreement between a client and solicitor under which the client pays less (or nothing, if 'no win, no fee') if the case is unsuccessful, but a full fee (usually with a 'success fee' or 'uplift') if the case is successful.

'After the event' policy: an insurance policy that provides cover for a possible lost case and a court order to pay the winner's legal costs. This is usually taken out as part of a conditional fee arrangement.

Study tips

Make sure you can distinguish 'before the event' and 'after the event' policies. Also, remember to be precise about conditional fee agreements: no win, no fee is not quite the same.

Key terms

Community Legal Service: a publicly funded network of organisations that provides and promotes civil legal services.

Community Legal Advice: provides free advice to those on low income or benefits.

Legal Help: free legal advice and help from a solicitor or an experienced legal adviser in civil law matters.

Help at Court: provides funding for a solicitor or adviser to represent a person in court in civil cases.

Legal Representation: provides State funding for taking a case to court; it will pay the legal costs not recovered at the end of a case.

Criminal Defence Service: provides legal advice and representation for people under police investigation or facing criminal charges.

State funding

Advice for civil cases

The **Community Legal Service** (www.clsdirect.org.uk) provides funds direct to solicitors and to other organisations such as the Citizens Advice Bureau. These organisations provide funds and promote civil legal services. This support is provided in a number of categories, from general information to advice and representation. These categories are known collectively as legal aid.

People often need legal advice – for example, in matters such as benefit claims, relationship breakdown, asylum and immigration, and community care issues. Sometimes it is enough to provide information leaflets or to direct people to other services, such as debt counselling or mediation. **Community Legal Advice** is available to those on low income or benefits. It is a free and confidential legal advice scheme via telephone or email.

Legal Help allows people with a low income and few savings to get free legal advice and help from a solicitor or an experienced legal adviser. The solicitor or adviser must have a contract with the Legal Services Commission. Legal Help is designed to cover everything up to and including the preparation of a case to go to court. It can also cover the costs of mediation in non-family cases. If money is won as a result of the case, that money must, in most cases, first be used to pay the solicitors' costs. This is known as the statutory charge.

Help at Court provides funding for a solicitor or adviser to represent a person in court. This might be used in representing someone who is being sued for a debt or who is defending eviction proceedings. Again, there are financial criteria to meet if a person is to get this assistance, just as there are criteria about the case itself: it must be a cost-effective method of dealing with the matter.

For other cases that a person might need to bring to court, there is **Legal Representation**. This is again subject to financial criteria, and the case must be one that the Legal Services Commission considers reasonable to fund. Legal Representation is also subject to the statutory charge. Funding can also be stopped if the solicitor involved does not think the case is strong enough. Types of cases that can be funded include consumer cases, such as claiming against the seller of faulty goods, or an appeal to the Employment Appeal Tribunal (but not for representation at an Employment Tribunal). Legal Representation will not usually pay for the costs of taking a personal injury case to court, as this is covered by conditional fee agreements.

There is also Controlled Legal Representation, which is only representation before a Mental Health Review Tribunal or an Asylum and Immigration Tribunal. In many cases there are no qualifying criteria, financial or otherwise.

Criminal cases

Legal aid in criminal cases is organised by the **Criminal Defence Service**, which arranges contracts with solicitors and barristers to provide state-funded advice and help.

This is available in three main forms:

Advice at the police station after arrest

If a person is in custody at any police station, they are entitled to legal advice and assistance free of charge.

The custody sergeant will ask the person if they have a preferred firm of solicitors or if they would like to speak to a duty solicitor.

The person is also entitled to speak to a solicitor on the phone free of charge. If circumstances warrant a formal police interview, the person can speak to the solicitor in person and in private before it takes place. There is no means or merit test for this scheme.

If the person is released from police custody pending further enquiries, the right to free legal advice continues until a final decision on a charge is made.

Free representation in the Magistrates' Court

This will be provided by the duty solicitor at the Magistrates' Court to persons in need of initial advice and representation – perhaps to argue for bail. There is no means test for this service.

Advocacy assistance

This scheme covers the cost of a solicitor preparing a case for court and initial representation – for example, the first hearing in the issuing of an ASBO. There is no means test for this scheme.

Representation Order

If a case is to go for trial, at either the Magistrates' or Crown Court, a person may be entitled to free representation under a Representation Order (Legal Aid). There are two criteria to be satisfied.

The court must agree that the case passes the 'Interests of Justice' test. The court first considers issues such as:

- whether or not the person is at risk of imprisonment
- whether they are subject to a Court Order
- if they are at risk of losing their livelihood or their reputation is at risk
- whether a substantial question of law is involved
- if they do not speak English, or may have difficulty understanding the court procedure for other reasons
- if witnesses need to be traced, or if expert witnesses need to be cross-examined.

Also, the application will be means-tested and a financial contribution may be required. The Order will cover the legal fees of the solicitor and any barrister who presents the case in court. Whether a person is entitled to the Order will be decided by the court.

Private Funding

If, for whatever reason, a person is not entitled to State funding, they can pay their lawyers privately.

Sources of legal advice

Often, the first place a person will go to get advice about a legal problem will be a solicitor – either their own that they have used before, or one who they contact specially for that problem. The solicitor may charge a fixed fee for giving the advice or make a charge depending on the amount of time taken.

Other sources of legal advice include the Citizens Advice Bureau, Law Centres, and a variety of companies, organisations and services (detailed on pages 128–9).

Citizens Advice Bureau

The Citizens Advice Bureau provides legal advice as part of its service. Whilst the Citizens Advice Bureau is a charity, it gains a substantial amount of income from its contracts with the Legal Services Commission to provide legal advice to people with debt, welfare benefits, housing, employment and immigration issues. The advice it gives is free, and where the problem requires further action, appropriate agencies or solicitors are contacted. Many bureaux work with local solicitors' firms, giving access to over 1000 specialist solicitors, working on a *pro bono* basis – that is, without charge. The Citizens Advice Bureau is also providing new ways of delivering legal advice, such as via the internet.

Law Centres

Law Centres have existed since the early 1970s. They are usually in less affluent areas, most often in cities with poor public services. There are more than 60 Law Centres throughout the UK (excluding Scotland). They are designed to help people access the legal system, especially those who would find it hard to do so. A Law Centre may take up a case where legal aid is not available, and they are often open outside normal office hours.

Law Centres specialise in social welfare law. This includes areas such as welfare rights, immigration and asylum, housing and employment rights. They are funded by a variety of sources. They hold contracts with the Legal Services Commission to provide casework services and they receive grant aid from local councils. They employ solicitors, barristers, legal advisers and community workers. Many lawyers volunteer to help in their nearest law centre as part of *pro bono* work.

The concept behind Law Centres is being developed, with Gateshead Community Legal Advice Centre being the first in a series of new networks and centres being established for people with the greatest need of legal and advice services. This is a joint service between Gateshead Citizens Advice Bureau and Gateshead Law Centre, which provides integrated services from basic advice to representation at court to help people with social welfare and family legal problems. This particular project was set up because the Legal Services Research Centre's national civil law and social justice survey found that:

▓ civil justice problems lead to further problems
▓ those experiencing the most problems were likely to be socially excluded
▓ only about half of those who have problems seek advice
▓ one in seven people who try to get advice fails to do so, mainly because the adviser couldn't help
▓ the more times a person gets referred on, the less likely they are to continue seeking advice.

The topic of funding and access to justice will be useful for the 'concepts of law' section in Unit 4 of the A2 specification.

Other sources of legal advice

There are many other places where a person can get initial advice about whether they have a claim and what can be done about it. These include:

▓ Trade unions – if a person is a member of a trade union, they may be able to obtain initial advice on a problem from the union, especially if it is an employment-related issue. The union may have arrangements with lawyers to provide advice to their members on other matters, such as personal injury claims.

- Insurance companies – a person may have taken out an insurance policy to cover loss or damage to his/her home, car or cycle. In the event of the person suffering personal injury in an accident, the insurance company may be able to give initial advice on a possible claim, or may have an arrangement with a firm of solicitors to give advice to their policy holders about the possibility of a claim.

- Motoring organisations – a person may be a member of a breakdown organisation such as the AA or RAC. In the event of the person suffering personal injury in an accident, the organisation may be able to give initial advice on a possible claim, or may have an arrangement with a firm of solicitors to give advice to their members about the possibility of a claim.

- Claims companies – these companies will often advertise their services in hospitals, on TV or in newspapers and magazines. If a person has an accident, they may contact such a company for an assessment of whether there is a possibility of a claim. If there is an initial likelihood of a claim, the company may refer the case to a firm of solicitors to pursue the claim in greater depth.

- Media – newspapers and magazines, TV and radio programmes will often have advice columns or sections to provide advice to specific readers about solving a legal problem and whether to pursue a claim. Similarly, there may be internet sites that a person can subscribe to, or be able to obtain free advice from, on whether he or she has the possibility of a claim.

- Charity – certain charities may be able to give advice on specific issues; for example, Shelter may be able to give advice on housing matters, and Mind on mental health matters.

- Local authority – some local authorities offer specific advice on certain issues, such as money advice clinics helping with debt and consumer-related problems.

- *Pro bono* – some local lawyers (solicitors and or barristers) may offer *pro bono* (for free) services on certain matters. Both the Law Society and the Bar Council run national schemes encouraging their members to offer these services.

Study tips

The general principles set out at the start of this topic can be used as a basis for evaluation of the legal profession and funding of legal services.

You should now be able to:

- understand the funding of legal services for an individual
- understand the sources of legal advice
- attempt past paper questions on funding and other sources of advice.

3 Evaluation of the legal profession, funding and other sources of advice

The provision of legal services is an issue that most people do not consider until they find that they have an obvious need for help from a lawyer. The person needing assistance then has to find and choose someone to help them. This is often done without any guidance as to the quality of the help or the relative merits of different providers.

In this topic you will learn how to:

- evaluate the legal profession
- evaluate legal funding
- evaluate sources of advice.

The essential principles relating to the provision of legal services have not changed since they were stated in the 1979 Royal Commission on Legal Services:

1 There should be equal access to the courts.

2 Equal access demands adequate legal services.

3 Financial assistance out of public funds should be available for every individual who, without it, would suffer an undue financial burden in properly pursuing or defending his rights.

4 The standard of legal services should be the same irrespective of whether or not provided at the public expense.

5 A free choice of lawyer should be available to each individual.

These principles need to take into account the fact that there is an unmet need for legal services, arising from a number of factors:

- There has been the creation of new categories of legal rights without the funding to enforce them: this relates in particular to social welfare law.

- People do not recognise their problem is a legal one that can be dealt with by a lawyer: an example of this is debt.

- There is still poverty in the UK, and poorer people often have a fear of lawyers' fees and high costs for legal services.

- There is general ignorance of funding methods available, despite the increase in advertising by the legal profession and other organisations such as accident helplines.

- There may be fear of authority and unfamiliarity with the surroundings: many people equate lawyers with the courts and the police, which makes them uneasy.

- Unfamiliar language is used – that is, legal jargon and technical terms.

- Lawyers may be inaccessible: this includes office hours usually matching times when people are at work.

- Lawyers in the area may be unavailable: this does not just affect rural areas but inner cities too. There are, for example, around 20 times more lawyers in Bournemouth than there are in the Huyton district of Liverpool.

- Solicitors' training emphasises the business side of being a solicitor, so the emphasis is on the most lucrative business rather than that which is unprofitable.

These general points need to be borne in mind when looking at the specific points made below.

Evaluation of the legal profession

The evaluation of the legal profession is largely concerned with an analysis of how the profession could be improved from the point of view of the user. Much of the criticism that has been levelled at the legal profession has had to be put on hold as the effect of recent changes is considered.

The work lawyers do

The large rise in the numbers of solicitors has led to a need for more work. All firms of solicitors face more competition from:

- each other
- accountants for tax work
- licensed conveyancers
- independent will-makers
- banks and building societies
- internet-based companies
- debt-collecting companies.

Some types of work are more profitable than others – for example, business and commercial affairs, commercial property and probate, wills and trusts are most frequently considered to be profitable, whilst welfare benefits are regarded as the least profitable and indeed often loss-making. Solicitors, unlike barristers, can choose the work they do, leaving some people without access to a lawyer. This situation is resolved where there is a Law Centre which specialises in welfare work and in other areas of low profitability.

Pay

The public perception of lawyers is that they are well paid, and for some that is true. However, how much can be earned will often depend on the success of the national (and increasingly international) economy.

Partners in some central London firms can earn several hundred thousand pounds per annum, whether the economy is performing well or not. Their clients are large national and international firms. If a firm manages to obtain a contract with the Criminal Defence Service or the Community Legal Service, and either have some high-profile cases or have a rapid turnover of cases, the firm may be able to earn considerable amounts. In 2010, it was reported that the highest-earning criminal firm received £9.3m from the Criminal Defence Service, and the highest earning civil firm received £9.9m from the Community Legal Service.

However, many provincial solicitors, whose work is private client based, will only earn the national wage. In a recession, non-contentious work – conveyancing, wills and probate, is very limited. For many civil personal injury cases, State-funded work has almost completely vanished. In criminal cases, fees have been regularly cut by the Government, making the work uneconomical.

For barristers, the picture is again mixed. It has been reported that almost 1000 barristers earned six figures in legal aid work in the year ending 31 March 2010; the highest criminal barrister received £928,000 and the highest civil barrister £442,000. Most barristers are self-employed; he or she may earn little, especially in the first five years of practice, yet still have to pay an amount towards the overheads in chambers.

From the consumer's view, the high cost of lawyers is seen as a deterrent to using the law. A person may well have a case, but whether financially it is worth pursuing is a different matter. The fact that some (a very small minority) of lawyers are very highly paid may make the consumer feel that they have no connection with the lawyer, and that they would rather avoid the situation. The article on page 132 discusses the wage difference between those working at the commercial bar and the publicly funded bar.

Barrister fees spiral ever up as the economy trundles ever down

As Britain lurches towards a double-dip recession, not everyone is struggling. Commercial barristers aren't the sort to broadcast their success – indeed, their discretion is such that they can get rather annoyed with journalists who ask them to put a figure on it – but it's no secret that they have been doing rather well of late.

Like the debt recovery game and the burglar alarm business, the commercial bar is counter-cyclical. Volumes of litigation spiral during the bust as individuals, companies and, increasingly, banks stake millions on court battles to decide who is to blame for excesses. Barristers with expertise in this sphere find themselves highly in demand.

An illustration of how rosy life is at the commercial bar right now is the recent decision by Wilberforce Chambers to up the amount it pays graduate recruits to a record £65,000 – half of which is tax free, thanks to a benevolent rule that exempts rookie barristers (or 'pupils') from paying income tax during their first six months of on-the-job training. Admittedly, some of this money can be drawn down in advance to cover barristers' law school fees, but with most in this elite bracket securing full scholarships from the inns of court, this is rarely necessary.

John Furber QC, head of Wilberforce's pupillage committee, says the rise from £48,000 was spurred by a motivation to 'remain competitive' amid concern that 'other sets' pupillage awards may be lifted again shortly'. But Wilberforce's rivals, several of which pay the previous top rate graduate salary of £60,000, deny that they have any such plans. A senior clerk at one of these chambers told me that he believed 'an extra five grand wouldn't sway recruits when they know they'll be earning half a million quid in a few years anyway'.

He wasn't exaggerating. Figures published by The Lawyer magazine show barristers at 11 separate sets of chambers generating average annual revenue in excess of £500,000, with Wilberforce leading the way with a whopping £800,000 (out of which around 20% must be deducted to account for the chambers expenses that apply to self-employed barristers). Even those at fashionable Matrix Chambers, which has a reputation for doing human rights work (but much of whose revenue is from private sources), rake in an average of £290,000 a year. Meanwhile, outside London they're doing pretty well, too, with revenue per barrister at Manchester's Kings Chambers and Birmingham's No 5 Chambers standing at £243,000 and £178,000 respectively.

At the publicly funded bar, the picture is very different. Indeed, it's so different that it's hard to believe we're talking about the same profession. Graduate recruits at legal aid barristers' chambers scrape by on the minimum pupillage award of £12,000, with many forced to supplement this with additional part-time work or financial assistance from their families. Earnings then climb to around £20,000–£30,000. A select few go on to make big money, but many senior criminal and family barristers find themselves earning not much more than £50,000 a year once chambers expenses have been deducted – a decent wage, but the sort of money their counterparts at the commercial bar could generate in a month. For a while now, with a few highly socially committed exceptions, the top law graduates have been steering clear of legal aid.

It hasn't always been like this. Going back a few decades, there was a much smaller gap between the publicly funded and commercial ends of the bar (which itself was much smaller: in 1960 it had just 2000 members, a figure that has since multiplied to around 15,000). In those days, it was common for barristers to do a mixture of different types of legal work, from criminal defence to company disputes. Then came the 1986 'Big Bang' of financial deregulation, which proved the catalyst for a group of barristers' chambers to rebrand themselves as commercial specialists. The ensuing growth of the City of London as a centre for financial services, allied to the Labour government's determination to see a greater proportion of the legal aid pot diverted to solicitors, cemented this fork in the road.

For some, the separation isn't a problem. 'Being frank, I don't think the state of the criminal bar is important for a commercial chambers – we trade independently on our excellence,' one senior individual at a top commercial set let slip to me a while ago. Others worry that the indirect benefits the commercial bar derives from its association with criminal justice – prestige, glamour and disproportionate political clout – could be eroded if the branches of the profession continue to grow apart. But as yet no one has come up with a way to reverse, or even halt, the divergence.

Looking ahead, with plans afoot to relax the restrictions on barristers performing activities currently reserved for solicitors, it seems likely that, over time, the publicly funded bar will merge with the legal aid section of the solicitors' profession, leaving commercial barristers to plough a solo path as law's elite. It's a risky message to be broadcasting for a profession that trades on its fairness.

www.guardian.co.uk/law/2011/dec/08/barrister-fees-spiral-up

Getting started

Combined with debt inevitably accumulated through university, qualifying and training, the financial outlook for many potential lawyers is uncertain. In many cases, the only way to progress is to take out more loans, even though there is no guarantee of success. For example, almost two thirds of bar vocational course students never even get a pupillage. Whilst pay is made during pupillage or a training contract, there is no guarantee of work after qualification. For barristers, only one third of pupils find a tenancy. Competition for training contracts and jobs as solicitors is fierce.

Evaluation of legal funding

Cost of state funding

Legal aid in England and Wales currently costs more than £2 billion per annum. This is nearly 50 per cent more than was spent on culture, media and sport. Successive Governments have been attempting to reduce the legal aid spending, but have only managed to contain it by reducing availability of legal aid.

Availability of state funding of civil cases

In the Select Committee on Constitutional Affairs Third Report in 2007, it was noted that legal aid suppliers had declined in numbers significantly. For example, family legal aid contracts have reduced by over a third since 2000, and cases starting declined from 410,916 cases in 2000–01 to 283,274 in 2005–06. This represents a huge reduction in access to justice for people with family problems, as firms throughout the country gave up legal aid work because of the poor rates of pay, the bureaucracy and costs of administering legal aid contracts, and the difficulties in recruiting and retaining suitably qualified staff.

The Mental Health Lawyers Association stated to the Select Committee that 'the number of Law Society Panel Mental Health Panel Specialists has declined by close to 25 per cent since 2000, whilst those mentally unwell clients requiring representation at Mental Health Review Tribunals has risen by over ten per cent in the same period'.

Sir Anthony Clarke, giving oral evidence to the Select Committee, expressed concern about unrepresented litigants in courts when he said:

> Actually, people with problems which give rise to civil dispute, especially in the mental health and housing fields, are extremely worthy of assistance and indeed may come from the very same families who find themselves before the criminal courts, so we are worried. In answer to your particular question, since that happened over the years there has been a big increase in litigants in person and it is very difficult for them.

www.publications.parliament.uk

These examples of lack of availability demonstrate that there remains an unmet need for legal services, and that the principles relating to access to justice are not being achieved.

Conditional fee agreements

These agreements are a mix of financial and legal matters, and are not always clearly understood by the non-lawyer. It is suggested that consumers are sometimes induced into signing conditional fee agreements inappropriately. Citizens Advice Bureau evidence suggests that the withdrawal of legal aid and the advent of conditional fee agreements has contributed to a system that involves relatively high legal costs and delays. In some cases, consumers are subjected to high-pressure sales tactics by unqualified people. Inappropriate marketing and sales practices are sometimes used, suggesting that solicitors are becoming 'ambulance chasers'.

The risks of conditional fee agreements are not always clearly explained at the outset. People are misled into thinking the system will be genuinely 'no win, no fee', but can often find that costs are hidden and unpredictable. Even the insurance against the costs of losing the case comes as a shock to some, who then finance the insurance with a high-cost loan that further erodes any compensation gained. The alternative of representing oneself in court is seen by many as impossible, so valid claims go unmade through fear and inertia.

The so-called compensation culture is focusing more people on the hope of money for nothing, rather than getting back to work after injury. Victims are not being helped to resume a normal life in both society and the workplace.

Conditional fee agreements create incentives for some solicitors to work only on high-value cases with good chances of success. They therefore sometimes refuse to take on strong smaller value claims which may nevertheless be of great significance to the client.

There is no effective regulation of conditional fee arrangements to provide protection on both quality of advice and costs. In particular, the activities of claims management companies seem to fall largely outside the system of regulation, yet they are increasingly the starting point for the claims process.

Evaluating sources of advice

If a person has a legal problem, they traditionally would have thought of getting initial advice from a solicitor or other legal professional. This has generally been the case because solicitors' offices could be found in most towns and cities, and many people may have had dealings with a solicitor in situations such as buying a house or business, making a will, and getting a divorce or separation. Once the solicitor has given the initial advice, he or she would then be able to follow the case through to a conclusion, especially if it involved court proceedings. Often solicitors firms had contentious and non-contentious departments, and the firm could offer clients an overall service, whatever their problem.

However, clients' needs have, over time, become more specialised, requiring advice in areas such as immigration, employment, housing and social benefits. Many solicitors have no expertise in these areas, which are often seen by many in the legal profession as time-consuming, and having limited reward. Further, many solicitors have limited experience in resolving disputes by methods of alternative dispute resolution. As a result, many solicitors have chosen not to offer advice in these fields.

As a result, other providers have developed expertise in giving advice in specialist areas, especially where a need has developed. For example, as mentioned above, the Gateshead Community Legal Advice Centre – working in conjunction with the local authority – gives free advice on issues such as family matters, employment, housing, welfare benefits, debt and community care – all issues of concern to some of the local population. Lawyers could, no doubt, develop expertise in these areas, but as a business it would not be economically viable for them to provide regular free advice to all who needed it. Similarly, charities such as Citizens Advice and Shelter have developed expertise in giving free or limited-cost advice in social welfare areas to anyone who needs it. Not every local authority has worked in conjunction with a Law Centre to give advice to local residents. However, the national charities have developed a network of advisers and clinics, and use the internet to make contact with those in need of advice. The charities and Law Centres have good records for bringing disputes to a satisfactory resolution, because of their reputation and independence. However, if a settlement is not possible, the adviser may, because of lack of funds, be unable to afford to support reference to a specialist and/or a court-based resolution.

Trade unions and membership organisations such as motoring organisations promote themselves as being able to offer legal advice when persuading people to join, and generally this will be included in the membership fee. Depending on the organisation, the areas that the advice can be given in may be limited. However, with the coming into force of Alternative Business Structures (see page 120), organisations may be able to offer more services that were once the preserve of lawyers. For example, the AA now offers to its members a variety of forms and standard letters to help deal with a legal dispute, as well as access to legal advice. The cost of the forms and advice is additional to the membership fee. Other promoters of ABS, such as the Co-op, will rely on their household name and reputation for attracting business that was traditionally dealt with by lawyers. A drawback to a member of the public dealing with these providers could be that there is limited possibility of face-to-face contact. The larger providers will be relying on centralised centres and email for communication.

Similarly, insurance companies do provide certain advice services for their members, and the cost of providing initial advice will be built into the insurance premium. If the case requires more than initial advice, the insurance company may then pass the case to a solicitors' firm on its panel. The same comments about lack of face-to-face communication can apply here too.

Claims companies have been accused of developing a 'compensation culture' by aggressively looking for business in personal injury claims, often through expensive advertising. It has been said that this drives up the cost of insurance, as compensation is often paid by an insurance company. However, without these claims companies many of those injured in an accident could be left without any form of compensation.

Evaluating criminal legal aid

When a person is arrested and taken to a police station for questioning, they are in an extremely vulnerable position, both emotionally and legally. Giving access to free legal advice provides some comfort, knowing that there is someone on your side who can give free independent advice during the detention. It also means that there is someone making sure that the police follow proper procedures during the detention and interviews. There used to be concerns about the availability of 24-hour/ 7-day-a-week cover, and the quality of such advice, which could be expensive for lawyers to provide. However, police station representatives are now required to be accredited, which means that the person giving the advice knows police station procedure and the suspect's rights.

Similar comments can be made about the vulnerability of the accused when he or she appears at court – both for first appearance at the

Magistrates' Court, and at subsequent trial. In theory, the prosecution has unlimited funds to instruct lawyers and to pursue a prosecution. Providing duty solicitors at Magistrates' Courts, and funding for representation at trial, does protect the vulnerable. In theory, the legal representation scheme allows those accused access to the best lawyers (both barristers and solicitors) available. It also means that the defence lawyers can fully investigate the law and facts of a case and put forward an appropriate defence in court.

However, criticisms can be made of criminal legal aid. For one thing, there are limitations on duty solicitors in the Magistrates' Court, as the duty solicitor scheme only applies to a first appearance; it also does not extend to minor motoring or non-imprisonable offences. A person convicted of either of these types of offences can still suffer a devastating loss of job or income, with limited ability to put forward a defence or to explain the effect of a conviction.

As far as the Legal Representation scheme is concerned, there are severe financial constraints placed on the criminal legal aid budget by the Government, at the same time that they are introducing more offences and putting pressure on the police to maintain law and order. For some offenders, Legal Representation comes at a cost because of the low financial eligibility limits, in which the accused's family income is considered rather than just his or her own. There may be high contributions required, and the tests for whether funding should be granted in the 'interests of justice' is interpreted narrowly by the courts. As a result of the pressure to save money, criminal lawyers are paid fixed fees for many types of lower-level cases, and some firms and barristers take the view that it is simply not economic for them to do this type of work. Alternatively, young inexperienced barristers may be representing offenders charged with quite serious offences.

The only alternative for someone who does not qualify for Legal Representation is to represent themselves in court (which is not encouraged) or to attempt to privately fund their lawyers. Even for lower-level offences this can be quite expensive, especially when it is likely to require the payment of dual fees – both solicitors and barristers – to conduct a trial.

You should now be able to:

- evaluate the legal profession
- evaluate legal funding
- evaluate sources of advice
- answer examination questions on the legal profession
- answer examination questions on funding of legal services and sources of advice.

8 The judiciary

> ### Key terms
>
> **Superior judges:** judges appointed to sit in the High Court and the appeal courts.
>
> **Inferior judges:** all judges who are not superior judges.
>
> **Lord Chief Justice:** head of the judiciary in England and Wales.

1 Judges

Judges perform a central function in the legal system. They have a number of different roles in both the delivery and the creation of the law. Judges can be seen as the pinnacle of the legal profession from which they are drawn. Unlike other countries, English and Welsh judges are not elected and are not trained to be a judge as an alternative to starting a career as a solicitor or a barrister. This chapter will look at the selection, appointment and role of different types of judges, and provide material to help consider how well they perform. It should be noted that the AQA Law specification does not require reference to judges in Scotland or Northern Ireland, just those in England and Wales.

Types of judge

There are many types of judge, and several different ways of categorising them. The most general distinction is between superior and inferior judges. **Superior judges** are those appointed to sit in the High Court and the appeal courts. Court of Appeal judges are also known as Senior Judges or, formally, Lords Justices of Appeal, and those sitting in the Supreme Court are known as Justices. All other judges are known as **inferior judges**. These include: Circuit Judges, who are full-time judges sitting in the County Court or Crown Court; Recorders, who are part-time judges sitting in the County Court and Crown Court; and District Judges, who sit in the County Court and Magistrates' Court.

Judges can also be categorised by the court in which they sit – for example, a Crown Court Judge or a High Court Judge. They can also be categorised as either full- or part-time, or even by their pay scale.

In addition, specific titles are assigned to a judge with a particular role in one of the courts, such as the Lord Chief Justice. You will have seen these titles in your study of the courts.

The Lord Chief Justice

The **Lord Chief Justice** is the head of the judiciary in England and Wales. The Constitutional Reform Act 2005 sets out his duties.

It should be noted that he is not responsible for the Supreme Court, as that is a court for the whole of the United Kingdom and not just England and Wales. He has more than 400 duties. Major duties include:

- ▨ representing the views of judges to Parliament and the Government
- ▨ provision and deployment of resources for the judiciary and the allocation of work of judges in the courts
- ▨ welfare, training and guidance of judges
- ▨ responsibility (along with the Lord Chancellor) for the Office of Judicial Complaints, which deals with complaints about judges
- ▨ hearing important criminal, civil and family cases, and many of the most important appeal cases; this helps him lead the judiciary, as he is closely involved with development of the law
- ▨ chairmanship of the Sentencing Guidelines Council, which aims to encourage consistency in sentencing

being President of the English and Welsh courts and, as such, being able to hear cases in any court in England and Wales; this means that he could hear a case in your local Magistrates' Court, if he wanted to!

The Master of the Rolls

The Master of the Rolls is the title of the judge ranking immediately below the Lord Chief Justice. He has a number of major responsibilities, including:

- acting as President of the Court of Appeal Civil Division, which he also organises. This means he is responsible for the deployment and organisation of the work of the judges of the Division. He normally sits with two other judges, often Lords Justices of Appeal. As the leading judge dealing with civil work in the Court of Appeal, he handles the most difficult and sensitive cases

- being consulted by the Government on the civil justice system and rights of audience in court

- officially authorising solicitors to practise. A solicitor is signed onto the Roll of Solicitors by him when first qualifying to practise as a solicitor. He also deals with professional rules and regulations dealing with solicitors and appeals against rulings of the Solicitors' Disciplinary Tribunal

- originally, being responsible for the safe-keeping of charters, patents and records of important court judgments written on parchment rolls. He still has responsibility for documents of national importance, being Chairman of the Advisory Council on Public Records and Chairman of the Royal Commission on Historical Manuscripts.

Justices of the Supreme Court

The Supreme Court is composed of the President, Deputy President and ten Justices of the Supreme Court. They are not subject to term limits, but may be removed from office on the address of Parliament. They retire at age 70, if first appointed to a judicial office after 31 March 1995, or at age 75 otherwise. The President and Deputy President of the court are separately appointed to their roles, rather than being the most senior by term of office. The Supreme Court includes senior judges from England and Wales, Scotland and Northern Ireland, as it is the final court of appeal for all these countries.

New justices appointed to the Supreme Court will not necessarily receive a life peerage. However, they are given the courtesy title of 'Lord' or 'Lady' upon appointment.

Lords Justices of Appeal

The Lords Justices of Appeal sit in the Court of Appeal. They usually sit as a bench of three judges and can make a majority decision. Generally in civil appeals, three Lords Justices will hear the case. In criminal appeals, there will again be three judges, though often Lords Justices will sit with High Court Judges or a specially nominated Circuit Judge. This gives a greater depth of knowledge of current sentencing and criminal trends, but still allows a lead to be taken where there is a necessary development of the law to be made. This is the last stage of appeal in many cases, and so these judges deal with most of the important cases and probably develop the law more than the House of Lords. The Lords Justices of Appeal's title is 'Lord/Lady Justice ...', or '... LJ' for short. There were 37 Lords Justices at 1 April 2011.

The Heads of Division, such as the Master of the Rolls and Lords Justices of Appeal, sometimes also sit with one or more High Court Judges in the Divisional Court, which hears appeals to the High Court from Magistrates' Courts and certain judicial review cases at first instance. This again helps develop the law and provides a consistency of approach to the application of the law.

High Court Judges

As of 1 April 2012 there were 108 High Court Judges appointed to deal with more complex and difficult civil and criminal cases. There were 71 judges assigned to the Queen's Bench Division. Judges of the Queen's Bench Division will try serious criminal cases, important civil cases of tort and contract law, and occasionally sit in the Court of Appeal hearing criminal appeals. Criminal trials will often be heard in major court centres around the country. Many civil trials and criminal appeals are heard in the Royal Courts of Justice in London. High Court Judges in the Family Division (19) and Chancery Division (18) will generally be based at the Royal Courts of Justice. High Court Judges are given the prefix 'The Honourable', and are referred to as 'Mr/Mrs Justice …'.

High Court Masters and Registrars

Masters and Registrars of the Supreme Court are the procedural judges for the majority of the civil business in the Chancery and Queen's Bench Divisions. They do not sit in open court, but in chambers (a private room within the court buildings) and do not dress in wig and robes. There is one Senior Master and nine Queen's Bench Masters. Outside London, their work is dealt with by District Judges or Deputy District Judges.

Circuit Judges

There were 665 Circuit Judges in post at 1 April 2011. Some of them are specialists either in criminal work, civil work or family work, or in the specialised courts such as the Commercial Court. There are some senior Circuit Judges who take on additional responsibilities, such as hearing appeals, and some who are semi-retired and sit part-time. These judges will often hear both criminal and civil cases in the Crown Courts or County Courts in the region for which they are appointed. England and Wales are divided into six regions: South Eastern, Midland, North Eastern, Western, Northern, and Wales and Chester.

District Judges

District Judges deal with the majority of cases in the County Courts, including the Small Claims Court, and District Registries of the High Court. There were 444 District Judges as of 1 April 2011. They are appointed to work on a specific circuit, and may sit at any of the county courts or District Registries of the High Court on that circuit. A District Registry is part of the High Court situated outside London, and deals with High Court family and other civil business.

District Judges (Magistrates' Courts)

District Judges (Magistrates' Courts), as the name suggests, sit in the Magistrates' Court. They are full-time salaried judges, as are other District Judges, but do the same work as lay magistrates. There were 137 of them as of 1 April 2011, and they are usually appointed to work in towns and cities. They sit alone, not as one of a panel of three as lay magistrates do. They hear criminal cases (usually the more serious or complex cases), youth cases and also some civil proceedings in Magistrates' Courts. They can deal with extradition proceedings and terrorist cases.

Non-salaried judges

There are a large number of part-time fee-paid (rather than salaried) judges, who are used to deal with the changing workloads of individual courts. It is a requirement for appointment as a salaried judge that the candidate has a number of years' experience as a part-time judge. The most numerous are Recorders (numbering about 1200), then Deputy District Judges (numbering a little over 700), and then Deputy District Judges (Magistrates' Courts) (numbering a little under 200). Recorders can hear both civil and criminal cases, and may sit in both the Crown Court and County Courts. Their work is similar to that of a Circuit Judge, but they will generally handle less complex or less serious cases. Deputies work in a similar manner to their full-time equivalents. There are also a few Deputy High Court and Circuit Judges and Deputy Masters and Registrars. Non-salaried judges are usually appointed for a fixed period of time.

The role and work of judges

The role of the judge in a civil case

The role of the judge in a civil case continues through many aspects of the case. At the start of the case is the role of case management. The main purpose of this is to ensure that the case proceeds as quickly and efficiently as possible. This will involve encouraging co-operation between the parties to the case, including arrival at a negotiated settlement or encouraging the use of an alternative method of dispute resolution. If this fails, then the role becomes one of controlling the different stages leading up to a trial, by setting appropriate time limits and dealing with matters that are urgent before the trial. This might include granting an injunction or joining another party in the case.

Before trying a civil case, the judge reads the relevant case papers and becomes familiar with their details. The vast majority of civil cases do not have a jury. The judge hears the case on his or her own, decides on the facts, applies the relevant law to the facts and then gives a reasoned judgement. To decide on the facts, the evidence has to be obtained and understood by the judge. This will be a mixture of written evidence that the judge will have to read, and oral evidence given to the court on oath. This oral evidence may well be subject to cross-examination, and the judge will have to decide what evidence is accurate and relevant to the case.

The judge must ensure that all parties involved are given the opportunity to have their case presented and considered as fully and fairly as possible. Even though the process is adversarial and not inquisitorial, the judge may ask questions on any point that he or she feels requires clarification, or is relevant but which has not been covered. The judge also decides on all matters of procedure that may arise during a hearing.

Once the judge has heard the evidence from all parties involved and any legal arguments, he or she delivers the judgment. This may be immediately or, if the case is complicated, the judgment may be given at a later date. The task of the judge is to decide on the appropriate remedy, if any, and on its precise terms. Usually the judge will then have to decide on the amount of damages to compensate a successful claimant for the losses suffered as a result of the defendant's actions. There are other orders that can be made, such as an injunction to prevent certain activities continuing or a declaration as to where the boundary between two pieces of land actually runs.

Once the judgement in the case has been delivered, the judge must deal with the costs of the case and decide on the amount that the unsuccessful party to the case must pay the successful one. The general rule is that the unsuccessful party will have to pay the successful party's costs, but the judge can depart from this rule if he or she thinks it appropriate to do so.

Study tips

Make sure you are clear about the differing roles of a judge in a civil and a criminal trial.

The role of the judge in a criminal case

The judge in a criminal trial is responsible for all matters of law, and for making sure that all the rules of procedure are properly applied. Before the criminal trial starts, the judge becomes familiar with the details of the case by reading the case papers. He or she may well have been involved in pre-trial matters, such as whether or not to grant bail and the plea and directions hearing. S/he will need to read various documents, such as the charges against the defendant, witness statements, details of exhibits and any previous documentation about the admissibility of evidence in the trial. At the start of the trial, the judge supervises the selection and swearing-in of the jury, and explains to the jury members what their role is in the trial. The judge will make it clear that they are only concerned with deciding the facts and coming to a verdict. He or she warns them not to discuss the case with anyone else.

Once the trial has commenced, the judge makes sure that all parties involved are given the opportunity for their case to be presented and considered fully and fairly. The judge is active during the trial, controlling the way the case is conducted according to the rules of evidence and procedure. As the case progresses, the judge makes notes of the evidence and makes any necessary decisions on legal issues – for example, whether evidence is admissible; if it is not, he or she will tell the jury to ignore that evidence.

Once all evidence in the case has been heard, the judge gives a summing-up to the jury. In this he or she sets out the law on each of the charges made, and states what the prosecution must prove if the jury is to find the defendant guilty on each charge. The judge refers to notes made during the course of the trial, and reminds the jury of the key points of the case. He or she will outline the strengths and weaknesses of the arguments for both prosecution and defence. The judge will then give directions to the jury members about their individual and collective duties before they retire to the jury deliberation room to consider the verdict. The judge will answer any questions or matters that might arise during the deliberations of the jury, and will advise the jury when a majority verdict is acceptable.

If the jury finds the defendant guilty, then the judge will decide on an appropriate sentence once he or she has considered all of the factors relevant to the case. The judge will then discharge the jury, and if the case has been particularly lengthy or distressing, excuse the jurors from any further jury service. If the jury delivers a verdict of not guilty, the judge will free the defendant, discharge the jury and make any appropriate order about the cost of the trial. If the defendant pleads guilty, then the judge's main function is to impose an appropriate sentence.

The work of judges outside court

Judges can perform a number of roles outside their normal court work. The main one is being the chairman of an inquiry. Under the Inquiries Act 2005, a minister can set up an inquiry that often has a judge as its chairman.

Because of the high cost and great length of public inquiries, there is often a reluctance to set one up. Notable recent inquiries have been:

the Hutton Inquiry, which was set up to investigate the death of Dr David Kelly and his role in the Iraq weapons of mass destruction pronouncements; and the McPherson Inquiry on the murder of Stephen Lawrence. At the time of writing, Lord Justice Leveson is chairing an inquiry on the role of the press and police in phone hacking.

An inquiry will issue an report to the minister, who can then choose whether to introduce legislation or take any action recommended.

Selection and appointment of judges

The Judicial Appointments Commission

The Judicial Appointments Commission was set up by the Constitutional Reform Act 2005 to select judicial office holders. The reform of the system of judicial appointments was part of a Government move to demonstrate judicial independence and to improve public confidence and the effectiveness of the appointment process. This was done by taking responsibility for selecting candidates for judicial office out of the hands of the Lord Chancellor and looking for a wider range of candidates than were traditionally appointed.

Qualities required to be a judge

The Judicial Appointments Commission identified five main qualities required for judicial office. Different types of judge may require a different balance in the qualities. The first quality is intellectual capacity, which will be evidenced in a high level of expertise in a candidate's chosen area of work, the ability to absorb and analyse information quickly, and an appropriate knowledge of the law and its underlying principles. This quality is required to ensure that all judges can deal with the intellectual demands of the job.

The second requirement involves the personal qualities of the candidate. These include integrity and independence of mind, sound judgement, decisiveness, objectivity, and an ability and willingness to learn and develop professionally. This is fairly obvious, given the nature of the role undertaken by a judge. The ability to learn is essential so that training and development of judges is speedy and effective.

The third quality is an ability to understand and deal fairly. A judge needs to be able to treat everyone with respect and sensitivity, whatever their background, and to be willing to listen with patience and courtesy to those involved in a court case. This is more than just being seen to be 'politically correct', it is a genuine need to understand the disparate nature and needs of members of society so that justice can be obtained.

The fourth quality is stated to be authority and communication skills. A judge needs to be able to explain the procedure and any decisions reached clearly and succinctly to all those involved. He or she clearly needs to know and understand them, which is another example of the first and second qualities. Judges also need the ability to inspire respect and confidence, and to maintain authority when challenged, which they will surely do when faced with a determined litigant, solicitor or barrister. This quality can be illustrated by a judge in the County Court about 50 years ago, who gave a young solicitor appearing before him a very hard time. The judge had not seen the solicitor advocate before and the young advocate was a little nervous, given the judge's reputation for being demanding and fiery. When a senior barrister who had been in court on that day saw the judge socially later, he enquired whether it had been necessary to be so tough on the young man. The judge explained that if the young man could not stand up for himself, he did not see how he could stand up for his clients. Modern judges are much more likely to be patient, but can still be intimidating!

The final quality is efficiency. Given the cost of the legal process, this is one way of being cost-effective, and requires a judge to work at speed and under pressure. This means a judge needs an ability to organise time effectively and produce clear, reasoned judgments quickly. This is key given the complaints made about judges in the past, such as the High Court Judge Sir Jeremiah Harman, who resigned after a 20-month delay in delivering a judgment. Three appeal court judges said his conduct in a 1998 case, 'weaken[ed] public confidence in the whole judicial process'. One of the lawyers involved in the case said he had written repeatedly to the judge asking for the judgment, and even considered taking out life insurance on him to cover lost legal costs if Harman died before giving his ruling. An ability to work constructively with others (including leadership and managerial skills where appropriate) is also required, particularly with respect to case and court management.

The Judicial Appointments Commission is required to appoint as judges people who are of good character. This requires a decision as to whether there is anything in the candidate's past conduct or present circumstances (for example, business connections) that would affect the application for judicial appointment. Thus a criminal conviction will normally be fatal to a candidate's application – indeed, the person description given to applicants makes this clear – unless it is well in the past, minor, and did not lead to imprisonment. Thus, minor motoring offences will normally be disregarded, but not, say, a conviction for grievous bodily harm. The Rehabilitation of Offenders Act 1974 does not apply to judges.

Financial correctness is looked for – a person who has been bankrupt may occasionally be appointed a judge, but difficulties with the taxman or with respect to VAT may result in an application being denied. This is to avoid a suspicion that the judge is dishonest or may be open to some form of blackmail or bribery.

When a judge has been appointed and later appears to fail to meet the criteria, then there is the likelihood of disciplinary action against the judge.

The stages in appointing a judge

The first stage is an advertisement. Most positions are advertised widely in the national press, the legal press and online. The Judicial Appointments Commission also runs roadshows and other outreach events. These are designed to explain the selection system to potential applicants and to encourage them to consider a judicial career, thus extending the likely range of candidates. Each appointment is started with an application form and information pack. The application pack includes details of the eligibility criteria and guidance on the application process.

Here is an example from an advertisement for a District Judge (Magistrates' Courts):

> To be eligible for appointment as District Judge (Magistrates' Courts) you must meet the following requirements.
>
> Statutory requirement
>
> **The statutory requirement for applicants is as set out in Courts Act 2003, Part 2 (Justices of the Peace), s22.**

> Her Majesty may, on the recommendation of the Lord Chancellor, appoint a person who has a 7 year general qualification to be a District Judge (Magistrates' Courts).
>
> A general qualification is within the meaning of s71 of the Courts and Legal Services Act 1990.
>
> In order to meet the statutory qualifications for appointment, persons who wish to rely upon their qualification as solicitors, including those holding full-time judicial office, must appear on the Roll of Solicitors.
>
> **Previous service in a judicial office**
>
> To be considered for appointment the Lord Chancellor expects applicants to have served in judicial office in a fee paid or salaried capacity for at least two years or to have completed 30 sitting days by 22 June 2007. Such service is not the only criterion. You will also need to demonstrate the qualities and abilities required for this office.

Extract from judicial post information pack 00316

Once the candidate has completed and returned the application form, it is checked to make sure of the candidate's eligibility for the post. At the same time, an assessment is made of the good character of the candidate.

Candidates are asked on their application form to nominate up to three referees. The Judicial Appointments Commission may also seek references from a list of Commission-nominated referees, which is published for each selection exercise. In all cases, references will form part of the information that the Judicial Appointments Commission uses to make final selection recommendations. Shortlisting is then done.

The next stage of the assessment will vary depending on the nature of the post to be filled. Candidates might be asked to attend a selection day, which could entail a combination of role-plays and an interview. For some specialist and the most senior appointments, there might be only a panel interview, as the candidate's ability as a judge at one level is already known. Interview panel members assess all the information about each candidate, prepare reports on their findings, and agree which candidates are best.

There is then a statutory consultation. This is required by the Constitutional Reform Act 2005, and means that the panel's reports on candidates are sent to the Lord Chief Justice and another person who has held the post or has relevant experience. The Commission considers all the information gathered on the candidates, and selects candidates to recommend to the Lord Chancellor for appointment. There are then final checks. For existing judges seeking promotion, this is with the Office for Judicial Complaints, to see that there are no complaints outstanding against the candidates. For all other candidates recommended for appointment, a series of good character checks are done with the police, Revenue and Customs and relevant professional bodies. The Lord Chancellor may also require candidates to undergo a medical assessment before the appointment is confirmed. This is a fair and open system and should result in the best candidates being appointed.

For most appointments specific qualifications are needed, although it is possible that some posts may be made attractive to academic lawyers who are not engaged in legal practice as a solicitor or barrister on a day-to-day basis. This is summarised in Table 8.1 on p145.

Table 8.1 *Judicial qualification requirements*

Type of judge	Qualifications
Justices of Supreme Court	15-year Supreme Court qualification or have held high judicial office for at least two years
Lords Justices of Appeal	Ten-year High Court right of audience or be an existing High Court Judge
High Court Judge	Ten-year High Court right of audience or have been a Circuit Judge for at least two years
Circuit Judges	Ten-year Crown Court or County Court right of audience qualification or be a Recorder or District Judge for three years
Recorders	Ten-year general qualification
District Judges	Seven-year right of audience

Normally, a judge will work his or her way up the ranks – for example, a District Judge can be promoted to Circuit Judge, a High Court Judge promoted to Lord Justice of Appeal and to Justice of Supreme Court. Occasionally, however, a person may be appointed to a higher-level post without going through this promotion – see the article below on Jonathan Sumption, who was appointed as Justice of the Supreme Court.

Two new judges have been appointed to the Supreme Court: Jonathan Sumption QC and Lord Justice Wilson

The choice of Sumption is seen as controversial since it is highly unusual for a barrister without extensive experience sitting as a judge to be raised to the benches of the Supreme Court. He has served intermittently as a recorder and deputy high court judge since 1991 and is reputed to earn more than £1m a year. In a letter to the *Guardian* in 2001, he said: 'You have accused me of the horrid crime of earning as much as eight high court judges and 69 refuse workers put together. I admit it ... I earn what I do because that is what my services are worth to the people who pay for them.' His 'puny £1.6m' income, he insisted, 'was not made at the expense of the public purse'.

The 62-year-old Eton-educated former Oxford don, who represented the government at the Hutton Inquiry, is acting as lead counsel for Roman Abramovich in the appeal court. The legal showdown is against Abramovich's rival, Boris Berezovsky, in a dispute over ownership of a share of the Russian oil company Sibneft. Effectively, Sumption has got permission to delay his ascent to the Supreme Court until after that case is heard, and is expected to join the bench after the case has finished.

Lord Phillips, the president of the Supreme Court, said 'Jonathan Sumption is widely acknowledged to be one of this country's leading advocates. He has demonstrated incisive intellectual rigour throughout his years as a barrister.'

Jonathan Sumption said: 'This is a challenging time for the development of the law, and I am honoured to have the opportunity of contributing to the work of one of the world's great common law courts.'

www.guardian.co.uk/law/2011/may/04/supreme-court-judges-wilson-sumption

Reasons to become a judge

Judges are usually former top solicitors or barristers. They have often started working part-time judicially to see if the life of a judge is attractive. A number of applicants are motivated by the idea of putting something back into the system, as well as desiring the personal prestige that comes with the title. Many applicants are already financially secure, and feel they can manage with the reduction in earnings that will come from the change, and look forward to a pension that is perhaps the best in the UK. A judge's salary is in the public domain: it can be found on the Department of Constitutional Affairs' website.

The salary has to be sufficient to attract appropriate candidates and also sufficient that there is no danger of financial pressures tempting a judge to accept a bribe or otherwise act in any way other than impartially. A judge's salary for 2012–13 ranges from the Lord Chief Justice, whose salary with effect from 1 April 2012 is £214,465, to a District Judge, whose salary with effect from 1 April 2012 is £102,921.

The judge's pension scheme is particularly favourable. Unlike most pensions, it is calculated on the basis of 1/40th of final salary for each year worked as a judge, up to a maximum of 20/40ths (50 per cent) of final salary, together with a lump sum of 2.25 times the final pension, various enhancements for retirement due to ill health, and some tax concessions on normal pension rules.

High Court Judges are expected to sit throughout the legal terms (189 days per year). The legal year traditionally begins in October, and courts sit for four terms during the year. In practice, judges work long hours, as well as during court vacations. They are required to deal with a variety of judicial business, such as reading case papers and preparing reserved judgments (judgments that are delivered in court some time after the end of the trial, so as to give time to reflect on the legal arguments and make a clearly reasoned decision) and to perform other public duties in addition to their actual sittings. However, this is often fewer days than many were working as a barrister or solicitor. Judges usually retire at age 70.

Training of judges

The Judicial Studies Board is directly responsible for training full- and part-time judges in England and Wales. It also oversees the training of lay magistrates and chairmen and members of tribunals. The Judicial Studies Board was set up in 1979 and its role is to carry out a number of stated objectives:

to provide high-quality training to full- and part-time judges in the exercise of their jurisdiction in civil, criminal and family law

- ■ to advise the Lord Chancellor on the policy for, and content of, training for lay magistrates, and on the efficiency and effectiveness with which Magistrates' Courts' committees deliver such training
- ■ to advise the Lord Chancellor and government departments on the appropriate standards for, and content of, training for judicial officers in tribunals
- ■ to advise the Government on the training requirement of judges, magistrates and judicial officers in tribunals if proposed changes to the law, procedure and court organisation are to be effective, and to provide, and advise on the content of, such training
- ■ to promote closer international co-operation over judicial training.

Much of the Judicial Studies Board's training work is carried out through its publications, such as the 8th edition of the *Guidelines for the Assessment of General Damages in Personal Injury Cases*, or specimen directions for use by judges in criminal trials. These publications are generally written by members of the judiciary at the Judicial Studies Board's request.

The current activities of the Judicial Studies Board are: initial training for new judges and judges who take on new responsibilities; continuing professional education to strengthen and deepen the skills and knowledge of existing judicial office holders; and delivering change and modernisation by supporting major changes to legislation and to the administration of justice.

The initial training of a judge on appointment is an intensive residential induction course. This lasts between four and five days. The course concentrates on the practical aspects of sitting as a judge and running a court. Much of the training is done through group discussions, role-play and practical exercises. Newly appointed judges also sit in with an experienced judge for at least
a week and, if they are to hear criminal cases, they must visit local prisons and the Probation Service.

Once new appointees have completed an induction course, they must attend annual training days – which are held locally in their regions – and are called back for continuation training by the Judicial Studies Board every three years. In addition, judges must attend further induction courses before being able to sit in certain types of case, for example, family law. Experienced judges also attend 'refresher' seminars, generally on a three-year cycle, in all the areas of law in which they sit. The Judicial Studies Board also organises training programmes in response to legislative change.

A mentoring scheme is being developed to help judges perform their role initially, and also to be able to progress up the judicial ladder. District Judges already mentor Deputy District Judges in the County Courts, and a range of other informal mentoring arrangements exists throughout the judiciary.

Dismissal and discipline

The Office for Judicial Complaints was set up by the Constitutional Reform Act 2005 to handle complaints about the personal conduct of all judges, and to provide advice and assistance to the Lord Chancellor and Lord Chief Justice in the performance of their new joint role of considering and deciding how to deal with complaints. The objective is that all judicial disciplinary issues be dealt with consistently, fairly and efficiently. The complaints must be about the personal conduct of the judge and not the actual decision made by him or her.

In the Office for Judicial Complaints' most recent report, from April 2010 to March 2011, there were 1638 complaints against judicial office holders; this includes magistrates, coroners and tribunal members, as well as the judiciary. Some 64% of these complaints were discounted as being outside the scope of the Office for Judicial Complaints, as they were about the judge's decision rather than his or her personal conduct.

Table 8.2 *Disciplinary action taken 2010–2011*

	Courts judiciary	Coroners	Magistrates	Tribunals	Total
Guidance issued/ warning/formal advice	12	1	7	4	24
Reprimand	3	0	24	1	28
Removal	0	1	22	6	29
Resignation	2	0	18	5	25
TOTAL	17	2	71	16	106

www.judicialcomplaints.gov.uk

The numbers in the table above should be seen in the context of there being 3600 members of the judiciary, over 29,000 magistrates, and 7000 tribunal judges and lay members. In addition to the disciplinary action shown, it is possible for the Office of Judicial Complaints to issue a reprimand for minor complaints. Copies of statements issued in respect of all complaints since 2008 appear on the website of the Office.

The ultimate sanction would be removal from judicial office, although for High Court Judges and above, judicial independence dictates that this would require a vote in both Houses of Parliament. Of course, the only way to complain about a judge's decision (rather than his or her personal conduct) is by way of an appeal.

It is highly unlikely to find a full-time serving judge needing to be removed. This has happened just once, in 1983, when a Circuit Judge, Judge Bruce Campbell, was removed from office after pleading guilty to several charges of smuggling whisky into England from Guernsey. In the last 200 years, only one High Court Judge has been removed from office on a vote in both Houses of Parliament. This was Sir Jonah Barrington in 1830. He misappropriated money belonging to litigants. A number of judges have retired or resigned to avoid the possibility of such action. Judges still manage to behave in inappropriate ways, and this appears to hinder their career prospects.

Judge found guilty after drunken fracas

A COUNTY Court judge remained defiant last night after being found guilty of causing a drunken fracas in a kebab shop.

David Messenger said he planned to appeal against his conviction for being drunk and disorderly.

He was also convicted of obstructing two police officers and criminal damage of a police cell.

He was found guilty by magistrates following a three-day trial and fined a total of £800, ordered to pay £188 in compensation for damaging the bell button in his cell and pay more than £6000 in court costs.

Messenger, 49, of Valley Bridge Parade, Scarborough, North Yorkshire, denied all the charges.

The judge was arrested at a takeaway in Scarborough, on May 2 and spent the night banging on his cell door, refusing to co-operate with officers and eventually damaging a cell bell button.

Messenger was arrested at the Best Kebab shop, in St Thomas's Street, after intervening in an incident that police were trying to sort out in the kitchen.

The court was told how Messenger called police officers 'ar******s' and said their behaviour would 'cost them £5000' as they marched him out of the kebab shop.

Asked if he wanted to contact anyone after his arrest he asked to speak to the Chief Constable.

As the officers were taking him from the building and attempting to put him into a police van he shouted to passers-by: 'Tell them I'm a solicitor and a county court judge.'

He was eventually taken to the police station where his lack of co-operation continued.

The court was told the 'booking in' procedure took 40 minutes as the defendant refused to give his personal details.

Once Messenger was locked in a cell, he spent the night banging on the door to such an extent that other prisoners had to be moved so they could get some peace.

Later, an officer found a button in the cell, which operated the bell, was damaged, the court heard.

Messenger told magistrates that he had described two police officers as 'ar******s' because he was shocked and frightened about being frogmarched out of a kebab shop. He said he had been 'unlawfully arrested'.

He said he could not believe what was happening to him after he tried to help a client who was involved in an incident at the kebab shop.

However, the magistrates said the evidence of the two police officers had been compelling and they had good reason to be concerned there would be a breach of the peace.

Dr Jones said: 'Their actions were entirely justified and perfectly reasonable.

'The way in which Mr Messenger responded was to behave in a totally inappropriate way.'

The court was told Messenger's convictions would mean the end of his 'judicial aspirations'.

Outside court, he continued to maintain his innocence and said he would carry on working as a solicitor.

He is not sitting as a judge at present.

He said: 'It's been a very difficult five months. I maintained my innocence throughout and I still do.'

A Department for Constitutional Affairs spokesman said: 'This judge has not been sitting and a report on the issue will be prepared for the Lord Chancellor, who will make a decision about his sitting in future.'

Northern Echo, *30 September 2003*

Conclusion

There are many types of judge, but all have the primary role of managing and deciding cases. Whilst a judge is appointed until the age of 70, there are still examples of those appointed who retire or resign before that age.

Activities

1. Using the internet, find other examples of complaints being made against judges for conduct in and out of court.

2. In a table, list (a) reasons why a lawyer might want to consider applying for a post as a judge, and (b) reasons why a lawyer might want to continue working in practice.

3. Read the article that starts on p148 and discuss whether the new system of judicial complaints is working.

You should now be able to:

- understand the operation of the judiciary
- attempt past paper questions on the judiciary.

2 Independence of the judiciary

The independence of the judiciary

The Universal Declaration of Human Rights enshrines the principles of equality before the law, of the presumption of innocence, and of the right to a fair and public hearing by a competent, independent and impartial tribunal established by law.

In order to ensure the right to a fair and public hearing, three basic principles are needed:

- Security of tenure: once appointed, a judge cannot be dismissed except for misconduct.

In this topic you will learn how to:

- define the term 'judicial independence'
- explain the meaning of separation of powers
- give examples of judicial independence and separation of powers.

■ Immunity from suit: a judge cannot be sued or prosecuted for his performance in court.

■ An independent judiciary: that is, independent of the State and, therefore, independent of influence on its decisions.

Security of tenure

As we have seen in the previous topic, full-time judges have security of tenure. Once appointed, a full-time judge remains in office until retirement unless he dies, resigns or is dismissed from office. Dismissal is very rare. However, there are an increasing number of complaints being made against judges. The fact that the systems in place result in few dismissals gives judges confidence in their ability to act as they think appropriate in every case. This is reinforced by the fact that the Office for Judicial Complaints cannot deal with any complaints about a judge's decision or about how he or she has handled a case.

Under the Judicial Discipline (Prescribed Procedures) Regulations 2006, there is provision for the Lord Chancellor or the Lord Chief Justice, upon receipt of information from any source which suggests that disciplinary proceedings might be justified, to refer that information to the Office for Judicial Complaints to be dealt with in accordance with their rules. This means that there does not have to be a formal complaint made by a member of the public, merely that information emerges that merits investigation. This can be from another judge, or as a result of a report in the press such as those referred to in the previous topic. This enables disciplinary proceedings to be started whenever there appears to be activity that suggests a judge is not behaving entirely properly, and will help protect against abuses that might occur where litigants are unsure of what to expect and are not represented by a solicitor or barrister.

The same Regulations suggest a large number of reasons why a complaint may be dismissed and not investigated at all, ranging from the fact that it relates to a judge who is no longer in office (hence some early resignations) to the complaint being vexatious (that is, it has been started maliciously and without good reason). This may explain why there have been so few disciplinary actions taken in comparison to the number of complaints. The result is that judges will feel secure and therefore independent of outside pressures unless they know that they have acted improperly.

Supporting the idea of security of tenure, judges can be confident that their salaries and pensions will be paid without interference by the Government or Parliament. This is because judicial salaries are paid from the Consolidated Fund, which neither Government nor Parliament can touch.

Immunity from suit

Any **immunity from suit** is contrary to a person's fundamental right of access to the court. Therefore, any immunity from suit has to be justified. This principle is found both in the common law and in the decisions of the European Court of Human Rights. The fact that judges cannot be sued for their court performance, and so have protection from negligence claims as a matter of policy, is central to the concept of an independent judiciary and therefore is the justification for the existence of this protection of a judge. It also gives a judge great peace of mind. As the number of negligence cases that are brought before the courts increases, this is one of the last areas of the law of negligence where no duty of care is owed.

If a judge makes an error in the course of a hearing, the correct procedure is to use the appeal system. This is consistent with the Office for Judicial

Complaints being unable to deal with a complaint based on complaints about a judge's decision or about how he or she has handled a case. It also preserves the independence of the judiciary, as senior judges do not count up how many appeals have been made from the decisions of particular judges.

Under the Court Settlement process (used in the Technology and Construction Court, which is part of the High Court Queen's Bench Division), it is made clear that the parties to the case agree that the Settlement Judge has the same immunity from suit in relation to a Court Settlement Process as the Settlement Judge would have if acting as a judge in the proceedings. This protects judges working towards alternative dispute resolution. Unfortunately, this is not clearly the case for mediators and conciliators.

The independent judiciary and the separation of powers

The idea of an independent judiciary stems from the doctrine of the **separation of powers**. For a political system to be stable, the holders of power need to be balanced against each other. In England and Wales, the holders of power are the Government, Parliament and the judiciary. The traditional theory, expounded by philosophers such as the Frenchman Montesquieu and the Englishman Locke, deals with three areas of power: legislative power (the power to make law); executive power (the power to carry the law into effect or oversee its enforcement); and judicial power (the power to make judgements and to apply the law in particular cases).

> **Key terms**
>
> **Separation of powers:** the idea that there are three powers in a State: legislative, executive and judicial.

There is obviously going to be some overlap between the three areas, and in England this overlap is demonstrated by the fact that it is the Cabinet of the Government that is the effective executive, while all the members of the Cabinet are also members of the legislature (Parliament). For some time, some of the judiciary (the Law Lords) offended the separation of powers as they sat in the parliamentary House of Lords. However, since 2009 the judiciary has been completely separated from the legislature. This is due to the establishment of the Supreme Court, and Justices of that court do not sit in the parliamentary House of Lords. Removal of a superior judge from office requires approval by the legislature, which also makes the law relating to the appointment of judges.

The Constitutional Reform Act 2005 limits the Lord Chancellor's role in the appointment of judges. Judges are effectively independent and have sufficient controls to ensure quality in their work. The controls also ensure that any hint of a lack of independence is dealt with effectively. This can be seen in the House of Lords case involving the extradition fight of Chile's former Head of State, General Pinochet. The claim was made that one of the Law Lords, Lord Hoffmann, was biased against General Pinochet because of Hoffman's links with the human rights group Amnesty International. Lord Hoffman's wife, Gillian, was also connected with Amnesty International. The original decision was reached by a panel of five Law Lords (by a 3:2 majority). In modern times, Supreme Court rulings cannot be appealed, but in this case arrangements were made for the case to be reheard by an appeal committee of the Law Lords, to ensure there was no hint of possible bias. The original decision showed no trace of bias, but justice through a truly independent judiciary had to be seen to be done.

Judges take the doctrine of the separation of powers to mean that they should not question the validity of an Act of Parliament; but the European Communities Act 1972 requires judges to give precedence to EU law over UK law where there is a conflict. Similarly, the Human Rights Act 1998 gives judges the power to declare that UK legislation does not comply with the requirements of the European Convention on Human Rights. The effect of this is to strengthen the independence of the judiciary, as judges can now, in certain circumstances, treat parliamentary-made law as ineffective. This has always been the case where judges have been able to interpret an Act of Parliament in such a way as to make the statute ineffective, as has been seen in cases such as *Fisher* v *Bell* (1960).

Conclusion

The principle of judicial independence is interlinked with the doctrine of separation of powers. Most constitutional theories require that the judiciary is separate from and independent of the Government, in order to ensure that the law is enforced impartially and consistently, no matter who is in power, and without undue influence from any other source. Judicial independence can be seen in the decisions the judges make, their security of tenure and their immunity from suit.

You should now be able to:

- understand the principle of judicial independence
- understand the doctrine of separation of powers
- attempt past paper questions on judicial independence and the separation of powers.

Activities

Attempt these sample questions on this topic:

1. Explain what is meant by the principle of judicial independence.

2. Discuss the importance of this principle of judicial independence.

In this topic you will learn how to:

■ evaluate the judiciary.

3 Evaluation of the judiciary

Evaluation of the composition of the bench

Where magistrates have been said to be middle class, middle aged and middle minded, it could be argued that judges are upper class, old aged and conservative in outlook. The judicial statistics for 2005 (revised August 2006) show that they fail to reflect society to a far greater extent than magistrates do.

There is still a great imbalance between the number of judges who were formerly barristers and those who were solicitors. Statistics suggest that 90 per cent of higher level judges are former barristers and 10 per cent former solicitors. When looked at from a gender point of view, the statistics show more women in posts at lower levels of the judicial hierarchy, which suggests that the gender imbalance will improve as promoted posts become available. This still is unlikely to match lay magistrates, who are almost 50:50 men and women.

The fact remains that the ethnic background of judges does not reflect the ethnic balance of people in England and Wales. There were three non-white judges of High Court rank or above as at 31 March 2010, although these figures have significantly improved over recent years as there are many more members of the lower ranks of the judiciary who have a non-white ethnic background.

In a report in 2002, the Labour research department found that the average age of judges was over 60, that two thirds of them had been to public school, and that 60 per cent had been to Oxford or Cambridge universities. In general, the higher the rank of judge, the more likely it was that the judge had been public school and been Oxbridge educated.

Table 8.3 *2010 Judicial gender statistics*

Post		Former Barristers	Former Solicitors	Total
Justices of the Supreme Court	Women	1	0	1
	Men	9	1	10
	Total	10	1	11
	% Women	10.00	0.00	9.09
Heads of Division	Women	0	0	0
	Men	5	0	5
	Total	5	0	5
	% Women	0.00	0.00	0.00
Lords Justices of Appeal	Women	3	0	3
	Men	34	0	34
	Total	37	0	37
	% Women	8.11	0.00	8.11
High Court Judges	Women	16	0	16
	Men	91	1	92
	Total	107	1	108
	% Women	14.95	0.00	14.81
Circuit Judges	Women	87	14	101
	Men	513	66	579
	Total	600	80	680
	% Women	14.50	17.50	14.85
Recorders	Women	185	16	201
	Men	987	45	1032
	Total	1172	61	1233
	% Women	15.78	26.23	16.30
District Judges (County Courts)	Women	17	93	110
	Men	30	308	338
	Total	47	401	448
	% Women	36.17	23.19	24.55
Deputy District Judges (County Courts)	Women	37	149	186
	Men	59	395	454
	Total	96	544	640
	% Women	38.54	27.39	29.06
District Judges (Magistrates' Courts)	Women	13	24	37
	Men	36	70	106
	Total	49	94	143
	% Women	26.53	25.53	25.87
Deputy District Judges (Magistrates' Court)	Women	16	25	41
	Men	44	66	110
	Total	60	91	151
	% Women	26.67	27.47	27.15

Source: Judicial Database 2010

Activities

1 What do these figures tell you about the gender of superior level judges (High Court and above)? Can you suggest a reason for your finding?

2 What do these figures tell you about the background (barrister or solicitor) of superior level judges? Can you suggest a reason for your finding?

3 What do these figures tell you about the gender of inferior level judges (below High Court)? Can you suggest a reason for your finding?

4 What do these figures tell you about the background of inferior level judges? Can you suggest a reason for your finding?

Table 8.4 *2010 judicial ethnic origin statistics*

		Not stated	White	Asian or Asian British	Black or Black British	Mixed	Other Ethnic Group	Total Minority Ethnic	Total in Post	% Minority Ethnic
Justices of the Supreme Court	Men	0	10	0	0	0	0	0	10	0.00%
	Women	0	1	0	0	0	0	0	1	0.00%
	Total	0	11	0	0	0	0	0	11	0.00%
Heads of Division	Men	0	5	0	0	0	0	0	5	0.00%
	Women	0	0	0	0	0	0	0	0	0.00%
	Total	0	5	0	0	0	0	0	5	0.00%
Lords Justices of Appeal	Men	13	21	0	0	0	0	0	34	0.00%
	Women	0	3	0	0	0	0	0	3	0.00%
	Total	13	24	0	0	0	0	0	37	0.00%
High Court Judges	Men	18	72	0	0	0	2	2	92	2.74%
	Women	5	10	0	0	1	0	1	16	9.09%
	Total	23	82	0	0	1	2	3	108	3.53%
Circuit Judges	Men	55	513	2	0	2	7	11	579	2.10%
	Women	16	80	1	2	0	2	5	101	5.88%
	Total	71	593	3	2	2	9	16	680	2.63%
Recorders	Men	238	744	18	10	11	11	50	1032	6.30%
	Women	51	138	3	5	2	2	12	201	8.00%
	Total	289	882	21	15	13	13	62	1233	6.57%
District Judges (County Courts)	Men	23	305	6	1	1	2	10	338	3.17%
	Women	10	92	3	1	2	2	8	110	8.00%
	Total	33	397	9	2	3	4	18	448	4.34%
Deputy District Judges (County courts)	Men	86	352	2	3	4	6	16	454	4.35%
	Women	61	115	7	2	1	0	10	186	8.00%
	Total	147	467	9	5	5	6	26	640	5.27%
District Judges (Magistrates' Courts)	Men	26	77	3	0	0	0	3	106	3.75%
	Women	11	25	1	0	0	0	1	37	3.85%
	Total	37	102	4	0	0	0	4	143	3.77%
Deputy District Judges (Magistrates' Courts)	Men	37	70	1	0	2	0	3	110	4.11%
	Women	12	26	2	0	0	0	3	41	10.34%
	Total	49	96	3	0	2	0	6	151	5.88%

As at 31 March 2010
Note: The database of the ethnic origin of the judiciary may be incomplete as (a) candidates are asked
to provide the information on a voluntary basis and (b) such details have only been collected since October 1991.

Source: Judicial Database 2010

Activities

1. What do these figures tell you about the ethnicity of superior level judges (High Court and above)? Can you suggest a reason for your finding?

2. What do these figures tell you about the ethnicity of inferior level judges (below High Court)? Can you suggest a reason for your finding?

Judges themselves talk of their isolation and the great feeling of responsibility in the post of a judge. Even where judges sit as a panel, this still holds true, as each appeal court judge and Law Lord writes an individual judgment or speech in making their decision. There is often a lead judgment to which some or all of the others agree in whole or in part.

The fact that judges are almost exclusively drawn from practising lawyers is positive, as it ensures that the judges start off being in touch with current practice and procedure. The fact that judges have a legal qualification (unlike most magistrates) means that they have a sound basic knowledge of the law and some procedures. However, not all judges come from the area of law in which they become a judge, and their training needs to be comprehensive and continuing.

Evaluation of the adequacy of training

The creation of the Judicial Studies Board has led to much improved training for judges. However, the revised appointment system has meant that it now has an increasing workload on top of its larger role in training magistrates and tribunal members. The increased emphasis on recruiting judges from more diverse backgrounds means that a greater range of skills needs to be developed in some judges. Some judges being trained have less courtroom experience than was the case under the old system of appointment.

Judicial Studies Board research in 2006 included a training needs analysis, which concluded that Circuit and District Judges needed training in judicial skills rather than substantive law. This would include training in those judicial skills that apply across the jurisdictions. The training would be annual rather than on a three-year-cycle, and would meet individual judges' needs as well as being assisted by technology.

The research also looked at the needs of senior judges. Its main recommendations included the following:

- there should be training of at least five days in the first year after appointment and at least two days per year after that
- the training should include training in judicial skills for those who seek it
- the induction package should be flexible and backed up by a formal programme of continuation training
- there should also be an annual two-day residential seminar for Queen's Bench Division judges, covering all aspects of serious crime.

The fact that so much training has been initiated by the Judicial Studies Board demonstrates that the prior lack of training is being addressed. It is positive that the training is aimed at all levels of the judiciary and includes existing judges. The concern is that some judges who most need training may not get it for some time, and that it is not always clear how the training fits into the appraisal, mentoring and disciplinary systems.

Evaluation of performance

The performance of a judge is very difficult to monitor objectively. The fact that, when the 2010/11 complaints were processed, disciplinary action was only taken against two judges, suggests that the performance of the judges was excellent given the number of hearings that took place. However, the fact that there were so many complaints to the Office for Judicial Complaints, even if 64% were discounted, suggests that there were many unhappy litigants. Equally, the number of appeals and cases that have come to an agreed settlement rather than going to appeal is not known, but the number of days sat by appeal court judges is indicative of some dissatisfaction. The only well-documented evidence of dissatisfaction comes from the newspapers. This usually relates to unduly lenient or harsh sentencing decisions or excessive damages being awarded. Examples are difficult to find, as most excessive damages cases are libel cases where the damages have been awarded by a jury, such as the case of Sonia Sutcliffe's claim against *Private Eye* magazine. However, in the so-called 'McLibel' case, which ended in 1997, there was no jury.

In that case, McDonald's won a partial victory in its libel trial against two environmental campaigners, Helen Steel and Dave Morris. They had published a leaflet entitled *What's wrong with McDonald's? Everything they don't want you to know*, accusing McDonald's of a series of unethical and environmentally destructive activities. At the end of the longest trial in English legal history, the judge, Mr Justice Bell, agreed that some of the claims made in the leaflet were unjustified. However, the judge's award of £60,000 damages to McDonald's conveyed to some that McDonald's had won the case on all bar a few minor points. In fact, most of the judge's findings of fact backed up the criticisms made in the leaflet. In March 1999, the Court of Appeal reduced the amount of damages awarded to McDonald's from £60,000 to £40,000. This shows that judges have a sound view about the amount of compensation to award, whereas a jury often makes excessive awards.

There was a later appeal in 2005 to the European Court of Human Rights. That court decided that the denial of legal aid constituted a violation of Steel and Morris's right to a fair trial. More importantly, the court decided that while the damages were relatively modest by British standards, because Steel and Morris were on a low income the amount was disproportionate and violated their right to freedom of expression. In that sense, the judges at the original hearing and on appeal had not really grasped the impact of the European Convention on Human Rights and its effect on the workings of the English legal system.

There are also examples of unduly lenient sentences being given. One

Fig. 8.1 *The original 'McLibel' case lasted ten years, making it the longest-running case in England's history*

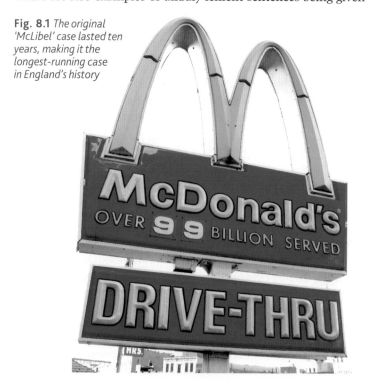

such was highlighted in a House of Commons debate in 1999, when the MP Teresa Gorman pointed out '... in the Ealing vicarage rape case. Three males were involved, two of whom abused her (the victim) in what even the judge referred to as a foul and disgusting way. They were given five-year sentences. A little bit was added on because they were there to commit a burglary. Nevertheless, one of those men was out after three years and the other served less than his five-year sentence. That is not uncommon. Many soft sentences are handed down by geriatric judges in our courts, often in cases that involve women and their sexual lives. Our courts are besmirched as a result of that and they need to do something about it.'

After the vicarage rape case, Lord Lane, who was then the Lord Chief Justice, said that the sentences had been too lenient. That is not surprising, because the third man in that case, who did not take part in the rapes but was involved in the burglary, was sentenced to 14 years' imprisonment. This contrast shows that the courts make dreadful mistakes and inconsistencies, however senior the judge might be.

Judges are sometimes seen as out of touch with questions such as, 'Who are the Beatles?' 'Who is Gazza?' asked Sir Jeremiah Harman in 1990, 'Is it an opera?' A judge sitting at Highbury, near Arsenal's home ground, did not know that Arsenal was an FA Premiership football club. In 1999, Judge Francis Aglionby stopped a 'Teletubby' theft case and asked, 'What is a Teletubby?' Finally, some judges realised that being in touch with society is important: the late Judge Michael Argyle QC, when asked if judges were out of touch, stoutly defended his peers. 'A lot of judges play golf. And if you play golf you couldn't possibly be out of touch.'

Behind the changes to the judicial system is a growing awareness that, to maintain confidence in the justice system, the judiciary needs to engage with the public. Society has moved on from the 1930s, when the Lord Chief Justice could say, 'His Majesty's judges are satisfied with the almost universal admiration in which they are held.' In 1999 the largest ever study of attitudes about judges and the justice system, funded by the Nuffield Foundation, revealed a lack of confidence across social class in the fairness of courts. Only 53 per cent of people believed they would get a fair hearing at court and 65 per cent agreed that 'judges are out of touch with ordinary people's lives'.

Evaluation of judicial independence

The current system of appointing judges is satisfactory, in that the judges are largely independent and are prepared to make decisions that are not popular with the Government of the day. The fact that the members of the judiciary remain in office when there is a change of Government supports this view, as do the changes to the process of appointing judges brought about by the Constitutional Reform Act 2005. Further, there is training and discipline carried out by the judiciary itself.

Conclusion

Whilst there are always criticisms of the judiciary, the systems in place ensure that, for the most part, the judiciary is effective and efficient, and that the lapses that occur can be corrected within the system.

Study tips

Do not make up examples of judicial errors. Examples should be sufficiently explained to demonstrate their source.

Study tips

Make sure you give examples and a reasoned justification for your evaluation of the judiciary.

Definitely no regrets: there is life beyond the High Court

[One difficulty that arises is that once a person becomes a High Court judge, there appears to be no going back as some judges may then refuse to have him appear as an advocate in their courts. However, in 2005, Sir Hugh Laddie announced that he was leaving the High Court Bench because he found it 'boring'. Since then he has gone to work part-time in a leading firm of intellectual property solicitors as a consultant and mediator. It means that he sees clients and can lecture and has taken up a part time post at University College London developing intellectual property law courses across the college.]

Laddie was a top patents silk when the 'tap on the shoulder' came in April 1995. 'I was at the Bar for 25 years. I had a truly stupendous time. I still think, if you're lucky and get a good practice, it's a great job.' But with the heavy and tiring workload – 'it was the only thing my wife and I would argue about' – he had no doubt about becoming a High Court judge. 'There was only one direction — down. You can't stay at the top for ever.'

For the first five years, he enjoyed it. But aspects jarred. 'One thing is that you are really isolated. You can go all day without speaking to another judge.' So he set up a common room where judges could meet weekly for teas. Laddie, who was senior judge of the Patents Court, also believed strongly that the courts should serve litigants, not the profession. 'That meant I was determined to try to cut costs to a point where I used to irritate people.

'Everyone has egos – it's a matter of how difficult you find it to control.' Laddie did not endear himself to counsel when, at the start of a case, having read the papers, he would make clear his preliminary views. 'Obviously I had provisional thoughts – it would be amazing if I didn't. Some would say: he's made up his mind. I hadn't, of course.'

Laddie also objected to sitting on Chancery cases beyond his expertise. Had he taken a case outside his field at the Bar, he'd have left himself open to a negligence action, he says. But the moment he was a judge he was expected to do just that. 'It was challenging – like high-wire walking – but I didn't think it fair for clients to be learning at their expense.' Most worrying were the cases involving unrepresented litigants, with applications 'in an area of law that I knew nothing about.'

He remains outspoken in his criticisms. Litigation is reserved for the 'rich, mad or destitute', he says. 'The slowness of it; the expense of it.' The Woolf reforms had not had an impact on costs: he believes one answer is less oral advocacy with time limits on counsel's speeches. He also favours keeping the courts running in the long vacation.

There were unfounded fears that his departure would prompt an exodus or that people would simply go for the job for the knighthood. 'If that's what they thought, there must be an awful lot of unhappy judges. The other answer is: scrap the knighthood. They don't have them in Australia and have perfectly good judges. Or give it to all judges. Many do just as good a job as a High Court judge. One or two others may leave before their time is up "because they now see there's a door". But most like the job and will stay.'

Laddie acknowledges the 'great privilege' he had working with 'some spectacular people', although the company, he adds, 'was not exactly a cross-section of the population' and conversation inevitably limited to cases. It also has 'immense status'. But if people want to leave, they should be able to. 'We abolished slavery a long time ago. If you don't like it, get out. Keep the job for people who really want to do it.'

http://business.timesonline.co.uk

You should now be able to:

- ■ evaluate the judiciary
- ■ answer examination questions on the judiciary.

Practice questions

Unit 1B questions in the AQA exam

Unit 1B together with Unit 1A constitutes Unit 1 of the AS specification. Unit 1A is about law-making and Unit 1B is about the legal system. Unit 1A and Unit 1B are examined together on one examination paper, which constitutes 50 per cent of the overall marks for the AS qualification and 25 per cent of the overall marks for the A2 qualification.

The Unit 1 examination is of 1.5 hours' duration. You must answer questions from three topics: one topic from Unit 1A; one topic from Unit 1B; and another topic, which may be from Unit 1A or 1B. There will be a choice of four topics in Unit 1A and four topics in Unit 1B.

Each topic is represented by one question, which has three parts. You must answer all parts of the question. Each part is normally worth 10 marks; the entire question is worth 30 marks, plus 2 marks for Assessment Objective 3.

All parts of each topic relate to the same topic area of the AQA Law AS specification – that is, the same chapter of this book. Parts (a) and (b) will normally be a test of your knowledge and understanding, and part (c) will normally be evaluative, requiring simple discussion of advantages and disadvantages of a topic.

Questions require essay-style answers. You should aim to include:

- correct identification of the issues raised by the question
- sound explanation of each of the points
- relevant illustration.

Illustration may be in many forms – for example, legislation, cases, research, statistics, and material from the media.

Chapter 5: The civil courts and other forms of dispute resolution

These example questions are taken from past exam papers. You must answer all three parts of the question.

Example question 1 (AQA, May 2011)

a) Josh has been badly injured in a road accident and intends to claim compensation for his injuries.

- Identify the civil courts (including relevant tracks and any any appeal courts) in which his claim for compensation could be heard.

  AND

- Briefly describe the process of negotiation which could be used as an alternative method of settling his claim.

  (10 marks)

b) Describe **either** the process of arbitration **or** the use of tribunals as a method of dispute resolution. *(10 marks)*

c) Discuss advantages **and** disadvantages of **either** the process of arbitration **or** the use of tribunals.
(10 marks + 2 marks for AO3)

Example question 2 (AQA, January 2012)

a) Describe the process of arbitration as a method of dispute resolution. *(10 marks)*

b) Outline what is meant by mediation **and** negotiation as alternative forms of dispute resolution. *(10 marks)*

c) Discuss advantages **and** disadvantages **either** of mediation **or** of negotiation. *(10 marks + 2 marks for AO3)*

Example question 3 (AQA, May 2012)

a) Describe the operation of tribunals as methods of dispute resolution. *(10 marks)*

b) Including appeal courts, outline the civil courts that can deal with a civil claim for negligence **and** briefly describe the process of negotiation. *(10 marks)*

c) Discuss advantages **and** disadvantages of using civil courts as a method of dispute resolution. *(10 marks + 2 marks for AO3)*

Chapter 6: The criminal courts and lay people

These example questions are taken from past exam papers. You must answer all three parts of the question.

Example question 1 (AQA, May 2012)

a) Describe how jurors qualify **and** are selected for service.
(10 marks)

b) Explain the work of lay magistrates.
(10 marks)

c) Discuss disadvantages of using lay persons in the criminal justice process.
(10 marks + 2 marks for AO3)

Example question 2 (AQA, January 2012)

a) **Either** describe how jurors qualify and are selected for service **or** describe the appointment **and** selection of lay magistrates.
(10 marks)

b) Explain the work of lay magistrates both in **and** out of court.
(10 marks)

c) Discuss advantages of using lay persons (jurors **and** lay magistrates) in the criminal justice process.
(10 marks + 2 marks for AO3)

Example question 3 (AQA, January 2011)

a) Outline the qualifications required for appointment as a lay magistrate. Briefly explain the training a lay magistrate has to undergo after appointment.
(10 marks)

b) Describe the role of a jury in a Crown Court trial.
(10 marks)

c) Discuss disadvantages of using a jury in a criminal trial.
(10 marks + 2 marks for AO3)

Chapter 7: The legal profession and other sources of advice and funding

These example questions are taken from past exam papers. You must answer all three parts of the question.

Example question 1 (AQA, May 2012)

a) **EITHER**

Briefly explain where a person arrested for a serious criminal offence could get legal advice and representation **and** outline how this could be paid for.

OR

Briefly explain where a person badly injured in an accident could get legal advice and representation for a civil claim for damages **and** outline how this could be paid for.

(10 marks)

b) Describe how a barrister is trained and qualifies for entry to their profession. *(10 marks)*

c) Discuss advantages **and** disadvantages of using solicitors and barristers to help resolve legal disputes.

(10 marks + 2 marks for AO3)

Example question 2 (AQA, January 2012)

a) Chloe has been badly injured in an accident and wants to claim compensation. Outline where she could get advice about a claim for compensation **and** outline how she could pay for bringing such a claim. *(10 marks)*

b) Explain how solicitors qualify. *(10 marks)*

c) Compare **and** contrast the work of solicitors and barristers.
(10 marks + 2 marks for AO3)

Chapter 8: The judiciary

These example questions are taken from past exam papers. You must answer all three parts of the question.

Example question 1 (AQA, May 2012)

a) Describe how judges are trained for their work.   *(10 marks)*

b) Describe the work of a judge **either** in a civil court claim for negligence **or** in a Crown Court trial.
     (10 marks)

c) Discuss why it is important for judges to be independent.
     (10 marks + 2 marks for AO3)

Example question 2 (AQA, January 2012)

a) Explain the role of a judge in **either** a Crown Court criminal trial **or** in a civil claim for negligence.   *(10 marks)*

b) Explain how judges are selected **and** appointed.   *(10 marks)*

c) Briefly discuss advantages **and** disadvantages of the methods of selection **and** appointment of judges.
     (10 marks + 2 marks for AO3)

Introduction

Unit 2A together with Unit 2B or Unit 2C constitute Unit 2 of the AS specification. Unit 2A is about Criminal Law and is compulsory. Unit 2B is about the Law of Tort and Unit 2C is about the Law of Contract. You must answer the questions on either Unit 2B or 2C, but not both, as well as the questions on Unit 2A. You can choose to study either Unit 2B or Unit 2C in addition to Unit 2A.

The Unit 2 examination paper constitutes 50 per cent of the overall marks for the AS qualification, and 25 per cent of the overall marks for the A2 qualification. The examination is of 1.5 hours duration. You must answer all the questions from Unit 2A and all the questions from either Unit 2B or Unit 2C. There is no choice of question in any of the sections.

The questions on each section are worth 45 marks each, plus 2 marks for Assessment Objective 3. Each question is divided into six parts, each part being worth up to 10 marks. You must answer all parts of the question. Each section stands alone, and there is no overlap between them.

The Criminal Law section is covered by Chapters 9 to 11 of this book. Some of the questions test your knowledge and understanding, and some test application of the law to the scenario that introduces the question. Some are a mixture of knowledge, understanding and application. There is a clear distinction on the examination paper.

Questions require essay-style answers. You should aim to include: correct identification of the issues raised by the question; sound explanation of each of the points; and relevant illustration. Illustration may be in many forms – for example, legislation, cases, research, statistics, and material from the media. Study tips are provided throughout each topic.

Key terms

Criminal law: the law that sets out the definitions of individual crimes.

Criminal process: the system used in a criminal case to manage the stages between the offence and conviction of the offender.

1 Introduction to criminal liability

Criminal law

Criminal law is concerned with the liability of an individual for wrongdoing against another individual, society, and/or the State. Not all wrongdoing is a crime, and some people consider that some crimes do not involve wrongdoing.

Society, through its lawmakers, has to decide what forms and types of conduct are criminal. Some forms of conduct, such as murder, have always been considered criminal. Other forms of conduct were criminal in the past but are no longer criminal, such as homosexual acts between consenting adults. Some activities have been made criminal, such as possessing certain types of drug. Some crimes have come into being to cover new situations, such as computer misuse.

The starting point for any criminal conviction is the criminal law. Crimes are defined either in an Act of Parliament or by reference to decided cases. This requires the use of the rules of statutory interpretation and the doctrine of precedent that are studied in Unit 1 of the AQA Law specification. The defendant's conduct must match the definition of the crime for him or her to be guilty. The definition of the crime usually has two parts to it: the *actus reus* and the *mens rea*. The *actus reus* is the guilty conduct and the *mens rea* is the guilty mind.

These terms are examined in more detail in later topics in this chapter.

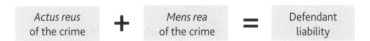

Fig. 9.1 *Link between the definition of a crime and the defendant's liability*

The criminal process

The **criminal process** has the function of deciding whether the crime has been committed by the accused and, if so, what sentence should be imposed. Reporting a crime is just the beginning. Police investigations, prosecution decision-making, court processes and sentencing can be a long and complicated business for both the victim and the defendant.

Once a person has been arrested and charged with a crime, they have to go to court to be tried and, if found guilty, to receive their sentence. The length and complexity of the process depends on the seriousness of the crime, whether the evidence is clear and how the defendant pleads. There are rules of procedure that set out the court in which the case will be heard, and the framework for deciding the case.

Fig. 9.2 *The criminal process*

■ **Link**

The aims of sentencing and the options available are dealt with in more detail in Chapter 11 (The criminal courts: procedure and sentencing), p192.

■ **Link**

These methods of tackling a question will be dealt with in more detail in the Unit 2A examination-style questions, at the end of Chapter 11.

When information about a case is received from the police, a Crown Prosecutor will read the papers and decide whether or not there is enough **criminal evidence** against the defendant, and whether it is in the public interest, to bring that person to court. There are rules of evidence that set out how the facts must be proved and the degree of certainty that is required. In a criminal trial, the burden is upon the prosecution to prove the guilt of the defendant beyond reasonable doubt. Juries in Crown Court trials are directed that, unless the evidence makes them satisfied so they are sure of guilt, their verdict must be one of not guilty. Magistrates also work to the same standard of proof.

Sentencing

Magistrates' Courts and the Crown Court have different **sentencing** powers. More serious cases are sentenced in the Crown Court and less serious offences are sentenced in the Magistrates' Court. When the defendant is convicted following a trial or a guilty plea, the court has a range of sentencing options available. These depend on the type, the seriousness and the circumstances of the crime, and on the maximum penalty available by law. When deciding upon the appropriate sentence, courts have guidelines to assist them. The judge or magistrate giving the sentence must consider the aims of sentencing: punishing the defendant, reducing crime, rehabilitating the defendant, protecting the public, and the defendant making reparation. The sentence will reflect a combination of these aims.

Examination of AQA Unit 2

The question paper for Unit 2 is divided into three sections. The first section, on Unit 2A, is compulsory and is the introduction to criminal law. Each section starts with a short scenario that sets the scene and is the basis of your discussions for some of the questions. Below is a scenario relating to the Criminal Law section, taken from the January 2012 AQA examination:

> Kai was using a mini digger to dig a trench on his drive. His neighbour, Lionel, saw what he was doing and started to make fun of Kai's efforts. Kai lost his temper and spun the digger round to scare Lionel. Unfortunately, he caught Lionel's jacket with the digger, pulling him down into a puddle. Lionel was not hurt, but did swallow some muddy water and started to vomit shortly afterwards. He went to the hospital where he was given an antibiotic injection. Unfortunately, Lionel suffered an allergic reaction to the antibiotic, which left him with permanent brain damage.

The questions are of two general types, theory-only and application. The application questions can be pure application, where the theory has been explained in a previous question; or application that requires some explanation of the law (theory) first. The examination paper states where theory-only questions end with the statement: 'Refer to the scenario when answering the remaining questions in this section'. This is usually after two theory-only questions.

Theory-only questions require an explanation of terms used, and no reference to the facts given in the scenario. Typical questions are:

1 Explain the meaning of 'mens rea'. *(8 marks)*
2 Briefly explain the meaning of and reason for strict liability. *(8 marks)*

Fig. 9.3 *Content of theory answer*

Application questions usually require you to select the appropriate law and apply the law to the facts given in the scenario. You should assume that the facts as stated in the scenario can be proved. A typical question, based on the scenario above, is:

3 Discuss the criminal liability of Kai with respect to the incident with the digger. (You should ignore the brain damage suffered by Lionel as a result of the injection.) (10 marks + 2 marks for AO3)

The two marks for AO3 (Quality of written communication) are usually awarded in the first question that is not theory-only.

Fig. 9.4 *Content of application answer*

Conclusion

Criminal law requires an understanding of the different aspects of the law that come into play in the criminal process. This Unit concentrates on the underlying concepts in criminal law and a little of the process. Your understanding of this will develop as you continue through the topics and chapters.

Activities

1 List two types of wrongdoing not mentioned in this topic that you believe should be a crime, and two crimes that you think should not be a crime. Compare your list with someone else, and discuss why you came up with those ideas.

2 Look at the criminal cases reported in your local newspaper and identify the stage in the process each has reached, or outline the process that will have been followed where a person has been found guilty.

You should now be able to:

- understand the underlying principles to the study of criminal liability
- understand how to use cases and statutes to justify your answers.

In this topic you will learn how to:

- identify the *actus reus* of a crime

- describe and give examples of how the law deals with acts that are not voluntary

- describe and give examples of circumstances in which a person can be criminally liable for an omission.

Key terms

Actus reus: the guilty act.

Link

For more information on the Offences Against the Person Act 1861 see p184 in Chapter 10.

Key cases

Pittwood (1902): here, a contractual duty created criminal liability for an omission when the defendant failed to act as required.

Dytham (1979): here, a person's public position created liability for an omission.

Miller (1983): the defendant's failure to minimise harm, caused by a dangerous situation he had created, created liability for an omission.

2 Actus reus

The defendant's conduct

As you have seen in the introduction, a criminal offence usually requires both guilty conduct (*actus reus*) and a guilty mind (*mens rea*). The **actus reus** of a crime is the act of the defendant. One of the offences that you will be studying is found in the Offences Against the Person Act 1861 s20, which states:

> Whosoever shall unlawfully and maliciously wound or inflict any grievous bodily harm upon any other person, either with or without any weapon or instrument …

The *actus reus* is any act of the defendant that: (i) is unlawful; and (ii) has the consequence of causing an injury to the victim that (iii) the law classifies as a wound or grievous bodily harm. You can see that the act might be a punch, a shot from a gun or hitting with an iron bar. All these appear to be voluntary deliberate acts of the defendant, and so would form the *actus reus* of s20.

Omissions

An omission, being a failure to act, is not an act. The law only makes a person liable for his failure to act where he has a duty to act. That duty can arise in a number of ways.

Where a person's contract requires him to act

A case involving a contract is **Pittwood (1902)**. In that case, Pittwood was employed as a gatekeeper at a railway crossing. One day he went for lunch, leaving the gate open. This meant that road traffic could cross the railway line. A cart crossing the line was hit by a train. One man on the cart was killed. Pittwood was convicted of manslaughter, based on his failure (omission) to carry out his duty to close the gate when a train approached. The duty to close the gate was part of his contract of employment. Note here that the defendant had a duty to act to close the gate. His failure to do so is an omission, but because he had a duty to act, the omission could form the *actus reus* of the offence.

Where a person's public position requires him to act

A case involving a person's public position is **Dytham (1979)**. In that case, a uniformed police officer saw a man who ended up being kicked to death. He took no steps to stop the attack, and drove away when it was over. He was convicted of the offence of misconduct in a public office, as he had omitted to act to protect the victim.

Where an Act of Parliament requires a person to act

There are many examples of this, ranging from the requirement to wear a seatbelt whilst driving a car, to neglect of (failure to look after) a child under the Children and Young Persons Act 1933.

Where a person fails to minimise the harmful consequences of his act

In **Miller (1983)**, Miller had been squatting in a house and fell asleep on a mattress whilst smoking a cigarette. He was awoken by the flames, but instead of putting the fire out, he simply got up and went into another room, where he found another mattress and went back to sleep. As a result, the house was damaged by fire. He was convicted of criminal damage. Once he awoke and realised what had happened, he had a duty to minimise the harmful effects of the fire, which he had omitted to do.

Where a person voluntarily takes on a duty

In **Stone and Dobinson (1977)** the defendants lived together, but were of low intelligence and had many personal difficulties. Despite this, Stone's sister came to live with them. The sister was anorexic, and although ill she refused to leave her room to seek medical attention. Stone and Dobinson made some effort to care for the sick woman, but did not call the medical services. Eventually she died. Stone and Dobinson were convicted of manslaughter, as they had taken on a duty of care by allowing the sister to live in their home and then omitted to make other arrangements for her, whilst knowing that she relied on them.

Voluntary conduct

The *actus reus* must be voluntary if the defendant is to be guilty. Everybody performs involuntary acts, such as closing their eyes whilst sneezing. This can be seen in **Hill v Baxter (1958)**, where the driver of a car suffered a heart attack. In this case, the court gave examples of situations where a driver of a car would not be driving voluntarily. These included being stung by a swarm of bees and being hit on the head by a stone. Such actions would not form the *actus reus* of a crime, and so a defendant could not be guilty.

It is clear that, if a strong person holds a knife in the hand of a weaker person and uses the knife to stab another person, then the weaker person could not be guilty of stabbing the victim. That would be because the act was not a voluntary deliberate act of the weaker person.

Conclusion

The *actus reus* of a crime is an essential ingredient of a crime. It is usually a voluntary deliberate act but can, in some circumstances, be an omission. The next topic examines whether the act caused the consequence required for the crime.

Key cases

Stone and Dobinson (1977): a person can take on responsibility for another and create liability for an omission if they fail to fulfil the duty.

Hill v Baxter (1958): an involuntary action does not form the *actus reus* of a crime.

Activities

1. Consider the following situation. You have been left to look after a friend's three-year-old daughter. Think of situations in which you would be liable and situations in which you would not be liable if the child were injured. Would it make any difference if you were a paid babysitter?

2. Take each of the cases mentioned in this chapter and make a table as in the example set out below. Note that you do not need to remember the dates of the cases.

Case	Key facts	Legal principle
Pittwood	Left crossing gates open and man was killed.	His omission to close the gates was part of the *actus reus* of the crime.

Practise writing a few sentences explaining each omission. Try to do this without notes and complete it in about seven minutes – this being the length of time you might have in the exam.

You should now be able to:

- understand the meaning of the term *actus reus*
- explain, using cases as examples, aspects of the term *actus reus*.

In this topic you will learn how to:

■ state the meaning of the term 'causation'

■ distinguish between factual and legal causation

■ describe and give examples of the meaning of factual causation

■ describe and give examples of the meaning of legal causation.

■ Key terms

Causation: the link between the defendant's act and the criminal consequence.

Factual causation: this is the 'but for' test: but for the defendant's act, would the consequence have occurred?

Legal causation: this is the 'operating and substantial cause' test to find the link between the defendant's act and the criminal consequence.

■ Key cases

White (1910): there was no factual cause of death because the actual cause was natural and not affected by the defendant's act.

Pagett (1983): this is an unusual result of the 'but for' test, but is quite logical.

■ Study tips

Make sure you don't confuse factual and legal causation. You should understand the distinction and be aware that both factual and legal causation is needed for there to be criminal liability.

3 Causation

The problem of causation

The *actus reus* of a crime is the defendant's guilty conduct. For many crimes, that act must have caused a particular consequence. **Causation** is part of the *actus reus* of a crime. The rules of causation are applied to decide whether the defendant's guilty act caused the required consequence in the definition of a particular crime. Thus in homicide, the defendant's act must have caused the death of the victim. In offences against the person, the defendant's act must have caused the injury that is relevant for the particular offence. If it does not, or the act is not unlawful, there is no criminal liability.

Crimes can be categorised as 'conduct' or 'action' crimes, where the act is the *actus reus* and the consequences are immaterial, or 'result crimes', where the *actus reus* must produce a particular consequence such as death or a particular type of harm.

In many cases, causation is not in issue. If I hit another person very hard over the head with an iron bar and their skull is then fractured, there is no question that I caused the broken skull. Where it is less clear, the prosecution must prove both factual and legal causation. These two terms will now be explored in more detail. Most of the cases involve homicide, but the principles apply equally to all cases where the prosecution has to prove that the defendant's act caused a particular consequence.

Factual causation

The defendant can only be guilty if the consequence would not have happened 'but for' his act. This can be seen in the case of **White (1910)**. In that case, White put the poison cyanide in his mother's drink, intending to kill her. She died shortly thereafter as a result of a heart attack. The poison had not taken effect at that time. Whilst he had intended to kill her and she had died, he had not caused her death and therefore could not be guilty of murder.

This principle can also be seen in an unusual way. In the case of **Pagett (1983)** the defendant used his girlfriend, Gail, as a human shield while he shot at armed police. The police fired back and killed Gail. Pagett was convicted of Gail's manslaughter, as she would not have died 'but for' his use of her as a human shield.

Legal causation

Once it is established that there is factual causation, the prosecution must also prove **legal causation**. This is so that there is little chance of the conviction of a truly innocent person. The link between the act and the consequence is known as the chain of causation, which must remain unbroken if there is to be criminal liability.

Suppose you invite a friend to visit you at your house. On the way to visit you, your friend is stabbed and seriously injured. It could be said that, but for your invitation, your friend would not have been stabbed.

Clearly, you are not guilty of causing the injuries, as your invitation was not the 'operating and substantial' cause of them. The 'operating and substantial' cause is the key test for legal causation, and several different aspects must be considered. The original injury must be the operating and substantial cause.

The general sequence of events is as set out in the diagram below:

Fig. 9.5 *Sequence of events in causation cases involving bad medical treatment*

The first case is **Jordan (1956)**. In that case, the defendant had stabbed the victim, who was taken to hospital. A week later, when the wound was almost healed, doctors gave him an incorrect injection and he died. As the medical treatment was 'palpably wrong', there was no legal causation and the defendant was acquitted. The original injury was not the operating and substantial cause of death, but the defendant would still be guilty of wounding.

The second case is **Smith (1959)**. In that case, two soldiers were involved in a fight. The victim received a stab wound that pierced his lung. The victim was taken to the medical station, where he died about one hour later. On being charged with murder, the defendant argued that the chain of causation between the stabbing and the death had been broken by the way in which the victim had been treated, in particular the fact that: (a) the victim had been dropped twice whilst being carried to the medical station; (b) the medical officer, who was dealing with a series of emergencies, did not realise the serious extent of the wounds; and (c) the treatment he gave him was 'thoroughly bad and might well have affected his chances of recovery'. The defendant was convicted of murder and appealed unsuccessfully. The court held that the defendant's stabbing was the 'operating and substantial cause' of the victim's death. In this case, the victim clearly died from loss of blood caused by the stab wounds inflicted by the defendant.

Rare medical complications can break the chain of causation, but only where the original injury is no longer having any real effect. In the case of **Cheshire (1991)**, where the victim was shot in the thigh and stomach, the victim died as a result of rare complications from a tracheotomy, which had not been spotted by the doctors. Even though the original wounds were no longer life-threatening, the tracheotomy given to help breathing problems and the rare complication were not seen as independent of the gunshot wounds. In other words, they were still the main reason for the tracheotomy and so the chain of causation was not broken.

Key cases

Jordan (1956): the test here is whether the medical treatment was 'palpably wrong'.

Smith (1959): here the original act was the operating and substantial cause of the consequence.

Cheshire (1991): in this case the actual cause of death was not seen as independent of the original act, so there was legal causation.

Key terms

Novus actus interveniens: literally, a 'new act intervening'. This breaks the chain of causation.

Intervening acts or events

Sometimes the sole cause of the death or injury seems to be a completely independent act. This is known as a **novus actus interveniens**, or 'new act intervening'. There are many ways in which a new act can break the chain of causation. Examples include an act of another person unconnected with the defendant's act, as in *Pagett*, or medical intervention as in *Jordan*.

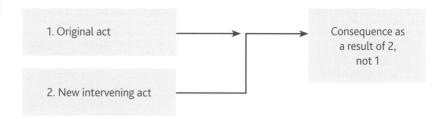

Fig. 9.6 *Novus actus interveniens*

Take your victim as you find him

The general principle is that you take your victim as you find him: in other words, the law does not take into account any particular characteristics of the victim. In *Watson* (1989) – outlined in Activity 1 on page 173 – it did not matter that the victim was an old man: if he was therefore more likely to suffer a heart attack, then that was a risk the defendant must take. This is clearly illustrated by the case of **Blaue (1975)**. The defendant had stabbed the victim, who was a Jehovah's Witness. The victim was rushed to hospital, where doctors told her that she would die if she did not have a blood transfusion. The victim refused on religious grounds and died from her wounds shortly after. The defendant argued that the victim's refusal of treatment was unreasonable and so broke the chain of causation. However, the defendant had to take his victim as he found her, meaning not just her physical condition, but also her religious beliefs. The question for the court was what caused the death. The answer was the stab wound, so the defendant caused the victim's death.

The victim's own act

If the defendant causes the victim to act in a foreseeable way, then the victim's own act will not break the chain of causation. This depends on whether the victim's conduct is reasonable or unreasonable. Contrast the cases of **Roberts (1971)** and **Williams (1992)**. In *Roberts* (1971) a girl who was a passenger in the defendant's car injured herself by jumping out of the car while it was moving. Her explanation was that the defendant had made sexual advances to her and was trying to pull her coat off. The defendant was convicted, as it was held that the correct test for causation in law was to ask whether the result was the reasonably foreseeable consequence of what the defendant was saying or doing. However, the chain of causation would be broken by the victim doing something 'daft' or so unexpected that no reasonable man could be expected to foresee it. In *Williams* (1992) the defendants gave a lift to a hitch-hiker and allegedly tried to rob him. The victim jumped from the moving car and died from head injuries caused by falling onto the road. Here, his own voluntary act was one that could be a *novus actus interveniens* and consequently break the chain of causation. It should of course be borne in mind that a victim may, in the agony of the moment, do the wrong thing.

Key cases

Blaue (1975): here, the victim's religious beliefs led to refusal of possible life-saving treatment. This is an example of the principle of take your victim as you find him.

Roberts (1971): the victim's own act was reasonable so there was causation.

Williams (1992): the victim's own act might be unreasonable and so break the chain of causation. The victim thus caused their own injuries.

Activities

1. It is not always easy to find out whether the defendant's act is the cause of the criminal consequence. In the case of *Watson* (1989), one of the questions before the court was 'did the defendant cause the victim's death?'

   Watson and another man burgled an old man's house at night. They knew he was very frail. When they saw him, they shouted abuse but took nothing. Shortly after, the police arrived, as did council workmen, who repaired a window broken by the burglars. Ninety minutes after the burglary, the old man had a heart attack and died. The court had to decide whether there was sufficient evidence that the burglars caused the heart attack, as anyone seeing him would have known he was frail.

   Discuss whether you think Watson caused the death of the old man.

2. Explain the causation issues in the past examination scenario set out below:

   Jamal, a man of Middle Eastern appearance, was walking to work when Sam ran up behind him. As he ran up, Sam shouted racial abuse and made suggestions that Jamal was a terrorist. Jamal was afraid that Sam was going to attack him, so he ran across the street without looking. Unfortunately, he ran in front of a moving car and suffered a badly broken leg.

3. Explain the causation issues in the past examination scenario set out below:

   Anna was walking alongside Tara, when she tripped Tara up with her foot. Tara fell over and grazed her knee. She ignored the graze until three days later, when her knee became swollen by an infection. She went to her doctor, who prescribed her a drug to deal with the infection. Tara's doctor did not check her medical records. Tara was in fact allergic to this drug, and was paralysed as a result of her reaction to taking the drug.

4. Using the general layout in Fig. 9.6 on p172, add the facts of the cases in this topic area and show whether the chain of causation has been broken.

5. Practice writing a few sentences explaining factual and legal causation. For legal causation, write sentences about intervening acts, medical intervention, the victim's own acts, and 'take your victim as you find him'. When you are confident that you can do this exercise correctly, try to do so without notes and complete it in about seven minutes – this being the length of time you might have in the exam. You can decide what you need to put in for factual causation and which case or cases you would use.

> **Study tips**
>
> There are many aspects to causation. Make sure you understand how the different aspects of causation relate to each other.

Conclusion

Once it has been established that the defendant performed an act, the *actus reus*, the prosecution then must prove that his or her act caused the criminal consequence. Causation has two parts to it, factual and legal causation. These are the elements you will need to explain if the exam requires you to deal with causation.

You should now be able to:

- understand the meaning of the term 'causation'
- explain, using cases as examples, the meaning of factual and legal causation.

■ Key terms

Mens rea: the guilty mind of the defendant.

Direct intent: this occurs where the consequence is the defendant's aim or purpose.

■ Key cases

Mohan (1976): this case is an example of, and gives a definition of, direct intent.

4 *Mens rea*

The general principle of *mens rea*

Many crimes need *actus reus* and also **mens rea**. The *mens rea* is the guilty mind, and is often the distinguishing factor between different crimes. For example, the main difference between s18 and s20 of the Offences Against the Person Act 1861 is the *mens rea* required. *Mens rea* must be distinguished from motive. Whilst the motive behind a criminal act may give an indication of the defendant's *mens rea*, it is generally irrelevant. Motive can be relevant in some crimes, such as a racially motivated assault, and can also be a factor that the court will take into account in passing sentence. In this specification, the only types of *mens rea* you need to study are intention and subjective recklessness.

Intention

Intention can be either direct intention or indirect (oblique) intention. The idea that a person will be guilty of a crime if he intends to perform a criminal act is perfectly reasonable. One definition of direct intent can be seen in the case of **Mohan (1976)**, where it was said that direct intention is a decision to bring about, so far as it lies in the defendant's powers, the criminal consequence, no matter whether the defendant desired that consequence of his act or not. It can be said to be the defendant's aim, purpose, or desire.

If I am angry and want to seriously injure someone, I might deliberately hit them on the head many times with an iron bar. This would be **direct intent** to cause grievous bodily harm. It is seen as direct intent, as the resulting injury is my aim or purpose. Note that use of a weapon is evidence of intention to cause injury, but not necessarily serious injury.

Difficulties arise when the defendant's aim is something different to the actual consequence. This is known as indirect or oblique intent: the defendant intended the act but not the consequences.

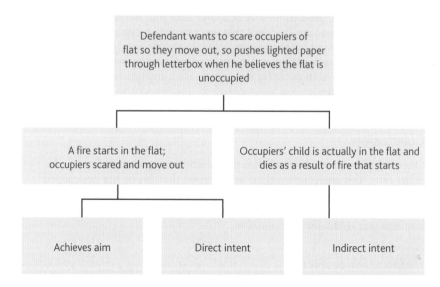

Fig. 9.7 *Distinction between direct and indirect (oblique) intent*

The jury in a criminal trial must have a clear direction from the judge as to how they should decide whether the defendant had the necessary intention, where direct intention isn't present and indirect intention is relied on by the prosecution. The leading case on this is **Woollin (1998)**. In that case, the defendant was feeding his three-month-old son when the baby choked on his food and the defendant lost his temper and threw the baby towards his pram. The baby hit the wall and suffered head injuries from which he died. Clearly, the defendant did not have direct intention to kill his son. The court stated a two-part test to decide whether the defendant had oblique intent. The test allows the court or jury to infer intention if:

a   the consequence is a virtually certain result of the act; and

b   the defendant knows that it is a virtually certain consequence.

A judge directing a jury on this point might say to the jury: 'You are not entitled to find that the defendant had the necessary intent to commit murder unless you are satisfied beyond reasonable doubt that death or serious bodily harm was a virtual certainty (barring some unforeseen intervention) as result of the defendant's actions, and that the defendant appreciated that such was the case.'

The following example might prove helpful:

> If I throw a large stone at point-blank range at a plate-glass window, it is only too easy – and you may think that it will almost invariably be correct – to infer that I intend to break the window. The lawyer's way of expressing this rather obvious proposition is to say that a man is presumed to intend the natural and probable consequences of his acts. But while the quest for truth will take account of this presumption it does not end there. You are looking for the actual intention and the actual state of knowledge and in order to discover them it is right to consider all the available evidence.

www.jsbni.com/Publications/BenchBook/Pages/2-13-Intention.aspx

Indirect intention was considered again in **Matthews and Alleyne (2003)**. In that case, the Court of Appeal stressed that the defendant's appreciation of death or serious bodily harm as a virtual certainty does not constitute the necessary intention for murder, but is something from which that intention can be inferred. The facts of that case were that Matthews and Alleyne pushed their victim from a bridge into a river, knowing that he could not swim. They watched him head towards the bank, but did not stay to see if he succeeded in getting out. In fact, he drowned.

Recklessness

Some crimes require the lower level of *mens rea* of **recklessness**. The type of recklessness that is used is subjective recklessness. This occurs where the defendant knows there a risk of the criminal consequence, is willing to take it and takes it deliberately. This is also difficult to establish, as it requires looking at what was in the defendant's mind. The leading case on this is **Cunningham (1957)**. In this case, the defendant had broken a pre-pay gas meter to steal the money in it, with the result that gas escaped into the next-door house.

The next-door neighbour became ill as a result. Cunningham was charged with administering a noxious substance to the victim. The court decided that the *mens rea* of the offence could be intention or recklessness to administer the noxious substance, and defined recklessness as 'being recklessness as to whether such harm should occur or not (that is the accused has foreseen that the particular kind of harm might be done, and yet has gone on to take the risk of it). It is neither limited to, nor does it indeed require, any ill will towards the person injured.' Cunningham was found not guilty as it could not be shown that he knew there was a risk of harming anyone.

Recklessness, like intention, is always stated to be 'recklessness as to...'. This '...' can be, for example, 'cause some harm' or 'cause serious harm', depending on the definition of the crime.

Conclusion

The *mens rea* of an offence is often quite difficult to prove. There have been many cases where the courts have struggled to find suitable words to direct the jury. The present rules on this are reasonably clear and can be applied in examination questions.

■ **Activities**

1. Consider whether any type of *mens rea* is shown in the following example:

   A young girl was struck twice by two airgun pellets whilst playing in the forecourt of a block of flats, which had been fired from a window by the appellant. He admitted to the police that he had fired a few shots out of the window, not in order to hit anyone, but to see how far the pellets would go. (Based on *Spratt* (1990).)

2. Practice writing a few sentences explaining intention and recklessness as types of *mens rea*. When you are confident that you have done this correctly, try to do so without notes and complete it in about seven minutes – the length of time you might have in the exam.

You should now be able to:

- understand the meaning of the term *mens rea*

- explain the meaning of intention as a form of *mens rea* using cases to illustrate the term

- explain the meaning of recklessness as a form of *mens rea* using cases to illustrate the term.

■ **Study tips**

Make sure you can distinguish between oblique intent and recklessness. A common fault is confusing these two.

In this topic you will learn how to:

■ identify the circumstances where there is coincidence of *actus reus* and *mens rea*

■ describe the cases involving continuing acts

■ describe the concept of transferred malice.

---

⑤ Coincidence of *actus reus* and *mens rea* and transferred malice

Coincidence of *actus reus* and *mens rea*

The general principle is that the *actus reus* and *mens rea* of a crime must occur at the same time. This is also called the contemporaneity rule. The idea is that a person cannot be guilty of a crime if he or she performs an act that causes a previously desired result. Thus, if I go out on Saturday with the intention of finding and injuring X, but fail do so, it does not make my activity on Tuesday a crime when I accidentally injure X in a car crash, not knowing that X was in the other car.

The courts have modified this rule so that a series of linked acts or omissions can be treated as a single continuing event. This establishes the coincidence of *actus reus* and *mens rea*. A simple example of this is the case of **Fagan v Metropolitan Police Commissioner (MPC) (1969)**.

In that case, the defendant accidentally stopped his car on a policeman's foot. When the policeman asked him to remove the car from his foot, he replied, 'F*** off, you can wait.'

The court found Fagan guilty of causing the injury to the policeman as leaving the car on the foot was seen as a continuing act. Even though he did not have the *mens rea* for the crime when he stopped the car on the foot (it was purely accidental), he did form the *mens rea* when he refused to move it and the act of placing the car on the foot remained.

> ■ **Key cases**
>
> **Fagan v MPC (1969):** here, there was a continuing act, so there was coincidence of *actus reus* and *mens rea* when the *mens rea* was later formed.

Fig. 9.8 Fagan *v* MPC

Sometimes the continuing act is a series of connected acts. This can be seen in a similar manner to the chain of causation considered in Topic 3 of this chapter; each act or omission is part of the continuing act, and the *mens rea* can be said to continue throughout. This can be seen in the case of **Thabo Meli (1954)**, where the defendant hit the victim over the head, intending to kill him. Believing the victim was dead and trying to make it look like an accident, the defendant threw the victim over a cliff, where the victim later died of exposure.

> ■ **Key cases**
>
> **Thabo Meli (1954):** here, the *mens rea* formed for the first act continued over a series of acts and a consequence some days later.

Fig. 9.9 In Thabo Meli, *the courts viewed the three separate incidents as one long continuing act*

Key cases

Church (1966): here, the *mens rea* continued despite the defendant's belief of a change of circumstances.

Mitchell (1983): this a good example of transferred malice to the victim through the original person attacked.

Latimer (1886): here, the *mens rea* was transferred from the intended victim to a bystander with whom the defendant had no argument and no intention to cause any harm whatsoever.

Pembilton (1884): in this case, the *mens rea* relating to hurting his victim could not be transferred to the window, as an offence against the person is a different type of offence to criminal damage.

Key terms

Transferred malice: Where the *mens rea* of the crime directed at one person is transferred to the unintended victim of the crime.

In *Thabo Meli* (1954) the *mens rea* continued throughout, as the defendant had set out to kill the victim. In **Church (1966)**, the defendant panicked, believing his victim was dead. This was not his desired consequence. What actually happened was the defendant had gone to his van with a woman for sexual purposes. She mocked his impotence and he had attacked her, knocking her out. The defendant panicked and, wrongly thinking he had killed her, threw her unconscious body into a river, where she drowned. He argued that all he had done wrong was to dispose of or conceal a dead body, and that the *mens rea* for the attack on the woman ended when he thought her unconscious body was in fact dead. The court decided that the *mens rea* continued even after he thought she was dead, so as to include her death from drowning.

Transferred malice

Transferred malice occurs when the defendant's *mens rea* is transferred from the intended victim to the actual victim. This can occur either by, for example, hitting one person and knocking them into another whom you have no intention of hitting, or by shooting at one person, missing, and injuring another. Thus in the case of **Mitchell (1983)** the defendant, having become involved in an argument whilst queuing in a post office, pushed an elderly man, causing him to fall accidentally on an elderly woman, who subsequently died in hospital from her injuries. The defendant unsuccessfully appealed on the ground that his unlawful act had not been directed at the victim. The court said that although there was no direct contact between the defendant and the victim, she was injured as a direct result of his act, and that the *mens rea* was transferred to the victim. There was, of course, also a crime committed against the person originally pushed over.

The principle can also be seen in the case of **Latimer (1886)**, where a person aimed to hit someone else with his belt, but missed and hit a bystander. The *mens rea* was transferred to the victim from the intended victim as the offence was clearly of the same type. There would have been no transferred malice if the belt had damaged an object such as a glass standing on the bar, as this would be a different type of offence. This can be seen in the case of **Pembilton (1884)**, where the defendant threw a stone at his intended victim, but missed and broke a window. The *mens rea* of intending to cause harm to the victim was not transferred to the window, so he could not be found guilty of criminal damage based on that *mens rea*.

Study tips

You can recognise the need to discuss this topic in applying the law to a given scenario where there is a time gap between different parts of the story.

Activities

1 Practice writing a few sentences explaining the law relating to coincidence of *actus reus* and *mens rea*. When you are confident that you have done this correctly, try to do so without notes and complete it in about five minutes, this being the length of time you might have in the exam.

2 Practice writing a few sentences explaining the law relating to transferred malice. As in Activity 1, you can then try to complete this exercise without using notes, within a time limit of five minutes. This will mimic the conditions you may have in the actual exam.

> **3** Consider the elements of coincidence of *actus reus* and *mens rea* in the following situation:
>
> Lyn had broken up with her boyfriend, Carl, and was very angry that he continued to climb onto the branches of a tree in the park next to her garden and shout at her when she was out in her garden. She went out one night and partly sawed through some of the branches on the tree, hoping that they would break and that Carl would fall and be injured next time he pestered her. Unfortunately, the next day, Jan, aged 6, climbed the tree. She fell and was seriously injured when one of the branches broke.

Conclusion

The general principle of coincidence between *actus reus* and *mens rea* is sometimes interpreted quite widely to ensure that there can be a conviction when someone is truly guilty. These interpretations include continuing acts and transferred malice.

You should now be able to:

- understand the meaning of the term 'coincidence of *actus reus* and *mens rea*'
- understand the meaning of the term 'transferred malice'
- explain those terms with the help of decided cases.

6 Strict liability

The general principle of strict liability

Crimes of **strict liability** are crimes where the definition of the crime includes an *actus reus* and no *mens rea*. Merely performing the act is sufficient to make a person guilty. There are many crimes of strict liability, many of which are purely regulatory and are not always seen by some sections of society as 'real' crimes. Many motoring offences are included in these crimes, and in many cases the decision to prosecute or not is seen, in part, as an indication of whether there is a truly wrongful act.

Strict liability offences were originally created to make it easier to prove guilt for business-related offences. In the 19th century, with the Industrial Revolution, there were many abuses of factory workers that were the subject of criminal law, but there were very few successful prosecutions, as showing *mens rea* on the part of the factory owner was very difficult. In addition, there was a view that as the magistrates were often factory owners as well, there was a temptation to find factory owners not guilty, and lack of *mens rea* was often the reason given. When *mens rea* did not have to be proved, conviction rates increased and so did factory safety.

Strict liability today

The vast majority of strict liability crimes are statutory offences. However, statutes do not always state explicitly that a particular offence is one of strict liability. Where a statute uses terms such as 'knowingly' or 'recklessly' then the offence being created is one that requires *mens rea*.

In this topic you will learn how to:

- explain the meaning of strict liability, giving reasons for its use
- state and explain examples of strict liability using decided cases and Acts of Parliament.

Key terms

Strict liability: these are crimes defined as requiring an *actus reus* only; *mens rea* has no relevance.

Sometimes, particularly in more recent statutes, it may be made clear that an offence of strict liability is being created. In many cases, it will be a matter for the courts to interpret the statute and decide whether *mens rea* is required or not.

The famous case of **Sweet v Parsley (1970)** was decided in the House of Lords, and established that the offence of being involved in the management of premises which were used for the smoking of cannabis was *not* an offence of strict liability under the Dangerous Drugs Act 1965. The facts were that Miss Sweet, a teacher, let out her cottage to students and only visited rarely to collect post and see that things were in order. She kept a separate room locked for her use when she visited the cottage. She knew nothing of the drug-taking and was acquitted when it was decided that an element of *mens rea* was needed for there to be a conviction for this crime.

In **Gammon (Hong Kong) Ltd v Attorney-General for Hong Kong (1985)**, the court considered the scope and role of strict liability offences in modern criminal law. The court started with the principle that in criminal law there is a presumption of *mens rea*. This means that it is presumed that all criminal offences require some form of *mens rea* unless the definition of the offence states the opposite. Unfortunately, as is seen in Unit 1, not all statutes are clear, so Lord Scarman laid down the criteria upon which a court should decide whether or not it is appropriate to impose strict liability. These criteria were as follows:

- There is a presumption of law that *mens rea* is required before a person can be held guilty of a criminal offence.
- The presumption is particularly strong where the offence is 'truly criminal' in character.
- The presumption applies to statutory offences, and can be displaced only if this is clearly or by necessary implication the effect of the statute.
- The only situation in which the presumption can be displaced is where the statute is concerned with an issue of social concern, and public safety is such an issue.
- Even where a statute is concerned with such an issue, the presumption of *mens rea* stands, unless it can be shown that the creation of strict liability will be effective to promote the objects of the statute by encouraging greater vigilance to prevent the commission of the prohibited act.

These criteria can be summarised as follows:

- presumption of *mens rea*
- truly criminal
- statute must clearly exclude *mens rea*
- only for public safety or social concern
- encouraging greater vigilance.

Examples of strict liability

Many cases of strict liability result in a very minor penalty, which makes one wonder why there was a prosecution in the first place. A typical case is **Alphacell v Woodward (1972)**, where the defendants were papermakers. There was an overflow from settling tanks which allowed polluted water to be discharged into a river.

Key cases

Sweet v Parsley (1970): this case is not one of strict liability as the House of Lords decided that the statute did not specifically exclude *mens rea*.

Gammon (Hong Kong) Ltd v Attorney-General for Hong Kong (1985): this case sets out the general criteria for a crime to be a crime of strict liability.

Alphacell v Woodward (1972): here, the defendant company was guilty even though the event could not be predicted. This encourages greater vigilance in business.

The overflow had happened because pumping equipment had become blocked. The company had alarm systems and a regular maintenance and inspection programme, but could not predict if and when there would be a blockage. Despite this, the company was found guilty and fined £20.

From the company's point of view, the main problem with a prosecution is often the hidden costs: engaging lawyers; non-productive time investigating the alleged offence and going to meetings about it; and bad publicity if there is a conviction (would you go to a fast food outlet that had just been prosecuted for selling unfit food?) Bad publicity affects future business, and fines affect profits. The result is that the real people punished are the shareholders, who may be far removed from the business. Consider **Smedleys v Breed (1974)**, where one tin of peas, out of millions of tins produced by the defendants, contained a caterpillar. The defendants were convicted under the Food and Drugs Act 1955, even though they had taken all reasonable care.

Sometimes the conviction and publicity will have little lasting effect on the defendant, but it serves as a reminder to others of their legal obligations. In **London Borough of Harrow v Shah (2000)**, the court held that the offence of selling a national lottery ticket to a person under 16 was a strict liability offence because the offence was not truly criminal but dealt with a matter of social concern (gambling by young people).

> ### Key cases
>
> **Smedleys v Breed (1974):** the defendant company was guilty, even though all reasonable care had been taken.
>
> **London Borough of Harrow v Shah (2000):** this is another example of the characteristics of a strict liability offence: it is not truly criminal, but is of social concern.

Fig. 9.10 *It is a strict liability offence to sell a lottery ticket to someone under the age of 16*

Key cases

Blake (1997): the characteristeric of strict liability in this case is that of public safety.

In **Blake (1997)**, investigation officers heard an unlicensed radio station broadcast and traced it to a flat, where the defendant was discovered alone standing in front of the record decks, still playing music and wearing a set of headphones. Though the defendant admitted that he knew he was using the equipment, he claimed that he believed he was making demonstration tapes and did not know he was transmitting. The court was told that pirate radio broadcasts might interfere with public service transmissions and so create a risk to public safety. The defendant was convicted as it was a crime of strict liability.

Conclusion

Strict liability offences require no *mens rea*. Even though these offences may seem unfair, the reasons behind strict liability usually make prosecution a just outcome. These reasons include:

- easier to prove
- takes less time in court
- encourages compliance with the law
- prevents defences being raised as an excuse
- makes regulation straightforward
- protects the public.

Study tips

If you use *Sweet* v *Parsley* (1970) as an example, do make it clear that the House of Lords decided the offence was *not* one of strict liability.

Activities

1 Look in your local paper and find examples of prosecutions for crimes of strict liability.

2 Find out as many offences as you can that are crimes of strict liability with respect to driving a car.

You should now be able to:

- understand the reasons for the use of strict liability
- describe the use of strict liability by reference to authority.

10 Non-fatal offences

In this topic you will learn how to:

- distinguish between common law offences and statutory offences

- distinguish between assault and battery

- describe, using authority, the *actus reus* of assault

- describe, using authority, the *mens rea* of assault

- describe, using authority, the *actus reus* of battery

- describe, using authority, the *mens rea* of battery

- apply the above to a given situation.

1 Introduction to the offences

The specification requires an understanding of five non-fatal offences. These are:

- assault
- battery
- assault occasioning actual bodily harm
- inflicting grievous bodily harm or wounding
- inflicting grievous bodily harm or wounding with intent.

Assault and battery are common law offences. This means that each of the offences is defined through decided cases only, and has no statutory definition. The other three offences are all set out in the Offences Against the Person Act 1861. You will need to refer to the Act precisely and then use decided cases to explain aspects of the statutory definition of each offence.

2 The nature of the offences

Assault and battery are two different offences that together are called common assault. The word 'common' is used because the definitions of the offences come from the common law – in other words, all the sources of this law are decided cases. The Criminal Justice Act 1988 s39 does not define these offences; it merely states the maximum sentence (six months) and establishes that the offences are summary offences – they can be tried only in the Magistrates' Court. They are the least serious of the non-fatal offences against the person.

The essential distinction between the two offences is that assault is about fear of suffering harm, whereas battery is the actual harm. It therefore follows that a person who is asleep cannot suffer an assault, but can suffer a battery. Both these crimes require *actus reus* and *mens rea*, and it is essential to be able to explain these accurately.

The three offences that we are concerned with in the specification are the more serious personal injuries offences. They are gradated in terms of seriousness, as can be seen in the diagram below.

Fig. 10.1 *The hierarchy of harm*

Assault occasioning actual bodily harm can be found in Section 47 of the Offences Against the Person Act 1861, and is the least serious offence. It is also the offence that, of the three, has the most convictions. The other two offences, being more serious, also include the possibility of a charge and conviction for the lesser offence. In some of the cases you may read about, you might wonder why a more serious charge was not brought against the defendant. The practical reason is that conviction and appropriate sentence is more important than a conviction for the more serious offence. It should also be noted that the maximum sentence under both s47 and s20 is five years' imprisonment; this gives the court plenty of scope to choose a suitable level of punishment.

Inflicting grievous bodily harm or wounding can be found in Section 20 of the Offences Against the Person Act 1861, and inflicting grievous bodily harm or wounding with intent can be found in Section 18 of the Offences Against the Person Act 1861.

The next step is to understand the distinction between the different offences, as it essential that you can apply these.

3 Assault

The *actus reus* of **assault** is any act that causes the victim to apprehend an immediate infliction of unlawful violence. This might be waving a fist at someone in an aggressive manner, or aiming a gun or a catapult at that person. The House of Lords in *Savage* (1991) stated that the *mens rea* is 'an intention to cause the victim to apprehend unlawful and immediate violence or recklessness whether such an apprehension be caused.'

The *actus reus* has the following elements:

1 causing the victim to apprehend violence
2 immediate violence
3 unlawful violence.

In the first element, causing the victim to apprehend violence, there is no need for any physical contact between the defendant and the victim. The emphasis is on what the victim thought was about to happen. So even if the defendant meant his threat as a joke, an assault is nevertheless committed if the victim is sufficiently frightened. This can be seen in the case of **Logdon (1976)**, where the defendant, as a joke, pointed a gun at the victim, who was terrified until she was told that it was in fact a replica. The court held that the victim had apprehended immediate physical violence, and the defendant had been at least reckless as to whether this would occur.

■ **Key terms**

Assault: intentionally or recklessly causing the victim to fear immediate, unlawful harm.

■ **Key cases**

Logdon (1976): the court decided that an assault could be by words and actions.

Fig. 10.2 *Pointing a replica gun at someone can be considered as an assault*

Logdon (1976) involved more than just words, as a replica gun was shown. In **Smith v Chief Superintendent of Woking Police Station (1983)** there were no words, merely actions. In that case, the victim was at home in her ground-floor flat, dressed in her nightdress. She was terrified when she suddenly saw the defendant standing in her garden, staring at her through the window. The court held him liable for assault, on the grounds that the victim feared immediate violence, even though he could not physically attack her as she was locked in.

Words alone, or even silence, can be assault. This is consistent with the law that was developed to deal with stalkers prior to the Protection from Harassment Act 1997. In **Ireland (1997)**, the making of silent telephone calls that caused psychiatric injury to the victim was capable of amounting to an assault in law, where the calls caused the victim to apprehend an immediate application of force.

The second element is that the violence threatened must be immediate. Immediate means as a part of the current activity. This can be seen in *Smith* v *Chief Superintendent of Woking Police Station* (1983), where the immediacy arose as the victim was behind glass, even though the defendant did not have immediate access to her. The immediacy in the telephone calls in *Ireland* (1997) is that the verbal contact made by the defendant with the victim caused the fear.

The reason that the victim could be held to fear 'immediate' unlawful personal violence in *Ireland* was that she could not know exactly where the defendant was when making the phone calls, and so could not rule out the possibility that he could get to her within a very short time.

The third element is that the threatened violence must be unlawful. Thus it is not a criminal offence for a policeman to threaten to handcuff someone or restrain them if they do not co-operate during an arrest.

The *mens rea* of assault stated in *Savage* (1991) was an intention to cause the victim to apprehend unlawful and immediate violence or recklessness whether such an apprehension is caused. This means:

- direct or oblique intention as to causing immediate, unlawful fear in the victim that he or she might suffer some harm;
- subjective (*Cunningham*) recklessness as to causing immediate, unlawful fear in the victim that he or she might suffer some harm.

In practice, the prosecution would rely on direct intention or recklessness.

> ### Activity
>
> Here is part of a scenario that relates to assault.
>
> Alan believed that Bhu, a fellow student, had stolen his mobile phone. Alan saw Bhu at college, went up to her and said, 'We sort out thieves like you.' Bhu hurried away in a panic.
>
> Practice applying the *actus reus* and *mens rea* of assault to the facts in the scenario.

4 Battery

The *actus reus* of **battery** is the unlawful application of force to another. The force involved can be very slight: indeed, it is suggested that touching a person's clothes may be sufficient. Typical examples are hitting someone or throwing a drink at someone. In **Thomas (1985)**, a school caretaker was charged with indecent assault after taking hold of the hem

> ### Key cases
>
> **Smith v Chief Superintendent of Woking Police Station (1983):** in this case, there was an assault by actions alone.
>
> **Ireland (1997):** it was decided that silence or words alone can be an assault.
>
> **Thomas (1985):** here, it was decided that touching a person's clothes can be a battery.

> ### Study tips
>
> Look for events such as shouting at someone or waving a weapon at someone, to consider whether assault should be discussed as an offence.

> ### Key terms
>
> **Battery:** the unlawful application of force to another person.

of a 12-year-old girl's skirt. Whilst the act was not indecent because there was no evidence of circumstances making it so, the court said that there can be no dispute that if you touch a person's clothes while he or she is wearing them, that is equivalent to touching him or her.

Consent can make the touching lawful. There is an implied consent in normal social situations, such as tapping someone on the shoulder to bring attention to something, or consent to touching in normal sporting activities. There is no consent when the touching goes beyond the rules of the sport, although in such cases the consequences are usually more severe than a battery.

The force can be applied only by an act, not an omission, which is why *Fagan* v *MPC* (1969) (p177, Chapter 9) was considered a continuing act. It is also possible to cause a battery by indirect force, as in the case of **Haystead (2000)** where the defendant punched his girlfriend, causing her to drop her baby onto the floor. He was convicted of battery on the baby.

The *mens rea* of battery was stated by the court in **Venna (1976)** as 'proof that the defendant intentionally or recklessly applied force to the person of another'. This is very similar to the *mens rea* of assault except as to the intended or reckless consequence. In *Venna* (1976), the defendant was arrested along with some friends for a public order offence. He struggled violently with the arresting officer, and he was judged to be reckless as to whether he caused some harm to the officer.

Battery only requires the slightest touching. Other offences may be more appropriate if the consequences to the victim are more severe.

■ **Activity**

For each of the cases listed in this section, set out the *actus reus* and *mens rea* of the offences disclosed by the facts.

5 Section 47 of the Offences Against the Person Act 1861

Section 47 of the Offences Against the Person Act 1861 states that:

> Whosoever shall be convicted on indictment of any **assault occasioning actual bodily harm** shall be liable to be imprisoned for any term not exceeding five years.

This offence is triable either way – that is, in either the Magistrates' Court or the Crown Court. The correct name for this offence is assault occasioning actual bodily harm, often referred to as ABH.

The *actus reus* has three elements:

- ▨ assault
- ▨ occasioning
- ▨ actual bodily harm.

The first element, assault, includes both assault and battery. The first essential part of the *actus reus* is to prove that there was an assault or battery as set out in the previous topic. This is usually not a problem, but can become one if the limitations on assault and battery are not taken into account.

The second element, occasioning, means bringing about the consequence. This is causation, which was discussed in Topic 3 of the previous chapter. One of the distinctions between s47 and the other offences under the

Offences Against the Person Act 1861 is the degree of harm caused. This aspect is vital, but sometimes is very straightforward and requires no discussion. Thus, if I hit someone with a stick and the victim is bruised where the stick hit them, there is no issue of causation and it would not need to be discussed further.

The third element is the key distinction. In **Chan-Fook (1994)** the court said that 'harm' means 'injury', and that 'actual' indicates that the injury should not be so trivial as to be 'wholly insignificant'. The court also said that 'bodily harm' is not limited to harm to the skin, flesh and bones of the victim. It includes the organs, nervous system and brain. It can include psychiatric injury, but it does not include emotions or states of mind that are not in themselves evidence of an identifiable medical condition. Where there is expert evidence of psychiatric injury, the injury is capable of being actual bodily harm.

The scope of the offence has been extended to include a person's hair in the case of **Smith (2006)**. In that case, the defendant cut off his former partner's pony-tail with a pair of scissors. The court said actual bodily harm is not limited to injury, and extends to hurt and damage so long as it is not trivial. It is not limited to the skin, flesh and bones but applies to all parts of the body, including the hair. It also seems that if paint or similar material were put on the hair, that could also be actual bodily harm.

In law there is a difference between battery, which is the slightest touching, and s47 actual bodily harm, where the injury is more than trivial. This means that bruising can fall within s47, but not s20 (see next topic) unless it is so severe as to be considered serious harm. In *Miller* (1954) it was stated as: 'Actual bodily harm includes any hurt or injury calculated to interfere with the health or comfort of the victim' and in *Chan-Fook* (1994) it was stated: 'The word "actual" indicates that the injury (although there is no need for it to be permanent) should not be so trivial as to be wholly insignificant.'

The *mens rea* of the offence is intention or recklessness as to assault or battery. This was made clear in the case of **Roberts (1971)**, where a girl who was a passenger in the defendant's car injured herself by jumping out of the car while it was moving. This is dealt with in more detail on p172 in Chapter 9. In that case, the defendant had the *mens rea* to cause a battery; the subsequent injuries were merely a consequence of his unlawful act, and so there was sufficient *actus reus* and *mens rea* for a conviction under s47. There need not be a separate *mens rea* for the actual bodily harm, so the requirements are exactly the same as those set out in Topic 3 of Chapter 9. This can be seen in **Savage (1991)**, the facts of which are set out in detail on the next page. In that case, the intention that was throwing of the beer was sufficient for the offence of battery; and as the result was something more serious, factually and legally caused by that act of the defendant, there is sufficient *mens rea* for the more serious offence under s47.

Key cases

Chan-Fook (1994): in this case, it was decided that 'harm' in s47 of the Offences Against the Person Act 1861 includes physical or psychiatric injury.

Smith (2006): in this case, it was decided that actual bodily harm can include all parts of the body including the hair.

Roberts (1971): this case is authority for the proposition that *mens rea* for s47 Offences Against the Person Act 1861 is intention or recklessness as to assault or battery.

Savage (1991): this case confirmed the *mens rea* for s47 Offences Against the Person Act 1861 is as set out in *Roberts* (1971) – that is, either intention or recklessness.

Study tips

Make sure you explain the elements of the offence and then apply the law to the facts to come to the conclusion.

Activity

Here is part of a scenario that relates to battery or actual bodily harm.

Zoe and Yasmin were both members of the same athletics club and competed in the same event. Zoe was furious that Yasmin was a better athlete than her. Zoe decided to injure Yasmin so she would not be able to compete in the next club championship. As they returned from a training run, Zoe tripped Yasmin, who fell down the steps leading to the changing room. Yasmin suffered minor bruising.

Practise applying the *actus reus* and *mens rea* of battery or actual bodily harm to the facts in the scenario, and decide which offence you think is more appropriate.

6 Section 20 of the Offences Against the Person Act 1861

Section 20 of the Offences Against the Person Act 1861 states that:

> Whosoever shall unlawfully and maliciously wound or inflict any **grievous bodily harm** upon any person, either with or without any weapon or instrument, shall be guilty of an offence …

This offence is triable either way – that is, in either the Magistrates' Court or the Crown Court. The correct name for this offence can be either malicious wounding or inflicting grievous bodily harm, often referred to as GBH, depending on the nature of the injuries to the victim.

The *actus reus* has three words/expressions that need explanation:

- unlawful
- wound
- grievous bodily harm.

The first element is that the act must be unlawful. In the context of s20, this usually means that there must have been no consent to the act. Thus, subject to age restrictions set out by statute, it is not an unlawful act to have a tattoo or a piercing. The issue is whether the consent is genuine; this is clearly of importance for those providing a tattoo or piercing service.

The second element is the definition of a wound. **Wounding** requires there to have been a break in the surface of the skin; this is both layers of the skin and is therefore seen to be an open wound, usually with blood loss. This can be seen in the case of **JCC v Eisenhower (1984)**, where the victim was hit by an airgun pellet in the eye. He suffered bruising and internal bleeding in the eye. The court decided there was no wounding, since there was no wound breaking the skin. Once the victim has bled, it will be a wound.

The third, separate, element is that of grievous bodily harm. This has been defined in various ways, such as 'really serious' harm. This means that it is a phrase that should be given its ordinary and natural meaning in the circumstances of the case. In the case of **Brown and Stratton (1998)**, the victim was a transsexual who went to the market stall where his father worked. The father felt humiliated to see his son as a woman and, along with his cousin, attacked the victim with a chair, causing a broken nose, three lost teeth and concussion. Together, these injuries were considered to be grievous bodily harm.

The *mens rea* required is set out in the definition above as 'maliciously'. Many older Acts of Parliament set out the *mens rea* of an offence as 'maliciously'. This was discussed in *Cunningham* (1957) and has been considered again in *Savage* (1991). The court transcript sets out the facts of *Savage* (1991) as:

> On 3 October 1989 in the Crown Court at Durham the appellant, Mrs Savage, was indicted and convicted on a single count of unlawful wounding contrary to s20 of the Offences Against the Person Act 1861, the particulars of the offence being that on 31 March 1989 she unlawfully and maliciously wounded Miss Beal. She was ordered to undertake 120 hours of community service. The victim, Miss Beal, was a former girlfriend of Mrs Savage's husband. There had been some bad

feeling between these two young women, although they had never previously met. On the evening of 31 March 1989 they were both in the same public house, but not together. Mrs Savage pushed her way through to the table where Miss Beal was sitting with some friends. She had in her hand a pint glass which was nearly full of beer. Having said 'Nice to meet you darling', she then threw the contents of the glass over Miss Beal. Unfortunately, not only was Miss Beal soaked by the beer, but, contrary to Mrs Savage's evidence, she must have let go of the glass, since it broke and a piece of it cut Miss Beal's wrist. The jury, by their verdict, concluded either that the appellant had deliberately thrown not only the beer but also the glass at Miss Beal or, alternatively, that while deliberately throwing the beer over Miss Beal, the glass had accidentally slipped from her grasp and it, or a piece of it, had struck Miss Beal's wrist, but with no intention that the glass should hit or cut Miss Beal.

It is clear that Mrs Savage did not intend to cause some harm to Miss Beal, but she had been reckless. The court confirmed that 'maliciously' meant intentionally or recklessly and she had been reckless.

Therefore, in order to prove that the defendant acted maliciously, it is sufficient to prove that he or she intended their act to result in some unlawful bodily harm to some other person, albeit of a minor nature, or was subjectively reckless as to the risk that his act might result in such harm.

There is no requirement that the intent or recklessness must be as to anything more than that some harm might occur. In other words, the defendant does not have to be reckless as to causing anything more than *some* harm.

The case of **Parmenter (1991)** went to appeal along with *Savage* (1991). In that case, the defendant had caused injury to his young baby by tossing him about in a way which would have been acceptable with an older child, but not with one so young. He did not realise that he might cause harm by this action. The House of Lords held that he could not be liable under s20 as he had not foreseen the risk of any harm. It was not necessary under s20 that he foresee the grievous bodily harm which must be caused, but the defendant must foresee that he might cause some harm.

7 Section 18 of the Offences Against the Person Act 1861

Section 18 of the Offences Against the Person Act 1861 provides:

> Whosoever shall unlawfully and maliciously by any means whatsoever wound or cause any grievous bodily harm to any person, with intent to do some grievous bodily harm to any person.

This offence is triable only on indictment, so will be tried at Crown Court only. The *actus reus* of the offence is either wounding or grievous bodily harm as set out in s20. The *mens rea* is that the defendant must be 'malicious' (see above, under s20) but in addition he or she must be proved to have had a further specific intent, in that it must have been the defendant's intention to do some grievous bodily harm to the victim. This can be seen in the case of **Belfon (1976)**. In this case, the

Study tips

Remember there are two aspects of this offence, grievous bodily harm and wounding. You should be able to distinguish between the two.

Activity

Here is part of a scenario that relates to s20.

John, a teacher, went to break up a fight, involving Ben, at the school gates. Ben left the fight with a knife in his hand. As he ran past John, Ben's knife slashed him in his side. This caused severe damage to one of John's kidneys.

Practise applying the *actus reus* and *mens rea* of s20 to the facts in the scenario, and decide whether wounding or grievous bodily harm is more appropriate.

Key cases

Parmenter (1991): in this case, the defendant could not be liable under s20 because he had not foreseen the risk of any harm.

Belfon (1976): it was decided in this case that for there to be a conviction under s18 of OAPA 1861, the defendant must have had the specific intent to do grievous bodily harm or resist arrest. Parmenter (1991): in this case, the defendant could not be liable under s20 because he had not foreseen the risk of any harm.

defendant had slashed the victim with a razor, causing severe wounds to his face and chest. The court said that, in order to establish the offence under s18, it was essential to prove the specific intent. References to the defendant foreseeing that such harm was likely to result or that he had been reckless as to whether such harm would result, would be insufficient.

Summary of offences

The table below summarises the three offences under the Offences Against the Person Act 1861.

Table 10.1 *The three offences under the Offences Against the Person Act 1861*

Offence	Actus reus	Mens rea
s47	Assault occasioning actual bodily harm	Intention or recklessness as to either putting the victim in fear of unlawful force or applying unlawful force
s20	Wounding or inflicting grievous bodily harm	Intention or recklessness as to some harm
s18	Wounding or inflicting grievous bodily harm	Specific intent to cause grievous bodily harm or resist arrest

Conclusion

The three offences under the Offences Against the Person Act 1861 and the common law offences of assault and battery have a number of overlapping essentials and a number of subtle differences. It is important to understand these, but also to recognise that the offences provide a framework for defining different levels of seriousness of harm that can occur.

Activity

1 Analyse the cases set out below and decide which offence or offences are disclosed by each set of facts, explaining and applying the relevant *actus reus* and *mens rea*:

a These are the facts of *Mowatt* (1968): the defendant attacked his victim by sitting astride him, raining a series of blows on his face, and lifting his head up and throwing it down again. The Court of Appeal upheld the defendant's conviction for inflicting grievous bodily harm, saying the offence required the defendant to have foreseen the risk of some physical harm.

b These are the facts of *Grimshaw* (1984): following an offensive remark in a pub, the woman defendant struck a man, her victim, who suffered serious eye injuries from the glass he had been holding.

Below is a summary of general points relating to your answer to application of the law to the problem scenario:

An exam question starting 'Discuss the criminal liability of ...' requires you to: select the relevant offence or offences; state the law for the *actus reus* and *mens rea* of the offence selected (you can refer back to other answers in your paper if you have explained the offence there); and then apply the law to the facts in the scenario, coming to a conclusion as to which offence or offences have been committed.

■ You should always refer to these offences by their correct names at least once in your answer. You can then use abbreviations to save time. This is best described in a manner similar to, 'The most appropriate offence in this case is assault occasioning actual bodily harm (ABH) under s47 of the Offences Against the Person Act 1861 (s47 OAPA).' If you then want to mention the expression 'assault occasioning actual bodily harm' again, you can say ABH. If you want to refer to another section of the Offences Against the Person Act 1861, you can refer to OAPA.

■ You only need to discuss causation in an answer where there is an issue relating to causation disclosed in the scenario.

■ In the examinations, you are expected to discuss and apply the law and not the charging standards. The only relevance they have is administrative.

You should now be able to:

■ describe, using authority, the offences in ss47, 20 and 18 of the Offences Against the Person Act 1861 and the common law offences of assault and battery

■ apply the law of the five offences to given situations.

---

11 The criminal courts: procedure and sentencing

Link

The basic structure for appeals is as set out in Figs 6.1 and 6.2 on p94 (Chapter 6).

Key terms

Summary offence: a criminal offence that can only be tried by a Magistrates' Court.

Either-way offence: an offence for which the accused may be tried by the Magistrates' Court or in the Crown Court, where the defendant will be tried by jury.

Indictable offence: a criminal offence that can only be tried by the Crown Court.

Arrest warrant: an order of the court for a person to be arrested in connection with a criminal offence.

Search warrant: an order of the court that permits the police to search premises to look for evidence in connection with a crime.

Bail: release of a defendant from custody until his or her next appearance in court.

1 Outline of criminal courts and appeal system

The criminal courts

Criminal offences are summary, indictable or either-way offences. **Summary offences** are relatively minor offences triable only in the Magistrates' Court. Most offences are summary – examples include common assault, threatening behaviour, and nearly all motoring offences. The maximum sentence is six months.

Either-way offences can, as the name suggests, be tried in either the Magistrates' Court or the Crown Court. The Crown Court tries the more serious offences, although most pre-trial matters are dealt with in the Magistrates' Court.

Indictable offences are the most serious offences, such as murder, rape or robbery, and are tried on indictment only. That means they must be tried in the Crown Court – before a judge, who rules on the law and passes sentence, and a jury of 12 members of the public, chosen at random, who decide on the facts if the defendant is guilty or not guilty.

There are different possible appeals from decisions in either the Magistrates' Court or the Crown Court.

The jurisdiction of the Magistrates' Court in criminal matters

The Magistrates' Court has the following criminal jurisdiction:

■ issuing **arrest** and **search warrants** – these will be applied for by the police, and are quite rare, as the police have such wide powers;

■ deciding on **bail** applications – when the defendant appears at court, it is the court's obligation to decide bail, not the police;

■ conducting sending-for-trial hearings – indictable-only offences such as murder are sent directly to the Crown Court for trial without the Magistrates' Court taking any action, apart from the decision on bail, public funding of the defendant, and the use of statements and exhibits. Where the case involves an either-way offence, the more usual form of committal for trial is committal without consideration of the evidence, known as a short committal. This means the defendant's case will be sent to Crown Court for trial without the magistrates making a detailed review of the evidence;

■ trying summary offences such as assault;

■ trying either-way offences that are to be tried summarily, such as theft.

The jurisdiction of the Crown Court

The Crown Court has the following jurisdiction:

■ trying indictable offences such as murder

■ trying either-way offences that are to be tried on indictment, such as theft

■ sentencing, where the case has been sent by the Magistrates' Court to the Crown Court for sentence

■ hearing appeals from the Magistrates' Court against conviction or sentence.

A Magistrates' Court summons looks like this:

Summons on Complaint (MCA 1980, ss 51, 52; MCR 1981, r98)

Magistrates' Court (Code   )

Date:

To the defendant:

Address:

You are hereby summoned to appear on
at   am/pm before the Magistrates' Court at
to answer the following complaint

Matter of complaint:

The Complainant is:

Address:

Date of complaint:

**Justice of the Peace
[Justices' Clerk]**

Fig. 11.1 *Magistrates' Court summons*

Table 11.1 *Summary of offences and the courts that hear them*

Offence	Type	Court
Assault	Summary	Magistrates'
Battery	Summary	Magistrates'
Section 47, Offences Against the Person Act 1861	Either-way	Magistrates'/Crown
Section 20, Offences Against the Person Act 1861	Either-way	Magistrates'/Crown
Section 18, Offences Against the Person Act 1861	Indictable	Crown

Classification of offences

Criminal offences are of three types: summary offences, either-way offences and indictable offences. Summary offences are the most minor offences, and can only be tried in the Magistrates' Court. The word 'summary' refers to the way in which the defendant is ordered to attend court, which is by a written order usually delivered by post.

Either-way offences, such as an offence under s47 of the Offences Against the Person Act 1861, can be tried in either the Magistrates' Court or the Crown Court. This is usually the defendant's choice but can be ordered by the magistrates. Indictable offences, such as under s18 of the Offences Against the Person Act 1861, are the most serious offences and can only be tried in the Crown Court.

The burden of proof in criminal offences

As has been seen, the general basis for imposing liability in criminal law is that the defendant must be proved by the prosecution to have committed the guilty act whilst having had the guilty state of mind for the crime with which he or she is charged. It is the responsibility of the prosecution to prove both of these elements of the offence to the satisfaction of the magistrates or jury. This is known as the **burden of proof**. The **standard of proof** is 'beyond reasonable doubt'. If this cannot be proved, the defendant will be acquitted. Active case management of criminal cases is designed to make cases proceed more quickly and lead to fewer cases collapsing. This means that the criminal justice system should become more cost-effective.

Activities

1. Review cases mentioned in the local paper and try to find out whether each is summary, either-way or indictable.

2. Choose one of the cases you have looked at in Activity 1 and outline the process that will have been followed, and note the courts where those processes took place.

You should now be able to:

- distinguish between different classifications of offence

- describe the burden of proof in a criminal case.

2 Outline procedure to trial

The principles behind the procedure

The main purpose behind the procedures is to ensure justice is done. The Criminal Procedure Rules 2011 set out the court rules. These rules are updated annually. The overriding objective is that criminal cases are dealt with justly. Dealing with a criminal case justly includes:

■ acquitting the innocent and convicting the guilty

■ dealing with the prosecution and the defence fairly

■ recognising the rights of a defendant, particularly those under Article 6 of the European Convention on Human Rights

■ respecting the interests of witnesses, victims and jurors and keeping them informed of the progress of the case

■ dealing with the case quickly and efficiently

■ ensuring that appropriate information is available to the court when bail and sentence are considered.

Starting a criminal case

The Magistrates' Court is the first court for all criminal cases. All prosecutions commenced by public prosecutors, including the police, are by charge administered either orally at a police station, or in writing. A written charge will be accompanied by a requisition requiring the defendant to appear in court on a specified date. These documents will be issued together by the police.

This procedure means criminal proceedings are no longer started by laying an information in a Magistrates' Court. The written charge and requisition are, in common with a summons, issued by post and are accordingly referred to collectively as a 'Postal Charge and Requisition'. This leads to the first hearing in the Magistrates' Court. The procedure depends on whether the person is accused of a summary offence, an either-way offence or an indictable offence.

All criminal cases involve aspects of:

■ bail

■ legal funding

■ plea

■ venue (the court involved)

■ the trial

■ sentencing of the guilty.

Types of criminal case and the procedure involved

Summary offences

These offences can only be dealt with by magistrates. On the first hearing date, the charge will be put and the defendant is required to enter a plea. Where a guilty plea has been entered, the magistrates may sentence there and then, or they may decide that a pre-sentence report should be obtained. If the latter, the case will be adjourned for this purpose for a period of three to four weeks.

If a not guilty plea is entered, either a trial date will be fixed there and then, or else the case will be adjourned for a period of weeks for a pre-trial review, at which a trial date will be fixed – taking into account the availability of all the witnesses and the likely length of the trial. Most trials will take place between two and three months after the pre-trial review. However, this will depend on how busy the particular court is, and the dates when all witnesses are available to attend. In the meantime, bail is renewed or reconsidered.

Either-way offences

These offences can be dealt with by either the Magistrates' Court or the Crown Court. Before any decision is made as to where the case will be tried, the magistrates will need to have an indication of the likely plea.

If a not guilty plea is indicated, the court clerk will ask the prosecutor to make representations regarding the complexity and/or seriousness of the offence(s), to enable the magistrates to decide whether they are able to deal with the case themselves. This is called 'mode of trial'.

If the magistrates decide that they are unable to deal with it, then the case will be sent to the Crown Court. Even if the magistrates decide that they can deal with the matter themselves, the defendant can still choose to go before a Crown Court.

If a guilty plea is indicated, then the magistrates will simply have to decide whether or not they have the power to impose an appropriate sentence. Where the case is to be sent to the Crown Court, then a decision as to bail will also have to be made.

Indictable offences

These offences can only be dealt with at the Crown Court. On the first hearing at the Magistrates' Court, the charge will be read out, but the defendant is not required to enter a plea until he appears in the Crown Court. The magistrates are then required to send the case to the Crown Court, and the later hearings will take place there. It is possible, however, to apply for bail at both the Magistrates' Court and the Crown Court.

Where a guilty plea has been entered in the Crown Court, the judge may sentence there and then, or he/she may decide that a pre-sentence report should be obtained and the case will be adjourned for this purpose for a period of about a month. Again, bail or remand will be considered.

Where a not guilty plea has been entered in the Crown Court, the case will be adjourned to a date for trial. Again, bail or remand will be considered.

Bail

Under the Bail Act 1976, there is a general right to bail. Bail can be granted by the courts or the police. Police bail can be given at a police station or under the Criminal Justice Act 2003, where police officers can grant bail following arrest at locations other than at a police station – a process known as 'street bail'. Court bail is dealt with through the Magistrates' Court.

Where bail is granted, the person is released from custody until the next date when they must attend court or the police station as stated on the bail notice. If bail is refused, this will be because the police or the court believes that the defendant, if released on bail, will abscond (not turn up to court), commit an offence, interfere with witnesses, or otherwise interfere with the criminal justice process. There are two types of bail: conditional bail and unconditional bail.

Her Majesty's Court Service
Bail Act 1976

Accused: .... Date of Birth: ....

Offences:..

DECISION OF THE COURT

☐ The accused is remanded to appear before the (..)

(above named) Youth/Magistrates' Court at........................... am/pm on ....

☐ The accused is committed/sent/transferred to the Crown Court at Cambridge/Peterborough/Northampton/

Norwich at.......................... am/pm on ....or such day, time and place as may be directed to the accused by the appropriate officer of the Crown Court

☐ The accused is granted unconditional bail

☐ The accused is granted bail/remanded to local authority accommodation subject to the following conditions:

Conditions to be complied with before release on bail | **Conditions to be complied with after release on bail**

☐ To provide Suret(y)(ies) ☐ To live and sleep each night at...

in the sum of £ ....(each) ☐ To be indoors at the above address between .... and ....

Continuous until (   ) ☐ To report to .... Police Station between .... and ....

☐ To surrender Passport to .... (daily) (on ....)

☐ To provide a security in the sum of ☐ Not to contact directly or indirectly ....

£ ....

Reasons to secure

☐ Surrender to custody

☐ That no offence is committed

☐ No interference with witnesses/ obstructing justice ☐ Not to go to ....

(except to attend court or see solicitor by prior arrangement)

☐ Accused makes him/herself available For the purpose of making report ☐ To keep any appointments with ....to enable enquiries or a report to be made

☐ The accused is refused bail and committed to custody/remanded to local authority accommodation

Exceptions to right on unconditional bail | **Reasons for applying exceptions**

All offences

☐ Serious nature of alleged offence (probable method of dealing with it)

☐ Arrested for absconding/breaching bail conditions ☐ Accused's character/antecedents/lack of community ties

☐ Custody for his/her protection/welfare ☐ Previous bail record

☐ Serving custodial sentence ☐ Strength of evidence

Imprisonable offences only ☐ Recent arrest and details not yet verified

☐ Believed would fail to surrender ☐ Behaviour towards/proximity to prosecution witness

☐ Believed would commit an offence ☐ No likelihood of co-operation for purposes of obtaining report

☐ Believed would interfere with witnesses or obstruct justice ☐ Already serving a custodial sentence imposed on ....

☐ Impracticable to complete inquiries or make report

☐ Impracticable to obtain sufficient information since arrest

☐ Either way/indictable offence committed on bail

Non-imprisonable offences only

☐ Previously failed to surrender and unlikely to surrender

S.23(5) CYPA 1969 The Court is of the opinion that only remand to remand centre/prison is adequate to protect public from serious harm

because ....

☐ I hereby certify that at the hearing today the Court heard full argument on an application for bail by or on behalf of the accused, before refusing the application and remanding the accused in custody under Section (5)(10)(18)(30) Magistrates' Courts Act 1980.

FAILURE TO SURRENDER TO BAIL OR COMPLY WITH YOUR BAIL CONDITIONS CAN RESULT IN YOUR ARREST

FAILURE TO SURRENDER TO BAIL IS AN OFFENCE PUNISHABLE BY IMPRISONMENT AND/OR FINE

Date: ....

(Clerk of the Court present during the proceedings)

1. White Copy - Register   2. Yellow Copy - Defendant   3. Blue Copy - CPS   4. Pink Copy - Court File

Fig. 11.2 *Bail notice*

Conditional bail

The police and courts can impose any requirements which are necessary to make sure that defendants attend court and do not commit offences or interfere with witnesses whilst on bail. Recommended bail conditions and the reasons for such conditions should be specific and justifiable. The conditions must be likely to be effective and capable of being enforced.

Bail conditions can be imposed before release on bail. These will be either surety, where the defendant or another person may be required to pay a sum of money up to that amount if the defendant does not attend the police station or court as required; or security, which is the same but secured on an asset such as a house. The security may be forfeited if bail is broken. Additionally, the defendant may have to surrender his or her passport.

Post-release conditions may also be imposed so that the defendant is likely to attend, and also is less likely to re-offend or interfere with witnesses. These conditions can include:

■ reporting to the police at given times
■ living at a stated address, which might be the defendant's home, the home of a relative away from the scene of the offence, or in a bail hostel
■ staying away from certain people or places
■ a curfew for which the court (but not the police) can order an electronic tag to be used.

If a defendant is reported or believed to have breached a bail condition, he can be arrested and brought before the Magistrates' Court, and may lose the right to bail and be placed on remand. Failing to appear at court as required is a criminal offence, and a defendant can also be prosecuted for this offence.

Unconditional bail

If the police or court think that a defendant is unlikely to commit further offences, will attend court when required and will not interfere with the justice process, he or she will usually be released on unconditional bail.

Legal funding and duty solicitors

Legal funding

There are three ways in which a person could be helped if he or she needs to be represented in court for a criminal offence:

■ A Representation Order – this covers representation by a solicitor and, if necessary, by a barrister in criminal cases. To qualify for a Representation Order in the Magistrates' Court, certain financial conditions must be met. These conditions are detailed in Unit 1B, Chapter 7 (p127). If the defendant meets the financial conditions, there is usually help with representation in a criminal case in the Magistrates' Court, as long as it is in the interests of justice that there is legal representation. This might be, for example, if the defendant is likely to go to prison or lose his or her job if convicted. In the Crown Court, it will automatically be in the interests of justice to be legally represented.
■ Advocacy Assistance – this covers the costs of a solicitor preparing your case, and initial representation in certain cases.
■ Other types of legal help, such as from motoring organisations.

Duty solicitors

A duty solicitor is a qualified criminal defence solicitor. He or she will either work directly for a firm, or will be self-employed. Duty solicitors are completely independent of the police and the courts. Each duty solicitor takes turns on a rota in up to six different local justice areas, depending upon where his or her office is based. These rotas cover police stations within those areas 24 hours a day, and courts within those areas Monday to Saturday throughout the year. It is the job of a duty solicitor to represent those people who do not have, or who have not requested, a specific solicitor.

Duty solicitors are paid by the Legal Services Commission for all cases they deal with, so their advice and representation is free for defendants.

Activities

1. Make a list of bail conditions that have been reported in the newspapers or that you have seen imposed on defendants in court. Decide why the bail was conditional or unconditional in each case, and, where conditional, why the conditions were imposed.

2. Jack was arrested after a person was attacked by a group of people outside a nightclub. The victim suffered severe injuries and is still critically ill. Jack was one of 15 people who were interviewed about the attack, but only Jack and two others were arrested and charged with an offence. The others are likely to be witnesses who will help confirm the images captured on CCTV. Jack is not known by the police to be a man of violence, but one of those arrested and charged has a history of violent attacks. Jack had been in the pub in the company of the other two charged and knows many of the witnesses. Consider the criminal process that will be followed in Jack's case, and the factors that will be taken into account in deciding whether Jack will be granted bail or not – and if so, what conditions might be imposed.

You should now be able to:

- describe the procedure from charging the accused to the start of the trial
- apply this procedure to a given situation.

3 Sentencing

The aims of sentencing

Once the defendant has been found guilty either by the magistrates or the jury, the court must decide on sentence. There is an underlying concept that justice requires consistency in sentencing. This principle means that similar crimes committed in similar circumstances by offenders whose circumstances are similar should be given similar sentences. This is important not only to the offender, but also to those directly affected by the crime and to the public, if there is to be public confidence in the criminal justice system.

When an offender is convicted following a trial or guilty plea, the court has a range of sentencing options available. The range of sentences available is discussed later on in this book. The range of sentences depends on the type, the seriousness and the circumstances of the crime,

In this topic you will learn how to:

- describe the aims of sentencing
- state and describe the different sentences available to a court in sentencing an adult offender
- explain what is meant by aggravating and mitigating factors
- apply the above to a given situation.

and the maximum penalty available by law. The judge or magistrates have a number of guidelines that are designed to help them make a decision. These guidelines, and the potential sentences available, can be seen in the light of the various traditional theories as to the purpose of a sentence. These are:

■ retribution
■ deterrence
■ prevention
■ rehabilitation.

The Criminal Justice Act 2003, s142, requires judges and magistrates dealing with an offender in respect of his or her offence to have regard to the following purposes of sentencing:

■ the punishment of offenders
■ the reduction of crime (including its reduction by deterrence)
■ the reform and rehabilitation of offenders
■ the protection of the public
■ the making of reparation by offenders to persons affected by their offences.

These follow the traditional principles, which will now be examined in turn.

Retribution

Retribution is based on the idea of revenge. This can be seen in the tabloid press demanding extreme sentences for notorious offenders that have come to the public eye – for example, a suspected child molester. In some ways, all punishment has this effect, as many individuals – and, often, society as a whole – feel better that someone has gone to prison for a long time. Retribution is one aspect of the view that a person who commits a serious crime such as murder should be executed. However, 'To take a life when a life has been lost is revenge, it is not justice': this quotation is attributed to Archbishop Desmond Tutu. Sometimes retribution may be part of the idea behind punishment, but it is not always the major principle behind the sentence.

The Criminal Justice Act 2003 starts with the principle of punishment and adds in the idea of reparation, which includes the compensation of victims through, for example, paying for damage caused in a case involving vandalism.

Deterrence

Deterrence can be an individual deterrent, where the sentence is designed to make the offender not wish to re-offend for fear of suffering the same or worse fate. An experiment with young offenders took place in the 1990s: a number of young offenders, who were likely to go to prison if they re-offended, were given a tour of an adult prison by serving prisoners. The result was a much lower than average reconviction rate, and for many it was seen as a turning point in their lives. There can also be a general deterrence, whereby the prospect of the potential punishment dissuades most people from offending. If the Government wanted to stop people parking illegally, it could make the offence a strict liability offence punishable by a minimum of ten years in prison. It is also thought that the likelihood of being caught is also a major deterrent, and that therefore better policing will help to reduce crime.

Prevention of crime

Prevention of crime works to protect the public by, for example, putting offenders in prison so they cannot re-offend during that time. It could be said that all sentences aim to prevent crime, by demonstrating the bad effect of conviction. However, it could also be argued that a criminal conviction tends to lead to other convictions, as employers are less willing to employ an ex-offender.

Rehabilitation

Rehabilitation involves offering offenders help to overcome problems that they face, thereby attempting to make it easier to avoid future offending. It can also be seen as 'curing' offenders. Much of rehabilitation is concerned with providing offenders with the skills to cope with life, and can be reflected in methods such as attendance of an anger-management course or driver retraining. This follows from having an individual sentence rather than a fixed tariff.

Types of sentence available

Sentences can be classified as:

- custodial (a sentence of imprisonment)
- community (for example, a community rehabilitation order)
- financial (a fine)
- discharge (the offender is found guilty but no further action is taken)
- other (for example, a driving ban).

Criminal offences can have different levels of seriousness – for example, non-fatal offences could be anything from scaring someone to nearly killing them. It is important to ensure that courts are consistent in their approach to sentencing. Sentencing guidelines, prepared by the Sentencing Council, set out a decision-making process for all magistrates and judges to follow.

Sentencing guidelines help judges and magistrates decide the appropriate sentence for a criminal offence. The sentence imposed on an offender should reflect their crime and be proportionate to the seriousness of the offence. There are sentencing guidelines for most offences. These guidlines set out sentence ranges to reflect different levels of seriousness; within each range, there is a starting point for the sentence. The guidelines also provide guidance on factors that the court should take into account, when deciding whether a more or less severe sentence should be imposed.

Custodial sentences

A **custodial sentence** is the most serious sentence, and is reserved for the most serious crimes. A custodial sentence can be imposed if the offence is so serious that neither a fine alone nor a community sentence can be justified for the offence. The sentence imposed by the court represents the maximum amount of time that the offender will remain in prison.

Despite these high-level criteria, the prison population in England and Wales is one of the highest in Europe, and continues to rise. A prison sentence can be suspended, which means that the prison sentence will not take effect unless there is a subsequent offence within a given period.

Key terms

Rehabilitation: this is the notion that the offender will be 'cured' of his criminal tendency and that there will be a restoration of, or improvement in, his ability to perform and function in society.

Custodial sentence: this is a sentence of imprisonment, which might be immediate or suspended (able to be implemented later if necessary).

Community sentences

Minor crimes are often dealt with by giving the offender a community sentence. While these sentences offer a suitable punishment, they concentrate on making sure that the person does not commit more offences.

www.direct.gov.uk

This government statement shows the purposes behind **community sentences** which the court can tailor-make for the individual. The idea is to combine punishment with changing the offender's behaviour and making amends. The range of options includes:

- compulsory (unpaid) work, so that something is put back into the community; here, the offender works for up to 300 hours on local community projects such as cleaning up graffiti under a local payback scheme
- programmes aimed at changing offending behaviour, such as anger management
- curfew, so that the offender must be at home between certain times such as 21.00–06.00; the offender must stay indoors, usually at their home, for the curfew period – a tag, worn on the ankle or wrist, notifies monitoring services if the offender is absent during the curfew hours
- exclusion from certain areas for a period of up to two years; there may be electronic monitoring of this too, via a tag
- residence requirement, where the offender must reside at a place specified – for example, an approved hostel or private address
- drug treatment and testing
- alcohol treatment for offenders who are alcohol-dependent and who might benefit from reducing or eliminating their dependency
- supervision, where the offender is required to attend appointments with an Offender Manager from the Probation Service; the subject of the supervision and the frequency of contact will be specified in a sentence plan
- attendance; the court can direct the offender to spend a total of between 12 and 36 hours at an attendance centre, on a number of occasions over a set period of time – here, the offender addresses their offending behaviour with others in a group; this also restricts the defendant's leisure time at the weekend, and can be used to prevent football hooligans attending matches, for example.

Financial sentences

A criminal fine is a simple financial penalty imposed on the defendant. A fine can be a fixed penalty, as with a fixed penalty speeding fine, or it can be given subject to a statutory maximum for the offence. A fine is the court's most frequently imposed penalty. Magistrates can impose a maximum fine of £5000, assuming that this sum is less than the statutory maximum for that offence.

Compensation orders are sometimes made. Some would argue that a compensation order is a financial penalty, although it is payable to the victim of the crime rather than the State and is designed to repay, for example, damage caused to the victim's property.

Discharge

There are two types of **discharge** that can form the court's sentence. The first is an absolute discharge, which is where the court takes no further action against an offender, but the offender's discharge will appear on his criminal record. The second type is a conditional discharge, which is where a defendant is convicted without sentence on condition that he does not re-offend within a specified period of time. This period can be between six months and two years. If another offence is committed during this time, the court can look at the old offence as well as the new one in deciding on the sentence to impose.

Other sentences

There are other sentences, such as a driving ban, that can be imposed. None of these is within the scope of the AQA Law 2 specification.

How the court goes about selecting a sentence

Once a defendant has been found guilty, the court's function is to impose the appropriate sentence. It is at this stage that the defendant's previous convictions will be made available, and it is likely that a pre-sentence report will be required for more serious offences. This report is prepared by the Probation Service. The Probation Service will be told how serious they consider the offence to be, and the purpose of the sentence. This might be related to any of the purposes of sentencing.

To compile the report, an officer from the Probation Service will interview the defendant. Usually this will be at the probation office, on a different day from the court hearing. The court will tell the Probation Service when it wishes to receive the report. The defendant will be either remanded in custody or be bailed.

A pre-sentence report will look at the reasons why the person committed the offence, their attitude to the offence and to any victims, and any other factors that affect their blameworthiness. These are aggravating and mitigating factors. The pre-sentence report will also include an assessment of the offender's risk of harm and risk of reconviction.

A judge or magistrate will use sentencing guidelines, which set out the process they should follow and the factors they should consider, to work out the appropriate sentence.

Factors include:

- the seriousness of the offence – looking at the harm caused, or intended to be caused, and the level of involvement and blameworthiness of the offender
- the offender's previous convictions
- aggravating factors – these are factors which may suggest that a higher sentence is appropriate, such as targeting a particularly vulnerable victim, or a racial or otherwise discrimatory motivation
- mitigating factors – these are factors which may suggest that a lower sentence is appropriate, such as having been provoked and showing immediate remorse
- personal mitigation – these are factors relating to the offender, such as having had no previous history of offending
- whether the offender pleaded guilty – admitting guilt would usually result in a lesser sentence

Key terms

Discharge: this is a sentence where the offender is found guilty of the offence, and the conviction appears on his or her criminal record. It may be absolute or conditional.

Study tips

If you visit a court, look out for the lawyers referring to mitigating and aggravating factors in their address to the court before the sentence is passed.

Fig. 11.3 *The magistrate reads out pronouncement cards, with the details for the case filled out, to announce the sentence in court*

1

Sentencing

Custodial sentence

We are sending you to [prison] [a young offender institution] for a total period of
.... days/weeks/months.

- [State each offence.
- State the term of custody.
- State whether concurrent or consecutive.]

[either]

The offence(s) is/are so serious that only a custodial sentence can be justified.
Our reasons are:
[State your reasons based on the following list:

- The aggravating or mitigating circumstances that determine the level of culpability and degree of harm caused (offence).
- Offender's personal mitigation (offender).
- Purpose(s) of sentence – punishment, reduction of crime, reform and rehabilitation, protection of the public, reparation.

SENTENCING 7

- The sentencing guidelines and the pre-sentence report.]

[or]

There has been a wilful and persistent failure to comply with your community order.

[or]

You have refused to agree to the making of a ....requirement on a community order.

[Where appropriate.] **We have reduced your sentence because you pleaded guilty. If you had not, it would have been ....**

........days will count towards this sentence.
[If the defendant has been remanded in custody or on a tagged curfew for more than 9 hours a day, your legal adviser will calculate the number of days to be taken into account. Where full entitlement has not been counted, reasons must be given.]

You will normally be released once you have served half your sentence. But if you commit an offence between your release and the end of your sentence, you can be returned to custody to serve the sentence in full and any sentence for the new offence(s).

Do you understand?

[Consider any ancillary orders.]

SENTENCING 8

www.sentencingcouncil.judiciary.gov.uk

- totality – in other words, where an offender is being sentenced for more than one offence

- the relevant law, including the maximum sentence.

These factors may be relevant in determining the type of sentence as well as the sentence length, requirements or amount. Different offenders may not be given the same sentence for the same type of crime depending on the circumstances of the crime and the offender. The factors taken into account in each case will vary depending upon the facts of each individual case.

Fig. 11.4 *Information about sentencing for ABH*

www.sentencingcouncil.judiciary.gov.uk

1 Using the scenario in Topic 2, Activity 2 (p199), and assuming that the injuries turned out to be less severe, Jack is convicted of assault occasioning actual bodily harm. Using the guidance in Fig. 11.3 on p204 and Fig. 6.3 on p100 (Chapter 6), consider what sentence might be imposed on Jack.

2 Look at each of the potential sentences available and consider which sentencing aim or aims is reflected.

■ Study tips

When applying the principles of sentencing, make sure you use the evidence given in the scenario.

You should now be able to:

■ understand the way in which a court sentences an offender

■ apply the principles of sentencing to a given situation.

Practice questions

Unit 2A questions in the AQA exam

In the Unit 2 examination paper, you must answer all the questions from Unit 2A (Criminal Law) and all the questions from either Unit 2B (Tort) or Unit 2C (Contract Law).

Each section is represented by one question, which has six parts. You must answer all parts of the question. Each part is worth up to 10 marks; the entire question is worth 45 marks, plus 2 marks for Assessment Objective 3.

Some of the questions test your knowledge and understanding, and some test application of the law to the scenario that introduces the question. Some are a mixture of knowledge, understanding and application. There is a clear distinction on the examination paper. Theory-only questions appear directly underneath the scenario; mixed theory and application questions are preceded by a specific instruction to refer to the scenario.

Example question 1 (AQA, June 2012)

This question is taken from a past exam paper. You must answer all six parts of this question.

> Ahmed was sitting in his house when a brick, thrown by Bryan, crashed through his window. Ahmed feared he was about to be attacked by Bryan's gang, which was noted for racist attacks. In a panic, Ahmed rushed out of his house and jumped into his van. He raced off to the police station and reversed wildly into a parking space. He failed to notice he had trapped Carl behind the van. When he did realise what he had done, he decided to leave Carl trapped, as he thought Carl was one of Bryan's gang. As a result, Carl suffered permanent damage to his spine. If he had been released immediately, his injuries would have been far less severe.

Actus reus usually depends on proof of an act, causation and a criminal consequence. *Mens rea* is also required for criminal liability, but there is an exception where the offence is one of strict liability.

1. Explain the meaning of causation in criminal law.   *(7 marks)*

2. Explain the meaning of the term '*mens rea*' in criminal law.   *(7 marks)*

   Refer to the scenario when answering the remaining questions in this section.

3. Ignoring liability for any property offences, discuss the criminal liability of Bryan for the incident with the brick.   *(8 + 2 marks for AO3)*

4. Outline the principle of coincidence of *actus reus* and *mens rea* (the contemporaneity rule). Briefly discuss the criminal liability of Ahmed for the serious injury to Carl's spine.   *(10 marks)*

5. Outline the procedure, up to the start of the trial, that would be followed if Bryan were charged with a summary offence. *(5 marks)*

6. Assuming Bryan has been convicted of an offence and is due for sentencing, outline the following:

   ■ the factors that the court would take into account when considering sentence

   ■ the range of sentences available to the court. *(8 marks)*

■ Example question 2 (AQA, January 2011)

This question is taken from another past exam paper. You must answer all six parts of this question.

> *Alan believed that Bhu, a fellow student, had stolen his mobile phone. Alan saw Bhu at college, went up to her and said, "We sort out thieves like you". As Bhu hurried away in a panic, Alan's friend, Carol, sprayed Bhu with red paint. A small amount of paint went into Bhu's eyes. She was taken to hospital where her eyes were treated to remove the paint. As she went home, and just before her sight was fully recovered, she tripped up a kerb and fractured her skull.*

Actus reus usually depends on proof of a voluntary act or an omission. *Mens rea* is also required for criminal liability, but there is an exception where the offence is one of strict liability.

1. Explain how there can be criminal liability for an omission. *(7 marks)*

2. What is strict liability? Outline the reasons for having offences of strict liability. *(7 marks)*

> Refer to the scenario when answering the remaining questions in this section.

3. Discuss Alan's criminal liability for his statement to Bhu, 'We sort out thieves like you'. *(8 marks)*

4. Discuss the criminal liability of Carol for the eye injury suffered by Bhu. *(8 marks)*

5. Outline the rules on causation, and briefly discuss whether Carol caused Bhu's fractured skull. *(10 marks +2 marks for AO3)*

6. Outline the procedure that would be followed before Alan's trial if he was charged with a summary offence. *(5 marks)*

Introduction

Chapters in this section:

Unit 2A together with Unit 2B or Unit 2C constitute Unit 2 of the AS specification. Unit 2A is about Criminal Law and is compulsory. Unit 2B is about the Law of Tort and Unit 2C is about the Law of Contract. You must answer the questions on either Unit 2B or 2C, but not both, as well as the questions on Unit 2A. You can choose to study either Unit 2B or Unit 2C in addition to Unit 2A.

The Unit 2 examination paper constitutes 50 per cent of the overall marks for the AS qualification, and 25 per cent of the overall marks for the A2 qualification. The examination is of 1.5 hours duration. You must answer all the questions from Unit 2A and all the questions from either Unit 2B or Unit 2C. There is no choice of question in any of the sections.

The questions on each section are worth 45 marks each, plus 2 marks for Assessment Objective 3. Each question is divided into six parts, each part being worth up to 10 marks. You must answer all parts of the question. Each section stands alone, and there is no overlap between them.

The Tort section is covered by Chapters 12 to 13 of this book. Some of the questions test your knowledge and understanding, and some test application of the law to the scenario that introduces the question. Some are a mixture of knowledge, understanding and application. There is a clear distinction on the examination paper.

Questions require essay-style answers. You should aim to include: correct identification of the issues raised by the question; sound explanation of each of the points; and relevant illustration. Illustration may be in many forms – for example, legislation, cases, research, statistics, and material from the media. Study tips are provided throughout each topic.

Liability in negligence

1 Introduction to liability in negligence

Negligence is an area of the law of tort. A tort, from the French word 'tort', which means wrong, is a civil wrong other than a breach of contract or a breach of trust. The purpose of the law of tort is to provide remedies when one person has been affected by another's acts or omissions and the law considers that a remedy should be available. The most usual remedy is damages (financial compensation), and that is the remedy being considered in this section.

Negligence requires three elements:

- a duty of care being owed to the claimant by the defendant
- that duty of care being broken, as the required standard of care has not been reached by the defendant
- that broken duty must have caused the loss complained of, and the loss must not be too remote a consequence.

These three elements are known as duty, breach and damage.

Civil law

Civil law is concerned with settling disputes between individuals, individuals' businesses and, sometimes, the Government. The key difference between civil and criminal law is that civil law is primarily designed to settle disputes, not punish wrongdoing. There are many areas of civil law, including the law of tort. Negligence is the one area of the law of tort that is to be studied in the AQA AS Law specification.

A civil case is started by the person who has suffered loss (the claimant) as the result of a wrong which only directly affects him or her. A typical negligence case is a claim for losses and injuries resulting from a car crash. The claim requires proof that the defendant was negligent. The claimant's usual remedy is financial compensation, known as damages. Thus, a successful claim in negligence against a driver who caused a car crash will result in damages paid to the claimant to cover his financial losses and to compensate for his injuries. There are other remedies available in the law of tort, but these are not relevant to the material in these chapters.

The civil process

The civil process is the procedure by which a claim makes its way through the court system, so that the court can decide whether the claim will succeed and, if so, what amount of damages should be awarded. The court processes and eventual award of damages can be a long and complicated business for both the claimant and the defendant, but the process is designed to keep delay to the minimum through case management. Once a person is advised that they are likely to have a good claim in negligence, the major consideration is to obtain sufficient evidence of the losses suffered. This is straightforward for a damaged car: it is the cost of repairs, or the market value of the vehicle if it is written off. Incidental costs such as renting an alternative vehicle whilst the car is being repaired also have to be proved, but again these are straightforward. Personal injuries are much more difficult to calculate, as is loss of future earnings.

Eventually, the claimant may have to go to court for some or all of the issues to be tried and, if the claim is successful, to calculate their award of damages. The length and complexity of the process depends on the nature of the injuries, whether the evidence is clear, and whether and how the defendant makes his defence and tries to establish that he has not been negligent. There are rules of procedure that prescribe the court in which the case will be heard and the framework for deciding the case. For many reasons, such as the length of time without compensation, the stress of a court case and the question of cost (especially as many claims are the subject of insurance, and the insurance companies have to take into account their overall financial status), most negligence cases are settled out of court.

Fig. 12.1 *The civil process*

There are rules of **civil evidence** that set out how the facts must be proved and the degree of certainty that is required.

The burden of proof is the obligation on a party to establish the facts in issue in a case to the required degree of certainty (the standard of proof) in order to prove their case. In a civil trial, the burden is upon the claimant to prove the liability of the defendant. The standard of proof is on a **balance of probabilities**. This is a lower standard of proof than in criminal cases, which is beyond reasonable doubt. The balance of probabilities has been defined as 'more likely than not' or '51 per cent'. Effectively, this is just a matter of convincing the judge that the claimant is right in his version of events. This is most likely to be relevant in assessing future losses or establishing that a particular loss was the result of the negligent act. Juries are not used in negligence trials, which take place in the County Court or High Court Queen's Bench Division.

Negligence

If a person is to succeed in a negligence case, there must be proof that the act of the defendant falls within the relevant definitions of what must be proved for a successful claim in negligence. There are three parts to any claim in negligence that must be proved:

- that a duty of care was owed by the defendant to the claimant
- that the defendant broke that duty of care; this means his act was not performed to the standard the law requires, which is that of the reasonable man
- that the broken duty caused the loss complained of, and that the law recognises that the loss is not too remote from the act.

So far as the material in this book is concerned, all the authorities for the law come from decided cases. This means that the law has been made by judges and has developed over the years. It is important that the latest interpretations of the law are used, although the historical background can sometimes be useful in explaining why today's law is as it is. Some areas of negligence have their basis in an Act of Parliament, but those areas are not part of the specification at AS.

Key terms

Civil evidence: the rules that set out how the facts of a civil case must be proved.

Balance of probabilities: the standard of proof in a civil case. It means that the claimant must prove his or her case is more likely than not to be as they presented it.

Study tips

Make sure you remember that all three elements – duty, breach and damage – must be proved before a claim for negligence can succeed.

How case law is used in answers to typical questions in AQA Unit 2

The examination paper for Unit 2 is divided into three sections. As we have seen, Unit 2A focuses on criminal law, and is compulsory. The choice of area of study of civil law is between tort and contract. Unit 2B is on the law of tort and, as in the other sections, all questions within it must be answered. The tort question starts with a short scenario that sets the scene and is the basis of your discussions for some of the following questions. A scenario, taken from the sample paper, is:

> Having bought herself a cheap sail board, Olga decided to teach herself to windsurf on a lake near her home. After several hours' practice, she began to tire and decided to have one last attempt at crossing the lake. She failed to notice Petra, who was fishing from a boat on the lake. Unfortunately, Olga crashed into the boat, which capsized, and Petra lost her fishing equipment, worth £3000, in the lake.

The questions are of two general types:

Theory-only questions

Theory-only questions require an explanation of terms used, but no reference to the facts given in the scenario.

A typical question is:

Negligence requires proof of duty, breach and damage. Explain how the law decides whether a duty of care is owed in negligence.

(8 marks)

Application questions

Application questions require you to select the appropriate law or principles of damages, and apply the law to the facts given in the scenario. You should assume that the facts as stated in the scenario can be proved.

A typical question (using the scenario of Olga and Petra) is:

Discuss whether Olga owed a duty of care to Petra.

(8 marks + 2 marks for AO3)

Note that this question also includes some marks for Assessment Objective 3 (written communication). These marks are usually awarded in the first questions that are not theory-only in each section of the paper.

You should now be able to:

- understand the role of the civil law
- understand the concept of negligence
- understand how to use authority in answering questions on negligence.

Link

For a diagram of how to structure a content of theory answer, see Fig 9.3 on page 167 (Chapter 9).

Link

For a diagram of how to structure a content of application answer, see Fig. 9.4 on page 167.

Activities

1. Think about your family and friends and remember accidents that have befallen them. Consider whether it is likely that someone had been negligent in the accident. Do you think one person was to blame?

2. Think about things you do every day, such as driving a car, riding a bike or playing football. What do you do to avoid being negligent?

2 The duty of care

The history of the test for a duty of care

The law of negligence has been developing for many years. The famous definition of negligence is 'the omission to do something which a reasonable man, guided upon those considerations which ordinarily regulate the conduct of human affairs, would do, or doing something which a prudent and reasonable man would not do'. This is the definition given by Baron Alderson in **Blyth v Birmingham Waterworks Co. (1856)**.

This definition is still relevant today, as it puts the idea of **the reasonable man** in the centre of negligence. What the reasonable man would do is to try to fulfil his duties to other people. This would include a duty of care owed to others. A duty of care is simply a duty to take care of others or to look out for them. The legal definition is a little more complex, as will be seen later. The law has struggled to define what a duty of care is, or at least how to decide the circumstances in which a duty of care is owed by one person to another. The famous case of **Donoghue v Stevenson (1932)** was an attempt to do this.

The facts of *Donoghue v Stevenson (1932)* were that Mrs Donoghue and her friend went to the Wellmeadow Café, Paisley, where her friend purchased ice cream, and ginger beer which, as was the fashion at the time, was to be poured over the ice cream as an iced drink. The ginger beer was contained in an opaque bottle, which meant that the contents could not be seen clearly. Mrs Donoghue drank some of the ginger beer. When the remaining ginger beer was poured into her glass, the decomposed remains of a snail came out of the bottle. This appalled Mrs Donoghue, and she became ill as a result of the sight and the ginger beer she had already drunk.

Mrs Donoghue had no direct claim against the manufacturer or the shopkeeper based on contract, because she did not buy the ginger beer. Mrs Donoghue's friend could claim against the café in contract, but had not suffered any loss apart from the fact that she had bought defective goods; she could get her money back, but nothing for Mrs Donoghue's illness. Therefore, Mrs Donoghue claimed damages against the manufacturer, Stevenson. Her claim was for the resulting shock and stomach upset, which she claimed was caused by drinking the ginger beer.

The court had to decide whether her claim against the manufacturer of the ginger beer could succeed. This led to Lord Atkin's famous statement:

> The rule that you are to love your neighbour becomes in law, you must not injure your neighbour; and the lawyer's question, 'Who is my neighbour?' receives a restricted reply. You must take reasonable care to avoid acts or omissions which you can reasonably foresee would be likely to injure your neighbour. Who, then, in law is my neighbour? The answer seems to be: persons who are so closely and directly affected by my act that I ought reasonably to have them in contemplation as being so affected when I am directing my mind to the acts or omissions which are called in question.

The neighbour principle was based on the command in the Bible to 'love thy neighbour', and Lord Atkin used that as his starting point for his attempt to set out a general principle that he could then apply to Mrs Donoghue's case. This made it clear that there could be liability without

In this topic you will learn how to:

- define a duty of care in terms of the neighbour principle

- state the three-part Caparo test for the existence of a duty of care

- explain each part of the Caparo test by reference to decided cases

- apply the Caparo test to a given situation.

Key cases

Blyth v Birmingham Waterworks Co. (1856): this case defined the meaning of the term 'negligence' in the famous statement by Baron Alderson.

Donoghue v Stevenson (1932): this famous case set out the neighbour principle in the law of negligence. This principle is the foundation of the modern law.

Key terms

The reasonable man: the expression used to describe the basis of the law of negligence: the typical ordinary person.

a contract, and gave the opportunity for the law to develop the rules of negligence. The law has developed these rules to the extent that there are a number of different areas of negligence that have developed in different ways. These are looked at in detail in A2 Law. The AS specification looks at the general concept of negligence only in relation to liability for physical damage and personal injury.

Donoghue v *Stevenson* (1932) was the first successful attempt to set out a general principle with respect to the concept of the duty of care. The principle set out was satisfactory, but as the world became increasingly complex and increasingly willing to take legal action, the test was seen to be too simple. This led to many other attempts to make a general test for the existence of a duty of care, but these, too, were unsatisfactory in various ways. The latest test comes from the case of **Caparo v Dickman (1990)**.

The three-part test in *Caparo* v *Dickman*

The case of *Caparo* v *Dickman* (1990) involved a claim by an investor who had lost money in a company. The investor claimed against the auditors of the company, as the auditors had produced inaccurate accounts. The court decided that the law should develop new categories of negligence incrementally and by analogy with established categories of negligence. This means that the court would first look at existing precedents, and if none could be found or adapted to fit the case in question, then, and only then, would a general test be applied to see whether a duty of care should exist.

The general test set in *Caparo* v *Dickman* (1990) requires three elements to be demonstrated:

- it was reasonably foreseeable that a person in the claimant's position would be injured
- there was sufficient proximity between the parties
- it is fair, just and reasonable to impose liability on the defendant.

Fig. 12.2 *Summary of three-part test from* Caparo v Dickman

All parts of the test must be satisfied if there is to be a duty of care owed by the defendant to the claimant.

Each part of the test must be looked at in turn.

The first part – foreseeability

This is an objective test: would a reasonable person in the defendant's position have foreseen that someone in the claimant's position might be injured? In *Donoghue* v *Stevenson* (1932) it can be seen that failing to stop a snail getting into a bottle will affect the consumer (Mrs Donoghue) of the contents. This is a consequence of producing food that has foreign bodies in it, and a reasonable person in the defendant's position (a soft-drink manufacturer) would foresee that the claimant (a consumer) might be injured.

It would equally apply, by analogy, to the caterpillar in the tin of peas in *Smedleys* v *Breed* (1974), noted in Chapter 9 (p181). So, if the consumer of the peas had not seen the caterpillar and had eaten it and become ill as a result, that person would have had a similar claim to Mrs Donoghue.

In fact, as we have seen, criminal action was taken against the manufacturer and, presumably, the consumer was unaffected by the caterpillar and got a refund from Smedleys.

A good example of the first part of the test can be seen in the case of **Kent v Griffiths (2000)**. In that case, it was decided that the ambulance service owed a duty of care to a member of the public on whose behalf a 999 call had been made. This was because it was reasonably foreseeable that a person in the claimant's position (an injured or sick person waiting for an ambulance to take them to hospital) would be further injured if the ambulance failed to arrive or took too long to arrive.

The second part – proximity

Proximity is related to the concept of foreseeability. Proximity just means closeness. There can be proximity by space, time or relationship. If I crash my car into yours, I am proximate in time and space, but not necessarily in relationship. If I crash into my son's car, although there is relationship it is not relevant to my liability, which is based on time and space. Relationship only becomes relevant when it makes the loss foreseeable to a person in the defendant's position. This is the basis of *Donoghue* v *Stevenson* (1932) – the relationship of manufacturer and consumer, or of anyone doing work for another (building a shed that later collapses, for example).

A good example of this can be seen in the case of **Bourhill v Young (1943)**. In that case, the claimant was getting off a tram in the centre of Edinburgh when she heard a motorcycle go past and almost immediately heard a collision. She did not see the accident and was in a safe place away from it when it happened. She decided to go and see what had happened and saw the dead motorcyclist and all the rest of the aftermath of the accident. She suffered shock from what she had seen and she claimed that the shock caused her to miscarry her baby. The defendant was found not to owe a duty of care to the claimant, as she was in a safe place and had not seen the accident but went to see the aftermath voluntarily. In proximity terms, there was no proximity in space as she was away from the accident even though she was nearby at the time.

The result might have been different if she had been related to the victim, as in the case of **McLoughlin v O'Brien (1983)**. Mrs McLoughlin was told of a serious accident involving her husband and children. She was nowhere near the accident when it occurred, but was told of it a short time afterwards. She rushed to the hospital where the family had been taken. Here she discovered that one of her children had died, the other was seriously ill and her husband, whilst alive, had not yet been cleaned up or sedated and was very distressed and in great pain. She suffered shock, and the court decided that the person that caused the accident owed a duty of care to her even though there was no proximity of time or space. The proximity of relationship was the deciding factor in establishing the duty of care in this case.

In most cases there is little issue of proximity, as the accident victim is part of the event. However, where a person learns about an accident later or sees it from a safe distance, and where the injury is psychiatric, (so-called nervous shock), then relationship is the key factor. This is explored in greater depth in A2.

The third part – reasonableness

The third part of the test – whether it is fair, just and reasonable to impose a duty of care – is really a matter of public policy. Traditionally, the courts were always concerned that any extension to the types of claim

Key cases

Kent v Griffiths (2000): this case is an example of foreseeability in that it is foreseeable that an injured person waiting for an ambulance may have more severe injuries if there is delay.

Bourhill v Young (1943): here there was no physical proximity as the claimant was in a safe place away from the accident, and whilst she could hear it, she could not see it. She later went to see the aftermath and then suffered her miscarriage.

McLoughlin v O'Brien (1983): the claimant was told of events and rushed to see her injured family. She then suffered shock. Even though there was no proximity of space and time, the relationship overrode this to make the defendant liable.

that could be brought before them would open the 'floodgates of litigation'. In other words, the concern was that there would be a huge number of claims and that the courts might be deceived into allowing a claim that had no validity. This was always a concern with nervous shock cases, and has been a consideration in other areas of negligence too. The fear was that – and is possibly justified by the impression that – the nation is much more claims-conscious today and some individuals are always looking to make some claim in the hope of getting money for nothing, or at least very little.

Today, the courts are looking at what is best for society as a whole. Thus, defendants who are in the public sector are more likely to find that claims against them will fail, as it is not fair and reasonable to impose liability on them. The police need to be able to act without undue worry about legal action in negligence against them. Thus, in the case of **Hills v Chief Constable of West Yorkshire (1988)**, the House of Lords refused to impose a duty of care on the police to the mother of the Yorkshire Ripper's last victim. The police had already interviewed and released the victim's killer before he killed again, but the court found no duty of care to potential victims of crime. This was partly on proximity grounds to an unknown member of the public but more on the policy consideration of allowing the police to work as efficiently as possible. This can be compared to *Kent v Griffiths* (2000). In that case the emergency service owed a duty of care to a known member of the public because it had assumed the responsibility for that person when the telephone call was taken.

In *Hills* v *Chief Constable of West Yorkshire* (1988), the police were found not to owe a duty of care to potential victims of crime and their families on policy grounds. This is an example of the reasonableness part of the Caparo three-part test.

However, the police do owe a duty of care in some circumstances. For example, they usually owe a duty of care to people taken into custody. In **MPC v Reeves (2001)**, the police took a man into custody who was a prisoner known to be at risk of committing suicide. Whilst in police custody, he hanged himself in his cell. The court found that the police owed him a duty of care.

There are limits to this duty of care, or at least as to whether the duty has been broken. This can be seen where the prisoner is not known to be a suicide risk, as in the case of **Orange v Chief Constable of West Yorkshire (2001)**. In that case, the increased risk of suicide among prisoners as compared with those in the community gives rise to an obligation, within the general duty of care owed by the police to a person in their custody for that person's health and safety, to take reasonable steps to identify whether or not a prisoner presented a suicide risk.

The obligation to take care to prevent a prisoner from taking his own life deliberately only arose where the custodian knew or ought to have known that the individual prisoner presented a suicide risk. In this case, because of the lack of any evidence to suggest that the police officers knew or ought to have known that a person in Orange's condition (he had been arrested for being drunk and disorderly) presented a significantly increased suicide risk, the judge concluded that the police had not been negligent in permitting Orange to retain his belt with which he committed suicide.

Similarly, the police do not owe a duty of care to a prisoner who is injured whilst making an escape attempt, as can be seen in the case of *Vellino v Chief Constable of Greater Manchester* (2001). This is partly because of policy (the injured person is committing a criminal offence and should not profit from their wrongdoing), and partly because an escaping prisoner is no longer under the control of the police.

In **Mitchell v Glasgow City Council (2009)**, a local housing authority summoned one of its tenants, who had been abusing and threatening one of his neighbours, to a meeting at which he was told that he could face eviction if his behaviour did not improve. The tenant left the meeting and within an hour had killed the neighbour. The House of Lords decided it was not fair, just or reasonable that the local housing authority should have had to warn the neighbour that the meeting had been arranged. This was done on the basis that a different judgement might open the floodgates to include, for example, social workers and private landlords.

Conclusion

Proof of the existence of a duty of care, where there is not an existing duty, requires all three parts of the test in *Caparo* v *Dickman* (1990) to be established by the claimant. Proof of the existence of a duty of care is not, however, proof of negligence. Breach of that duty and resulting damage must also be proved.

Activities

1. Practice writing a few sentences explaining each element of the Caparo three-part test. You should do this by stating the test and using a decided case to show how that part of the test works. When you are confident that you have done this correctly, try to do so without notes and complete the exercise in about seven minutes – this is the length of time you might have in the exam.

2. Look at the facts of *Donoghue* v *Stevenson* (1932). Imagine that case was coming before the court for the first time today. Apply the Caparo three-part test to the facts and decide whether a duty of care would be found to exist.

3. Consider the scenario below, taken from a past examination paper, and decide whether a duty of care exists in that case.

   Yannick and Zoe, university students, were at a music festival organised by XS Ltd. They were sitting on the ground in the main tent, listening to a band, when one of the tent supports became detached and the tent collapsed. Yannick suffered severe head and neck injuries.

You should now be able to:

- understand the legal requirements for the existence of a duty of care
- describe and apply the Caparo test in examination-style questions.

3 Breach of duty

The nature of breach – the reasonable man

Once it has been established that a duty of care exists, the claimant must satisfy the court that the defendant broke that duty of care by failing to reach the standard of care required. The standard of care is that of the 'reasonable man', which comes from the definition from Baron Alderson in *Blyth* v *Birmingham Waterworks Co.* (1856), set out at the start of Topic 2.

The reasonable man is the ordinary person performing the particular task: he is expected to perform it reasonably competently. Thus, when I am riding my bicycle, I am expected to be a reasonably competent cyclist; when I am building a wall, a reasonably competent wall builder

Key cases

Mitchell v Glasgow City Council (2009): there is no duty of care to warn others of meetings which may lead to trouble, as it is not fair and reasonable to do so on the basis of extending possible liability to many others.

Study tips

When applying the Caparo test, say why each part is or is not present in the scenario. You must give a reason for your decision, not just assert, for example, that it is fair, just and reasonable.

In this topic you will learn how to:

- describe the 'reasonable man' test
- list the factors that affect the standard of care of the reasonable man
- state and explain relevant examples for each of the above factors
- apply the test to a given situation.

and so on. This is an objective standard: the peculiarities of the person performing the task are irrelevant.

Types of reasonable man

There are a number of variations of reasonable man. The standard expected will depend on the individual skills expected. We have already seen that the standard varies with the task, but does it also vary depending on whether the defendant is a professional? There are four types to consider:

- the ordinary person doing a task
- the learner
- the professional
- young people.

The ordinary person doing a task

The defendant is expected to be a reasonably competent person performing the task. This is straightforward when dealing with everyday people doing everyday tasks. In **Wells v Cooper (1954)**, a man fitted a new door handle to the outside of the back door of his house. The door was at the top of some steps. The door was difficult to close on the day the accident happened, as there was a high wind blowing against the door. The claimant was leaving the house and pulled hard on the door to shut it. The handle came away in his hand and he fell down the steps and was injured. The court decided that a reasonably competent carpenter would have done the work to a similar standard as the man doing DIY on his house, so he had reached the standard of a reasonably competent person attaching a door handle.

The learner

For learners, there are some surprising but logical results. In **Nettleship v Weston (1971)**, the claimant was a non-professional driving instructor and the defendant was a learner driver. The learner driver was on her third lesson in her car, which did not have dual controls. She failed to straighten up the car after turning a corner at a road junction and hit a lamppost, injuring the passenger/instructor. The court decided that the learner driver's standard of driving should be that of the reasonably competent driver, not the standard of a learner driver.

Key cases

Wells v Cooper (1954): the standard of care required is of the reasonably competent person doing the job in question. Here, a man doing DIY was expected to reach the standard of a reasonably competent professional doing the job.

Nettleship v Weston (1971): the standard of care expected of a learner driver is the same as that of any driver. This is logical from the point of view of those injured, and because there is compulsory insurance.

Fig. 12.3 Nettleship *v* Weston

The decision is perfectly logical. First, the defendant must be insured by law and if not insured, personal injuries might be covered by the Motor Insurers' Bureau. Second, any claimant would find it unjust if he were told 'Sorry, I am not liable to pay you compensation as I am only on my first lesson and you cannot expect me to be as good a driver as someone who has passed their driving test.'

However, it might be that the person teaching the learner may also have been negligent in how they performed that task. This principle will apply to others in training too, such as chefs, beauticians, etc.

The professional

The position is just as logical when dealing with a professional. When you go to hospital for an operation, you expect the same standard from your surgeon whether it his first operation ever or not. This is no different to the learner driver.

The principle for professionals is established by asking two questions:

- Does the conduct of the defendant fall below the standard of the ordinary competent professional?
- Is there a substantial body of opinion within the profession that would support the course taken by the defendant?

If the answer to the first question is 'no' and to the second question is 'yes', then the correct standard has been reached and the defendant has not broken his duty of care.

The test looks at whether, for example, a surgeon is operating to the standard expected under a known and accepted procedure. This can be seen from the case of **Bolam v Friern Barnet Hospital Management Committee (1957)**.

Bolam was suffering from mental illness and was advised by a consultant attached to the defendants' hospital to undergo electro-convulsive therapy. This is a form of electric shock treatment. He signed a form of consent to the treatment but was not warned of the risk of breaking a bone whilst strapped down and being given electric shocks. On the second occasion of receiving the treatment, Bolam suffered a broken bone. The hospital did not use relaxant drugs that would have reduced the risk of breaking a bone. Among the medical experts, however, there were two bodies of opinion – one favoured the use of relaxant drugs as a general practice, and the other confined the use of relaxant drugs to cases where there were particular reasons for their use which were not present in Bolam's case. The hospital had reached the standard expected by following the standard procedure and so had not broken their duty of care.

It should be noted that a court could decide that the practice of the entire profession is wrong and thus a duty of care would be broken even though following normal practice. This was seen in the case of **Bolitho v City and Hackney Health Authority (1997)**.

Finally, it should be noted that where a reasonable man cannot know that a standard procedure is in fact dangerous, he will not break the duty of care. This is because the reasonable man is not expected to know and protect against risks of harm that are not yet known scientifically. Once the risk is known, there can be a breach of duty. This is illustrated by the case of **Roe v Minister of Health (1954)**. In that case, the claimant was injected with an anaesthetic contained in glass ampoules which were, prior to use, immersed in an antiseptic solution. The object of this was to minimise the risk of infection. Unfortunately, the

Key cases

Bolam v Friern Barnet Hospital Management Committee (1957): The standard of a professional is judged by the standard of the profession. In this case, following either of two accepted medical methods was said to be acceptable in reaching the standard of care expected.

Bolitho v City and Hackney Health Authority (1997): A consistent body of expert medical opinion may still be ignored by the judge, if heor she can be sure that no logical basis for the opinion has been shown in the case.

Roe v Minister of Health (1954): The reasonable man cannot take precautions against unknown risks. He will only break his duty by failing to take precautions when the risk becomes known.

claimant suffered permanent paralysis from the waist downwards as the anaesthetic had been contaminated by antiseptic that had seeped through invisible cracks in the ampoules. At the time, the risk of this happening was not appreciated by competent anaesthetists in general, and such contamination had not happened before. Therefore the duty of care owed by the hospital to the patient had not been broken.

Young people

Where the defendant is not an adult, the standard expected is of a reasonable person of that age. In **Mullin v Richards (1998)**, Teresa Mullin and Heidi Richards were friends and were sitting side by side at their desk in school. They were playing around, hitting each other's white plastic 30 cm rulers as though in a play sword fight, when one or other of the rulers snapped and a fragment of plastic entered Teresa's right eye, with the result that she lost all useful sight in that eye. Teresa sued Heidi (and the school) in negligence. The court of appeal decided that Heidi was only expected to meet the standard of a reasonable 15-year-old schoolgirl, not that of a reasonable man (adult). The court decided she was not to be in breach of duty, as she had reached the standard of behaviour required of a 15-year-old schoolgirl.

Lady Justice Butler-Sloss, referring to a previous case, said:

> ... in the absence of relevant statutory provision, children, like everyone else, must accept as they go about in society the risks from which ordinary care on the part of others will not suffice to save them. One such risk is that boys of twelve may behave as boys of twelve; and I would say that girls of fifteen playing together may play as somewhat irresponsible girls of fifteen.

Factors affecting the standard of care of the reasonable man

When the court looks at whether a duty of care has been breached, it bases the standard on the reasonable man performing the task in the circumstances. A number of factors that can be considered to raise or lower the standard expected: would the reasonable man take more or less care doing the task in certain situations? This is logical because a reasonable person (whatever he is doing) may take greater risks in an emergency, and take more care when the risk of harm is greater. For example, I may well damage a person's clothing or cause minor injuries when pulling a person from a burning car; equally, I will be more careful when carrying a young baby than when carrying a sack of potatoes.

Questions to be asked to see whether the standard of care should be raised or lowered include:

■ Are there any special characteristics of the claimant?
■ What is the size of the risk?
■ Have all practical precautions been taken?
■ What are the benefits of taking the risk?

Are there any special characteristics of the claimant?

The reasonable man takes more care where the situation demands it. This factor relates to risks known to the defendant as a result of peculiarities of the claimant. This is illustrated by the case of **Paris v Stepney Borough Council (1951)**. Here, the claimant was employed as a fitter in a garage. His employer, the local council, knew he had the use of only one eye. While he was using a hammer to remove a bolt on a vehicle, a chip of metal flew off and entered his good eye. This resulted

■ **Key cases**

Mullin v Richards (1998): the standard expected of a young person is that of a reasonable person of their age.

Paris v Stepney Borough Council (1951): where a defendant knows of an increased risk to the claimant, more care must be taken. The council knew he only had one good eye, so needed to do more than usual to protect the other.

■ **Study tips**

Make sure you do not confuse claimant and defendant.

in his becoming totally blind. The council did not provide goggles for him to wear as, in 1950, it was not common practice for employers to supply goggles to men employed in garages on the maintenance and repair of vehicles. Had Mr Paris been fully sighted, the council might not have broken its duty of care. Because the council knew he was blind in one eye when it employed him, the court decided that the council owed him a higher standard of care because of this known increased risk.

This principle applies equally to illness. In **Walker v Northumberland County Council (1995)**, the claimant was a social services manager who had been forced, because of local authority funding shortages, to take on a far higher volume of work than he could cope with. He suffered several weeks of being unable to work because of a stress-related illness. This then became a special characteristic of Mr Walker known to the defendant. When he returned to work, the local authority made little or no effort to improve his situation. The claimant then suffered another long period of illness. The court referred to the principle in *Paris* v *Stepney Borough Council* (1951) that the standard of care expected of an employer is raised if the employer knows that an employee is more likely to suffer injury. Thus, the claimant was owed a higher standard of care, which had been broken.

Another example of this is that a higher standard of care is expected by organisers and sports coaches to disabled athletes because of their special needs; this can be seen in the case of **Morrell v Owen (1993)**.

What is the size of the risk?

The principle is that the greater the risk, the more care needs be taken. To some extent, this is an extension of the ideas behind the previous factors. The reasonable man takes more precautions where the risk is greater, but does not take precautions against highly unlikely events. The classic case on this factor is **Bolton v Stone (1951)**. During a cricket match, a batsman struck a ball that hit a person who was standing outside her house on the road outside the ground. The ball was hit out of the ground over a protective fence 5 metres high. The distance from the striker to the fence was about 70 metres, and to the place where the person was hit was nearly 100 metres. The ground had been used as a cricket ground for about 90 years, and only on six occasions in the previous 30 years had a ball been hit out of the ground in that direction, and no one had previously been injured. The court decided that the risk of injury to a person from a ball being hit out of the ground was so small that the probability of it happening would not be anticipated by a reasonable man. Therefore the cricket club had not broken its duty of care, as it had reached the appropriate standard of care. The club had clearly thought about the risk and provided a reasonable solution by erecting the fence.

A combination of this factor and a person with a disability can be seen in the case of **Haley v London Electricity Board (1964)**. A blind man was walking along the pavement on his way to work. He was using his white stick to go along a route he knew very well. The electricity board had opened a trench and warned of it in the then-conventional manner of laying a tool on the ground to force people to walk round it. The blind man did not notice the tool with his stick and fell over it into the trench. The court decided that it was reasonably foreseeable that a blind person might be in the area as about 1 person in 500 is blind or partially sighted. Thus, the reasonable man would take

Key cases

Walker v Northumberland County Council (1995): where an employee has already had time off work with an illness or injury, the employer must then take more care to avoid a repeat or more serious illness. In this case it was stress-related.

Morrell v Owen (1993): a higher standard of care is expected by organisers and sports coaches to disabled athletes, because of their special needs.

Bolton v Stone (1951): the reasonable man takes precautions against reasonable risks, not fantastic possibilities. The likelihood of a cricket ball clearing the protective fence at the ground and injuring a passer-by was not a risk the reasonable man would protect against.

Haley v London Electricity Board (1964): a reasonable risk to protect against is one that is statistically likely to occur. In this case, a blind pedestrian was not adequately warned of a trench across the pavement.

precautions to prevent such an accident happening, as it was a reasonable risk to protect against and not a fantastic possibility. Of course, today's procedure for warning of such an obstacle protects against this risk.

Have all practical precautions been taken?

It follows from the previous factor that a defendant will have acted reasonably if he has taken reasonable precautions. Thus, the fence around the cricket ground in *Bolton* v *Stone* (1951) was a reasonable precaution, but the tool left on the ground was not in *Haley* v *London Electricity Board* (1964). The idea behind this factor is that the reasonable man will do all he reasonably can to prevent harm coming to others.

In situations that are unexpected, this may not always prevent an accident, but the key is the reasonableness of the action taken. In **Latimer v AEC (1952)**, the defendant's factory was flooded after an exceptionally heavy rainstorm. The water, mixed with some oil, made the floor very slippery. The defendant put up warning signs, passed the message round the workforce, and used all its supply of sand and sawdust to try to dry the floor. Despite this, the claimant slipped and was injured. The defendant owed a duty of care to the employees, but had not broken the duty, as all reasonable practical precautions had been taken in the circumstances of the accident.

What are the benefits of taking the risk?

This factor is sometimes called public utility. The idea is that there is a lower standard of care when reacting to an emergency. This is consistent with the idea of fair, just and reasonable in the third part of the test to establish a duty of care. The most famous example of this is **Watt v Hertfordshire County Council (1954)**. This case concerns firefighters who were injured by lifting gear when travelling in a vehicle not specifically fitted for carrying that gear. The vehicle that the firefighters should have used was adapted to carry the gear. However, that vehicle was already in use attending an emergency when the call came to go to another emergency where a woman was trapped under a heavy vehicle. The court held that the firefighters were ready to take the risk of using the vehicle to save life. The court must 'balance the risk against the measures' and the benefit of saving the woman was greater than the risk of injuring the firefighters by using a vehicle not suited to carrying the heavy gear, which moved and crushed a firefighter. Thus, the duty of care owed by the council to its employee firefighters had not been broken.

In another recent case, **Day v High Performance Sports (2003)**, Ms Day, a reasonably experienced climber, fell while climbing on an indoor climbing wall belonging to the defendant. She suffered serious brain injury. At a height of 9 metres (30 ft), she had discovered she was not tied to her top rope, and had to be rescued by the duty manager because she was 'frozen' in her position. The court recognised that this was an emergency situation and that the circumstances of the emergency had to be taken into account. In fact, the centre was one where a concern for safety was prominent, and workshops on safety were given to employees. The court concluded that the climbing centre had not broken its duty of care, and had reached the standard of care of a reasonably competent climbing centre.

The approach of the courts is very realistic when an emergency arises as the courts want to encourage rescuers, but also want to make sure

---

■ **Key cases**

Latimer v AEC (1952): one factor in deciding whether the defendant has acted as a reasonable man is taking all practical precautions. After a flood, this was doing the best to mop up, and warning the employees in the factory.

Watt v Hertfordshire County Council (1954): the benefits of saving a woman's life outweighed the risk of injury to a firefighter when using the best, but still unsuitable vehicle in an emergency.

Day v High Performance Sports (2003): the standard of care can be lower when making a rescue, in this case on a climbing wall.

employers are not put off encouraging employees to effect a rescue by the threat of being sued in negligence because they had not taken all reasonable precautions.

Conclusion

Breach of duty is concerned with the question of whether the defendant has reached the standard of care of a reasonable man. There are a number of factors that are relevant to this duty, which raise or lower the standard expected.

Activities

1. Explain how the law decides whether a duty of care has been breached, including how any *two* risk factors may affect the court's decision. Your answer might include:

   - the meaning of the reasonable man

   - the objective test

   - special characteristics of the defendant – the position of professionals and learners and children.

   You need to use appropriate cases to explain the points.

   This should be followed by an explanation using cases of the meaning of any two risk factors and the effect they have on the standard of care.

2. Think about things you do and decide what standard of care is required. Situations could include driving a car, babysitting, and taking a person in a wheelchair shopping. In order to do this exercise, you need to decide on the people to whom you would owe a duty of care and then decide the standard of care owed to each of those people.

3. Consider the following case and decide whether there is a duty owed and the standard of care required, concluding with a decision as to whether any duty of care owed has been broken.

   On 26 August 2000, the Saturday before the late summer Bank Holiday, Mary Abrew, a pensioner in her mid-60s living in Thornton Heath, was shopping in the Thornton Heath branch of Tesco, when, in aisle 23, she slipped on some dried spaghetti that had apparently been spilt onto the floor near the shelves which she was approaching. She was helped to her feet by an employee of the defendants, and taken by that employee to the first aid room, where she was treated with the utmost courtesy, and the incident was entered in the incident book in her presence. (These are the facts of *Abrew* v *Tesco* (2003).)

Study tips

Make sure that you start from the reasonable man test. Breach of duty does not need a repeat of the Caparo three-part test.

You should now be able to:

- understand the concept of breach of duty

- describe and apply the test for the standard of care in negligence.

4 Damage caused by the defendant's breach

General principles

At the start of this chapter, it was seen that the third aspect that must be proved if there is to be liability in negligence is that the broken duty caused the loss complained of, and that the law recognises that the loss is not too remote from the act. This is often referred to as **damage** and must be distinguished from **damages**, which is the amount of compensation awarded.

There are two parts to damage: causation and remoteness. Causation is the idea that the defendant must have caused the loss complained of. This is causation in fact. This is the same concept as in criminal law, but is illustrated by examples from the law of negligence. If no loss is caused then there is no claim in negligence. Remoteness concerns whether the loss is reasonably foreseeable: causation in law. Both must be proved following a broken duty of care if there is to be liability for a claim in negligence.

This can be illustrated by the following diagram:

Fig. 12.4 *Causation and remoteness*

Key terms

Damage: the resulting loss to a claimant from a breach of a duty of care.

Damages: the amount of compensation payable to the claimant who has proved the defendant has been negligent.

Key cases

Barnett v Chelsea and Kensington Hospital Management Committee (1968): this is an example where there was no causation in fact, as the hospital could not have done anything to save Barnett's life. The cause of death was the original poisoning, not the hospital's failure to examine him properly.

Causation in fact

Causation in fact is the starting point. If there is no causation in fact, there is no point in considering whether there has been causation in law. Causation in fact is determined by the 'but for' test. The test is satisfied if it can be said that, but for the defendant's act or omission, the claimant would not have suffered the loss or harm. A different way of stating the test is to ask whether the prohibited result would have occurred if the defendant had not acted. If the prohibited result would still have occurred, even without the defendant's actions, then something other than the defendant's actions caused it and factual causation is not present.

This is clearly illustrated in the case of **Barnett v Chelsea and Kensington Hospital Management Committee (1968)**.

The facts of the case are that the defendants managed a casualty department at a hospital. One night, three night-watchmen arrived at casualty, complaining to a nurse on duty that they had been vomiting for three hours after drinking tea. The nurse reported their complaints by telephone to the duty medical casualty officer, who instructed her to tell the men to go home to bed and call their own doctors if they still felt ill in the morning. The casualty officer did not speak to the men or offer to examine them, which would have been normal practice. The men then left, and, about five hours later, one of them died from poisoning by arsenic. It seems that the arsenic had got into the tea, probably as a result of the mugs or teapot being used for mixing poison by someone else at the workplace. The medical opinion was that the claimant was likely to have died from the poisoning even if he had been admitted to the hospital wards and treated with all care for the five hours before his death.

The judge stated in his decision, 'My conclusions are: that the plaintiff, Mrs Bessie Irene Barnett, has failed to establish, on the balance of probabilities, that the death of the deceased, William Patrick Barnett, resulted from the negligence of the defendants, the Chelsea and Kensington Hospital Management Committee, my view being that had all care been taken, still the deceased must have died. But my further conclusions are that the defendants' casualty officer was negligent (owed a duty of care and broke it) in failing to see and examine the deceased, and that, had he done so, his duty would have been to admit the deceased to the ward and to have treated him or caused him to be treated.'

In other words, the hospital owed the deceased a duty of care; the hospital broke the duty of care by not reaching the standard of the reasonably competent hospital; but the hospital had not caused the death of the deceased, as its failure to examine him had not been proved to be the factual cause of his death. It should be noted that the judge stated that the hospital had been negligent, and only ruled out liability for the death. This means that the hospital could be liable for any other losses following from its failure to examine the deceased. Note also how the judge specifically referred to the standard of proof as being 'on the balance of probabilities'.

Multiple causes

It is not always straightforward to establish that the defendant's act or omission caused the loss about which the complaint is being made. Sometimes there is more than one possible cause. The courts have started to use a modified rule on the grounds of public policy where there are 'special circumstances', and otherwise a claim would not succeed. This was set out in the case of **Fairchild v Glenhaven Funeral Services Ltd (2002)**.

This case decided that a worker who had contracted mesothelioma (a form of cancer caused by exposure to asbestos dust) could sue any of his previous employers following multiple exposures to asbestos caused by employers' negligence, even though the claimant could not prove which particular exposure had been the cause of the disease. It is understood that just one fibre from asbestos can cause the disease, but not every fibre inhaled will cause the disease. As a result of this uncertainty, the court decided that all possible exposures to asbestos could have triggered the disease, and if any and all employers were not to be held to be the cause of the disease, the claimant would not succeed. It was, therefore, unjust on policy grounds to leave this type of claimant without a remedy in law.

However, where there are a number of possible causes, the claimant must still prove the defendant's breach of duty caused the harm or was a material contribution.

Intervening events

As with criminal law, an intervening act can break the chain of causation. As has been seen, the intervening act is known as a *novus actus interveniens* (new act intervening) and can be seen diagrammatically as:

Fig. 12.5 *Diagram of* novus actus interveniens

The defendant's act may be said to cause the claimant's damage, in that it satisfies the 'but for' test, but a second factual cause is the real cause of the damage. For example, suppose your head was injured at school by a tile

> ### Key cases
>
> **Fairchild v Glenhaven Funeral Services Ltd (2002):** the normal rule on causation can be modified on policy grounds where there are 'special circumstances'. Here, this was because it is impossible to prove when asbestos actually entered the system to cause illness.

> ### Study tips
>
> The law on multiple causes is very complex and no more than an awareness that there is a problem for the law is needed.

falling off the roof (because the roof was badly maintained), and you were taken to casualty by a teacher. On the way to casualty, the teacher's car was hit by a bus that was being driven badly, causing you leg injuries. It could be said that 'but for' the tile falling off the roof you would not have suffered the leg injury. However, the real cause of the leg injury is the bus, not the tile. The bus is the *novus actus interveniens*. This means the injury to your head is caused by the tile, the injury to your leg by the bus.

Many of the cases we have looked at have an element of an intervening act in them, and it is often argued that if there is duty and breach, the intervening act prevents liability. These arguments were used in *MPC* v *Reeves* (2001) (the case where a prisoner was known to be at risk of committing suicide) and *Orange* v *Chief Constable of West Yorkshire* (2001) (the case where the prisoner was not known to be a suicide risk). In *Orange* it was a *novus actus interveniens* and in *Reeves* it was not.

The principle applied is whether the resulting damage was a foreseeable consequence of the original act. The cases often appear to be decided on the basis of producing a just result, as each set of facts are very different.

In **Smith v Littlewoods (1987)**, the defendants purchased a cinema with a view to demolishing it and replacing it with a supermarket. They closed the cinema and employed contractors to make site investigations and do some preliminary work on foundations, but then left the cinema empty and unattended but locked. Vandals started a fire in the cinema which seriously damaged two adjoining properties, one of which had to be demolished. The court decided that a reasonable person in the position of the defendants would not foresee that if he took no action to keep the premises fully secured, rather than just locked, in the short time before the premises were demolished, that they would be set on fire and that would result in damage to neighbouring properties. The defendants had not known of vandalism in the area or of previous attempts to start fires, so the events that occurred were not reasonably foreseeable by the defendants. They therefore owed no duty to the claimants, the vandalism being a *novus actus interveniens*.

Remoteness of damage – the test of reasonable foreseeability

Where there is factual causation, the claimant may still fail to win the case because the damage suffered may be too remote. The breach of duty may have significant results, but the defendant will not be liable for everything that can be traced back to the original act. This is a similar concept to legal causation in criminal law (see Chapter 9).

Clearly, there are some far-fetched results that are not foreseeable and therefore are not recoverable. For example, consider the negligent driving of someone who bumped into the back of my car – there are almost infinite consequences: the car suffers very minor damage (a broken tail light); I might miss the train; I might not be on time for the interview to which I was travelling when the accident occurred; I might not get the job because I was late for the interview; I might then be unemployed for many months; I might have to sell my car to cover living expenses as I have little income (being unemployed); I might then buy an old cheap car that does not have modern safety features; I might crash that car and be injured, become depressed and commit suicide – all because of a minor traffic accident. The law has to draw the line and say that some events are too remote to be considered to have been caused by the negligent act.

■ **Key cases**

Smith v Littlewoods (1987): vandals breaking into an unoccupied, but secured, building and setting fire to it was a new act intervening when vandals were not common in the area.

■ **Key terms**

Remoteness of damage: the defendant is liable for damage only if it is the foreseeable consequence of the breach of duty.

Fig. 12.6 *Diagram of* novus actus interveniens

The test is that the defendant is liable for damage only if it is the foreseeable consequence of the breach of duty.

The case that this principle stems from is *Overseas Tankship (UK) Ltd* v *Morts Dock and Engineering Co. Ltd* (1961), usually known by the name of the ship involved: **The Wagon Mound**. In that case, the defendant spilt a quantity of oil whilst refuelling another ship. The oil spread over the water to the claimant's wharf, which was some distance away. The claimant was carrying out repair work to a ship. This involved welding. Molten metal (part of the welding) from the claimant's wharf fell on floating cotton waste, which smouldered and then ignited the oil on the water. The claimant's wharf was severely damaged by fire. The defendants did not know, and could not reasonably have been expected to know, that the oil could be set alight when spread on water. They had made enquiries about the possibility of fire as soon as the oil was noticed, and suspended welding whilst the situation was checked. They were told that it was safe to continue, and took precautions to stop flammable waste falling into the water. Despite this, the fire started. The court decided that the damage by the oil was foreseeable, but the damage by the fire was too remote and was not foreseeable.

Remoteness of damage – the kind of damage must be reasonably foreseeable

The principle here is that as long as the type of damage is foreseeable, it does not matter that the form it takes is unusual. A classic example of this is **Bradford v Robinson Rentals (1967)**. The claimant was required by his employer to take an old van from Exeter to Bedford and collect a new one. The weather was very cold and there was advice not to travel unless it was necessary. The vans had no heater and the windscreen kept freezing over, so Bradford had to drive with the window open. The old van's radiator leaked and had to be topped up regularly. Bradford suffered frostbite. It was foreseeable that he would suffer some cold-related injury, so the defendants were liable for his frostbite even though that is very unusual. The reason for the claimant succeeding is that frostbite is merely an extreme form of injury from being cold.

Similarly, in **Hughes v Lord Advocate (1963)** the claimant succeeded. Two boys took a paraffin warning lamp down an unattended open manhole. On emerging from the hole, one of the boys knocked the lamp back into the hole, causing an explosion, and suffered severe burns. Since the risk of injury by burning was foreseeable, this extremely unlikely form of burning meant that there was factual and legal causation, and the boys' claim succeeded. This is another example of case law helping develop safety standards, as this method of warning is no longer used.

Key cases

The Wagon Mound No. 1 (1961): damage by the spilt oil was foreseeable; damage by fire was not foreseeable and was therefore too remote.

Bradford v Robinson Rentals (1967): as long as the type of damage is foreseeable, it does not matter that the form it takes is unusual. In this case, frostbite was an extreme form of injury from the cold.

Hughes v Lord Advocate (1963): another example of a claimant succeeding for injury caused by an extreme type of harm (an explosion and fire being an extreme type of a burn).

Key cases

Doughty v Turner Asbestos (1964): the claimant was injured when a lid was knocked into a vat of molten metal and the vat erupted. Scientific knowledge could not predict the eruption, so the event was unforeseeable. The claim failed.

Smith v Leech Brain (1962): the claimant had a pre-cancerous condition. He was splashed on the lip by some molten metal. The burn turned into a cancer as a result of his condition. His claim succeeded.

Gabriel v Kirklees Metropolitan Council (2004): this example of how a judge should apply the reasonable foreseeability test involved children playing on an unfenced building site.

However, in **Doughty v Turner Asbestos (1964)**, the claimant was burned when an asbestos lid was knocked into a vat of molten metal; the lid slid into the liquid with no noticeable effect for a few minutes. However, a chemical reaction then caused a violent eruption that scientific knowledge at the time did not expect to happen. It could be foreseen that knocking things into the liquid might cause a splash of molten metal, but this was an event of a wholly different type from that which could have been foreseen. Therefore, the claim failed as the result was not reasonably foreseeable.

Remoteness of damage – take your victim as you find him

This is similar to the concept in criminal law. A person's liability in negligence is not extinguished or lessened because the claimant had a pre-existing condition that made the injuries worse. A case that illustrates this principle is **Smith v Leech Brain (1962)**.

In that case, the claimant suffered a very minor splash by molten metal that caused a burn on his face. The burn triggered his pre-existing cancerous condition, and the claimant developed cancer. Some minor injury at least was foreseeable. His extreme reaction was a result of his condition and as the principle is that you take a person as you find them, the claim succeeded.

Remoteness of damage – a recent example of how a judge should apply the principle of reasonable foreseeability

In **Gabriel v Kirklees Metropolitan Council (2004)**, the claimant was six years old. He was walking past a building site owned by the local council in Huddersfield, when he was hit in the eye by mud thrown by children playing on the site. The site was not fenced at that time. It was decided that the correct way to assess whether the council was liable in negligence involved the following tests:

- whether it was reasonably foreseeable that children would go onto the construction site
- whether, whilst on the construction site, it was reasonably foreseeable that the children would play there
- whether it was reasonably foreseeable that, in playing on the site, they would throw whatever came to hand
- whether in playing with material on site it was reasonably foreseeable that they might cause injury to those passing by on the pavement.

The original judge had not followed these tests, and so a retrial was ordered. Thus it can be seen that the idea of reasonable foreseeability is still the backbone of the modern test.

Conclusion

Damage caused by the defendant's breach has two principles that equate to factual and legal causation. Factual causation is the 'but for' test. Legal causation is the idea of remoteness of damage, which has a test of reasonable foreseeability.

Activities

1 The text on p226 on *novus actus interveniens* states, 'These arguments were used in *MPC* v *Reeves* (2001) and *Orange* v *Chief Constable of West Yorkshire* (2001). In *Orange* it was a *novus actus interveniens* and in *Reeves* it was not.' Consider why that was the case.

2 Practice writing a few sentences explaining the idea of the causation and remoteness of damage. You should do this by stating the tests and using a decided case to show how that part of the test works. When you are confident that you have done this correctly, try to explain remoteness of damage without notes and complete the exercise in about seven minutes – this is the length of time you might have in the exam. An examination question might be: 'Damage in negligence involves the rules of factual causation and the rules of remoteness of damage. Explain these rules.'

3 Consider the scenario below, taken from a past examination paper, and consider whether there is duty, breach and damage in this case.

Seema was an amateur mountain-bike racer who was preparing for the Student Championships in Austria. She bought some expensive new wheels from Spokes Ltd that had been made to their new design. Whilst she was training abroad, a design fault in her new front wheel caused the tyre to burst and she crashed, breaking several bones. She can no longer ride competitively.

Study tips

Always use negligence cases for causation in this part of the specification rather than those learned for criminal law.

You should now be able to:

- understand the concept of damage
- describe and apply the test for damage
- decide, giving reasons, whether a person has been negligent or not in a given situation.

13 The courts: procedure and damages for negligence cases

Key terms

Court of first instance: the court that first tries a case.

Small claims track: a straightforward claim for damages of less than £5000 or, if personal injuries, less than £1000.

Fast track: a claim of between £5000 and £25,000, with limited oral evidence, that is likely to be completed in less than one day.

Multi-track: a claim that does not fall within small claims or fast track; it is likely to be complex and/or high value.

1 Outline of civil courts and appeal system for a negligence case

The civil courts

The majority of negligence cases are heard in a County Court. The manner in which each case is dealt with depends on the nature and size of the claim. The largest claims are heard in the High Court (Queen's Bench Division). Usually, appeals go to the Court of Appeal (Civil Division). For most legal cases in England and Wales, the Supreme Court is the final point of appeal.

The basic structure is set out in the diagram below:

Initial hearing	First appeal	Final appeal
County Court	Court of Appeal	Supreme Court
High Court	(Civil Division)	

Fig. 13.1 *Court structure for a negligence case*

The courts of first instance

A **court of first instance** is the court where a case is first tried. The court of first instance will be either the County Court or the High Court. The County Court and the High Court have different jurisdictions, so will hear different cases. The courts hope most cases will be settled out of court or by alternative dispute resolution, with only a minority actually being tried. In the 2005–06 County Court Annual Report, Lord Justice Thomas, Senior Presiding Judge for England and Wales, wrote:

> **The division between the County Court and the High Court**
>
> The figures in this report reflect solely the work of the county court. However, in reality, outside the Royal Courts of Justice there is very little distinction in practice between the way in which High Court and county court work is done. We have in practice a 'single civil court', but unfortunately the figures in this report do not reflect this. A distinction is still perpetuated between the High Court and the County Court, even for reports such as this.

He went on to quote from the report for South Wales: 'There is no rational reason why a case is issued one or the other. Practitioners frequently issue and pursue personal injury cases worth a seven-figure sum in the county court.'

The reality is that the cases are heard according to the track into which they fit. The courts are responsible for case management, with all cases allocated to one of three 'tracks' (**small claims, fast track, multi-track**) according to their value and complexity. If a negligence case is to be heard in the High Court, it is heard in the Queen's Bench Division.

In early 2012, there has been a consultation about changing the track limits and the courts to be used, but at the time of writing no definite proposals have been formulated.

Appeals

Either side of a civil case can appeal against the judge's decision based on supposed errors of law or fact. If the appeal is from the decision of a District Judge, the first appeal will normally be to a Circuit Judge. Such appeals are usually on procedural matters or smaller claims in the County Court. Thereafter, appeals go to the Court of Appeal with a further appeal to the Supreme Court. The leapfrog procedure, which bypasses the Court of Appeal, is only used where the case is of great legal importance, and will take the appeal directly to the Supreme Court.

The appeals do not take the form of a complete rehearing, but a consideration of the documentary evidence in the case and the judge's notes of witness evidence. Appeal judges rarely change the trial judge's finding of fact, as the trial judge will have seen the way the witnesses behaved whilst on oath in the witness box. The appeal court has three options: it may affirm the original judge's decision, which means that the result is totally unchanged; it may vary the decision, usually by changing the amount of damages awarded; or it may reverse the judgment in the first hearing by finding in favour of the other party (usually the party making the appeal).

Claims involving small sums and appeals to the Supreme Court require leave of the court, either from the court where the appeal is coming from or the court it is going to. Leave to appeal just means permission to appeal.

The burden and standard of proof

In civil law cases the burden of proof is on the claimant to prove his claim on a balance of probabilities. There is a lower standard than that in criminal cases. This means that the party bearing the burden of proof, the claimant, must demonstrate that it is 'more likely than not' that the defendant has been negligent. The burden of proof is the obligation on a party to establish the facts in issue in a case to the required degree of certainty (the standard of proof) in order to prove their case. In a civil trial, the burden is upon the claimant to prove the liability of the defendant. The standard of proof is on a balance of probabilities.

There are, however, two exceptions to the rule that the claimant must prove his case. The first is that, if the defendant has been convicted of a crime based on the same event, the claimant's case in negligence will be satisfied as a court has already been satisfied that the defendant caused the wrongful act beyond reasonable doubt, which is a higher standard. This comes from the Civil Evidence Act 1968. Thus, a claim for personal injuries arising from a car crash where the driver has been convicted of dangerous driving will not require proof of the driver's negligence. The driver would then have to prove he or she was not negligent – an impossible task one would assume, given the conviction! The only issue before the court is the amount of damages to be awarded.

A more important exception is **res ipsa loquitur**. This literally means 'the thing speaks for itself'. The idea is that the accident causing the damage complained of would not have happened unless someone had been negligent and the thing that caused the accident was wholly under the control of the defendant. This can be seen as a three- part test:

1 The thing that caused the harm was wholly under the control of the defendant.

2 The accident that caused the damage complained of would not have happened unless someone had been negligent.

> ■ Key terms
>
> *Res ipsa loquitur*: this literally means 'the thing speaks for itself'. It is a rule whereby negligence can be inferred from the fact that the accident happened.

3 There is no other explanation of the injury caused to the claimant.

The classic example is **Scott v London and St Katherine's Docks (1865)**. The claimant was walking along the dock when he was hit on the head by a sack of sugar that had fallen from an overhead crane. The claimant did not have to prove that the dock company was negligent as the required elements for *res ipsa loquitur* were present:

■ the thing that caused the harm was under the control of the defendant – the sack of sugar fell from a crane controlled by the dock company;

■ sacks of sugar do not fall from cranes unless someone has been negligent;

■ there is no other explanation of the injury caused to the claimant.

Since these conditions are fulfilled, the claimant does not have to prove his case. The burden of proof shifts to the defendant, who has the opportunity to prove that he or she was not in fact negligent – in other words, that there was some other explanation for the accident.

The modern explanation of *res ipsa loquitur* was summarised in *Bergin v David Wickes Television Ltd* (1994) as simply a convenient label for a group of situations in which an unexplained accident is, as a matter of common sense, the basis for an inference of negligence. *Res ipsa loquitur* has been successfully used in cases involving a car knocking over someone on the pavement and an aircraft crashing on take-off.

A particularly clear case is **Mahon v Osborne (1938)**. In that case, the claimant went into hospital for an abdominal operation, and after the operation he remained in pain and died when he should have made a recovery. In fact, a swab had been left inside his body. *Res ipsa loquitur* applied, as a swab is not left inside a body unless someone has been negligent, the swab is wholly under the control of the hospital, and there is no other explanation for the incident. It should be noted that this rule is particularly helpful to a claimant who was not even conscious when the event happened.

There are occasions where the defendant can show that he or she was not negligent and so the claimant does not succeed despite using *res ipsa loquitur*. In **Pearson v North Western Gas Board (1968)**, the gas main outside the claimant's house exploded, killing her husband and destroying the house. The gas board was able to show it had not been negligent as it had taken all reasonable precautions to deal with gas leaks. There had been particularly cold weather and this had caused the ground to freeze and then buckle during the thaw. This had caused the pipe to fracture. Having regular inspections and 24-hour emergency call-out teams was a sufficient standard of care, so the board had not been negligent.

Conclusion

Most negligence cases are heard in a County Court. The actual timing and venue will depend on the track to which the case is allocated. Whichever track the case is allocated to, the claimant has to prove his or her case on a balance of probabilities. This may be easier where *res ipsa loquitur* can be established, which shifts the burden of proof to the defendant.

You should now be able to:

■ describe appeal routes in the civil courts

■ understand procedure of negligence cases in the civil courts.

2 An outline of the procedure of a negligence case up to trial

In this topic you will learn how to:

- describe the procedure from the start of court action to trial
- apply the above to a given situation.

Personal injury case

Claim form

Limitation period. three years from date of accident or date of knowledge to issue court proceedings

Instruct solicitor

Initial instructions taken; terms of business letter and initial letter of instruction sent to client

Initial investigations

Statements taken from client and any witnesses

Letter of claim sent to defendants

Three months to investigate liability

If defendant admits liability then matter will proceed in relation to quantum only ← Defendant admits/denies liability → *If defendant denies liability then the matter wil proceed in relation to both liability and quantum via court proceedings*

High value cases; claimant and defendant may instruct own medical experts ← Joint medical expert instructed

Medical expert will examine and prepare a report on client

Valuation of case

Depending on seriousness of injuries a barrister may be instructed to advise as to the value of the case

Negotiations

If negotiations do not produce settlement, issue court proceedings

Fig. 13.2 *Flow chart of activities before issue of proceedings in a personal injuries claim*

Starting a negligence case

Once it has been established that court proceedings need to be started (most claims are settled by negotiation without the need to go to court), the formal procedure must be set in motion. Claims where there are personal injuries and the claimant does not expect to be awarded more than £50,000 must be started in the County Court. All other claims may be started in either the County Court or the High Court. Most claims are started in the County Court, and we will now concentrate on claims starting here. The first step is to complete a claim form. Information about this is available online to download, or can be collected from one of over 200 court offices in the country.

This form is simple to complete, requiring names and addresses for claimant and defendant, brief details of the claim (such as 'Damages for personal injuries caused when the defendant knocked down the claimant on a pedestrian crossing'), and the value of the claim. The purpose of this is to establish the fee payable and to help establish the choice of court and track. If the claim is expected to be worth less than £5000 in total, with some element being personal injuries and there being some losses that have a fixed value (for example, replacement of ruined clothes, loss of earnings for a week whilst recovering), the claimant would put: 'My claim includes a claim for personal injuries and the amount I expect to recover as damages for pain, suffering and loss of amenity is not more than £1000.'

The particulars of claim on side two of the form will give details of the claim being made. This may be sent separately within 14 days, but most simple claims have it included. The particulars of claim give a simple statement of the facts on which the claimant bases the claim. This might include the time, date and place of the accident, and an outline of why the claimant considers the defendant has been negligent.

The fee payable depends on the size of the claim. In the example in the preceding paragraphs, the fee would be £175 (as at May 2012).

There is also the possibility of having the fee lessened, or pay no fee at all in certain cases for claimants with low income and few assets.

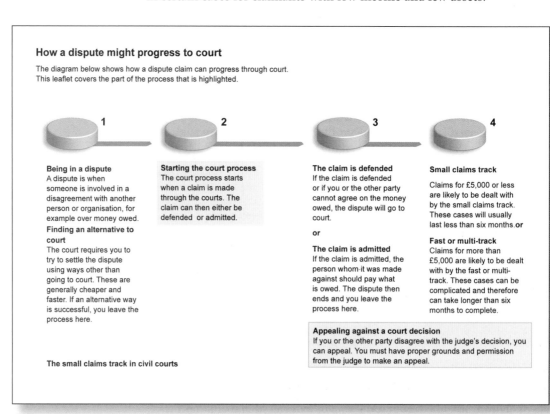

Fig. 13.3 *A diagram showing how a dispute might progress to court*

The three tracks

The court rules and practice direction explain the limits of the tracks. There are three tracks: small claims, fast track and multi-track. Which court and judge will hear the case depends on the scope and size of the case.

Small claims	Fast track	Multi track
▨ Up to £5000	▨ £5000–£25,000	▨ Over £25,000
▨ Personal injury up to £1,000	▨ Trial up to one day	▨ Complex cases
▨ Simple cases	▨ Moderately complex cases	

Fig. 13.4 *The three tracks*

The small-claims track is the normal track for claims of a monetary value of less than £5000. It is also the track for cases in which the financial value of any claim for damages for personal injuries is less than £1000. Personal injuries include claims for pain, suffering and loss of amenity. There will be no complex issues involved. This type of case is usually heard by a District Judge.

An example of a small-claims track case is where a horse jumped over a broken fence in the field in which he was grazing and ran into a parked car. The car suffered £2000 of damage. The car owner claims the owner of the horse had been negligent by not keeping the horse securely fenced in. This would be small-claims track, as the value of the claim is less than £5000 and there are no complex issues of law or evidence and no personal injury claim (if there were one it would have to be less than £1000).

The fast track is the normal track for a claim that does not fall within the small-claims track and has a claim value of less than £25,000. In addition, the trial must not be expected to last more than one day and there is limited oral expert evidence. There may be some complex issues involved. This type of case is also usually heard by a District Judge.

A fast-track case might be a claim following a road accident where a pedestrian had been knocked down whilst crossing the road. The injuries were straightforward – some bruising and a broken leg – and the medical evidence is all in written reports. The issues for trial might be amount of special and general damages, and whether the accident was caused by the injured person. This would be supported by witness statements rather than oral evidence. The documentary evidence would usually be receipts for expenses and damage items such as spectacles and loss of earnings. This is likely to be a fast-track case as the issues are straightforward, the value is probably between £5000 and £25,000, and the expert evidence is written.

Any claim that is not within the scope of small-claims track or fast track is a multi-track case. A multi-track case would be more complex and also (usually) involving a larger sum of money. Multi-track cases are almost always heard by a Circuit Judge.

This might be following a road accident where the claimant is a 17-year-old person who has suffered multiple injuries and is unlikely to make a full recovery from the injuries. Questions the court might have to decide could include: whether the injuries were caused by the person who had hired the car to the driver involved in the accident due to not

> ## Study tips
>
> Make sure you know the differences between the tracks, and check that the limits have not changed.

maintaining the car properly (was the seat belt defective?) rather than the driver; whether the injured person knew the driver had taken drugs and would therefore be unfit to drive; and what the effect of the accident is on the claimant's future earnings. This would be fast track because of the value of the claim, the complex nature of the evidence – some expert evidence might not be written – and the likely length of a trial.

Between allocation and trial

After the case has been allocated, the court sets a date for the trial. This date will be at least 21 days later, and the actual date will depend on what other directions need to be made. These other directions include providing copies of documents to the other party or parties to the case, and copies of experts' statements. The stage is now set for the trial.

Conclusion

The procedure from issue of a claim up to trial is designed to bring the claim to a conclusion fairly and speedily. The aim of the civil justice system is to reduce the average time a claim takes to be resolved and thus reduce the criticism that the law is very slow. The aim is to reduce the time from over a year at the end of the 1990s to about 30 weeks on average for a fast-track case. The procedure is relatively straightforward and is backed up with much help and guidance online, in leaflets and at court offices.

Activities

1. Set out below is a slightly expanded past examination question. Using the information in the scenario, complete a claim form as far as possible and explain to the claimant how the case would proceed up to any trial.

   Having bought herself a cheap windsurfer, Ursula Langer decided to teach herself to windsurf on a lake near her home. After several hours' practice, she began to tire and decided to have one last attempt at crossing the lake. She failed to notice Vera Unsworth, who was fishing from a boat on the lake. Unfortunately, Ursula crashed into the boat, which capsized, and Vera lost her expensive fishing equipment in the lake. The equipment cost £2000 and the boat needed £400 worth of repairs. Vera suffered some injuries, including being cut by a fish hook which imbedded itself in her cheek. She now has a permanent scar and has been advised that she is likely to be awarded £1500 in damages for her injuries.

2. A friend of yours has just been involved in a minor car accident that appears to have been the fault of the other driver. Write a short guide tthat explains to him how he might take legal action to recover the cost of repairs to his car.

3. If the case in Activity 1 above were heard today, explain which track would be used.

Study tips

Make sure that you present the order of events in a clear, logical manner using the correct legal terminology. It is usually a good idea to plan your answer first, as the planning exercise will help you get the procedure in the correct order.

You should now be able to:

- understand the procedure up to trial in a case of negligence

- apply the procedure in a given situation.

Court proceedings

All court cases vary slightly but this is a general overview

Fig. 13.5 *Flow chart of fast-track case up to trial*

In this topic you will learn how to:

- state the meaning of the term 'compensatory damages'

- distinguish between general and special damages

- distinguish between pecuniary and non-pecuniary damages

- distinguish between lump sum and structured settlements

- apply the above to a given situation.

3 Damages

The purpose of damages

Damages in a negligence case are compensatory. The purpose is to put the claimant in the position he or she would have been in had the negligent event not occurred. This means that the claimant will have his actual losses repaid and will also get a further sum of money to compensate for future losses. It is relatively easy to compensate the victim of a car crash for a damaged car, but much harder to compensate for personal injuries and the effect of the accident on life in the future. The purpose of damages is to do this as fairly as possible. The law is not concerned with punishing the defendant, only with compensating the victim of the defendant's negligent event.

As the claimant is not expected to profit from the award of damages (they are compensatory, although it can be argued that some claimants do gain financially), the claimant must follow the general principle of mitigation of loss. This means minimising the loss by taking reasonable action to do so. An example of this might be replacing a car that has been written off as soon as possible, rather than hiring a car for many weeks as part of the claim against the defendant. This is often reflected in guidelines given by employers to their staff following losses that might result in an insurance claim, as insurance companies operate the principle of mitigation of loss. An example of this is set out below.

> In the event of flood damage on premises for which you are responsible, you should take sensible actions to mitigate the loss such as:
>
> 1. Clean or mop up the affected areas as best you can.
>
> 2. If necessary, turn off gas, mains water stop cock, but do not switch off electricity supply unless clearly advised by a qualified electrician that circuits are unsafe. If you have to switch off the electricity, arrange for emergency supply of refrigeration and freezing appliances if there are perishable goods.
>
> 3. Identify items lost and prepare lists for costing. You should expect these lists to be closely scrutinised. No action should be taken to replace or repair damaged items until agreed by the Insurance Section.
>
> 4. Try to protect key/critical equipment from further deterioration; retrieve important documents/items. No items should be disposed of until Loss Adjusters have given approval.
>
> 5. If possible, copy any computer files to portable storage to prevent further damage.
>
> 6. Ensure safety checks are made of power and light circuits before turning the power back on and arrange for safety checks of all equipment. Retain all evidence of safety testing, dated and signed. Keep a list of the time and date and actions taken by you.

In practice, the claimant does not have to be too careful about ensuring mitigation of loss; the key criterion is that the action taken by the claimant is reasonable. Thus, in a case involving an unwanted pregnancy resulting from a negligently performed sterilisation, it was not reasonable to expect the claimant to undergo an abortion.

Since damages are compensatory, the claimant can only receive damages once, even if several people contributed to the accident. Similarly, the amount received can be reduced where the court considers the claimant is partly responsible for his losses. This is known as contributory negligence, and the reduction is in proportion to the claimant's own proportion of blame. Contributory negligence is not part of the AQA AS specification, so will not be explored further.

Where the event has resulted in personal injuries, it is usual to get a preliminary idea of the amount (technically called 'quantum') of damages likely to be awarded. This helps negotiation and often avoids the need to start proceedings. Whilst this is time-consuming, it can often result in an earlier settlement of the claim, or at least an interim payment to help the claimant with immediate expenses.

When calculating the quantum of damages, there are two types of damages: special and general. Special damages reflect losses that are particular to the claimant in the event that has occurred, and general damages are those that are presumed to follow from the negligence. A distinction is also made between pecuniary and non-pecuniary losses. **Pecuniary losses** are those involving financial loss such as loss of earnings (any claim for lost wages is for net wages – again, so the claimant does not make a profit) or damage to goods. **Non-pecuniary losses** are compensation for those things that do not have a ready financial value, such as pain and suffering after an injury.

Special damages

Special damages are compensation for the financial losses incurred up to the date of the trial. These losses must follow from the negligent event and the losses that are particular to the claimant rather than those that can be foreseen to affect any claimant. The things included can all be given an exact figure. This includes medical expenses such as prescription fees and hospital charges. For example, the driver of a vehicle involved in a road accident may be charged for any emergency medical treatment provided by a doctor and any hospital involved. The driver's insurance company will usually pay this charge without affecting their no-claims bonus.

Also included is loss of earnings up to the date of trial. This is straightforward where the claimant is salaried and has sick pay arrangements that do not cover full pay for the duration of time off work. Deductions are made for benefits actually received; if that were not the case, the claimant would make a profit as a result of the negligence. Where the claimant has had irregular overtime or works for varying hours each week, the calculation is less clear and would have to take into account the history of earnings and the likelihood of missed overtime and work. The usual calculation is to take the average earnings from the previous 26 weeks' earnings. Loss of future earnings is part of general damages, and will be considered there.

Damage to goods such as repairing a car or replacing ruined clothes are easy to calculate as special damages, as there is evidence of the cost from receipts. A car that is written off would attract damages of the market value before the accident. This principle is applied to all such losses that occur as a result of the negligent act.

General damages: the principle

General damages are designed to cover anything that does not have a readily quantifiable figure that can be put on it. There are three major areas that need to be explored:

- pain, suffering and loss of amenity
- future medical care and personal assistance
- loss of future earnings.

Pain, suffering and loss of amenity

Pain, suffering and loss of amenity are very difficult to calculate. The damages awarded under this heading include the physical and mental suffering of the claimant, the injury itself, and the reduction in the quality of life of the claimant – known as loss of amenity. The Judicial Studies Board lays down guidelines with respect to the size of the award for different injuries. This allows for a general consistency in approach, but provides some range for different levels of severity. Having the range of figures available also helps claimants and defendants to settle the claim without the need to go to court. There are many calculators available on the internet.

Some examples of typical awards of damages for physical injuries are:

- infertility in a woman who already has children: £10,000–£20,000
- moderate knee injury: £8000–£14,750
- total loss of sight in one eye: £27,000–£30,000.

The court takes into account many factors when making the overall calculation, as every claimant's injuries are different even if there are similar outward appearances (such as loss of a limb). The factors taken into account include:

- time spent in hospital and the number and type of treatments
- whether the injury is temporary or permanent, and if temporary, the length of time it will affect (or has affected) the claimant
- loss of expectation of life – how much shorter the claimant's life is likely to be
- loss of quality of life – how much worse the claimant's is as a result of the accident
- inability to have children and loss of marriage prospects
- cosmetic injury and the effect that has on the claimant
- psychological and emotional damage, such as depression
- whether there is continuing pain and discomfort and a greater likelihood of serious disease later; in this case, there can be an award of provisional damages, with further damages later with the onset of the disease.

Loss of amenity is the effect of the injury on everyday activities and on the claimant's enjoyment of life. This, therefore, covers things such as not being able to do the housework and being unable to perform personal care activities such as shaving, as well as being unable to follow a sport or recreation, such as cycling or driving.

Future medical care and personal assistance

Personal assistance follows on from the concept of loss of amenity and the inability to look after oneself fully. The problem for the courts is when a member of the victim's family becomes the carer and has to lose earnings as a result. In many such cases there is a claim for compensation in respect of the care provided to the claimant by family members or friends free of charge. This type of care happens naturally and so the claimant can be awarded damages for the care and domestic assistance. This money is then used for the carer.

Even with relatively minor cases, an award of damages can be made for care, particularly where the victim is a child. This can be seen from the case of **Giambrone v JMC Holidays (2002)**, where 652 people staying at a hotel in Majorca on a holiday provided by the defendant tour operator suffered food poisoning, giving rise to the claims. Many of the victims of the food poisoning were children, and their parents were successful in claiming damages for the extra care they had to carry out.

Key cases

Giambrone v JMC Holidays (2002): Parents of children who suffered food poisoning at a hotel in Majorca successfully claimed damages for the extra care they carried out.

Loss of future earnings

Loss of future earnings is very difficult to predict, and depends on the evidence that can be provided and the arguments that can be made to reduce the claim. There are many firms offering forensic and investigative services who become expert witnesses in such cases. The problem is illustrated by a simple example. Suppose an 18-year-old AS Level student was involved in a car crash that resulted in his paralysis and reduced mental abilities. Earnings at the time of the accident are likely to be very low, perhaps from a part-time job at a supermarket checkout. The argument made on his behalf would be that he had a very bright future, would get good results (this could be based on AS results, progress tests and Units taken at A2), and has received an offer of a place at university, and so on. After the accident, he has limited capacity for employment, and is currently still a part-time supermarket checkout operator. How would you calculate his future lost earnings?

The answer is not clear and relies on likely outcomes based on the evidence and not fanciful outcomes: after all not every teenage guitar player will become an enduring rock musician earning millions! This is one reason why most claims are settled by negotiation without going to court.

In many cases, a formula is used to help make the calculation.

Fig. 13.6 *Loss of earnings calculator*

This formula works on the principle that the income from the capital sum of damages invested will produce the lost earnings, and that the capital will also be used up during the expected working life used in the calculation. This is on the basis that the damages awarded are compensation and that the claimant will not make a profit. However, these calculations are not accurate, and some claimants benefit while others do not. Clearly, a claimant who dies before the end of the anticipated period would benefit, but similarly, a claimant who far exceeded his life expectancy would lose out. The courts do take into account loss of life expectancy and, under the Damages Act 1996, the expected rate of return from investments.

Suppose a 30-year-old man suffered an accident following which he could no longer work. His income was £20,000 and it was decided that he was unlikely to work for the next 30 years. In theory, he would be awarded £20,000 × 30 = £600,000. In practice, because of the effect of using capital and other factors, the multiplier is rarely more than 18, so the maximum award is likely to be £20,000 × 18 = £360,000.

Method of payment of damages

Traditionally, all damages were paid as a lump sum. This meant that the claimant received his payment and did with it as he wished. A lump sum could then be invested and the interest earned would give the defendant much more than he would have earned had he not been injured. This is the reason for the reduction in the multiplier for calculating an award for loss of future earnings, and all other payments that are to represent money for the claimant's future needs.

Lump sum payments are entirely appropriate for loss of or damage to goods, but periodical (e.g. monthly) payments are more appropriate where the claimant is going to need a regular income during his or her life. Damages for personal injuries paid in this way are known as a structured settlement and are dealt with in the Damages Act 1996.

A structured settlement is usually paid by the defendant's insurer. Once a lump sum figure has been agreed, some of that sum takes the form of periodic payments 'structured' to meet the claimant's individual needs. The lump sum, or part of it, is effectively spent on getting these payments made through an annuity provided by a financial institution. Thus the payments can be guaranteed to increase with inflation and to continue for the rest of the claimant's life. There can be tax advantages to this as damages are tax-free.

The main advantages of a structured settlement are greater certainty and security compared to the traditional lump sum, and the fact that the claimant does not have to manage his lump sum or pay someone to do that. The structured settlement is therefore an excellent solution where the victim is a child or is so severely injured that management of a large sum of money would be an unnecessary burden. Structured settlements, based on an annuity, also solve the problem of a claimant living for a very short or a very long time and being over- or under-compensated by the lump sum system.

Conclusion

The basic idea of damages as financial compensation for the claimant's loss is quite simple. It becomes more complicated where non-financial losses are involved, such as personal injuries, and where the value cannot easily be calculated, such as care costs and future earnings. The payment of damages is usually by way of a lump sum, but large claims are increasingly paid though a structured settlement. It should be noted that structured settlements are usually used only when the general damages would be a very large amount.

Activity

Using the scenario in the Activity 1 on p236:

1 Identify the type of damages that can be claimed in this case.

2 Explain how the court would go about calculating the amount of damages in this case.

You should now be able to:

- understand the principles behind an award of damages

- apply the principles in examination questions.

Practice questions

Unit 2B questions in the AQA exam

In the Unit 2 examination paper, you must answer all the questions from Unit 2A (Criminal Law) and all the questions from either Unit 2B (Tort) or Unit 2C (Contract Law).

Each section is represented by one question, which has six parts. You must answer all parts of the question. Each part is worth up to 10 marks; the entire question is worth 45 marks, plus 2 marks for Assessment Objective 3.

Some of the questions test your knowledge and understanding, and some test application of the law to the scenario that introduces the question. Some are a mixture of knowledge, understanding and application. There is a clear distinction on the examination paper. Theory-only questions appear directly underneath the scenario; mixed theory and application questions are preceded by a specific instruction to refer to the scenario.

Example question 1 (AQA, June 2012)

This question is taken from a past exam paper. You must answer all six parts of this question.

> *Eve was a trainee hairdresser. After work on a Thursday, she met Fran and told her that, this week, she had started to learn to colour hair and showed her a range of products that she used. Fran asked Eve if she would colour her hair ready for Friday evening out. Eve agreed and they went to Fran's home to colour Fran's hair. Despite warnings on the colour containers, Eve did not make any tests on Fran and used too much colour. As a result, Fran's skin became very painful and blistered. She lost a number of modelling assignments. If she is successful, it is estimated that Fran's total damages are likely to amount to around £20,000.*

Negligence requires proof of duty of care, breach of duty, and damage.

1. Explain how the law decides whether a duty of care has been breached, including how any two risk factors may affect the court's decision. *(8 marks)*

2. Damage in negligence involves the rules of factual causation and the rules of remoteness of damage. Explain these rules. *(8 marks)*

Refer to the scenario when answering the remaining questions in this section.

3. Outline the principles on duty of care and discuss whether Eve owed a duty of care to Fran. *(8 marks + 2 marks for AO3)*

4. Discuss whether Eve was in breach of her duty of care to Fran. *(8 marks)*

5. Outline the three-track case management system used in the civil courts and identify which track and which court are most likely to be used in a claim that Fran could make against Eve. *(5 marks)*

6. Assuming Eve were found liable in negligence, explain how the court would calculate an award of damages to Fran. *(8 marks)*

Example question 2 (AQA, June 2011)

This question is taken from another past exam paper. You must answer all six parts of this question.

> *Robyn fitted a handrail over the bath for Elsie, her elderly and very overweight aunt. A few days later, when Elsie was getting out of the bath, the handrail came away from the wall. Elsie fell backwards into the bath and suffered severe head injuries. If this matter were to be taken to court, it is estimated that a successful claim in negligence would result in damages exceeding £100,000, excluding the minor damage to the bathroom.*

Negligence requires proof of duty of care, breach of duty, and damage.

1. Explain how the law decides whether a duty of care is owed in negligence. *(8 marks)*

2. Breach of duty requires the claimant to prove that the defendant has fallen below the standard of care of the reasonable man. That standard is assessed by taking into account one or more of the risk factors. Briefly explain **three** risk factors. *(8 marks)*

3. Briefly explain how the principle of *res ipsa loquitur* applies in negligence cases. *(5 marks)*

   Refer to the scenario when answering the remaining questions in this section.

4. Discuss whether Robyn owed a duty of care to Elsie.
   (8 marks + 2 marks for AO3)

5. Assuming that Robyn owed a duty of care to Elsie, discuss whether she was in breach of that duty. *(8 marks)*

6. Assuming Robyn were found liable in negligence, explain how the court would calculate an award of damages to Elsie. *(8 marks)*

Introduction

Unit 2A together with Unit 2B or Unit 2C constitute Unit 2 of the AS specification. Unit 2A is about Criminal Law and is compulsory. Unit 2B is about the Law of Tort and Unit 2C is about the Law of Contract. You must answer the questions on either Unit 2B or 2C, but not both, as well as the questions on Unit 2A. You can choose to study either Unit 2B or Unit 2C in addition to Unit 2A.

The Unit 2 examination paper constitutes 50 per cent of the overall marks for the AS qualification, and 25 per cent of the overall marks for the A2 qualification. The examination is of 1.5 hours' duration. You must answer all the questions from Unit 2A and all the questions from either Unit 2B or Unit 2C. There is no choice of question in any of the sections.

The questions on each section are worth 45 marks each, plus 2 marks for Assessment Objective 3. Each question is divided into six parts, each part being worth up to 10 marks. You must answer all parts of the question. Each section stands alone, and there is no overlap between them.

The Contract section is covered by Chapters 14 to 15 of this book. Some of the questions test your knowledge and understanding, and some test application of the law to the scenario that introduces the question. Some are a mixture of knowledge, understanding and application. There is a clear distinction on the examination paper.

Questions require essay-style answers. You should aim to include: correct identification of the issues raised by the question; sound explanation of each of the points; and relevant illustration. Illustration may be in many forms – for example, legislation, cases, research, statistics, and material from the media. Study tips are provided throughout each topic.

14 Formation of contract

Key terms

Civil law: the law concerned with the relationship between individuals.

1 Introduction to formation of contract

Contract is an area of **civil law**. A contract is an agreement that the law will recognise. The purpose of the law of contract is to decide whether there is a valid contract or not, and to provide remedies when one person has been affected by another's failure to perform their part of the contract. The most usual remedy is damages (financial compensation), and that is the remedy considered in this section. A valid contract starts with the acceptance of an offer made to the person accepting the offer.

Civil law

As discussed, civil law is concerned with settling disputes between individuals: 'individuals' including businesses and, sometimes, the Government. The key difference between civil and criminal law is that civil law is primarily designed to settle disputes, not deal with punishing wrongdoing. There are many areas of civil law, including the law of contract. Contract is one area of civil law that is to be studied in the AQA AS Law specification.

A civil case is started by the person who has suffered loss (the claimant) as the result of a wrong that only directly affects him. A typical contract case is a claim for losses for failure to deliver goods, such as bread to a restaurant. The claim requires proof that the defendant had a contract with the claimant and that he or she did not carry out their part of the bargain. The claimant's usual remedy is financial compensation, known as damages. Thus, a successful claim for failure to deliver bread under a contract with a restaurant will result in damages paid to the restaurant claimant to cover the financial losses – which might be the cost of getting bread elsewhere or, in some circumstances, possible loss of trade. There are other remedies available in the law of contract, but these are not relevant to the material in these chapters.

The civil process

The civil process is the procedure by which a claim makes its way through the court system so that the court can decide whether the claim will succeed and, if so, what amount of damages should be awarded. The court processes and eventual award of damages can be a long and complicated business for both the claimant and the defendant, but the process is designed to keep delay to a minimum through case management. Once a person is advised that they are likely to have a good claim in contract, the major consideration is to obtain sufficient evidence of the losses suffered. This is straightforward for non-delivery of an item; it is the difference between the contract price and the market value of the item at the time of breach of contract. Any incidental costs would have to be proved, but, again these are straightforward. Contracts involving services are much more difficult to calculate, as is loss of future business.

Eventually, the claimant may have to go to court for some or all of the issues to be tried and, if the claim is successful, to calculate their award of damages. The length and complexity of the process depends on the nature of the claim, whether the evidence is clear, whether and if so how the defendant makes his defence, and whether or not he or she tries to establish that he had not broken the contract. There are rules of procedure that set out the court in which the case will be heard and the framework for deciding the case. For many reasons, such as the effect of publicity on the businesses involved, the stress of a court case and the question of cost, many contract cases are settled out of court. A successful claimant needs to prove that a contract existed and that it has been breached.

Fig. 14.1 *The civil process for a contract case*

There are rules of **civil evidence** that set out how the facts must be proved and the degree of certainty that is required. In civil law cases, the burden of proof is on the claimant to prove the liability of the defendant. The standard of proof is on a **balance of probabilities**. This means that the party bearing the burden of proof, the claimant, must demonstrate that it is 'more likely than not' that the defendant has proved his case. The burden of proof is the obligation on a party to establish the facts in issue in a case to the required degree of certainty (the standard of proof) in order to prove their case. This is most likely to be relevant in assessing future losses or establishing that a particular loss was the result of the breach of contract. Juries are not used in contract cases, which take place in the County Court or High Court Queen's Bench Division or the Commercial Court.

Contract

A **contract** is an agreement between two parties that the law will enforce. The central part of the concept is that of agreement made voluntarily between the parties to the contract. If a person is to succeed in a contract claim, there must be proof that there is a valid contract and that the contract has been broken. There are four elements that need to be considered in the formation of a valid contract:

- that there has been a valid offer made by one party to the contract
- that there has been a valid acceptance of the offer – together, offer and acceptance constitute an agreement
- that there is an intention to create legal relations – in other words, an intention to have a legally enforceable contract
- that there has been consideration – the idea that each party has given up something or contributed something to the agreement; if one party contributes and the other does not, then there is a gift rather than a contract.

You will study breach of contract: if a contract has been performed satisfactorily, there will be no dispute and so no possibility of the courts being involved. Two aspects of breach of contract are studied: actual breach, where the defendant fails to perform his or her side of the contract; and anticipatory breach, where the defendant states he or she will not perform his or her part of the contract when the time comes for them to do so.

So far as the material in this book is concerned, most of the authorities for the law come from decided cases. This means that the law is judge-made and has developed over the years, and that the rules of precedent studied in Unit 1 are used. It is important that the latest interpretations of the law are used, although the historical background can sometimes be useful in explaining why today's law is as it is. There are a few areas that have their basis in an Act of Parliament, and those areas require the Act of Parliament to be interpreted in accordance with the rules of statutory interpretation that are studied in Unit 1.

How case law is used in answers to typical questions in AQA Unit 2

The examination paper for Unit 2 is divided into three sections. As we have seen, Unit 2A is on the introduction to criminal law, and is compulsory. The choice of area of study of civil law is between tort and contract. Unit 2C is on the law of contract and, as in the other sections, all questions within it must be answered. The contract question starts with a short scenario that sets the scene and is the basis of your discussions for some of the following questions. A scenario, taken from the sample paper, is:

> Umar wanted to buy a large quantity of mobile phones for his shop. He phoned Mobiles plc, who agreed to supply him with a quantity of phones for £60,000. Mobiles plc immediately realised they had been using an old price list and tried to contact Umar on the phone, but failed to reach him. Mobiles plc therefore posted a new price list to Umar, which he received the next day. Mobiles plc refused to supply the phones at £60,000 and Umar refused to pay the revised price of £70,000. Mobiles plc's new prices were the same as other suppliers of the phones.

The questions are of two general types:

Theory-only questions

Theory-only questions require an explanation of terms used, but no reference to the facts given in the scenario.

A typical question is:

Explain the difference between an offer and an invitation to treat.

(8 marks)

Application questions

Application questions require you to select the appropriate law or principles of damages, and apply the law to the facts given in the scenario. You should assume that the facts as stated in the scenario can be proved.

A typical question (using the scenario of Umar and Mobiles plc) is:

Briefly discuss the legal effect of each stage of negotiations between Umar and Mobiles plc, and decide whether those negotiations resulted in a valid contract with Mobiles plc.

(8 marks + 2 marks for AO3)

Note that this question also includes some marks for Assessment Objective 3 (written communication). These marks are usually awarded in the first question that is not theory-only in each section of the paper.

1 Think about what you have bought today. Each time you bought something you made a contract. How did this contract take place? What do you think the situation might be if you put a coin in a vending machine or clicked to buy something from a website?

2 Think about contracts that have gone wrong, such as buying a DVD that would not play. Was there a breach of contract and what was done about it?

You should now be able to:

- understand the role of the civil law
- understand the concept of contract
- understand how to use authority in answering questions on contract.

In this topic you will learn how to:

- define an offer

- distinguish between an offer and an invitation to treat

- describe the rules that decide when an offer comes to an end

- apply the rules to a given scenario.

2 The offer

What is an offer?

An **offer** is the starting point for a contract. It is essential to understand what amounts to an offer and when the offer comes into existence. The difficulty is in deciding whether a statement amounts to an offer or whether it is just a statement preparatory to an offer (known as an **invitation to treat**).

Much of the law is found in precedents set in the 19th century, so the facts may seem rather dated. Most of the law is based on sensible ideas and is easy to apply, providing a logical approach is taken.

The next essential aspect of an understanding of the operation of the law is to look for communication of the offer. Unless a person knows about an offer, it cannot be acted upon. Once it is known to exist, the essential point is to establish the duration of an offer, as it can only be accepted whilst the offer remains open. Once the offer has ended, it cannot be accepted and so it cannot be the basis of a contract. A new offer would then have to be made to start the process of forming a contract. The contract is formed when an offer has been accepted.

Fig. 14.2 *Duration of an offer*

█ Key terms

Offer: an offer is a statement of the terms upon which the person making the offer is willing to enter a contract: it can be verbal or written.

Invitation to treat: an invitation to treat is merely an indication of a willingness to start negotiations, and is not an offer.

An offer or an invitation to treat?

An invitation to treat is merely an indication of a willingness to enter negotiations. This is not always understood by the general public.

In 1999, Argos was inundated with orders on its website when, as the result of a software error, a 21-inch TV set was mistakenly priced at £3 rather than the correct price of £299.99. By the time the price was corrected, hundreds of people are reported to have already placed orders for the TV set. As many people placed multiple orders – one customer was reported to have ordered 1700 of the TV sets – the total cost of the orders was allegedly around £1m. Argos spoke with its lawyers and with the Advertising Standards Authority, and decided that it would not honour the orders placed. This was partly on the basis that acceptance of the orders had not been confirmed and that therefore there was no contract to sell at the £3 price.

Argos was correct that the advertisement on the internet was just an invitation to treat: it was following precedents that have been set for many years. Therefore, there was no offer that could be accepted and thus no contract between the customers and Argos. This is a logical decision for many reasons – for example, there are usually a finite number of articles for sale. If you advertised your car for sale, you only have one to sell and you would be in legal difficulties if the advert were an offer as each person telephoning to accept would create a contract, only one of which you could fulfil.

Generally, an advertisement in a newspaper or magazine is not an offer but an invitation to treat. There are a number of examples of cases setting the precedent that such advertisements are an invitation to treat and not an offer. One such case is **Partridge v Crittenden (1968)**. This was a criminal case where an advertiser in a newspaper advertised 'bramble finch cocks and hens 25/– [£1.25]' It was an offence under the Protection of Birds Act 1954 to offer wild birds for sale. The defendant was found not guilty as he did not offer the birds for sale; there was merely an invitation to treat.

The same conclusion is reached with respect to goods in a shop window. This can be seen in **Fisher v Bell (1961)**, another case involving a criminal prosecution. A shopkeeper in Bristol was prosecuted because he had a flick knife in his shop window with a price label on it. It was a criminal offence under the Restriction of Offensive Weapons Act 1959 to offer such knives for sale. The shopkeeper was found not guilty as he was not offering the knife for sale; it was merely an invitation to treat. Again, it is a logical decision, as the shopkeeper may wish to choose the person to whom he sells the goods.

The idea of choosing to whom a shopkeeper wants to sell goods is even more important in a self-service shop such as a supermarket. There are many restrictions on those who can buy certain types of goods, ranging from alcohol, potential weapons such as chef's knives, solvents and other dangerous items, to lottery tickets. In all such cases, the seller has the right to refuse to sell the item to the potential customer, as the advertisement of the lottery or the display of bottles and cans of alcoholic drink are not offers, just invitations to treat. The customer makes the offer and the shopkeeper decides whether to sell or not, often after establishing that the buyer is of the appropriate age.

■ **Study tips**

Make sure you can distinguish an offer from an invitation to treat.

■ **Key cases**

Partridge v Crittenden (1968): an advertisement for the sale of protected birds was not an offer.

Fisher v Bell (1961): a knife with a price label on it in a shop window was not an offer but an invitation to treat.

Fig. 14.3 *The display of goods does not constitute an offer to sell*

Pharmaceutical Society of Great Britain v Boots Cash Chemists (Southern) Ltd (1952): goods in a self-service store are an invitation to treat, not an offer.

Thornton v Shoe Lane Parking (1971): a ticket from an automatic machine in a car park involved the car park owner making the offer, and the customer accepting the offer by putting money in the machine.

Chapelton v Barry UDC (1940): a pile of deckchairs for hire on a beach was an offer that the customer could accept.

Thus, in the case of **Pharmaceutical Society of Great Britain v Boots Cash Chemists (Southern) Ltd (1952)**, the well-known high-street shop was prosecuted for offering medicines for sale when a pharmacist was not present. This was an offence under the Pharmacy and Poisons Act 1933. Boots was found not guilty as the court decided that the offer was made by the customer at the point of sale – that is, the counter or checkout till. This is reflected in the practice of assistants in pharmacies of seeking approval from the pharmacist before selling some medicines.

There are some variations on this principle, again based on common sense. Where a person buys something from a vending machine, it can be said that the offer is made by the owner of the machine and that it is the buyer from the machine who accepts the offer and makes the contract come into existence. This has some implications for cigarette machines and access to them by those who are under the legal age for buying cigarettes.

However, it would be impractical to use any other principles on vending machines, and this can be seen in the case of **Thornton v Shoe Lane Parking (1971)**. In that case, the court decided that a contract was formed by a customer entering a car park via an automatic barrier. On the facts, Mr Thornton put money in a machine to open the barrier and was given a ticket. It would be the same if he had just taken a ticket and paid on exit as is more common today. Lord Denning said, 'The offer is made when the proprietor of the machine holds it out as being ready to receive the money. The acceptance takes place when the customer puts the money in the slot.'

An even more unusual example of an offer can be seen in the case of **Chapelton v Barry UDC (1940)**, where the act of taking a deckchair from a pile of deckchairs and sitting on it formed the contract where a local council hired deckchairs to people on its beach. The offer was the placing of the pile of deckchairs that could be taken. There would not be an offer if the deckchairs were secured and an attendant had to release one to a customer who requested it. In the last case, it would be the customer making the offer and the attendant accepting it on behalf of the council.

It should also be noted that just giving information does not amount to an offer – it is a common courtesy to reply to an enquiry should the person owning the item decide to sell. There are a number of cases that involve this point, and each one is decided on the key aspects of the evidence. The most famous of these cases is **Harvey v Facey (1893)**. In this case, the claimants were interested in buying some land and sent a message, 'Will you sell us Bumper Hall Pen [the land]? Send lowest cash price.' The defendants replied, 'Lowest cash price for Bumper Hall Pen £900.' The claimants then replied, 'We agree to buy Bumper Hall Pen for £900.' The court decided that there was not a contract, as the original message was merely a request for information.

Finally, a statement is not an offer if it is not definite in the terms it uses. In **Gibson v Manchester City Council (1979)**, the council's response when asked by Mr Gibson whether he could buy his council house was, 'the corporation may be prepared to sell the house to you at the purchase price of £2725 less 20 per cent'. The court decided that this reply was not an offer, but an invitation to treat. The word 'may' indicated a lack of certainty so there was not an offer. The uncertainty showed that negotiations were still continuing, not that there was a readiness to make a contract.

Key cases

Harvey v Facey (1893): a response to a request for information is just an invitation to treat not an offer.

Gibson v Manchester City Council (1979): a statement is not an offer if the words you use show uncertainty as to whether there is a willingness to make a contract.

Carlill v Carbolic Smoke Ball Co. (1892): an advertisement could contain an offer if it was clearly meant to be taken seriously.

Table 14.1 *Cases distinguishing offers and invitations to treat*

Invitation to treat	Offer	Case
Advertisement in newspaper		*Partridge* v *Crittenden*
Goods in a shop window		*Fisher* v *Bell*
Goods on a supermarket shelf		*Pharmaceutical Society of Great Britain* v *Boots Cash Chemists (Southern) Ltd*
	Dealing with an automatic machine	*Thornton* v *Shoe Lane Parking*
	Barry UDC placing the pile of deckchairs with the terms of hire alongside	*Chapelton* v *Barry UDC*
Response to a request for information		*Harvey* v *Facey*
Uncertain words ('the corporation may ...')		*Gibson* v *Manchester City Council*

Communication of the offer

An offer cannot be accepted unless the person who is seeking to accept it knows of its existence. Thus if I offer a reward for finding my missing cat, a person who returns the cat but is unaware of the offer cannot claim the reward. Similar problems arise with answerphones that do not play back messages and fax machines that fail to print out. This has implications for potential purchasers who are responding to an invitation to treat who do not realise that they have failed to communicate with the person making the invitation. However, they will have no legal claim as there is no contract.

There is one famous case that illustrates a number of points, but is unusual because the offer was made to anyone and everyone rather than to a specific person. This is the case of **Carlill v Carbolic Smoke Ball Co. (1892)**. In that case, Mrs Carlill claimed the reward offered by the Carbolic Smoke Ball Co. for anyone who used its smoke ball (a sort of medicinal vaporiser or inhaler), but caught influenza. The company refused to pay, stating that

Study tips

There are many cases on the law on offer and acceptance. Make sure you know the legal point for which each case is authority.

Fig. 14.4 *The advertisement in* Carlill v Carbolic Smoke Ball Co.

the so-called offer of £100 was a mere marketing 'puff' and not intended to have any basis for a contract. Mrs Carlill argued that it was an offer which she had accepted by buying and using the smoke ball in accordance with the instructions. Mrs Carlill won the case, as the court decided that it was an offer that could be taken seriously and was not just an advertising gimmick. The court also said that an offer could be made to the whole world, and that anyone hearing the offer could accept: it just had to have been communicated to the individual claiming to have accepted it. Mrs Carlill apparently lived to the age of 96. She died in 1942 of … influenza.

Ending an offer

As an offer can only be accepted whilst it is open, it is important to know when an offer comes to an end. It can come to an end in the following ways:

■ lapse of time

■ revocation

■ rejection

■ counter offer

■ death.

Lapse of time

Some offers are made for a fixed period of time, such as seven days or one month. At the end of that period, the offer lapses and comes to an end. Most offers do not have any fixed time limit and so will come to an end after a reasonable time. What is reasonable will depend on all the circumstances. It is clear that a short period would be appropriate for something perishable such as a cake, and a long period for something large and complex such as a ship. In the case of **Ramsgate Victoria Hotel v Montefiore (1866)**, the defendant offered to buy shares in the Ramsgate Victoria Hotel on 8 June. On 23 November, the company tried to accept the offer but the defendant no longer wanted to buy the shares. The court decided that the five-month gap after the offer was too long, and so the offer had lapsed and could not be accepted.

Revocation

A person who makes an offer can revoke (withdraw) his offer at any time before it has been accepted. For this to happen, the person to whom the offer was made must receive notification of the withdrawal, at which point he can no longer accept the offer. A withdrawal of an offer can even occur during any period when the offer is said to be open, and an example of this is **Routledge v Grant (1828)**. In that case, Grant made an offer to buy Routledge's house, the offer to remain open for six weeks. Grant decided not to buy the house three weeks later, and told Routledge he was withdrawing his offer. Two weeks later, Routledge tried to accept the offer. The court decided that the offer had been withdrawn, so it could not be accepted.

Revocation can be implied by other actions. Once an offer for an object is accepted, it cannot be accepted again. However, where the offer has been made to more than one person, there are potential difficulties, as there could be two contracts with respect to one object. Suppose I offer my car for sale to Y and Z at a price of £1000 even though the market price for my car is £1500. If I agree to sell to Y, I will need to tell Z that the car I offered to sell him was in fact sold or I risk being sued for breach of contract. If Z found out from a reliable source I had sold the car, he would also know that the offer had ended. This can be seen from the case of **Dickinson v Dodds (1876)**, where Dodds offered to sell his house to Dickinson. The offer was open until Friday. On Thursday afternoon, Dickinson heard from someone else, whom he knew to be reliable, that Dodds had sold the property to someone else. On the Friday morning, Dickinson delivered a formal acceptance to Dodds but the court decided that the offer made to Dickinson had been revoked on the Thursday when he heard of the sale of the house. There was no longer an offer in existence to accept, and so no contract could be formed. Hearing about the sale from a reliable source is the implied revocation of the offer.

The situation where one person wants an offer to remain open for a period of time is quite common, as the time period is to be used for getting financial and other plans drawn up. So as to make sure that the offer will remain open, a separate contract has to be made. This is usually a contract to keep the offer open for an agreed fixed period in exchange for an agreed sum of money. This is known as 'buying an option'.

Rejection

Once an offer is rejected, it cannot be accepted and the offer comes to an end. The person to whom the offer is made does not have a second chance to accept the offer. If he or she attempts to accept the offer, he is in fact making a fresh offer that the person who originally made the offer can accept or reject. The rejection must be a clear rejection, and not just a request for more information as in the case of *Harvey* v *Facey* (1893). In **Stevenson v McLean (1880)** there was an enquiry from a person to whom goods had been offered for sale as to whether he could have two months' credit. There was no reply, so assuming that there would be no credit, he accepted the offer, being prepared to pay cash. The court decided that this enquiry about credit was not a rejection of the offer or a counter offer, and the offer remained open and had been accepted.

Counter offer

A counter offer both rejects the original offer and creates a new offer that can then be accepted or rejected. This commonly takes place during negotiations. If I were selling my car, the sequence might be like this:

- Advertisement to sell car for £2000: this is an invitation to treat (*Partridge* v *Crittenden*).
- X offers to pay £1800 for the car: an offer.
- I refuse, saying I could go to £1950: rejection of X's offer of £1800 and new offer made by me at £1950.

This process then continues until agreement is reached or there is no sale. Note I cannot go back to X and 'accept' his offer of £1800, as that offer ended when I originally rejected the offer and made an offer to sell at £1950.

A case that illustrates counter offer is **Hyde v Wrench (1840)**. The facts of that case were:

- 6 June: Wrench offered to sell his farm to Hyde for £1000; Hyde offered £950.
- 9 June: Wrench rejected Hyde's offer.
- 21 June: Hyde tried to accept the offer to sell at £1000. Wrench refused to sell at £1000, as his original offer had ended with Hyde's counter-offer of £950.

Key cases

Dickinson v Dodds (1876): where a reliable person informs the person to whom an offer has been that the offer has ended, it is as if the revocation of the offer had been made by the person who had made the offer.

Stevenson v McLean (1880): an enquiry about whether credit was available did not reject the offer, which could still be accepted.

Hyde v Wrench (1840): a counter-offer ends the original offer. In this case this occurred in negotiations over the price to be paid for a farm.

Study tips

When explaining the theory of the ending of an offer, deal with all the ways it can be ended. When discussing an offer and acceptance problem, select the appropriate method for the facts in the scenario.

Death

In English law, contracts can be enforced against a dead person's estate, if necessary by suing the deceased's executors or administrators. However, an offer made by a person who dies before the offer ends cannot be accepted if the person to whom the offer is made knows of his death. If he does not know of the death, then the offer can still be accepted. This is logical as it could otherwise provide hardship for the family of a business owner who died, as contracts in the course of negotiation would have to be restarted. Obviously if the contract involves a service to be provided by the deceased, the contract will not be valid, as performance of it would be impossible.

Conclusion

An offer is a statement of the terms on which the person making the offer is willing to be bound, whereas an invitation to treat is only preliminary to that. Once an offer is open it can be accepted by the person to whom it has been made until the point where the offer ends. There are a number of different ways in which an offer can end, although it is most usually by lapse or acceptance.

Activities

1. Practice writing a few sentences distinguishing an offer from an invitation to treat. You should do this by stating each distinction and using a decided case to demonstrate each distinction. When you are confident that you can do this accurately, try to do so without notes and complete the task in about seven minutes – this is the length of time you might have in the exam.

2. Make a chart of the ways in which an offer can come to an end and give your own example of how each would occur.

You should now be able to:

- understand the nature and duration of an offer
- decide whether there is a valid offer in a given situation.

In this topic, you will learn how to:

- define acceptance
- describe when acceptance takes place
- apply the rules of acceptance to a given situation.

Key terms

Acceptance: the final expression of assent to the terms of an offer.

3 Acceptance

What is acceptance?

Once an offer is accepted, there is a contract between the person making the offer and the person accepting it, provided the other essentials of formation of consideration and legal intention are present. The **acceptance** has to be positive and unqualified. In other words, it is responding to the offer by saying 'Yes', and not 'Yes, but' or 'Yes, if'. The words can be said or written. Acceptance can be by conduct – in other words, by doing something – but it cannot usually be by doing nothing. Acceptance must usually be communicated to the person making the offer. This is the most crucial aspect of acceptance, as that communication establishes if and when the contract comes into existence.

Methods of communication of acceptance

The usual methods of acceptance do not present any problems. A verbal statement that is clearly heard and understood fulfils the requirements. The acceptance takes place as soon as the acceptance is heard by the person making the offer. If it is not heard, there would be no acceptance. There are potential difficulties where acceptance is by conduct, by post or by electronic methods.

Conduct

In general, silence or inaction cannot be an acceptance as some positive act is needed. An example of this is seen in the case of **Felthouse v Bindley (1862)**, where the sale of a horse was being negotiated by letter and message. Eventually, Felthouse wrote saying that if he heard nothing further, he would consider the horse sold to him for a stated price. The court decided that this was just another offer that the seller could accept or reject, and was not an acceptance, as acceptance required positive conduct.

This principle is reflected in legislation such as the Unsolicited Goods and Services Act 1971 and the Consumer Protection (Distance Selling) Regulations 2000 (as amended). This legislation states that someone who receives goods they did not request does not have to pay for them, and may be able to keep them if the sender of the goods does not collect them. In other words, just retaining the goods does not accept any offer to sell such goods, which it could be argued had been made.

Positive conduct can be acceptance where that is a method of communication set out in the offer. This can be implied in the offer – for example, starting to use goods sent on approval. It can also be seen in the case of *Carlill* v *Carbolic Smoke Ball Co.* (1892), where Mrs Carlill's use of the smoke ball was sufficient to accept the offer of the reward as the company clearly did not expect individual users to contact the company.

Communication of acceptance by post: the postal rules

The postal rules developed during the 19th century as the postal service became reliable and the main means of communication between businesses that were at a distance from each other. There is a risk that a letter may go missing, so the court had to decide where the loss should fall. The following rules were set out:

- The postal rules only apply to letters of acceptance, not to offers, revocation of offers or counter-offers.
- The postal rules only apply if the post is the usual method of communication between the parties involved in the contract, or is specifically stated as the only or an accepted method of communication of acceptance.
- Acceptance takes place when a correctly stamped and addressed letter is posted (the principle is based on the fact that once a letter is posted, it cannot be got back).
- The claimant must be able to prove the letter was posted. This is reflected in a certificate of posting from a post office or a signed statement by the person putting the letter in the letter box.

These rules were first clarified in the case of **Adams v Lindsell (1818)**. The facts are best seen in date order:

- 2 September: Lindsell wrote to Adams offering to sell some wool, asking for a reply 'in the course of post'.

Key cases

Felthouse v Bindley (1862): a statement that if nothing further was heard then a contract would be made was not sufficient to be the positive act required for acceptance.

Adams v Lindsell (1818): the postal rules state that a letter of acceptance takes effect at the moment of posting.

■ Study tips

When applying the law on acceptance, at least consider whether the postal rules apply.

■ 5 September: Adams received the letter and sent a letter of acceptance.

■ 8 September: Lindsell sold the wool to someone else.

■ 9 September: Lindsell received Adams' acceptance letter.

The court set out the postal rules and decided that the offer for the sale of the wool had been accepted by Lindsell on 5 September when Lindsell posted his letter of acceptance, thus there was a contract.

This principle has been confirmed as the law in several cases since then, and in the 1980s it was used as the basis of a corporate promotion video made by an insurance company. The scenario was posting a letter accepting life insurance on the way to run a marathon and then dying during the marathon. The deceased's widow was paid in full by the life insurance company, even though he had died before the acceptance of the offer had reached the insurance company.

Electronic and instantaneous forms of communication

The advent of technology meant that the postal rules had to be reconsidered in the light of electronic communication. It is accepted that telephone is instant verbal communication, just as though the parties were in each other's presence. If the call was not heard because of a fault, it appears there would be no communication of acceptance. This will be a question of evidence, but does not usually present a problem as most businesses keep written notes of important telephone calls and it is business practice to send confirmation of an order.

■ Key cases

Entores v Miles Far East Corporation (1955): communication by telex machine takes place when the message is received rather than when sent. It is not the same as using the post.

The first case on this was **Entores v Miles Far East Corporation** (1955). In this case, the question was when a telex machine communication was made. The court decided that the acceptance by telex took place when it was received. A similar decision was arrived at in *Brinkibon* v *Stahag Stahl* (1983).

Whilst this still seems to be the law for telex and fax communications, all other electronic communications are now covered by the Electronic Commerce (EC Directive) Regulations 2002. Regulation 11 states that an order and the acknowledgement of receipt of it (these can be taken to be the offer and acceptance) are deemed to be received when the person to whom they are addressed is able to access them. This covers all contracts made with internet companies. This suggests that acceptance would not in fact take place until business hours have begun; this is, of course, subject to any term set out in the offer as to when acceptance takes place.

How to approach an offer and acceptance problem

All offer and acceptance problems require the same logical approach:

■ Identify the sequence of events and list them in chronological order.

■ Identify each event as an invitation to treat, offer, counter offer, revocation of offer, acceptance, etc., as appropriate.

■ State the reasons why you identified the event as you did, using decided cases to back up your argument.

■ Identify when the offer opens and when it ends.

■ Identify whether there is an acceptance within that period (if so, there is a contract).

■ Come to a conclusion.

Note that problems involving consideration and legal intention have other issues that may need to be identified and dealt with too.

Here is a sample question, together with an outline answer following the template just described:

The scenario:

> On 29 April, Richard placed an advertisement in the local paper offering his car for sale for £17,000. Jennifer telephoned Richard on 1 May and offered to buy the car for £15,000. Richard said he was not prepared to accept such a low price, but kept Jennifer's details. On 8 May Richard had still not sold his car and wrote to Jennifer offering to sell it to her for £16,000. Jennifer received the letter on 9 May. On 10 May, Jennifer wrote back stating that she would not pay more than £15,500 for the car. On 11 May Jennifer wrote another letter to Richard saying that she accepted his offer and would pay £16,000 for the car. Richard received both of Jennifer's letters on 12 May but refused to give the car to Jennifer as he had found another buyer who would pay him £16,500.

The approach:

29 April – advertisement (£17,000) – invitation to treat – *Partridge* v *Crittenden*.

1 May – offer (£15,000) – Jennifer to Richard – Richard can accept or reject it; he rejects it instantly on the telephone, ending Jennifer's offer.

8 May – offer (£16,000) Richard to Jennifer – offer open when Jennifer receives the letter (9 May).

10 May – rejection of offer in the letter from Jennifer to Richard by counter-offer (*Hyde* v *Wrench*) – rejection takes place when this letter is received by Richard (12 May).

11 May – acceptance of offer in the letter from Jennifer to Richard – acceptance takes place when put in the post box as the postal rules apply (post is usual mode of communication, evidence of posting and correct address, etc. as letter arrived the next day) – *Adams* v *Lindsell*. Contract therefore made as acceptance takes place whilst the offer is still open (it is open till 12 May). If Richard does not sell the car to Jennifer he will be in breach of contract.

The conclusion:

Acceptance is agreeing to the terms of the offer, and requires understanding of when the acceptance takes place as the consequences are a legally binding contract. One consequence might be the need to insure the item bought from that moment as it then belongs to the buyer.

Activities

1. Here are the facts of *Byrne* v *Van Tienhoven* (1880). Van Tienhoven, a Cardiff businessman, offered goods to Byrne, a New York trader, at a fixed price in a letter of 1 October. Byrne accepted as soon as he received the offer. On 8 October Van Tienhoven had sent a letter revoking the offer. The letter of 1 October arrived on 11 October. On 12 October, Byrne sent a telegram accepting the offer and a confirmatory letter of acceptance on 14 October. The letter of 8 October arrived on 20 October and the letter of 14 October arrived on 30 October.

   Apply the methodology for solving offer and acceptance problems to those facts.

2 Practice writing a few sentences explaining acceptance by post and acceptance by conduct. You should do this by explaining each type of acceptance and using a decided case to demonstrate each type. When you are confident that you can do this accurately, try to do so without notes and complete the task in about seven minutes – this is the length of time you might have in the exam.

You should now be able to:

- understand when acceptance takes place
- apply the rules on offer and acceptance to a given situation.

In this topic you will learn how to:

- explain the term 'intention to create legal relations'
- distinguish between the rules for commercial and domestic agreements
- state relevant cases and examples.

Key terms

Intention to create legal relations: the parties to a contract must intend the agreement to be legally binding. This is implied in commercial agreements, but presumed not to exist in social and domestic agreements.

Study tips

In most contracts, legal intention is not an issue. However, you need to be able to distinguish between commercial and domestic arrangements as seen in the cases.

Key cases

Jones v Vernons Pools (1938) and Appleson v Littlewoods Pools (1939): in both cases, a claim that money had been won on a football pool coupon could not be enforced in the courts as the football pool coupon clearly stated it was 'binding in honour only'.

4 Intention to create legal relations

Background

So far we have looked at the formation of the agreement that forms the contract. Any agreement includes an offer and an acceptance, but the law will not enforce such an agreement if there is no **intention to create legal relations**. Whilst some may try to avoid the use of the courts to settle disputes, it is an essential principle that there is an intention that legal rights and duties will follow from a commercial contract. Everyone expects to have some legal rights should goods bought turn out to be defective or services ordered not provided. The law presumes that there is an intention that such contracts will be legally binding.

However, it is equally clear that we do not expect our domestic arrangements to be legally binding, with the prospect of a court case in the event of failure. I do not expect my children to sue me if I am late in paying their pocket money; if a friend fails to turn up and give me a lift to a venue for an evening out, I, again, will consider that I have no legal right to claim damages. The law will take the same view, and presume that there is no intention to create legal relations in domestic or social arrangements.

There are some situations where these two presumptions will be rebutted; in other words, the law will find a legally binding contract in what appears to be a domestic arrangement or the law will find no intention to create legal relations in a business arrangement.

Commercial agreements

The general principle is that an intention to create legal relations is presumed in commercial agreements. This can be rebutted by the words used in the agreement. There are some older cases where the agreements had specific terms referring to 'honour clauses', but these are rarely seen in today's commercial world and are likely to be interpreted very strictly by the courts. The agreement must be quite clear as to the nature and effect of this restriction. A clear, express statement excluding legal intention can be seen to have been effective in the following examples.

A football pool coupon

In **Jones v Vernons Pools (1938)** and in **Appleson v Littlewoods Pools (1939)** claims were made by claimants who believed they had a winning coupon. In both cases, the courts refused to deal with the claim as the coupon clearly stated 'binding in honour only' and the claimants had signed the coupon.

A sale of a house 'subject to contract'

It is quite usual to see a house sale board with the addition 'sold, subject to contract' added to it. This is reflecting the situation that an agreement has been reached between the owner of the house and the prospective purchaser, but that a written contract has not yet been completed. The delay may occur while the purchaser checks financial and other details. A contract to sell land, and therefore a house, has to be evidenced in writing to be legally valid under the Law of Property Act 1925. The idea of 'sold, subject to contract' is common practice in such transactions, but can still lead to unpleasant disputes where a house seller ignores the agreement and then sells to another person for more money. The seller is legally, but arguably not morally, correct in taking this action. It should be noted that some commercial agreements are also made 'subject to contract', where the agreement is a basic intent to proceed with the need to draw up precise terms. In these cases, it is a matter of interpretation as to whether or not a contract exists.

Social and domestic arrangements

Social and domestic arrangements are not usually legally binding. The exceptions to the rule are those where there is a more formal situation. Two matrimonial cases illustrate this.

In **Balfour v Balfour (1919)**, Mr Balfour worked in Ceylon (modern-day Sri Lanka), and came to England with his wife on holiday. He later returned to Ceylon alone, but his wife stayed in England for health reasons. He promised to pay her £30 per month as maintenance whilst she stayed in England, but he stopped paying her when the marriage broke down. The court decided she could not take legal action for the promised maintenance payments as, amongst other reasons, the agreement was a purely domestic arrangement that they didn't intend to be legally binding. It would then be a question in divorce proceedings for the court to decide what payments he should make to her.

In **Merritt v Merritt (1970)**, the situation was different because the husband and wife were already living apart when the agreement was made. Mr Merritt left his wife, and shortly after he left they met to make arrangements for the future. He agreed to pay £40 per month maintenance, out of which she would pay the mortgage. When the mortgage was paid off, he would transfer the house from joint names to the wife's name. He wrote this down and signed the paper, but later refused to transfer the house. The court decided that they must have intended the agreement to be binding, as they would base their future actions on it and had put it in writing. Therefore there was a legally binding agreement rather than a purely domestic arrangement.

This principle has been applied to many other domestic arrangements, including parental support for students at university. For such an agreement to be a contract, there needs to be something much more formal, such as a deed (a formal written and witnessed document).

Finally, there can be social arrangements that are legally binding, such as an agreement to share winnings in a lottery syndicate. These arrangements are usually set out in writing and signed, which again helps the evidence that the agreement is meant to be legally binding. This can be seen in the case of **Simpkins v Pays (1955)**. Mrs Pays, her granddaughter, and Mr Simpkins, a lodger, shared a house. They all contributed one third of the stake in entering a weekly competition in the *Sunday Empire News*. On 27 June 1954, the competition was to place, in order of merit, eight women's fashions. They took it in turns to pay the entry fee and fill in the form and send it off. That week, a prize of £750 was won for correctly placing

Key cases

Balfour v Balfour (1919): a domestic arrangement to pay maintenance was not intended to be legally binding as it was a domestic arrangement during a marriage. The fact that the marriage failed later did not make it legally binding retrospectively.

Merritt v Merritt (1970): a more formal written agreement between husband and wife as to some financial arrangements following a marital split can be legally binding.

Simpkins v Pays (1955): an agreement to share winnings in any prizes won in a competition or lottery is legally binding as the exercise is a sort of joint enterprise.

the fashion items in order – but as Mrs Pays had entered the form that week, she refused to share the prize. The court decided that the arrangement was a joint enterprise to which cash was contributed in the expectation of sharing any prize. Thus, each was entitled to a one-third share of the winnings.

A similar case arose in Scotland in 2002, with the same outcome. This was the case of *Robertson* v *Anderson*, where two women set off together on 21 November 1997 to play bingo at the Mecca Bingo Hall in Drumchapel. The defendant won a big prize. When she declined to share it with the claimant, proceedings were brought for payment of half the winnings, alleging that there had been an agreement to 'go halfers'.

Conclusion

Generally there is presumed to be an intention to create legal relations in commercial agreements and no intention in social or domestic arrangements. There are exceptions, but they are quite clear and seem to have been sensible decisions.

Activities

1. Consider the agreements you have made today and decide whether each is legally binding or not.

2. Practice writing a few sentences explaining intention to create legal relations and distinguishing between business and social agreements. You should do this by explaining both business and social agreements and the exceptions to the general rule, using a decided case to demonstrate each type. When you are confident that you can do this accurately, try to do so without notes and complete the task in about seven minutes – this is the length of time you might have in the exam.

You should now be able to:

- understand the meaning of intention to create legal relations
- apply the rules to a given situation.

In this topic you will learn how to:

- define consideration
- explain the term 'past consideration'
- state relevant cases and examples.

5 Consideration

What is consideration?

Consideration means that each party to a contract must give something of some value. This is because the law is concerned with bargains and not gifts. This has been defined by Sir Frederick Pollock as follows: 'An act or forbearance of one party, or the promise thereof, is the price for which the promise of the other is bought, and the promise thus given for value is enforceable.' The idea in the definition is that each party to the contract does something of some value for the other: either a positive act, such as giving something or doing some work; or forbearance – that is, not doing something. Consideration must be present for any valid contract unless the agreement is made by a deed (a form of legal document). There are a number of aspects of consideration that need to be understood.

Types of valid consideration

There are two types of valid consideration: executed consideration and executory consideration. **Executed consideration** is the term used to describe the status of a person's promise in a contract where that part of the bargain has been performed. For example, if A agrees with B to pay B £10 to wash A's car, and B washes the car, B's consideration is executed – that is, complete – because he has then performed his side of the bargain. He can then hold A to his promise to pay the £10.

Executory consideration is the term used to describe the status of a person's promise in a contract where that part of the bargain has not yet been performed. Thus in the previous example, it would be the payment of the £10 that had not yet happened.

Consideration must have some value

As the law is concerned with bargains and not gifts, the consideration must have some value but does not have to be of equal value. The whole point of business is to get more for your goods than you paid for them; clearly this is not equal value. Thus, contract law recognises the rule that consideration must be sufficient but need not be adequate.

The idea of adequacy is that there must be some economic value, but not necessarily equal value. This can be seen in the case of **Chappell v Nestlé (1959)**, where chocolate bar wrappers were taken as part payment for a record as part of a promotion. It was acknowledged that used chocolate bar wrappers have little value, but there was some value, all that is needed. This is reflected today in the use of vouchers that are often described as having a value of 0.0001 pence.

Past consideration is not valid consideration

Past consideration is not a valid form of consideration. It is defined as something already done at the time the agreement is made. Where the consideration is past, there will not be a valid contract. An example of this can be seen in the case of **Re McArdle (1951)**. In this case, a person died and in his will left his assets in equal shares to his five children. The wife of one of the children paid out of her own money for alterations to one of the houses that were included in his assets. The children wrote to the wife, 'In consideration of your carrying out certain alterations … we hereby agree to repay you [£488] from the estate.' The court held that the promise of payment did not create a contract as the alterations were over and done with by the time the promise of payment was made, so in relation to that promise her 'consideration' was past. In other words, she had given no consideration for the promise of payment, there was no contract, and she could not claim the £488.

This is different where A requests some performance from B before the contract comes into existence, but on the common understanding that there will be a contract and that there will be a payment. An example is asking a plumber to fix a leak in an emergency. A case that illustrates this is the very old case of **Lampleigh v Braithwaite (1615)**. Braithwaite killed someone and then asked Lampleigh to get him a pardon from the king. Lampleigh got the pardon and gave it to Braithwaite, who promised to pay Lampleigh £100 for his trouble. The court decided that although Lampleigh's consideration was past (he had got the pardon), Braithwaite's promise to pay could be linked to Braithwaite's earlier request and treated as one agreement. Therefore, it could be implied at the time of the request that Lampleigh would be paid and so was valid consideration.

Consideration must move from the promisee

This means that the person making the promise must provide the consideration. It does not matter that the contract was made for the benefit of another person. Thus, if A agrees to wash B's car if B pays £10 to C, there is no promise that is enforceable by C, as he or she has given no consideration for the £10. This basic rule has been altered by the Contracts (Rights of Third Parties) Act 1999 so that a person who is not a party to a contract can enforce the contract if he or she is named in the contract or he gains a benefit from it. There are a number of possible examples of how this applies, such as where a person has ordered goods on the internet to be delivered to someone else, where someone makes a group booking for an event or travel, and where someone has bought the bride and groom a wedding present from a wedding list in a shop.

Conclusion

All contracts require consideration. It is important to know what amounts to consideration and what does not. The main basis of the principle is that the law is concerned with bargains and not gifts.

Activities

 Identify whether the consideration in the example below is executed or executory.

Umar agreed with Mobiles plc that they should supply him with 1000 mobile phones for £60,000. Mobiles plc has now delivered the phones, but Umar has not yet paid for them.

2 Practice writing a few sentences, explaining consideration and distinguishing good consideration and past consideration. Then attempt this practice examination question:

Explain the meaning of the term consideration, including an explanation of past consideration.

You should now be able to:

- understand the concept of consideration
- apply the rules to a given situation.

15 Breach of contract and the courts: procedure and damages

1 Breach of contract

Introduction

A breach of contract occurs when one party to the contract fails or states that he or she will fail to perform part or all of their side of the bargain.

If the breach has serious consequences for the innocent party, he or she will have the choice of ending or continuing with the contract, as well as claiming damages; if the breach is only trivial, the innocent party must continue with the contract, although he can claim damages for any losses. Consider the difference between an electrician who has made a contract to renew all the electrical circuits, lights and sockets in a landlord's two houses, who fails to renew: (i) one socket in one house; and (ii) the electrical circuits in the upstairs of one house. These are both breaches of contract, as they both result in loss to one party to the contract. The first is a minor loss in having to get a socket renewed: a relatively small cost, even if it is essential work. But the second is much more serious and expensive to rectify, and would probably end the contract. The landlord may well agree a small reduction in the price he is paying for the minor failure and expect other work to continue. However, he or she may lose confidence in the electrician after the major failure and not wish them to continue to work on the second house. The first essential therefore is to decide which breaches are sufficiently serious that the innocent party can choose to end the contract.

Types of term

The law decides whether a breach of contract is serious enough by deciding which type of term in the contract has been broken. A term in a contract is known as either a **condition** or a **warranty**. A warranty is not the same as the promise made by manufacturers of goods in relation to repair or replacement if it should fail within a fixed period of time, often 12 months. A term that can be either a condition or a warranty depending on the nature of the failure is known as an **innominate term**.

A condition is a term of the contract that goes to the heart of the contract. If I rent a car, one term of the contract that will be a condition is that the car will actually go and stop. If it does not, then clearly I would want to end the contract and either rent a different car or go elsewhere. The failure to provide a car that goes and stops would be a breach of condition of a contract, and I would be entitled to treat the contract as ended. If the problem was easily fixed, I might delay renting the car and continue the contract, but seek damages as compensation for the delay. In law it is my choice if a condition has been broken.

A warranty, on the other hand, is a minor term of the contract. If it is broken, loss will result, but the main purpose of the contract will still be achieved. If I rent a car and the rental company offers me one that has a CD changer, if the CD changer does not work I will still have a useable car, but would expect to pay less and to be compensated for any CD of mine that I loaded that could not be recovered from the broken changer. This would be a warranty and I would have to continue with the contract, but would expect compensation.

Key terms

Condition: a term of the contract that, if not performed, will go to the heart of the contract. Breach of a condition gives the innocent party the right to end the contract, if he or she chooses, in addition to the right to claim damages for any losses.

Warranty: a minor term of the contract that, if not performed, will cause loss but does not go to the heart of the contract. Breach of warranty will not end the contract but will give rise to a claim for damages.

Innominate term: a term in a contract that can be treated as either a condition or a warranty, depending on the nature of the breach of that term.

Two cases that illustrate the distinction between a condition and a warranty are **Poussard v Spiers and Pond (1876)** and **Bettini v Gye (1876)**. In *Poussard* v *Spiers and Pond*, an opera singer made a contract to sing in an opera. She failed to attend the first six performances and was replaced for the entire run of the opera. She could only be replaced if her failure to attend was a breach of condition. The court decided that this was a breach of condition, as her role was central to the performance and a replacement singer would not want to perform only for a few days. The promoters could therefore replace the singer without paying compensation, as she had broken a condition of her contract.

In *Bettini* v *Gye*, an opera singer made a contract to perform from March to July and was also required to attend six days of rehearsale before performances were due to start. He failed to attend the first two days of rehearsals. This was a breach of warranty and not a breach of condition, as his failure to attend only caused some inconvenience; other parts of rehearsal could continue without him, and the promoters would not lose much, if any, money. They could not treat the contract as ended and replace the singer. Damages were the only remedy available. If the promoters had refused to use the singer in the performances, they would have broken their side of the contract and the singer could then have taken legal action against them for damages.

Actual breach and anticipatory breach

Breach of contract can occur in two ways: actual breach and anticipatory breach. Actual breach occurs either through poor performance of the contract, where there is performance of the contract but the work is done badly or the goods are substandard; or by non-performance, where the work is not done or the goods are not provided at all.

Anticipatory breach occurs where one party to the contract states or otherwise indicates that there will not be performance of the contract. This is usually that goods or services will not be provided. As soon as this has happened, the person affected can start legal action under the contract. This would occur in the situation where a person told a mobile-phone provider that he did not wish to continue with the contract after two months of a 12-month contract. An example of this can be seen in the case of **Hochster v De La Tour (1853)**, where a tour guide was told that his services would not be required despite the contract for him to work in two months' time. Here the guide had a choice: he could wait and see if the guide work was in fact wanted after all on the due dates, or treat the contract as ended and take immediate legal action to recover damages for his losses.

The consequences of breach of contract

Whatever type of breach has occurred, the party to the contract affected by the breach automatically has a right to damages. That party can also treat the contract as repudiated and take no further action under the contract where the breach is a breach of a condition, or an innominate term that has been broken in a serious way so that it is in effect a breach of condition.

Conclusion

Breach of contract can either end the contract because the breach is serious, or be a minor breach where damages are payable. Breach can be actual breach – the breach has happened – or anticipatory breach, a statement of intention not to perform the contract in the future.

> **Activities**
>
> **1** Distinguish between actual breach and anticipatory breach, giving examples of each type of breach.
>
> **2** John has booked to go on holiday to Malta in the summer. The tour company has recently written to him to tell him that the holiday is not now available to him as too many people have booked on the same holiday. Explain John's legal rights.

You should now be able to:

- understand the concept of breach of contract
- apply the rules to problem situations.

2 Outline of civil courts and appeal system

Initial hearing	First appeal	Final appeal
County Court	Court of Appeal	Supreme Court
High Court	(Civil Division)	

Fig. 14.1 *Court structure for a contract case*

In this topic you will learn how to:

- ▓ draw a diagram of the civil court structure showing appeal routes
- ▓ state the jurisdiction of each court
- ▓ distinguish between different classifications of cases in contract
- ▓ describe the burden of proof and the standard of proof in a civil case
- ▓ apply the above to a given situation.

The civil courts

The majority of contract cases are heard in the County Courts. Simple money claims can all be dealt with online using the Money Claim Online scheme. The manner in which each case is dealt with depends on the nature and size of the claim. The largest claims are heard in the High Court, Queen's Bench Division. Part of the Queen's Bench Division is the Commercial Court. Usually, appeals go to the Court of Appeal (Civil Division). For most legal cases in England and Wales, the Supreme Court is the final point of appeal.

The courts of first instance

A court of first instance is the court where a case is first tried. The court of first instance will be either the County Court or the High Court. The County Court and the High Court have different jurisdictions, so will hear different cases. The courts hope most cases will be settled out of court or by alternative dispute resolution, with only a minority actually being tried. In the 2005–06 County Court Annual Report, Lord Justice Thomas, Senior Presiding Judge for England and Wales wrote:

> **The division between the County Court and the High Court**
>
> The figures in this report reflect solely the work of the County Court. However, in reality, outside the Royal Courts of Justice there is very little distinction in practice between the way in which High Court and County Court work is done. We have in practice a 'single civil court', but unfortunately the figures in this report do not reflect this. A distinction is still perpetuated between the High Court and the County Court, even for reports such as this.

Money Claim Online is part of the County Court and was set up in 2001 to support Government policy in making justice affordable and accessible to all. This online service allows County Court claims to be issued for fixed sums up to £100,000 by individuals and organisations over the internet, anywhere, anytime. Its use is growing enormously each year.

Apart from Money Claim Online, the reality is that the cases are heard dependent on the track into which they fit. The courts are responsible for case management, with all cases allocated to one of three 'tracks' (namely, small claims, fast track and multi-track) according to their value and complexity. If a contract case is to be heard in the High Court, it is heard in the Queen's Bench Division. The Commercial Court is part of the Queen's Bench Division. It deals with complex cases arising out of business disputes, both national and international. In the Commercial Court there is particular emphasis on international trade, banking, commodity and arbitration disputes. All Commercial Court cases are treated as multi-track cases; these are explained later.

Whilst there are few cases in the Commercial Court (fewer than 100 went to trial in 2005), they are often quite lengthy. The procedure is successful because the number of full trials is about 10 per cent of the number of cases started. For example, the case *Man Nutzfahrzeuge Aktiengesellschaft* v *Freightliner Ltd* began on 11 January 2005 and continued for 18 weeks. It involved a dispute about the acquisition of a company. The existence of the Commercial Court is important because many international contracts contain a term that any dispute will be settled in accordance with English law in the English courts. This is good for the business of UK law firms and barristers.

The three tracks

Small claims
- Up to £5000
- Personal injury up to £1000
- Simple cases

Fast track
- £5000–£25,000
- Trial up to one day
- Moderately complex cases

Multi track
- Over £25,000
- Complex cases

Fig. 14.2 *The three tracks*

■ Link

The three tracks are discussed in more detail on pp235–6 (Chapter 13).

■ Link

For information on appeals, see Chapter 13 (The courts: procedure and damages for negligence cases), p231.

As outlined in Chapter 13, cases are heard in the court appropriate to the track into which they fit. The courts are responsible for case management, with all cases allocated to one of three 'tracks' (small claims, fast track or multi-track) according to their value and complexity. If a contract case is to be heard in the High Court, it is heard in the Queen's Bench Division, some large cases being allocated to the Commercial Court.

Which court and judge will hear the case depends on the scope and size of the case. Multi-track cases are almost always heard by a Circuit Judge, the others more often by a District Judge. A number of factors are taken into account in deciding the track, apart from the normal financial limits set out above. These include the complexity of the case and the amount of oral evidence that will be given.

An example of a small-claims track case is a dispute about the performance of a custom-built computer system that cost £4000. This would be small-claims track as the value of the claim is less than £5000 and there are no complex issues of law or evidence. It might be fast-track if specialist IT evidence were required to decide the case.

A multi-track case would be more complex and also (usually) involving a larger sum of money. This might involve a dispute about the construction of a new office block that appears to have been built with substandard foundations.

The burden and standard of proof

As we have seen in Chapter 14, in civil law cases the burden of proof is on the claimant to prove his or her claim on a balance of probabilities. There is a lower standard than in criminal cases. This means that the party bearing the burden of proof, namely the claimant, must demonstrate that it is 'more likely than not' that the defendant has been negligent. The **burden of proof** is the obligation on a party to establish the facts in issue in a case to the required degree of certainty (the standard of proof) in order to prove their case. In a civil trial, the burden is upon the claimant to prove the liability of the defendant. The **standard of proof** is on a balance of probabilities.

As most cases are for non-payment of a debt, there is often little need for complex evidence unless the defence is that the debt was not paid becuase the goods were faulty. These simple cases are usually dealt with following the Money Claim Online procedure and are rarely defended, so the claimant quickly obtains a default judgment, which he can then try to enforce against the defendant.

Conclusion

Most contract cases are heard in the County Court. The vast majority start as a Money Claim Online. The actual timing and venue will depend on the track to which the case is allocated. Whichever track the case is allocated to, the claimant has to prove his or her case on a balance of probabilities.

In early 2012 there was a consultation about changing the track limits and the courts to be used, but at the time of writing no definite proposals have been formulated.

> ### Activity
>
> Practice writing a few sentences explaining how damages are calculated. You should do this by explaining each aspect of damages, and referring to relevant case law. When you are confident that you can do this accurately, try to do so without notes and complete the task in about seven minutes – this is the length of time you might have in the exam.

You should now be able to:

- describe appeal routes for contract cases in the civil courts
- apply knowledge of court procedure to a given situation.

> ### Study tips
>
> Make sure you know the differences between the tracks, and check that the limits have not changed.

> ### Key terms
>
> **Burden of proof:** the obligation to prove that the defendant committed the crime.
>
> **Standard of proof:** the level to which the evidence must be proved to gain a conviction.

In this topic you will learn how to:

- describe the procedure from the start of court action to trial

- apply the above to a given situation.

3 An outline of the procedure of a contract case up to trial

Starting a contract case

Once it has been established that court proceedings need to be started (most claims are settled by negotiation without the need to go to court), the formal procedure must be initiated. Claims where there are personal injuries and the claimant does not expect to be awarded more than £50,000 must be started in the County Court. All other claims may be started in either the County Court or the High Court. Most claims are started in the County Court and many use the Money Claim Online procedure. We will now concentrate on claims starting in the County Court. The first step is to complete a claim form. Information about this is available online to download or can be collected from one of over 200 court offices in the country.

This form is simple to complete, requiring names and addresses for claimant and defendant, brief details of the claim (such as 'Damages for breach of contract resulting from the failure of the defendant to complete building works at the agreed time'), and the value of the claim. The purpose of this is to establish the fee payable and to help decide the choice of court and track. The claimant needs to assess the value of his claim. This is easy for an unpaid debt, but for other claims it is more difficult. If the claim is not for a fixed amount of money (an 'unspecified amount') under 'Value' the claimant would write, 'I expect to recover' followed by whichever of the following applies to the claim:

- 'not more than £5000'
- 'more than £5,000 but not more than £25,000'
- 'more than £25,000'
- 'I cannot say how much I expect to recover'.

This is done to select the relevant track. The particulars of claim on side two of the form will give details of the claim being made. This may be sent separately within 14 days, but most simple claims have it included. The particulars of claim give a simple statement of the facts on which the claimant bases the claim. This will include the date and terms of the contract and an outline of why the claimant considers the defendant has broken his contract and the loss that resulted.

The fee payable depends on the size of the claim. There is also the possibility of having the fee lessened or paying no fee at all in certain cases for claimants with low income and few assets.

This claim form is then served on the defendant, usually by post. In addition to the claim form, the defendant is sent forms for use in dealing with the claim made. At this stage, the claimant chooses which County Court he or she wishes to start the claim in, although the claim may be transferred to a different court later in the process.

The defendant receives the claim form

Assuming the defendant's details and address are correct, the claim form and defendant response pack will not be returned to the court by the Post Office and will be deemed to have been received by the defendant. The defendant's response pack includes an admission form so that the defendant can admit the claim, a defence form to be completed if the claim is not admitted, and an acknowledgement of service form that confirms receipt of the claim. This means that the defendant can do nothing and not reply to the claim at all, admit all or part of the claim, or dispute all or part of the claim. The defendant must do this within 14 days of receiving the claim.

If the defendant does not file a defence within 14 days or any extension the court may give, the claimant can file for a default judgment and effectively win the case. The court will then only be concerned with awarding the appropriate amount of damages and costs. This can be done either by allocating the case to the small claims track or to a disposal hearing in those cases where the claim is more complicated.

In many cases, the defendant may attempt to settle the claim by making an offer of payment. The great majority of claims are settled without the need for a court hearing. However, the defendant may dispute the claim, in which case the defendant may well just complete an acknowledgement of service, as this will give additional time to complete the defence (from 14 to 28 days). In these circumstances, the defendant may instruct a solicitor. The defendant will then complete his or her defence and send it to the court.

The claimant receives the defence

When the claimant receives the defence, the court will also send an allocation questionnaire to all parties to the case. The purpose of this is to establish the location, track and timing of a trial. Any allocation fee becomes payable at this point. This is another incentive to negotiate a settlement of the case, as the expense of taking the case forward mounts up. There will also be a trial fee payable.

The court will keep records of when the allocation questionnaires are due to be returned and if they have in fact been returned. This is part of case monitoring. Case monitoring is where judges receive support from court staff in carrying out their case management role. The court uses a computerised diary monitoring system to record court orders and requests, the deadline for the return of documents such as the allocation questionnaire, and whether the deadline has been met.

Once the allocation questionnaires have been completed, a procedural judge (normally a District Judge) will allocate the case to the appropriate track. If a party to a case does not comply with a court order or time limit, that party may be struck out of the action. The effect of this is that the party would be unable to take further part in the case and would lose any right to claim or defend the court action. This is part of judicial case management, which aims to keep the process moving along at a reasonable speed and help reduce the average time taken to deal with a claim.

Between allocation and trial

After the case has been allocated, the court sets a date for the trial. This date will be at least 21 days later, and the actual date will depend on what other directions need to be made. These other directions include providing copies of documents to the other party or parties to the case, and copies of experts' statements. The stage is now set for the trial.

Conclusion

The procedure from issue of a claim up to trial is designed to bring the claim to a conclusion fairly and speedily. The aim of the civil justice system is to reduce the average time a claim takes to be resolved and thus

> **Link**
>
> A flowchart of a fast track case up to trial can be found in Chapter 13 (The courts: procedure and damages for negligence cases), Fig. 13.2, p233.

■ Study tips

Make sure that you present the order of events in a clear and logical manner, using the correct legal terminology. It is usually a good idea to plan your answer and then write it out. The planning exercise will help you get the procedure in the correct order.

reduce the criticism that the law is very slow. The aim is to reduce the time from over a year at the end of the 1990s to about 30 weeks on average for a fast-track case. The procedure is relatively straightforward and is backed up with much help and guidance online, in leaflets and at court offices.

Activity

Set out below is a scenario from a sample examination question. Using the information in the scenario, complete a claim form as far as possible and explain to the claimant how the case would proceed up to any trial.

Umar wanted to buy a large quantity of mobile phones for his shop. He phoned Mobiles plc, who agreed to supply him with a quantity of phones for £60,000. Mobiles plc immediately realised they had been using an old price list and tried to contact Umar on the phone, but failed to do so. Mobiles plc therefore posted a new price list to Umar, which he received on the next day. Mobiles plc refused to supply the phones at £60,000 and Umar refused to pay the revised price of £70,000. Mobiles plc's new prices were the same as other suppliers of the phones.

You should now be able to:

- understand the procedure up to trial in a contract dispute
- apply the procedure in a given situation.

In this topic you will learn how to:

- state the meaning of compensatory damages
- describe the rules for calculation of damages for damage to property
- describe the rules for calculation of damages where there is a market for the goods involved
- describe the principle of mitigation of loss
- describe the rules on causation and remoteness of damage
- apply the above rules to a given situation.

4 Damages

The purpose of damages

Damages in contract are compensatory. The purpose is to put the claimant in the position he or she would have been in had the contract been properly performed. This means that the claimant is entitled to the benefit of the bargain. It is easy to calculate the loss where a bill has not been paid, but much harder to calculate where services have not been performed or goods not delivered, as there are losses that could be said to be a consequence of the failure to perform or deliver.

Consider, for example, what losses there might be if the copy of this book that you are reading were delivered late, or the losses that would follow from a cancelled restaurant reservation. The purpose of damages is to calculate this as fairly as possible. The law is not concerned with punishing the defendant, only with compensating the victim of the defendant's breach of contract.

Calculation of damages

The court has to take into account a number of factors when awarding damages. The first thing is the easiest: the amount payable for what is known as the 'loss of the bargain'. The idea is to put the claimant in the same situation as if the contract had been performed. For example, in a contract to buy for £400 a television normally costing £500 and where the television is either defective or is not delivered, the claimant will be entitled to damages reflecting the difference between the price paid under the contract and the actual value of the non-delivered or defective television. This will usually involve the return of any money paid and the difference between the contract price and the general selling price of the television at the date the contract was broken – in other words, £100.

There are also consequential losses that are more difficult to calculate. The extent of the losses that can be claimed depends on whether the consequence is too remote to be recovered or not. The principles behind this will be discussed later in this topic, but the basic principle is that the loss is foreseeable. Thus if a television is defective and catches fire, it is foreseeable that other goods may be damaged by the fire. This damage would also be recoverable. The damages would reflect the value of the other goods that were damaged.

Additionally, there will be costs incurred by the claimant as a result of sorting out the consequences. A simple example of this is the additional costs incurred in getting another television to replace the one that was defective – in that case, it could be the cost of an additional trip to the shop or a delivery charge for a replacement television bought over the internet.

Where a business is claiming a loss of profit, it will have to show how the broken contract affected its earnings. This is usually done by calculating the loss of profits on the basis of previous profits, contracts made and the consequences of those contracts being broken. The detail of a claim can be seen from the case of *Wiseman* v *Virgin Atlantic Airways* (2006), where the claimant was wrongly not let on board an aircraft in Port Harcourt, Nigeria, flying to Stansted Airport in England. It was another 12 days before he could return to England. The successful claim resulted in damages of around £2300, which was based on:

1 hotel bill for the additional stay

2 restaurant bills for the additional stay

3 taxi fares in and out of town for the purpose of trying to rearrange his flight to England

4 postage and telephone calls.

However, nothing was awarded for:

1 expenses incurred by his fiancée who had arranged to meet him at Stansted

2 the breakdown of their relationship, which is not a recoverable type of damage even if that was caused by the breach of contract

3 the additional expenses of his Nigerian friends who had come to see him off

4 his hurt feelings and the alleged damage to his reputation

5 a robbery suffered during the time he was delayed in Nigeria; this was a supervening event not caused by the delay.

In exceptional cases, there can also be damages for emotional distress following a breach of contract. This relates to consumer contracts and particularly holidays. Lord Denning said in the case of **Jarvis v Swan Tours (1973)**, 'It has often been said that on a breach of contract, damages cannot be given for mental distress … I think those limitations are out of date. In a proper case, damages for mental distress can be recovered in contract … One such case is a contract for a holiday, or any other contract to provide entertainment and enjoyment.' *Jarvis* v *Swan Tours* was a case where a winter sports holiday had failed to live up to expectations with respect to the activities on offer. The original trial judge awarded damages of approximately half the cost of the holiday. However, on appeal, twice the cost of the holiday was awarded even though that sum could not possibly reflect the actual financial loss. This seems to be contrary to the basic principles of an award of damages, but is the just result which is reflected in the quotation from Lord Denning.

Study tips

Most calculations of damages are straightforward. For example, a breach by failure to deliver, where the cost of the goods has risen from £10 to £15, is the difference between the contract price and the market price at breach – that is, £5. Possible other losses depend on the knowledge the defendant has of the claimant's situation.

Key cases

Jarvis v Swan Tours (1973): damages could be awarded for mental distress following a breach of contract. This is particularly relevant to holidays.

Mitigation of loss

The claimant must do his or her best to keep the losses he has suffered to a minimum. Thus in *Wiseman* v *Virgin Atlantic Airways* (2006), the claimant could not do nothing or be extravagant. Chartering an aircraft to fly out from England to Nigeria and collect him would have been irrecoverable, as it would not have been keeping his losses to a minimum. In practice, the claimant does not have to be too careful about ensuring mitigation of loss. The key criterion is that the action taken by the claimant is reasonable, so Wiseman did not have to buy the cheapest meal available or walk into town rather than take a taxi.

Causation and remoteness

The general principle is that the loss complained of must have been caused by the breach and must not be too remote. The rule with respect to **causation** is that the breach of contract must be the main cause of the claimant's loss: in other words, but for the defendant's breach of contract, the claimant would not have made the loss. For example, if I have made a contract to have my new car delivered on Friday and it is not delivered on Friday, I would then have to hire a car until delivery took place. The cause of my loss is the defendant's breach of contract in not delivering on the stated day. If, however, the car was delivered late because I was not able to pay for it on Friday, as my bank had failed to deliver the funds to pay for it on time, the cause of my loss is the bank's failure, not the seller of the car.

With remoteness of damage, it would clearly be impossible to make the defendant liable for all the consequences of the breach as they could be, arguably, never ending. The decision the law has to make is where to draw the line. Remoteness is the test used by the courts to decide whether losses resulting from a breach of contract are recoverable. The first case to really establish the law was **Hadley v Baxendale (1854)**. In that case, the claimants needed to have the main shaft that powered their mill repaired, as it had broken. Until it was repaired, the mill could do no work, and so they were losing money. It could be repaired only in London; they hired the defendant to take it from Gloucester by the next day. For some unexplained reason, the shaft took several days to arrive. The delay caused continuing losses.

The question before the court was whether the defendant was liable for the money that the Hadleys had lost while the mill was without its shaft. The court decided that since the defendant did not necessarily know that the mill would be idle until the shaft could be returned (they might have had a spare shaft), the defendant was not liable for the loss. The decision was based on the 'foreseeability' test for contract breaches: you cannot be held liable for losses that you could not reasonably have anticipated. This test has been restated in various ways on many occasions. Two categories of loss are recognised:

- Direct or normal loss: loss of a type that would usually arise from a breach of contract. This is assumed to have been in the 'reasonable contemplation' of the parties at the time they made the contract.
- Indirect or abnormal loss: loss of a type that is out of the ordinary. This is recoverable if, at the time of making the contract, the defendant knew it could happen in the event of breach. The defendant must also have accepted responsibility for that risk. Acceptance of risk is often implied from knowledge that the defendant has in relation to the situation.

There are a number of cases that have looked at these abnormal losses. The first to be considered is **Victoria Laundry v Newman Industries (1949)**. In that case, the defendants contracted to sell a new, larger, boiler to the claimants, which the defendants knew was required for immediate use. Delivery was made five months late. The claimants lost not only the £16 a week profit that they could have made from normal customers, but also a £262 a week dyeing contract with a government department. The court decided that the £16 per week was recoverable as it was a normal loss, but the £262 was not recoverable as the defendants did not know about the government contract.

The case of **The Heron II (Czarnikow v Koufos) (1969)** shows that business people know of, and are therefore responsible for, losses occurring in normal business situations. In that case, the defendants were ship owners who made a contract to carry a cargo of sugar to Basra for the claimant. They knew a great deal about the claimant client and the world of business: they were sugar merchants; there was a sugar market in Basra. What they did not know was whether the claimant intended to sell the sugar as soon as the ship arrived. The ship arrived in Basra nine days late as a result of the defendants' fault. In the course of those nine days, the price of sugar fell significantly in the market and the sugar was sold for much less than it would have done had the cargo arrived on time. The claim was for the loss of profit on the sugar. The court decided that the claimant was entitled to their lost profit. Even though the ship owner did not know of the intention to sell the sugar immediately, 'If he had thought about the matter he must have realised at least that it was not unlikely that the sugar would be sold in the market at market price on arrival.' The defendant is liable for such loss as a reasonable man, knowing what the defendant knew or ought to have known, would consider 'not unlikely' to result.

A typical modern example is *Hotel Services Ltd* v *Hilton International Hotels* (2000), where the court decided that the claimant was allowed to recover both the costs of the removal of defective mini-bars and the consequent loss of profit from their non-availability. These were both direct losses.

> ### Key cases
>
> **Victoria Laundry v Newman Industries (1949):** the claimant could recover damages for their normal lost profit, but not for an especially valuable contract the defendant did not know about.
>
> **The Heron II (1969):** the claimant could recover damages for late delivery of a cargo of sugar as the defendant knew the cargo and that there was a market for it. This was an ordinary, known risk.

> ### Study tips
>
> Remeber that application requires an explanation of how the law is used in connection with the facts, so that you produce a reasoned conclusion.

> ### Activity
>
> Using the scenario in the activity on p272 in Topic 3, outline how the court would calculate an award of damages to Umar in the situation given.

You should now be able to:

- understand the principles behind an award of damages
- apply the principles in examination questions.

Practice questions

Unit 2C questions in the AQA exam

In the Unit 2 examination paper, you must answer all the questions from Unit 2A (Criminal Law) and all the questions from either Unit 2B (Tort) or Unit 2C (Contract Law).

Each section is represented by one question, which has six parts. You must answer all parts of the question. Each part is worth up to 10 marks; the entire question is worth 45 marks, plus 2 marks for Assessment Objective 3.

Some of the questions test your knowledge and understanding, and some test application of the law to the scenario that introduces the question. Some are a mixture of knowledge, understanding and application. There is a clear distinction on the examination paper. Theory-only questions appear directly underneath the scenario; mixed theory and application questions are preceded by a specific instruction to refer to the scenario.

Example question 1 (AQA, June 2012)

This question is taken from a past exam paper. You must answer all six parts of this question.

> Greta wanted to make an appointment with her dentist, Hari. Greta telephoned on 1 May and asked Hari to leave a number of possible times on her voicemail. Hari replied by leaving a message on Greta's voicemail later that day. When Greta listened to her voicemail on 2 May, she decided that the suggestion of 4:00 pm on Monday was perfect. She texted back immediately, stating that 4:00 pm on 12 May was fine. Unfortunately, Greta had not listened to all Hari's voicemail, which finished with 'All times are for the week beginning 5 May.' Greta then lost her phone, so did not pick up Hari's text sent on 3 May, stating that 12 May was no good. Josh, another patient of Hari's, failed to arrive for his pre-booked appointment because he overslept.

A valid contract requires an offer, acceptance, an intention to create legal relations and consideration.

1. Explain the rules which apply to the ways in which an offer can be accepted.

   (8 marks)

2. Explain the meaning of the term consideration, including an explanation of past consideration. *(8 marks)*

   Refer to the scenario when answering the remaining questions in this section.

3. Briefly discuss the legal effect of each stage in the negotiations between Greta and Hari, and decide whether those negotiations resulted in a contract. *(10 marks + 2 Marks for AO3)*

4. Briefly explain what is meant by breach of contract. Assuming there was a contract between Josh and Hari, briefly discuss whether Josh was in breach of that contract when he failed to arrive for his pre-booked appointment.
(8 marks)

5. Outline the three-track case management system used in the civil courts, and identify which track and which court are most likely to be used in any claim that Hari could make against Josh. *(5 marks)*

6. Explain how the court would decide the amount of damages to be awarded to Hari if Josh were found to be in breach of contract for missing his appointment. *(6 marks)*

Example question 2 (AQA, June 2011)

This question is taken from another past exam paper. You must answer all six parts of this question.

> Ian, a club owner, e-mailed Jay, a singer, to arrange for him to perform at his club. Jay replied by e-mail, indicating that his fee would be £500. Ian thought this was too much. He e-mailed back asking if the fee would be lower if Jay used the club sound system. Jay replied, saying his fee would be slightly less. Ian did nothing for two weeks until Jay released a CD, which became an immediate hit. Realising the performance would now sell out, Ian immediately e-mailed Jay stating that he would pay £500 and suggesting a range of dates for the performance. Jay replied saying that his fee was now £2000.

A valid contract requires an offer, acceptance, an intention to create legal relations and consideration.

1. Explain the differences between an offer and an invitation to treat. *(8 marks)*

2. Briefly explain any three ways in which an offer may come to an end.
(8 marks)

> Refer to the scenario when answering the remaining questions in this section.

3. Discuss whether there is a contract between Ian and Jay.
(8 marks + 2 marks for AO3)

4. Explain what is meant by consideration and how it would apply if the court decided there was a contract between Ian and Jay. *(8 marks)*

5. Outline the three-track case management system used in the civil courts and briefly explain which track is most likely to be used in any claim that Ian could make against Jay. *(5 marks)*

6. If Jay were to be in breach of contract, explain how the court would calculate an award of damages to Ian. *(8 marks)*

Index

Acknowledgements

The authors and publisher are grateful to the following for permission to reproduce photographs and other copyright material in this book:

p6 Handguns extract reprinted from the World Council of Churches; p8 AllOut; p10 www.parliament.uk; p11 www.parliament.uk; p13 bis.gov.uk; p20 ajfi/Shutterstock; p22 Nicholas Kane/Arcaid/Corbis; p25 World Economic Forum/Remy Steinegger; p27 Railways Act 2005 reprinted under Crown copyright PSI License C2008000256; p28 corbs83/Flickr; p28 Richard Klune/Corbis; p31 Hastings Borough Council bylaw on dog fouling; p31 The Smoke-free Regulations Act 2006 reprinted under Crown copyright PSI License C2008000256; p37 Nuclear Consultation was flawed extract reprinted with permission from The Times/NI Syndication; p44 Djtm/Wikimedia; p46 Puposes of Climate Change and Sustainability Act 2006 reprinted under Crown copyright PSI License C2008000256; p50 Extract from Report on the Interpretation of Statutes (1969) reprinted under Crown copyright PSI License C2008000256; p53 Lord Denning verdict reprinted under Crown copyright PSI License C2008000256; p55 Court of Justice of the European Union; p56 Adrian Pingstone; p57 Paul Doyle/Alamy; p63 Purity ring is not intimately linked to religious beliefs extract reprinted with permission from The Times/ NI Syndication; p96 Justices of Peace in England and Wales reprinted under Crown copyright PSI License C2008000256; p100 Sentencing guidelines reprinted under Crown copyright PSI License C2008000256; p104 Janet Chapman jailed for holiday extract reprinted with permission from ©Daily Mail; p108 Controversy flares over magistrate aged 19 extract reprinted with permission from the Yorkshire Evening Post; p114 Chris/Wikimedia; p116 Typical day of a barrister extract reprinted with permission from the Bar Council; p117 Bar statistics extract reprinted with permission from the Bar Council; p120 Wait for ABS is over: Tesco law is here extract © Guardian News & Media Ltd (2012); p122–3 All take and no give? extract reprinted with permission from The Times/NI Syndication; p122 Cockburne v Atkinson, Dacre and Slack extract reprinted under Crown copyright PSI License C2008000256; p132 Barrister fees spiral ever up extract © Guardian News & Media Ltd (2011); p133 Sir Anthony Clarke oral evidence to Select Committee extract reprinted under Crown copyright PSI License C2008000256; p143 Advertisement for a district judge extract reprinted under Crown copyright PSI License C2008000256; p145 Jonathan Sumption QC appointment extract © Guardian News & Media Ltd (2011); p148 Disciplinary actions taken against judges reprinted under Crown copyright PSI License C2008000256; p148–9 Judge found guilty after drunken fracas extract reprinted with permission from Northern Echo © Newsquest Media Group 2003 (2012); p153–4 Judicial Statistics extracts reprinted under Crown copyright PSI License C2008000256; p156 Sam Smith/Wikimedia; p158 Definitely no regrets extract reprinted with permission from The Times/NI Syndication; p181 Magnus D/Wikimedia; p184 Vaclav Volrab/Shutterstock; p193 Magistrates' Court summons reprinted under Crown copyright PSI License C2008000256; p197 Bail notice reprinted under Crown copyright PSI License C2008000256; p202 Community sentences definition reprinted under Crown copyright PSI License C2008000256; p204 Guidance for sentencing extract reprinted under Crown copyright PSI License C2008000256; p205 ABH guidance reprinted under Crown copyright PSI License C2008000256; p230 Division between County Court and High Court reprinted under Crown copyright PSI License C2008000256; p234 Diagram of how a dispute might progress to court reprinted under Crown copyright PSI License C2008000256; p252 joyfull/Shutterstock; p254 Carbolic Smoke Ball Co.

AQA examination questions are reproduced by permission of the Assessment and Qualifications Alliance.

Every effort has been made to trace the copyright holders but if any have been inadvertently overlooked the publisher will be pleased to make the necessary arrangements at the first opportunity.